Dyslexia Across Languages

Dyslexia Across Languages
Orthography and the Brain–Gene–Behavior Link

edited by

Peggy McCardle, Ph.D., M.P.H.
Eunice Kennedy Shriver National Institute for Child Health &
    Human Development
National Institutes of Health
Bethesda, Maryland

Brett Miller, Ph.D.
Eunice Kennedy Shriver National Institute for Child Health &
    Human Development
National Institutes of Health
Bethesda, Maryland

Jun Ren Lee, Ph.D.
National Taiwan Normal University
Taipei, Taiwan

and

Ovid J.L. Tzeng, Ph.D.
Academia Sinica
Taipei, Taiwan

·P·A·U·L·H·
BROOKES
PUBLISHING CO®

Baltimore • London • Sydney

·PAUL·H·
BROOKES
PUBLISHING C⍛.

Paul H. Brookes Publishing Co.
Post Office Box 10624
Baltimore, Maryland 21285-0624
USA

www.brookespublishing.com

Typeset by Aptara, Inc., Falls Church, Virginia.
Manufactured in the United States of America by
Sheridan Books, Inc., Chelsea, Michigan.

The following were written by a U.S. Government employee within the scope of his or
her official duties and, as such, shall remain in the public domain: Preface, Section III
Integrative Summary, Section V Integrative Summary, and Conclusion. The opinions
and assertions contained herein are the private opinions of the authors and are not to be
construed as official or reflecting the views of the U.S. Government.

The views expressed in this book are those of the authors and do not necessarily represent those of the National Institutes of Health, the *Eunice Kennedy Shriver* National
Institute of Child Health and Human Development, or the U.S. Department of Health
and Human Services.

1006846740

Library of Congress Cataloging-in-Publication Data
Dyslexia across languages: orthography and the brain-gene-behavior link/edited by
Peggy McCardle . . . [et al.].
    p.   cm.
  ISBN-13: 978-1-59857-185-1
  ISBN-10: 1-59857-185-0
  1. Dyslexia—Cross-cultural studies.   2. Dyslexia—Physiological aspects.
  3. Neurobiology.   I. McCardle, Peggy D.
    LB1050.5.D917   2011
    371.91′44—dc23   2011022954

British Library of Congress Cataloguing in Publication data are available from the
British Library.

Contents

About the Editors

Peggy McCardle, Ph.D., M.P.H., Chief, Child Development & Behavior Branch at the *Eunice Kennedy Shriver* National Institute for Child Health & Human Development (NICHD), National Institutes of Health, 6100 Executive Boulevard, Suite 4B05, Bethesda, Maryland 20895-7510

Dr. McCardle has been a classroom teacher, university faculty member, and hospital clinician. At NICHD, in addition to her oversight of the branch, she directs the research program on Language, Bilingual and Biliteracy.

Brett Miller, Ph.D., Program Director of the Reading, Writing, and Related Learning Disabilities Program at the *Eunice Kennedy Shriver* National Institute for Child Health and Human Development, National Institutes of Health, 6100 Executive Boulevard, Suite 4B05, Bethesda, Maryland 20895-7510

Dr. Miller previously held the position of Associate Research Scientist at the Institute of Education Sciences, U.S. Department of Education, where he oversaw programs in adult literacy and math and science learning.

Jun Ren Lee, Ph.D., Experimental Psychologist, Department of Educational Psychology & Counseling, National Taiwan Normal University, 162, Heping East Road, Section 1, Da-An District, Taipei 106, Taiwan

Dr. Lee is an experimental psychologist by training. He is working on the issues of reading acquisition, reading disabilities, reading instruction, and bilingualism.

Ovid J.L. Tzeng, Ph.D., Cognitive Neuroscientist, Academia Sinica, No. 128, Sec. 2, Academia Road, Nankang District, Taipei 115, Taiwan

Dr. Tzeng is a cognitive neuroscientist who is recognized for his works on memory and language processing. Emphasizing reading as a biological system, he investigates reading acquisition and skilled reading processes from a neuroplasticity perspective, using various neuroimaging techniques, in order to uncover their universal and language-specific principles.

About the Contributors

Yusra Ahmed, Department of Psychology, Florida State University, 1107 West Call Street, Tallahassee, Florida 32306

Ms. Ahmed is a graduate student in the Developmental Psychology program, where she is studying the developmental relationship between reading and writing skills as well as the development of normal and abnormal reading. She is the coauthor of several articles in peer-reviewed journals and book chapters.

Leena Alho-Näveri, M.S., University of Jyväskylä, Post Office Box 35, FIN-40014, University of Jyväskylä, Finland

Ms. Alho-Näveri is working on the Eteva joint municipal board, which provides services for people with intellectual and developmental disabilities in Finland. She works mainly with adolescents and adults; her special field is autism spectrum disorders. Her work consists of different evaluations, consulting, and therapeutic work.

Mikko Aro, Ph.D., Professor, Department of Education/Special Education, University of Jyväskylä, Post Office Box 35, FIN-40014, University of Jyväskylä, Finland

Dr. Aro's educational background is in child neuropsychology. His main research interests are reading disabilities and development of reading skills.

Diane August, Ph.D., Senior Research Scientist, Center for Applied Linguistics, 4646 40th Street, NW, Washington, D.C. 20016

Dr. August is the principal investigator or co-investigator for a number of large federally funded studies that investigate the development of literacy in high-poverty elementary school children.

Ellen Bialystok, Ph.D., Distinguished Research Professor, York University, Department of Psychology, 4700 Keele Street, Toronto, Ontario M3J 1P3, Canada

Dr. Bialystok studies the effect of experience on cognitive ability across the lifespan. The majority of her research has examined the effect of bilingualism on children's language and cognitive development.

David Braze, Ph.D., Linguist and Senior Scientist, Haskins Laboratories, 300 George Street, Suite 900, New Haven, Connecticut 06511

Dr. Braze's research focuses on the cognitive bases underlying the apprehension of combinatorial meaning in speech and print. He employs online methods, including monitoring eye movements during reading, to collect moment-by-moment indicators of comprehension bottlenecks and to explore how comprehension challenges inherent to texts interact with individual differences in the cognitive underpinnings of reading skill.

Stanislas Dehaene, Ph.D., Professor of Experimental Cognitive Psychology, Collège de France, Head, Inserm–CEA Cognitive Neuroimaging Unit, NeuroSpin center, CEA/SAC/DSV/I2BM, Bât 145, Point Courrier 156, F-91191 Gif/Yvette, France

Dr. Dehaene's research investigates human cognitive functions such as reading, calculation, and language, with a particular focus on conscious versus nonconscious processing.

R. Holly Fitch, Ph.D., Associate Professor of Neuroscience, University of Connecticut, Department of Psychology/Behavioral Neuroscience, Box U-1020, Bousfield Building, Babbidge Road, Storrs, Connecticut 06269

Dr. Fitch conducts studies on the role of early injury and genetic manipulation (risk genes) in anomalous brain development and associations with subsequent deficits in sensory processing and learning and memory. Models assessed include early hypoxia-ischemia typical of low birthweight and premature populations, as well as manipulation of neuronal migration genes implicated in dyslexia.

Ram Frost, Ph.D., Professor of Psychology, The Hebrew University, Department of Psychology, Jerusalem 91905, Israel

Dr. Frost's research focuses on the cognitive processes involved in visual word recognition, investigating what is universal in the reading process across diverse languages and what aspects of reading are unique to each language's orthographic and morphological system.

Albert M. Galaburda, M.D., Emily Fisher Landau Professor of Neurology, Beth Israel Deaconess Medical Center, 330 Brookline Avenue—KS274, Boston, Massachusetts 02215

Dr. Galaburda reported on the first studies of changes in the brain in developmental dyslexia and has published more than 200 articles, chapters, and books on the subjects of language and the brain, brain lateralization, and developmental dyslexia.

Tomi K. Guttorm, Ph.D., Researcher, Department of Psychology and Agora Center, University of Jyväskylä, Post Office Box 35, FIN-40014, University of Jyväskylä, Finland

Dr. Guttorm works in the Oulu University of Applied Sciences. His research focuses on developmental psychophysiology, early identification and intervention of reading difficulties, and motivation and learning in adulthood.

Debra Jared, Ph.D., Associate Professor, University of Western Ontario, Department of Psychology, London, Ontario N6A 5C2, Canada

Dr. Jared's primary research interest is in reading. She has conducted research on word recognition in monolinguals and bilinguals with a focus on phonological processing. She has also been involved in a large-scale study examining reading development in children who were in the process of becoming biliterate and was formerly an associate editor of the *Journal of Memory & Language*.

Clinton L. Johns, Ph.D., Postdoctoral Scholar, Haskins Laboratories, 300 George Street, New Haven, Connecticut 06511

Dr. Johns studies language comprehension in mature readers with a particular focus on the processes that are involved in understanding pronouns and other referring expressions.

Yulia Kovas, Ph.D., Department of Psychology, Goldsmiths College, University of London, SE14 6NW, United Kingdom

Dr. Kovas has a degree in philology from the State Pedagogical University of St. Petersburg. She received a B.Sc. in psychology from Birkbeck College, University of London, in 2003; a M.Sc. in social, genetic, and developmental psychiatry from King's College in 2004; and a Ph.D. from the SGDP Centre in 2007. In addition to the lectureship at Goldsmiths College, Dr. Kovas is an honorary researcher at the Institute of Psychiatry, where she leads the mathematics research on the Twins Early Development Study, exploring gene–environment interplay in shaping individual variation in mathematics interest and achievement. She is also involved in cross-cultural collaborations with Russia and China that focus on genetic and environmental influences on individuals.

Judith F. Kroll, Ph.D., M.A., A.B., Distinguished Professor of Psychology, Linguistics, and Women's Studies, Director, Center for Language Science, Pennsylvania State University, Department of Psychology, 641 Moore Building, University Park, Pennsylvania 16802

Dr. Kroll, along with Annette de Groot, co-edited *Tutorials in Bilingualism: Psycholinguistic Perspectives* (1997, Lawrence Erlbaum Associates) and the *Handbook of Bilingualism: Psycholinguistic Approaches*

(2005, Oxford University Press). She serves on a number of editorial boards, including *Journal of Memory and Language, Journal of Experimental Psychology: Learning, Memory, and Cognition, International Journal of Bilingualism,* and *Psychological Science.* The research that she and her students conduct concerns the acquisition, comprehension, and production of two languages during second-language learning and in proficient bilingual performance.

Anuenue Kukona, M.A., Department of Psychology, University of Connecticut and Haskins Laboratories, 406 Babbidge Road, Unit 1020, Storrs, Connecticut 06269
    Mr. Kukona is a Ph.D. student in language and cognition at the University of Connecticut. He has interests in language processing, dynamical systems, self-organization, and individual differences research.

Chia-Ying Lee, Ph.D., Institute of Linguistics, Academia Sinica, #128, Sec. 2, Academia Road, Nankang, Taipei 11529, Taiwan
    Dr. Lee works in the Brain and Language Laboratory at the Institute of Linguistics at Academia Sinica in Taiwan. Her central research interest is to understand the cognitive and neural basis of Chinese visual word recognition and reading by using an interdisciplinary approach, including behavioral, neuroimaging (functional magnetic resonance imaging), and electrophysiology (event-related potential/magnetic resonance imaging) measurement.

Phil D. Liu, Ph.D., Assistant Professor, Department of Psychology, Fudan University, No. 220 Handan Road, 10th Floor, Art Building, Shanghai, China
    Dr. Liu's research interests focus on cognitive development, especially language and literacy development and difficulties, as well as metalinguistic processing and developmental models.

Joseph J. LoTurco, Ph.D., Professor of Physiology and Neurobiology, University of Connecticut, 75 North Eagleville Road, Storrs, Connecticut 06269
    Dr. LoTurco completed his Ph.D. in neuroscience at Stanford University and his postdoctoral studies at Harvard Medical School in the Department of Genetics. For the past 16 years, his research at the University of Connecticut has focused on defining the cellular patterns and molecular mechanisms required for normal growth and function of the cerebral neocortex.

Gigi Luk, Ph.D., Rotman Research Institute, Baycrest, 3560 Bathurst Street, Toronto, Ontario M6A 2E1, Canada
    Dr. Luk's research focuses on the cognitive and linguistic consequences of bilingualism in the lifespan. She takes a dynamic

approach to examine these consequences in brain structures, brain functions, and behavior.

Heikki Lyytinen, Ph.D., Professor of Developmental Neuropsychology, Department of Psychology, University of Jyväskylä, Agora Center, Box 35, 40014, University of Jyväskylä, Finland

Dr. Lyytinen's recent research has focused on longitudinal study of children at familial risk for dyslexia—Jyväskylä Longitudinal Study of Dyslexia—which he has led from the beginning, when the children followed intensively were born more than 15 years ago. His earlier work focused on psychophysiology and he now concentrates on the development of tools for preventively helping children identified to be at risk for dyslexia (for more, see heikki.lyytinen.info).

James S. Magnuson, Ph.D., Associate Professor, University of Connecticut, Department of Psychology, Unit 1020, Storrs, Connecticut 06269

Dr. Magnuson received an A.B. in linguistics from the University of Chicago and a Ph.D. in brain and cognitive sciences from the University of Rochester. His work focuses on language comprehension, language learning, and language disabilities.

Jon K. Maner, Ph.D., Associate Professor, Department of Psychology, Florida State University, 1107 West Call Street, Tallahassee, Florida 32306

Dr. Maner's interests include human cognition and evolutionary psychology, as well as quantitative approaches to behavioral science.

Catherine McBride-Chang, Ph.D., Professor, Psychology Department, The Chinese University of Hong Kong, Shatin, N.T., Hong Kong, China

Dr. McBride-Chang is the author of more than 100 peer-reviewed journal articles and two books. She has a primary research focus on reading development and impairment in children across cultures.

W. Einar Mencl, Ph.D., Director of Neruroimaging Research, Haskins Laboratories, 300 George Street, New Haven, Connecticut 06511

Dr. Mencl is interested in reading, language processing, and music perception. He uses functional magnetic resonance imaging to investigate these neurocognitive processes and better understand their failure and potential remediation.

Prakash Padakannaya, Ph.D., Professor, Department of Psychology, University of Mysore, Manasagangotri, Mysore 570006, Karnataka, India

Dr. Padakannaya's research focuses on reading, phonological awareness, and orthography using behavioral, brain imaging, and eye-tracking techniques.

Charles A. Perfetti, Ph.D., Distinguished University Professor of Psychology and Director of the Learning Research and Development Center, University of Pittsburgh, 3939 O'Hara Street, Pittsburgh, Pennsylvania 15260

Dr. Perfetti's research on reading and language is published in more than 180 journal articles and two books, and he has co-edited four books on literacy topics. He is the 2004 recipient of the Distinguished Scientific Contribution Award of the Society for the Scientific Study of Reading.

Robert Plomin, Ph.D., MRC Research Professor in Behavioral Genetics and Deputy Director, King's College London, MRC Social, Genetic, and Developmental Psychiatry Centre, Institute of Psychiatry, DeCrespigny Park, London SE5 8AF, United Kingdom

Dr. Plomin is conducting a study of twins born in England from 1994 to 1996 (Twins Early Development Study) focusing on developmental delays in early childhood and their association with behavioral problems. His research combines quantitative genetic and molecular genetic approaches to understand the interplay between genes and environment in behavioral development.

Kenneth R. Pugh, Ph.D., President and Director of Research, Haskins Laboratories, 300 George Street, New Haven, Connecticut 06511

Dr. Pugh holds faculty appointments in the Department of Psychology at University of Connecticut and Department of Linguistics at Yale University.

Nallur B. Ramachandra, Ph.D., Professor, Department of Studies in Zoology, University of Mysore, Manasagaotri, Mysore 570 006, India

Dr. Ramachandra works in the field of genetics and genomics of *Drosophila nasuta* systems—evolution of new cytoraces and their speciation—and human genetic disorders such as grandmother's age and Down syndrome, congenital heart diseases, asthma, type 2 diabetes, and dyslexia.

Ulla Richardson, Ph.D., Linguist, University of Jyväskylä, Agora Center, Post Office Box 35, 40014, University of Jyväskylä, Finland

Dr. Richardson's research focuses on language development and phonological and orthographic processing in dyslexia. Her current work centers on developing and studying the effects of a computerized intervention method on reading skills. From 2005 to 2009, she led the international Graphogame research project funded by a Marie Curie Excellence grant, and she has previously worked with Professor Usha Goswami in London and Cambridge on the research project Linguistic Factors, Phonological & Orthographic Processing in Dyslexia.

Glenn D. Rosen, Ph.D., Associate Professor of Neurology, Department of Neurology, Beth Israel Deaconess Medical Center, E/CLS-643, 330 Brookline Avenue, Boston, Massachusetts 02215

Dr. Rosen received his undergraduate degrees in biology and psychology from Swarthmore College and his Ph.D. in developmental psychobiology at the University of Connecticut. His lab is interested in identifying genes and gene networks that modulate normal variation in brain development.

Christopher Schatschneider, Ph.D., Professor of Psychology, Department of Psychology, Florida State University, 1107 West Call Street, Office C234V, Tallahassee, Florida 32306

Dr. Schatschneider is a professor of psychology at Florida State University and an associate director of the Florida Center for Reading Research. His research focuses on early reading development, methodology, and statistics.

Mark S. Seidenberg, Ph.D., Hilldale Professor and Donald O. Hebb Professor, Department of Psychology, University of Wisconsin–Madison, 1202 West Johnson Street, Madison, Wisconsin 53706

Dr. Seidenberg has studied reading for 30 years, with a focus on using computational models to understand how children learn to read, the mechanisms involved in skilled reading, impairments that interfere with becoming a reader, and the brain bases of it all. He thinks that learning to read is more like learning a first language than most people believe, and he can tell you why English and Chinese are alike.

Ayumi Seki, Ph.D., Department of Regional Education, Tottori University, 4-101 Koyama Minami, Tottori, Tottori 680-8551, Japan

Dr. Seki is an associate professor in the department of special needs education. Her background is pediatric neurology and she works at clinics for children with developmental disorders and learning disorders. Her main research interest is the biological mechanisms of reading acquisition in Japanese orthographies in both nonimpaired children and children with reading difficulties. She worked for a year at Haskins Laboratories as a Fulbright Scholar.

Donald Shankweiler, Ph.D., Department of Psychology, University of Connecticut, Unit 1020, 406 Babbidge Road, Storrs, Connecticut 06269

Dr. Shankweiler is Emeritus Professor of Psychology at the University of Connecticut and a Research Scientist at Haskins Laboratories, where he has long pursued an interest in the developmental problems of speech and reading and their neural bases. He and his associates study eye movements in reading to gain insight into how sentences are read and comprehended in real time by readers at various levels of skill. They are also exploiting cognitive neuroimaging as a tool to study how the brain is changed by experience with written language.

Linda S. Siegel, Ph.D., ECPS, University of British Columbia, 2125 Main Mall, Vancouver, British Columbia, V6T 1Z4 Canada

Linda Siegel holds the Dorothy C. Lam Chair in Special Education at the University of British Columbia. She has published studies in a number of aspects of learning disabilities, including cognitive processes, assessment, definition, and early identification and intervention. She has also published a number of studies of children learning English as a second language.

Shelly D. Smith, Ph.D., Professor of Pediatrics, 985960 Nebraska Medical Center, Omaha, Nebraska 68198

Dr. Smith received her Ph.D. in Medical Genetics at Indiana University and has certification as a Ph.D. Medical Geneticist through the American Board of Clinical Genetics. Her research interests are gene identification for hereditary deafness and communication disorders, particularly dyslexia, language impairment, and speech sound disorder.

Whitney Tabor, Ph.D., Associate Professor of Psychology, Department of Psychology, University of Connecticut, U-1020, 406 Babbidge Road, Storrs, Connecticut 06268

Dr. Tabor studied mathematics as an undergraduate, linguistics in graduate school, and language processing as a postdoctoral student. He has combined these viewpoints in a dynamical systems approach to language processing that offers a valuable new approach to language disorders. Instead of starting with order and distorting it to account for aberrant behavior, he takes disorder as the starting point and considers how order arises (or fails to arise) out of it.

Yaching Tsai, Research Assistant, Chinese University of Hong Kong

Yaching Tsai graduated from the National Taiwan Normal University and did graduate work in linguistics at the University of Venice and the Chinese University of Hong Kong. Among her translations into Chinese is the recent essay by M. Tomasello, Origins of Human Communication.

Jessica Brown Waesche, Ph.D., Florida Center for Reading Research, 1107 West Call Street, Tallahassee, Florida 32306

Dr. Waesche received a Ph.D. in Clinical Psychology from Florida State University. She works for the Florida Center for Reading Research as an assistant in research.

Richard K. Wagner, Ph.D., Robert O. Lawton Disttinguished Professor of Psychology, Department of Psychology, Florida State University, Room A205, 1107 West Call Street, Post Office Box 3064301, Tallahassee, Florida 32306

Dr. Wagner is a researcher and teacher in the psychology department at Florida State University as well as an associate director of the Florida Center for Reading Research. His research interests center on the development of reading, reading disability, and assessment.

William S-Y. Wang, Professor, Department of Electronic Engineering, Chinese University of Hong Kong, Shatin, Hong Kong, China

Dr. Wang is Professor Emeritus at the University of California at Berkeley. He is an honorary professor of Peking University and an academician of Academia Sinica, Taiwan. He works in research at the intersection of linguistics, cognitive neuroscience, and evolutionary theory.

Julie A. Van Dyke, Ph.D., Senior Research Scientist, Haskins Laboratories, 300 George Street, Suite 900, New Haven, Connecticut 06511

Dr. Van Dyke earned her Ph.D. in cognitive psychology from the University of Pittsburgh and her M.Sc. in computational linguistics from Carnegie Mellon University. Her research focuses on identifying the memory mechanisms that support language comprehension with an emphasis on understanding how failed memory retrieval and interference lead to poor comprehension. She is developing new methods to study individual variability in retrieval ability and susceptibility to interference in clinical populations and nondyslexic poor readers.

Johannes C. Ziegler, Ph.D., Director of Research, Laboratoire de Psychologie Cognitive, Aix-Marseille Université, 3 Place Victor Hugo, 13331 Marseille Cedex 3, France

Dr. Ziegler's main interests concern the scientific study of reading including dyslexia, reading development, skilled reading, and computational modeling of reading.

The Dyslexia Foundation and the Extraordinary Brain Series

The Dyslexia Foundation (TDF) was begun in the late 1980s. It was founded by William H. "Will" Baker in collaboration with notable researchers in dyslexia. Through the generosity of the Underwood family and the Baker family, funds were provided to support the establishment of the first Dyslexia Research Laboratory at Beth Israel Hospital, Harvard Medical School, Boston, Massachusetts; the laboratory opened in 1982 with a goal of investigating the neural underpinnings of dyslexia. Baker became Director of Research for the Orton Dyslexia Society and at the urging of Dr. Albert M. Galaburda and others convened top researchers from cognition, neuroscience, and education in a 1987 meeting. That meeting was held in Florence, Italy, under the auspices of the Orton Dyslexia Society, with generous support from Caryl Frankberger and Emily Fisher Landau. The meeting was a symposium at which ideas were presented and discussed, with sufficient time to disagree, to identify research challenges, and to brainstorm solutions. With that meeting, the concept of a dyslexia symposium series was born. In the spring of 1989, the National Dyslexia Research Foundation (later renamed The Dyslexia Foundation) was formed to focus more specifically on research, as the Orton Society continued its primary focus on treatment and education. In 1990, the new foundation sponsored the next symposium in Barcelona, Spain. With this second symposium—the first to be held under the foundation's auspices—the Extraordinary Brain Series was born.

This volume celebrates the 11th symposium in the Extraordinary Brain Series. Nine of the first ten symposia have resulted in volumes that reflect the papers presented and the discussion that was spurred by those presentations. The series makes accessible to all researchers the current thinking of scholars across disciplines as they tackle various aspects of the behavior, neurobiology, and genetics of dyslexia and learning to read and write. This—the 10th such volume—is focused on dyslexia as it is recognized and dealt with across languages and differing orthographies. Following is a listing of the 11 symposia and the 10 related volumes:

I. June 1987, Florence, Italy. Symposium Director: Albert M. Galaburda.

Galaburda, A.M. (Ed.). (1990). *From reading to neurons.* Cambridge, MA: Bradford Books/The MIT Press.

II. June 1990, Barcelona, Spain. Symposium Director: Albert M. Galaburda.

Galaburda, A.M. (Ed.). (1992). *Dyslexia and development: Neurobiological aspects of extraordinary brains.* Cambridge, MA: Bradford Books/Harvard University Press.

III. June 1992, Santa Fe, New Mexico. Symposium Director: Paula Tallal.

Chase, C., Rosen, G., & Sherman, G.F. (Eds.). (1996). *Developmental dyslexia: Neural, cognitive, and genetic mechanisms.* Mahwah, NJ: Lawrence Erlbaum Associates.

IV. June 1994, Kauai, Hawaii. Symposium Director: Benita Blachman.

Blachman, B.R. (Ed.). (1997). *Foundations of reading acquisition and dyslexia: Implications for early intervention.* Mahwah, NJ: Lawrence Erlbaum Associates.

V. June 1996, Kona, Hawaii. Symposium Director: Drake Duane.

Duane, D. (Ed.). (1998). *Reading and attention disorders: Neurobiological correlates.* Mahwah, NJ: Lawrence Erlbaum Associates.

VI. June 1998, Kona, Hawaii. Symposium Director: Barbara Foorman.

Foorman, B. (Ed.). (2003). *Preventing and remediating reading difficulties: Bringing science to scale.* Baltimore: York Press.

VII. June 2000, Crete, Greece. Symposium Director: Maryanne Wolf.

Wolf, M. (Ed.). (2001). *Time, fluency, and dyslexia.* Baltimore: York Press.

VIII. October 2001, Johannesburg, South Africa. Symposium Director: Frank Wood.

Multilingualism and dyslexia. No publication.

IX. June 2004, Como, Italy. Symposium Director: Glenn Rosen.

Rosen, G. (Ed.). (2005). *The dyslexic brain: New pathways in neuroscience discovery.* Mahwah, NJ: Lawrence Erlbaum Associates.

X. June 2007, Campos do Jordao, Brazil. Symposium Directors: Ken Pugh and Peggy McCardle.

Pugh, K., & McCardle, P. (Eds.). (2009). *How children learn to read: Current issues and new directions in the integration of cognition, neurobiology, and genetics of reading and dyslexia research and practice.* New York: Psychology Press, Taylor & Francis Group.

XI. January 2010, Taipei, Taiwan. Symposium Directors: Peggy McCardle, Ovid J.L. Tzeng, Jun Ren Lee, and Brett Miller.

McCardle, P., Miller, B., Lee, J.R., & Tzeng, O. (Eds.). (2011). *Dyslexia across languages: Orthography and the brain—gene—behavior link.*

Preface

Peggy McCardle, Jun Ren Lee, Ovid J.L. Tzeng, and Brett Miller

Dyslexia is in most countries a recognized condition of specific difficulty in learning to read, yet the etiology is still debated and how (and even whether) this condition manifests in certain languages is poorly understood. In particular, there is still much to be learned about issues of dyslexia identification and manifestations in nonalphabetic languages and the potential differences between Asian languages with nonalphabetic orthographies (e.g., Chinese, Japanese) versus alphabetic languages with varied orthographic depth.[1] Because there has been so little work looking at dyslexia and reading and writing ability across languages and orthographies, a major international symposium was organized.

In January 2010, The Dyslexia Foundation's 11th Extraordinary Brain Symposium was held near Taipei, Taiwan. It was jointly sponsored by The Institute for Cognitive Neuroscience (National Yang Ming University) and The Dyslexia Foundation (TDF) and represented a joint celebration of the past 20 years of progress on dyslexia awareness and dyslexia research. This symposium marked the 20th anniversary of the establishment of the Laboratories for Cognitive Neuroscience of the National Yang Ming University in Taipei as well the 20th anniversary year of TDF.

Scientifically, this important symposium provided the opportunity to examine current research into the identification, manifestations, and potential differences in dyslexia across languages. The topics discussed at the meeting hold important implications for basic foundational research on the etiology or etiologies (behavioral, neurobiological, and genetic) of dyslexia and potential comorbid conditions as well as for applied research on the nature of optimal reading instruction and reading and language remediation. In addition, because bilingualism and/or second (or additional) language learning has become increasingly important globally, understanding not only fundamental differences across languages but also the implications of dyslexia for speakers of multiple languages and multiple types of languages has never been more important, both intellectually and economically. The education of all children—which enables them to have employment and career choices—may rest on the outcomes of such research.

---

[1]Orthographic depth is the degree to which a language deviates from a one-to-one sound—symbol correspondence, with one-to-one being the shallowest degree.

In examining the current research in this area and the need for future research, three themes emerged: the importance of basic research, interdisciplinary collaboration, and comparisons across and among languages. Basic research on the neurobiological and genetic underpinnings of how children learn to read and write—and the nature and causes of problems with such learning—is essential. Without understanding how children learn and recognizing when they are having problems, we cannot develop effective interventions or optimal instructional approaches. Research testing the effectiveness of instructional approaches and interventions is part of a cycle of research that feeds back to continuously refine, change, and critically improve interventions and to better our understanding of how to tailor specific instructional or intervention techniques to individual student needs. As they develop and implement interventions, researchers are continuously using what they and their colleagues have learned in order to refine programs and approaches to teaching all children to read as well as to ameliorate the learning situations of those with reading disabilities.

Team-based approaches are the norm today in many areas of science. Dyslexia research is no exception. Interdisciplinary, collaborative research is essential in order to be able to address the many factors involved in a comprehensive study of dyslexia; its possible manifestations; and the neurobiological, developmental, cognitive, and educational ramifications of this reading difficulty. Those imaging various aspects of brain function use a variety of techniques, and each neuroimaging technique has its own strengths and weaknesses in studying reading and writing abilities. To build a coherent picture of brain function during these high-level cognitive tasks, researchers must be able to communicate across methods and approaches and when possible to use different methods with the same individuals in order to maximize what we can learn. Similarly, there are many levels of genetic analysis, from behavioral through cellular and molecular; the information must be brought together at some point to build a coherent picture. It is important that across the broad domains of neurobiology, genetics, and behavior, researchers communicate, share information, and find ways to work collaboratively to bring their various approaches to bear. We are all studying the same problem from various perspectives, which ultimately must converge if we are to reach our explanatory goals.

Finally, if we are to be able to truly address the similarities and differences in how dyslexia is revealed, we must compare studies in various languages and in those who speak and read and write proficiently or are learning to speak and read and write in more than one language. Because of differences in orthographic depth and other cross-language differences, how and at what point in learning dyslexia manifests differ across languages. Therefore, cross-linguistic and bilingual/second-language learner studies are key to addressing empirically the differences in behavioral phenotypes, the differential potential and real manifestations of dyslexia in various languages, and similarities and differences in the neurobiology and genetics of dyslexia across languages.

Two major areas—etiology, and ascertainment and measurement— are fundamental to how research might address the three themes of basic research, interdisciplinary collaboration, and the importance of cross-language and multilingual studies. How etiology and ascertainment are dealt with directly affects how research is conducted across languages and laboratories and how the behavioral, neurobiological, and genetic contributions to dyslexia are measured and analyzed.

Etiology must be studied across languages, in both monolingual and bilingual individuals, and across multiple levels of analysis. It must be studied while taking into account the genetic determinants as well as the neurobiological and behavioral and cognitive characteristics of those who manifest reading difficulties and the impact of environmental and developmental factors on how reading difficulties manifest over time. Such explorations should seek to determine whether in fact different etiologies result in the same or different phenotypes, whether the same etiology might manifest different behavioral phenotypes, or whether etiologies can be used to predict specific behavioral phenotypes. These same questions should be addressed with regard to whether etiology might in some way predict specific developmental trajectories because we know that the manifestation of reading difficulty changes with development over time. Children with reading disabilities in English, for example, may exhibit quite different characteristics in second grade, in fourth or fifth grade, or in high school. Similarly, children whose native language is alphabetic versus nonalphabetic may differ both in the timing of when dyslexia might be most apparent as well the particular ways in which it might be recognized in those languages.

Ascertainment and measurement are crucial to all areas of research. Researchers must have clear reasons for who is included or excluded in studies, as well as what will be measured, how it will be measured, and why. Cross-language research presents particular challenges in measurement and methodology. Comparable measures do not always exist in various languages and may need to be developed; comparability of measures across languages is a key challenge that must be addressed such that the same constructs are measured. Areas to be measured must be common across languages, whether these are being measured in the same individual in various languages or in different individuals in different languages. Researchers must clearly indicate in both their research plans and their publications how subjects were ascertained for inclusion in studies, what specific skills and subskills were measured, and what specific measures were used. If researchers could agree on a few core areas of agreement across laboratories—such as how subjects could be ascertained and what measures or types of measures were to be used across studies—this agreement would greatly facilitate cross-linguistic comparisons and the convergence of evidence to inform both theory and practice.

At the symposium, researchers were charged with considering several empirical questions that were considered crucial to moving the field forward. They were also charged with developing a specific research agenda to share with the broader fields of dyslexia, cognitive science, neuroscience, genetics, and education and special education research. Participants were asked to consider how reading difficulties manifest in languages with different characteristics (alphabetic versus nonalphabetic, differing orthographic depth, differing phonological and morphological characteristics), how genetic profiles interact with environment to influence the manifestation of reading difficulties, and whether there are unique neurobiological and/or behavioral characteristics that are thought to be universal to dyslexia. They were also asked to consider the incidence and prevalence of dyslexia among speakers of various languages and how the characteristics of those languages might affect those statistics.

At the symposium, researchers shared their work, their views, and their best ideas on all of these questions. Discussion was rich and often highly energized. What you will find in this volume are not just papers developed from the talks those researchers presented, but papers that were thoughtfully developed based on both the presentations the authors made and the discussions that ensued throughout the week. We also present to you a research agenda for the continued study of dyslexia across all languages, across orthographic depth, and across varying orthographies requiring different learning strategies, different instructional approaches to reading and writing, and differing techniques for identifying those with dyslexia. We hope that both the symposium and this volume will contribute to more and stronger interdisciplinary collaborations, to more and better research on dyslexia across languages, and ultimately to convergent findings that can guide us all in ensuring that all children, in all languages, are given the optimal opportunities to learn to read and write—regardless of language!

Preface

Peggy McCardle, Jun Ren Lee, Ovid J.L. Tzeng, and Brett Miller

在多數的國家裡，讀寫障礙者是指在學習閱讀時有著特殊困難的人，它的病源還是一個熱烈討論的議題，而科學家對於不同書寫系統裡閱讀障礙者的行為表現異同，更是所知有限。特別是在非拼音文字的國度裡，例如中文或日文，這些屬於口語語音與文字對應較不一致的書寫系統，其閱讀障礙者的徵狀與檢測方式，還有許多待解的謎題；而這些徵狀與檢測方式，可能因為文字系統的差異與拼音文字系統所出現的徵狀和所需的檢測方式而有所不同。這些，都是科學研究者急於想要得到答案的議題[1]。但相關的研究實在太少，所以舉辦這個國際研討會的目的就是希望瞭解不同語言與書寫系統裡，閱讀發展、書寫、讀寫障礙的異同。

2010年元月，美國閱讀障礙基金會在台北舉辦第11屆「卓越大腦國際研討會」。該研討會是美國閱讀障礙基金會與臺灣陽明大學認知神經科學實驗室共同舉辦。一方面，此研討會慶賀閱讀障礙基金會於過去20年裡，在宣導閱讀障礙與促成閱讀障礙研究進展所達成的貢獻，另一方面，也慶祝陽明大學認知神經科學實驗室（原先創立於中正大學心理學研究所）在台灣成立20週年。

從科學研究的角度而言，這個重要的研討會提供了檢驗不同語言在閱讀障礙鑑定、行為表現異同的重要討論平台。在研討會裡所討論的議題，對於閱讀障礙的基礎研究，閱讀障礙與其它疾病可能的共病狀況，以及應用研究都有重要的影響。研討會討論了多項議題，其中基礎研究包括行為、神經生物與基因方面的研究；在應用研究則包括閱讀障礙的教學、閱讀以及語言的矯治。除此之外，因為全世界各國家對於雙語或第二語言學習的重視，此一研討會除了檢視不同語言裡閱讀歷程的差異，也檢視閱讀障礙者的異同，相關知識的進展，對於學習多種語言，或是學習單一語言裡的不同面向，都能夠有所啟發。這不僅對於知識發展，甚至對於經濟上而言，都是極為重要的；學童將來在工作以及職業上的基礎能力，是透過教育施行達成，而優質的教育，正是基於這些研究的成果。

在檢視閱讀障礙研究在過去、現在與未來的需求上，有三個主題盤旋在我們的腦海裡：基礎研究的重要性、跨領域合作，以及跨語言比較。

在基礎研究裡，有兩個根本的議題：神經生物運作與遺傳對於學童在學習閱讀與書寫的影響，以及閱讀與書寫障礙的特性與成因。如果沒有對於閱讀障礙的特性以及成因有所瞭解，就沒有辦法發展出最佳化的教學以及有效的補救教學。在基礎研究的支持下，教學以及介入補救的研究，就可以經由不斷的修正、改變教學方式，達成有效教學的目標。很重要的，這樣的發展模式，最終的目的必須能夠提供針對個別學生在

---

[1] 組字規則深度是指稱一個語言裡口語語音與文字符號的對應程度。如果是一對一的對應狀況，稱為最淺顯對應的文字系統。

教學或是介入需求的處理方式。當研究者能夠不斷的修正以及發展教學方案，方有機會能使得每一個學生具備基本的閱讀能力，以及增進閱讀障礙者在這些基礎能力上的表現。

團隊合作已經是科學研究的常態，閱讀障礙研究也不例外，跨領域的協同合作，對於閱讀障礙方能有全面的瞭解，這包括閱讀障礙者在神經生物上、發展上、認知上、教育上的徵狀。不同的腦功能儀器各有其專擅之處，也有其不足之處。運用不同腦功能儀器、不同研究取向進行研究，有時甚至是針對同一受試者施行不同儀器的研究，才能擴大研究者對於大腦在高等認知運作的瞭解。同樣的，在遺傳領域的研究，也是涵蓋多個層次，包括從行為到分子生物的運作。結合不同層次的分析資訊，才能形成一個共通、完整的瞭解。很重要的是，不管是行為研究、神經生物研究或是遺傳研究取向切入，研究者必須分享、溝通訊息，並且應該要密切地合作。畢竟，不同研究取向想要解決的問題是一致的，形成跨領域的合作，方能對於瞭解閱讀障礙產生最大的效益。

最後，為了要瞭解不同書寫系統裡，閱讀障礙者的共通性與特殊性，必須進行跨語言的研究，以進行比較。跨語言比較的研究議題裡，除了障礙者外，還必須包括能夠順利運作書寫和閱讀的人，或是正在學習和書寫另一個語言的人。不同文字系統裡，因為字音和字形對應的差異、構詞上的差異，學習障礙者在何時，以及如何產生困難會是關鍵的議題。所以，不管是跨語言研究，或是雙語研究，檢視學習者在行為徵狀、神經生物、和遺傳上是相似與差異性，將是基本的議題。

兩個關鍵議題包括病源，以及確認閱讀障礙的方式與測量將會是基礎研究、跨領域合作以及跨語言比較研究的根本。這兩個議題，決定了跨語言以及跨實驗室的研究進行模式，也決定了資料分析的方式。

病源的研究必須基於跨語言的比較上，不但要比對單語者以及雙語者的語言發展歷程，更要分析不同語言層次的語言特徵。這些研究都要考慮閱讀障礙者的遺傳因素以及神經生物和行為/認知的特徵。此外，對與時俱增的環境影響和發展的歷程也要一併考量。在病源的解釋上，必須考量是否不同的病源可能導引出相同或相異的表現型、相同病源可能導致不一樣的表現型、或是能夠利用對於病源的了解，推估特定行為表現的出現。同樣的，由於發展的因素，閱讀障礙者在不同年齡的徵狀可能有差異，對病源的瞭解是否能夠推估發展的軌跡，也就是閱讀障礙者隨成長所帶來的行為改變，也是重要議題。例如說，在英文裡的閱讀障礙者，他/她在二年級、四年級或五年級、高中時，可能有不一樣的徵狀。同樣的，非拼音文字可能在出現明顯閱讀障礙徵狀的時間點與拼音文字不同，這當然會影響不同語言裡，辨識出閱讀障礙者的年齡。

確定研究對象和測量對於所有的閱讀研究領域都是核心的成分。研究者必須決定誰符合研究的條件，如何測量、什麼時候測量，以及這些決定是基於什麼理由。從事跨語言的研究者進行研究時，在測量以及研究法上，面臨特別的挑戰。不同語言裡，不一定具備測量相同概念架構的測量工具，即使名稱相同，也必須考量測量的內容是否相同。發展出不同語言裡各自可以使用的測量工具，且這些工具必須是在同樣的架構以及程序下所發展的，這會是進行跨語言比較的關鍵。除此之外，不管是在單一受試者身上測量不同語言的基礎能力，或是在不同語言下各自測量各自的測驗，測量的面向必須是不同語言裡共通的。研究者必須在研究計劃書以及論文裡，清楚地表達受試者的條件、行為以及認知能力的測驗方式、以及使用哪些測試。在跨國領域的研究裡，如果各國的研究者能夠建立共識，摸索出一致的受試者徵求標準、測量的工具，那將會大幅地增進對於跨語言比較研究的瞭解，以及能夠提供理論與實務的共構證據。

在這個研討會裡，主辦單位請研究者除了需要考量推動整個領域前進的關鍵問題外，也必須思考能夠讓認知科學、神經科學、遺傳學、教育及特殊教育者共同研討的新議題。主辦單位同時也邀請所有的參與者思索不同語言閱讀障礙的行為徵狀、遺傳與環境的互動如何影響閱讀障礙者的行為表現，以及不同語言裡的閱讀障礙者是否具有共通的神經生物或行為特徵。不同國家的參與者，必須考量閱讀障礙在各自國家的發生率與盛行率，並要思索不同語言的特徵、檢測標準，如何影響這些的調查數據。

在這個研討會裡，研究者分享他們的工作內容、觀點以及對於所有問題的最佳概念。在研討會裡的討論是豐富的，且通常是令人興奮的。從這一本書裡，讀者不只會看到研究者呈獻他們在研討會裡分享的內容，同時也包括與他人討論後的成果。在書裡，我們也提出一些重要的研究議題，希望能對未來的研究有所啟發，它涵蓋跨語言、文字的閱讀障礙研究、思索跨語言不同學習需求的可能性、思索閱讀以及書寫裡的不同教學取向、和檢測閱讀障礙的不同方式。我們衷心希望不管是研討會或是這本書，能夠促進跨領域的合作、能夠讓研究者更瞭解不同語言裡閱讀障礙的行為徵狀以及病源。當然，我們更希望能夠讓所有學童，不管是在任何國度裡，都能因為研究的進展，獲得學習閱讀以及學習書寫的最佳教學環境與條件，充分地發揮其潛力。

Acknowledgments

The editors of this volume wish to acknowledge the generous support and assistance of many organizations and individuals in making possible both the highly successful international symposium from which this volume is drawn and the volume itself. In Taiwan, we thank these organizations for their generous contributions of time, effort, and financial support:

Ministry of Education

National Science Council

Academia Sinica

National Yang-Ming University

National Central University

National Taiwan Normal University

Also in Taiwan, we wish to acknowledge with honor and gratitude the following distinguished guests and sponsors of the symposium and the preceding reception:

Dr. Lou-Chuang Lee, Minister, National Science Council

Dr. Tsong-Ming Lin, Deputy Minister, Ministry of Education

Dr. Yan-Hwa Wu Lee, President, National Yang-Ming University

Director Rosemary W. Ho, Wu Chien-Shiung Education Foundation

Mrs. Li Ma Leong, Wu Chien-Shiung Education Foundation

Chairman Cher Hu, D-Link Charity Foundation

Dr. Daisy L. Hung, Director, Institute of Cognitive Neuroscience, National Central University

TECO Technology Foundation

And a very special thanks must go to the Aboriginal Children's Drum Art Performance Team, Chin-Ai Elementary School, Nan-Tou County, Taiwan, for their colorful and inspiring performance at the reception preceding the symposium, and to Ms. Vigo Hsu from *Scientific American* (Chinese Edition) for her help in photographing and recording all the activities at the symposium.

In the United States, we wish to thank The Dyslexia Foundation and its founder and president William H. "Will" Baker and to acknowledge generous contributions from Helen U. Baker, Joan McNichols, the Linden Hill Institute, and the Brehm School.

Special thanks must go to Stefany Palmieri and Rose Lee for their dedicated work in arranging the details of the conference, to Stefany for expert onsite management and assistance, and to Rose for assistance in making sure that the details needed for the volume were provided in an accurate and timely way.

Such major endeavors as the symposium and this volume could not have happened without the dedicated efforts of many researchers and faculty. Therefore, we wish to express our gratitude to the following individuals: Erik Chihhung Chang, Jie-Li Tsai, Chia-Ying Lee, Denise Hsien Wu, Wen Jui Kuo, Shih-Kuen Cheng, Chi-Hung Juan, and I-Hui Hsieh.

Finally—and perhaps most important, as they represent our next generation of scholars—we wish to acknowledge and thank the graduate students from the Taiwanese universities supporting the symposium. These young scholars were tireless in handling all of the technology issues, assisting with logistics at the site, and ensuring that the symposium went smoothly while also attending all symposium sessions and interacting with the presenters and audience. These graduate students made a significant contribution to the success of the symposium: Miao-Hsuan Yen, Chun-Hsien Hsu, Ying-Ying Cheng, Wan-Hsuan Lin, Esther Yi-Chen Lin, Ming Lo, Yuchun Chen, Yu-Yin Lian, Yalin Chen, Yihui Hung, Jing-Yi Shyong, Hui-Chuan Chang, Ting-Ting Chang, and Hsin-Ching Wang.

Acknowledgments

本書的編輯者特別感謝許多機構組織及個人慷慨的支持與協助。他們的支持與協助，不僅讓一個聲名卓著的國際學術研討會，能成功的在臺灣舉辦，其研討會的議題，也成為本書的基本架構。所發表的論文經修正及整合後，完成本書的出版。

在臺灣的機構組織方面，包括教育部、國科會、中研院、陽明大學、中央大學，臺灣師範大學以及東元基金會，都資助了研討會的舉辦。

在臺灣的個人方面，國科會主任委員李羅權博士、教育部次長林聰明博士、陽明大學前校長吳妍華博士、吳建雄學術基金會董事何薇玲女士以及梁馬利女士、友訊慈善基金會董事長胡雪女士，以及中央大學認知神經科學研究所所長洪蘭博士也都積極參與。如果不是這些人的支持，就不可能完成此研討會以及開幕酒會。

編輯羣也特別感謝南投縣仁愛鄉親愛國小的鼓隊，他們在開幕酒會精彩的表演，為此研討會揭開序幕，中文版「科學人」雜誌編輯許碧純小姐，利用相機記錄了整個研討會的活動，讓我們得以回味研討會的點點滴滴。

在美國方面，編輯羣特別感謝閱讀障礙基金會以及其主席威廉．貝克先生、海倫．貝克女士、瓊安．尼可拉斯女士、霖敦高地組織，以及布拉罕學校的支持。

如果沒有美國閱讀障礙基金會的史蒂芬尼．蒲瑪麗小姐在會前的協調聯繫，以及臺灣曾志朗政務委員辦公室李如蕙小姐在會議期間以及此書完成期間鉅細靡遺的協助，本書不可能完成。

此次研討會以及本書的完成，還要歸功於許多來自臺灣認知神經科學實驗室的研究人員，這包括張智宏、蔡介立、李佳穎、吳嫻、郭文瑞、鄭仕坤、阮啟弘與謝宜蕙。

最後，也會是最重要的一群人，因為他們代表下一世代的研究人力，也因為他們確保了整個研討會平順的進行，他們不僅是研討會的工作人員，也是會議的參與者。他們參與了研討會所有的演講。會議期間，他們也與報告者以及聽眾有熱烈的互動。這些研究生包括顏妙璇、徐峻賢、鄭盈吟、林宛萱、林依禎、羅明、陳昱君、連育吟、陳亞琳、洪意惠、熊靜儀、張惠娟、張荸荸，以及汪心淨。

當然，非常清楚的，本書編輯羣也要感謝研討會的報告者，以及之後的論文撰寫者。因為他們的參與以及無私的奉獻，本書才得以完成。

To readers—those who read well and those who struggle to read, in one language or many languages, in alphabetic or nonalphabetic orthographies

僅將此本書獻給所有的閱讀人：閱讀能力佳者或是閱讀有困難者，不管是在單一語言或是多語的狀況，也不管是在拼音文字或是非拼音文字的狀況

INTRODUCTION
The Alphabet and the Sinogram
Setting the Stage for a Look Across Orthographies
William S-Y. Wang and Yaching Tsai[1]

LANGUAGE: SPOKEN AND WRITTEN

Although we share a common ancestry with the chimpanzee, our closest living relative, there is a huge chasm between how chimpanzees communicate and how we communicate. The differences started accumulating after our lines diverged some six million years ago. When, exactly, early *Homo sapiens* acquired language is a question that is often asked. The answer of course depends on how we define *language.* Human communication focused on the increasingly differentiated sounds we made with our mouths. Some of the vocal sounds we inherited from our ancestors, building upon the cyclic movements of our jaw used in chewing food, gradually became articulated as syllables constructed from vowels and consonants. When these early syllables were uttered with meanings shared in a community, the first words were born together with an infrastructure of phonology. When our ancestors varied these words slightly for different but related meanings, such as *lion* versus *lioness,* they invented morphology. When they associated different orders of the same words with different meanings, such as *lion saw monkey* versus *monkey saw lion,* they invented syntax.

The emergence of human language crossed several such phase transitions, and it is impossible at present to know the details of this trajectory, which may have been quite different for the many communities scattered in the ancient world; compare Freedman and Wang (1996) for a polygenetic scenario. However, whatever the scenario for

[1]This chapter is based on remarks presented by the first author at the Extraordinary Brain Symposium (January 16–22, 2010, Taiwan). Due to space limitation, much of the symposium presentation cannot be included here. The symposium was indeed extraordinary and highly successful because it was organized with contributions from many disciplines and from many distinct languages. We thank the organizers of the Symposium and The Dyslexia Foundation for their invitation and colleagues at the symposium for their many helpful discussions. Our work at the Language Engineering Laboratory (LEL) is supported in part by the Shun Hing Institute of Advanced Engineering of the Chinese University of Hong Kong, and the Research Grants Council of Hong Kong SAR. We thank members of the LEL for their collaboration, especially Manson Fong, James Minett, Yang Ruoxiao, and Zhang Caicai for helping us improve this paper in various ways. Special thanks to Peggy McCardle for her invaluable contributions to the symposium and for her excellent editorial suggestions on this chapter.

the prehistoric interactions, it is reasonable to infer from archeological evidence that by some 40,000 years ago, human communication had evolved to something like the languages we speak today, at least in some communities; see Davidson (2010). That is, they had phonology, morphology, and syntax, as well as hundreds if not thousands or tens of thousands of words.

We must not take such dates too seriously, of course, though they are useful as rough guidelines. Language did not suddenly materialize out of thin air. It is grafted on many of the sensory-motor, cognitive, and social skills that had been evolving for millions of years and that we share to varying extents with our chimpanzee relatives today. In recent years, writers have been using terms like *overlaid* (Sapir, 1921), *tinker* (Jacob, 1977), *mosaic* (Wang, 1982, 2007), *exaptation* (Gould, 1991; Gould & Vrba, 1982), *recycle* (Dehaene, 2005), and *reuse* to express this idea. Anderson (2010) discusses *reuse* and compares its various interpretations. Darwin was studying orchids and writing the following words a century and a half ago, but they apply to both spoken language and written language:

> Thus throughout nature almost every part of each living being has probably served, in a slightly modified condition, for diverse purposes, and has acted in the living machinery of many ancient and distinct specific forms. (Darwin, 1862, p. 348)

Written language came much later than spoken language; indeed, the majority of the world's languages do not have writing systems even today. Speech sounds can be heard only in an immediate area, and they disappear as soon as they are uttered. Written texts overcome these limitations in space and time—they can be carried to distant lands and passed on from generation to generation. It has been said of our species that our humanity came with spoken language and our civilization came with written language. Not all visual symbols qualify as writing or orthography, even if they have well-defined meanings. Traffic signs on roads, gender figures on washroom doors, icons on the computer screen, symbols for numbers—these all bear clear messages, but they are not part of a complete system that maps directly to a corresponding spoken language. Unlike orthography, they are pronounced differently in different languages.

The correspondence between a spoken language and a written language is not complete. For instance, intonations express a variety of attitudes, such as doubt, irritation, joy, or sadness, most of which are not indicated in writing. In English, for example, some of these intonations can be approximated by punctuation marks. Moreover, the use of *space* to separate syllables or words on the printed page, as well as many ways of capitalization in various languages, provide information typically absent in spoken language. For example, words in the grammatical category of nouns are all capitalized in written German. In principle, however, a writing system should be able to represent anything that can be said, even though the mapping between the spoken and the written may be quite complex.

Around 10,000 years ago, our ancestors gradually changed from roving tribes of hunter-gatherers to people with sedentary lives, built villages, and began agriculture. From clay, they made pottery as well as tablets that could be inscribed on. The earliest precursors of writing on clay represented numbers and domesticated animals, presumably for keeping records and for trading. These were excavated in West Asia and dated to some 9,000 years ago. From such humble beginnings came the Western tradition of writing, including the early Sumerian cuneiform, the Egyptian hieroglyphics, the Phoenician script, and others, which evolved step by step to the various kinds of alphabetic writing we have in the world today.

THE ALPHABETIC TRADITION

The word *alphabet* was formed by joining the names of the first two letters of the Greek alphabet, *alpha* (α) and *beta* (β). The Latin alphabet is the Roman adaptation of the Greek alphabet and is the most widespread among modern languages today. The idea of the alphabet deeply impressed no less a scholar than Galileo, who considered it the crowning glory of all human inventions:

> But of all other stupendous inventions, what sublimity of mind must have been his who conceived how to communicate his most secret thoughts to any other person, though very far distant, either in time or place? And with no greater difficulty than the various arrangements of two dozen little signs upon paper? Let this be the seal of all the admirable inventions of man. (Galileo, 1632)

As writing systems were transmitted from culture to culture, they took on different forms. One parameter that varies among alphabetic systems is how vowels are written. The distinction between vowels and consonants is universal among all spoken languages, which typically include many more consonants than vowels (Wang, 1971); there is even the possibility that these two classes of sounds are processed separately in the brain (see Caramazza, Chialant, Capasso, & Miceli, 2000). However, languages differ in how vowels are written. In one type of alphabetic writing, of which Arabic is an example, vowels are optional: they may not be written at all. In another type of alphabet, such as is used in many Indic orthographies, vowels are obligatory: they are always written, but as diacritic marks appended to the consonants. These two types have been named *abjad* and *abugida*, respectively (Daniels, 1992; Daniels & Bright, 1996). In contrast to these two types of alphabetic writing—vowel-optional and vowel-diacritic, respectively—vowels are written as full letters, as consonants are, in the Latin alphabet; thus, it may be considered a third type of alphabet: full alphabet.

Table I.1. Vowel sounds in American English

Front	Central	Back	Diphthong
he		who	
hid		hood	
hay	hud	hoe	
head		hod	
had	hard		hi, how, hoy

For example, in English vowels are written on the line much as consonants are. But the mapping between vowel sounds and vowel letters is quite complex. Whereas there are only five vowel letters that English adopted from the Latin alphabet, there are many more distinct vowel sounds. We can easily verify this by considering a set of words such as shown in Table I.1.

Such a complex relationship between the 5 vowel letters of the written language with the 14 vowel sounds of the spoken language is obviously a burden for readers who need to establish a GPC (grapheme–phoneme correspondence) as they try to retrieve the meaning of what is being read. The burden is all the heavier for learners of the English language, whether as native tongue or as a foreign language.

From the viewpoint of GPC, the burden is heavier still when we note that the vowels in most words alter their phonetic values according to their morphology. Thus the stressed vowels in words such as "tut *o* rial" and "manag *e* rial" are reduced to an indistinct schwa sound [ə] when the stress moves away; that is, "tutor" and "manager." But note that the vowel letter in *tutor* tells us how the second vowel should be pronounced when it does carry the stress.

Alternations affect many vowels in a different way in the following set of words, even when the stress does not move:

sanity > sane	*shepherd > sheep*	*fifth > five*
gratitude > grateful	*kept > keep*	*Christmas > Christ*
opacity > opaque	*serenity > serene*	*divinity > divine*
tabular > table	*obscenity > obscene*	*linear > line*
chastity > chaste	*left > leave*	*hid > hide*

English spelling was largely fixed around 1475, when Caxton first introduced printing to England. Spoken language is always changing, and English is no exception. More than five centuries have passed since Caxton, and Modern English is very different from the Middle English of Chaucer.

The vowels in words illustrated in the previous example, such as *sane, sheep,* and *five,* changed their pronunciations several hundred years ago in a systemwide sound change that has been called the Great Vowel Shift; see Wang (1968) for an analysis of this shift. (It is also due to this shift that the name "China" is pronounced with a diphthong [aⁱ] in English, yet it is pronounced with a high front vowel [i] in other

European languages, in agreement with the name of the first Chinese empire which is its probable source, "Qin"; compare French "Chine.") On the other hand, these same vowels were shortened but preserved their vowel height when these words took on certain suffixes, namely -ity in sanity, -itic in Sinitic, -herd in shepherd, and -th in fifth.

Many people have complained about English orthography, and various attempts have been made to reform it, perhaps the best known being that of the writer George Bernard Shaw. Abercrombie (1981) gives a brief historical review of these efforts. Also noteworthy in this regard is the progress that has been made in the science of speech sounds. Our understanding of the speech chain has deepened on several fronts—how the sounds are produced, their acoustic structure, how they are perceived, and the neuropsychology underlying both the production and the perception. We realize now that the goal set by Alexander Melville Bell (1867)—for his universal alphabet to teach the sounds of all languages—is much more ambitious than he realized. Speech sounds are continuous along many different acoustic dimensions, and different languages slice up these continua in different ways. A phonetic feature that is lexically distinctive in one language may not be distinctive in another. For example, the phonetic feature that distinguishes "peel" from "pill" in English is not distinctive in Spanish.

In any case, because a desired end product of the reading process is the words and their combined meanings, it is not clear that attention to all the phonetic details is helpful. English spells the plural suffix in cats and dogs the same way: -s. A more faithful GPC would require us to spell them as cats and dogz, thereby obscuring the identity of the suffix. Similarly, a "shallower" orthography with high GPC would require us to spell the pairs of words with different vowels: sanity and seyn, shepherd and shiyp, hid and hayd. Phonetic fidelity, in the sense of GPC, is only part of the story, but it is surely less important than the preservation of morpheme identity. After all, it is the morphemes that will lead us to the meaning, not the phonetics per se.

An interesting new phenomenon that has arisen in writing English, and in alphabetic writing in general, has to do with numerous innovations found among casual communications on the Internet: abbreviations such as "ruok" for "are you ok?" or emoticons such as ":-)" for a happy face (Crystal, 2001). The phenomenon is too recent for us to assess its ultimate effect on the evolution of written language; much depends on future technological developments.

THE WORLD OF THE SINOGRAM

In contrast to the Western tradition and its various alphabetic writings, the Chinese tradition developed along a different route. The earliest specimens are inscriptions preserved on bronzeware, pieces of pottery (potsherds), and shells and bones. The inscriptions on turtle shells and ox scapulae were discovered only around the beginning of the

20th century, and systematic excavations were begun by archeologists only in the 1920s. Previous to this discovery, countless pieces were ground up for medicinal purposes in the superstitious belief that these inscriptions marked them as bones of the dragon.

Many decades of dedicated scholarly research have enabled us to read most of these inscriptions. Like the habits of many ancient peoples who practiced divination in many parts of the world—most famously at Delphi in ancient Greece—these inscriptions were mostly questions addressed to God, and records were kept of the divinations. Hence they are also called *oracle bone inscriptions*. Heat was applied to processed parts of these oracle bones, and the cracks thus produced were divine responses interpreted by the royal shaman (Chang, 1980; Keightley, 1978). Typically, the inscriptions dealt with prospects of winning a war, appropriate weather for planting crops, likelihood of a successful childbirth, and so forth.

Such inscriptions date to more than 3,000 years ago during the Shang Dynasty and extend a little into the succeeding Zhou Dynasty, several millennia later than the earliest extant writing in West Asia. However, judging by the maturity of these inscriptions and the number of distinct symbols used, experts agree that this orthographic tradition must have started considerably earlier (Cheung, 1983). Nonetheless, no evidence is available so far that is fully convincing of an earlier date than these oracle bone inscriptions, even though occasionally archeologists report likely precursors on potsherds, especially those found in well-known Neolithic sites such as Banpo (半坡) and Dawenkou (大汶口). One such recent report is that of Li X-Q, Harbottle, Zhang, and Wang (2003), who titled their paper "The Earliest Writing? Sign Use in the Seventh Millennium BC at Jiahu." This report has particular significance because the signs were inscribed on tortoise shells, rather than on potsherds.

Because reading is a relatively new function for the brain in evolutionary time, it has been hypothesized that the cortical circuits of this region have been exapted from their earlier function of tracking or "reading" natural trails—a skill that doubtless was highly adaptive for prehistoric hunters. Skills developed from tracking patterns of animal footprints on the ground have been transferred to reading graphic patterns on a printed page (Dehaene, 2009; Dehaene, chapter 6 in this volume).

This line of reasoning is reminiscent of the speculation advanced by China's first lexicographer, Xu Shen (許慎), some 2,000 years ago when he described how the legendary Cang Jie (倉頡) "examined the tracks made by birds and beasts . . . and created writing."[2] Xu also went

---

[2]Here is a fuller quote from the original text from Xu's preface to his great dictionary: 「倉頡之初作書也，蓋依類象形，故謂之文。其後形聲相益，即謂之字。文者，物象之本；字者，言孳乳而寖多也。著於竹帛謂之書。」 We see from this quote that before paper and printing, writing was mainly done on bamboo and silk. This ancient work has been reproduced numerous times over the past two millennia. The quote here is taken from p. 761 of the 1965 version of 說文解字段注, published by 藝文印書館 in Taiwan.

on to say that "the first graphs Cang Jie created imitated the shapes of the categories; these graphs were called *wen* (文). Later, shapes and sounds were combined to form *zi* (字)." In modern Chinese, the first graphs and all the later combinations have been lumped together and called *wenzi* (文字), or simply *writing*.

The unit of Chinese writing—a set of strokes assembled in a square architecture—is popularly known as the Chinese *character*. A more precise term that we use here is *sinogram*. Similarly, although popular descriptions frequently characterize Chinese writing as ideographic or pictographic, a more precise term is *logosyllabic*, as the majority of sinograms are actually phonograms, as we discuss shortly. Due to the early emergence of the sinogram and the broad reach of the Chinese civilization, the sinogram has exerted a profound influence over much of East Asia and parts of Southeast Asia. For two millennia, Vietnamese was written in sinograms, either directly imported from China or in locally created variants, until 1910, when the French colonialists decreed that all public documents be transcribed into *quốc ngữ* (literally, *national language*) based on the Latin alphabet. A lesser known case is that of the Dungan (東干), who emigrated to Kirghistan in the 19th century and replaced their sinograms with a Cyrillic script (Husmann & Wang, 1991).

Korea began to replace the sinogram in the middle of the 15th century, when they invented an ingenious writing system called *Hankul*[3] (literally, *Han writing*). This system is remarkable and unique in that each syllable is represented by the square architecture of the sinogram, and the component graphs actually represent consonants, vowels, and sometimes distinctive features of the language as well. So the system is simultaneously alphabetic and syllabic. The name of the script, Hankul, is written as 한 글. In the left syllable, the circle and the two horizontal lines above it, ㅎ, is the consonant *h*; the short horizontal line together with the vertical line ㅏ is the vowel *a*; and the bent line at the bottom of the square, ㄴ, is the consonant *n*. The right syllable is written vertically downward. The bent line on top, ㄱ, is *k*; the horizontal line, ㅡ, in the middle is *u*; and the remainder below, ㄹ, is *l*.

Japanese and Korean are both Altaic languages; their grammars differ from that of Chinese in fundamental ways in both morphology and syntax, despite much shared vocabulary. Altaic languages are typically rife with sequences of suffixes that cannot be easily written in sinograms, which function primarily as content words. Rather than abandoning sinograms altogether, Japanese adopted a hybrid approach

---

[3]A potential source of confusion lies in the first syllable of these words: *hanzi* in Chinese, *kanji* in Japanese, and *hankul* in Korean. In the first two cases, the *han-* and the *kan-* are two pronunciations of the same morpheme, 漢, the name of one of China's great dynasties, which was roughly a contemporary of the Roman Empire. 漢 is also the name of China's major ethnic group. The Korean *han-*, on the other hand, though homophonous, is a different morpheme, 韓, and refers to the Republic of Korea. This same morpheme is also the name of various kingdoms of ancient China.

for its script. On the one hand, some 2,000 sinograms are kept for daily use in Japan, a few with minor modifications on the original ones imported from China. These are called *kanji,* or Han writing. For instance, the sinogram for Buddha in Chinese is 佛, based on an ancient phonetic transcription of the word imported from India. But in Japanese, the corresponding kanji is written as 仏. More important, based on the square architecture of the sinogram, the Japanese have invented a syllabary of some 50 symbols, most of which represent syllables of the CV type; that is, a consonant followed by a vowel. The Japanese syllabary is called *kana,* a common form of which is called *hiragana.*

The word *hiragana* is written ひらがな, and the four symbols correspond to the four syllables. Note that for the third symbol there are two little dots in the upper right corner; these are diacritics for phonetic voicing. These dots indicate that the *k* in *kana* should be pronounced [g] because of its phonetic environment, much as the *s* in English *dogs* should be pronounced [z], though it is not marked as such. The two scripts, kanji and kana, are used simultaneously in Japanese writing in complementary ways, with kana mostly representing various grammatical morphemes to glue the sentences together and kanji representing most of the content words. It is of great theoretical interest that these two coexisting scripts can be selectively impaired in Japanese aphasics (Sasanuma, 1974).

Consider once again ancient China and the Han dynasty. Xu Shen pioneered a classification of the 9,000 or so sinograms that he compiled in his dictionary by introducing a system of 540 radicals called *bushou* (部首) in Chinese. The idea is that every sinogram belongs to a unique radical and can be found under its radical in the dictionary and by counting the number of residual strokes. The system of radicals has great philosophical interest because it is an orthographic representation of the knowledge of the world, insofar as the totality of sinograms is a representation of the world one can write about. By the time the authoritative *Kangxi Dictionary* was compiled in the 18th century, the system had been reduced to 214 radicals. And with the wholesale simplification of sinograms in the 1950s, which was officially sponsored by the government, the system of radicals was further reduced. The influential dictionary *Xinhua Dictionary,* in its 1992 edition, has reduced the system further to 189 radicals. Although the great majority of the radicals are also independent sinograms with their own sound and sense, a handful are not.

The simplification of the 1950s has an effect on the how phonetics represent the pronunciations of their host sinograms. As examples, the traditional sinograms for *factory* and *large* are 廠 (*chang3*) and 廣 (*guang3*);[4]

---

[4]The numerals at the end of pinyin spellings of Putonghua (common speech, also known as Mandarin in mainland China, Hong Kong, and Macau) words indicate their tones.

their simplified counterparts are 厂 and 广, thereby removing their phonetic clues, which are 敞 (*chang3*) and 黄 (*huang2*), making them no longer phonograms. As a contrast, the simplified sinograms for *protect* and *Chinese* are 护 (*hu4*) and 华 (*hua2*), with the phonetics 户 (*hu4*) and 化 (*hua4*); these are phonetically more transparent than their traditional counterparts, 護 and 華. The simplification also altered the relations of some sinograms to their original radicals and thereby their semantic associations. In the previous two examples, the radicals are different between the respective traditional and simplified forms.

In Figure I.1, 12 radicals are illustrated in gray because they occur in different host sinograms. Each radical has an approximate or fuzzy meaning: the three dots on the left side of the left top sinogram indicate *water,* and the standing cross in the sinogram to the right indicates *wood.* Because the world of meanings is vast and nondiscrete, each radical can offer only a vague hint for the meaning of its host sinogram. For this reason, for most cases we also refer to the radical as the semantic of the host sinogram.

These sinograms are selected because they are all phonograms, in the sense that in each the remaining partial is a phonetic—an independent sinogram with its own pronunciation (except for the two in the bottom row). The phonetic in the left top sonogram, 羊, for instance, is an independent sinogram pronounced *yang2,* meaning *sheep*—the two horns are still visible from its earlier iconic form. But here the partial is serving as a phonetic, so its meaning is irrelevant. The total sinogram is therefore pronounced *yang2;* it means *ocean.* Coincidentally, like the word *logosyllabic,* the approximate meaning of this sinogram is indicated by its radical on the left side, and its syllabic pronunciation is indicated by its phonetic on its right side. Phonograms are the most prevalent type of sinogram; according to various estimates, as much as 80% of the sinograms in Putonghua are phonograms, even though in

Left	洋	water	松	wood
Right	切	knife	頂	head
Top	草	grass	竿	bamboo
Bottom	煮	fire	盟	vessel
Outside	圓	encircle	裏	clothing
Inside	斑	graph	瓣	melon

Figure I.1. Radical positions.

many cases the phonetic can only approximate the pronunciation of its host sinogram. (However, because the definition of *phonogram* varies among reports, a rigorously collected and publicly accessible database would be very helpful for future research.)

In the top right sinogram, the radical (or semantic) on the left means *wood*. The phonetic on the right is pronounced *gong1*, but the host sinogram is pronounced *song1*, with a different initial consonant, and means *pine*. A perfect match in pronunciation between the phonetic and its host sinogram occurs in only about a third of the phonograms in Putonghua (Zhou, 1978). This low rate is perhaps to be expected because a lot of sound changes have occurred over the centuries, which could take a phonetic and its host sinogram along divergent paths of phonetic development. For similar reasons, dialects vary in the degree to which the pronunciations of the phonetic and its host sinogram agree. Indeed, vibrant dialects like Cantonese often create new sinograms based on regional need (Cheung & Bauer, 2002).

Using S for semantic/radical and P for phonetic, the top two sinograms may be described geometrically as SP. But the semantics may appear on the right, as in the two sinograms 刀 and 頁 in the second row of the figure, meaning *knife* and *head*. These sinograms therefore have the geometric description of PS. Similarly, the semantics may appear at top or bottom, outside or inside, as illustrated in the figure. Of all the geometric types illustrated here, SP sinograms by far constitute the majority.

It used to be thought that reading Chinese was a straightforward process going directly from the graphs on paper to the meanings represented by these graphs. Tzeng, Hung, and Wang (1977) disabused us of this overly simplistic misconception with a series of experiments that conclusively demonstrated "speech recoding" in reading Chinese, regardless of whether the sinograms being read are phonograms. Their paper was a turning point in helping launch many studies of the Chinese and Japanese scripts from an experimental perspective (see Hardyck, Tzeng, & Wang, 1977, 1978, and many others).

With the recent technological breakthroughs in computer graphics and brain imaging, we are now in a new era of research on questions of reading. The studies of Lee and colleagues (2007) and Hsu, Tsai, Lee, and Tzeng (2009) have been particularly effective in using the temporal resolution of electroencephalography (EEG) to examine effects of combinability, consistency, and regularity in recognizing sinograms. Also using EEG, Hsiao, Shillcock, and Lee (2007) explore whether the left and right halves of a sinogram—of either the SP or PS structure—may actually fall differently on a split fovea and project to different brain hemispheres. (See also Ellis & Brysbaert, 2010.) These EEG studies have yielded a great deal of information on sublexical processing of the sinogram. We now know that both the radical and the phonetic and their frequencies of occurrence play significant roles in how the brain accesses their host sinograms.

The studies of Kuo and colleagues (2001), Siok, Perfetti, Jin, and Tan (2004), and Lee, Huang, Kuo, Tsai, and Tzeng (2010) have discovered important information regarding which parts of the cortex are more involved in processing sinograms by capitalizing on the spatial resolution of functional magnetic resonance imaging (fMRI). Comparing the brain scans of normal and dyslexic readers, Siok and colleagues (Siok et al., 2009) discovered a region in the left middle frontal gyrus (LMFG) that may be of special significance for reading Chinese. It is intriguing that this region is close to various cortical areas involved with motor control, hinting at a closer connection between reading and writing for sinograms than for alphabetic writing. Because the sinograms are graphically much more complex than letters of the alphabet, Chinese school children typically spend a great deal of time in learning to write them correctly, if not elegantly, thus involving extensive practice of motor skills. Indeed, it is not unusual for a Chinese person to try to recall a forgotten sinogram by tracing its shape with a finger on his or her palm. (This habit sometimes even generalizes to Chinese bilinguals who might trace difficult English words on their palms.)

These studies harnessing the new technology of brain imaging are the leading edge of many ongoing and future waves of research, which will surely bring deeper understanding of the ability to read sinograms. This new understanding will in turn lead to a more balanced knowledge of reading and writing in our species.

READING AND WRITING

Ultimately, our knowledge of reading and writing, normal as well as impaired, must come from the convergence of results from at least three disciplines: linguistics, neuroscience, and psychology. Marcus Raichle (2010), a pioneer in the technology of brain imaging, gives us a current appreciation of the complexity of visual cognition in informational–theoretic terms, of which reading is a special instance:

> Of the virtually unlimited information available in the world around us, the equivalent of 10 billion bits per second arrives on the retina at the back of the eye. Because the optic nerve attached to the retina has only a million output connections, just six million bits per second can leave the retina, and only 10,000 bits per second make it to the visual cortex.
>
> After further processing, visual information feeds into the brain regions responsible for forming our conscious perception. Surprisingly, the amount of information constituting that conscious perception is less than 100 bits per second. Such a thin stream of data probably could not produce a perception if that were all the brain took into account; the intrinsic activity must play a role.
>
> Yet another indication of the brain's intrinsic processing power comes from counting the number of synapses, the contact points between neurons. In the visual cortex, the number of synapses devoted

> to incoming visual information is less than 10 percent of those present.
> Thus, the vast majority must represent internal connections among
> neurons in that brain region. (Raichle, 2010, p. 47)

From the 10 billion bits per second (bits/sec) made available at the
retina, the amount of information is dramatically pruned to a mere
100 bits/sec at the stage of conscious perception at the cortex—a reduction of 100 millionfold! There are many way stations along this route
that participate in this information reduction or filtering, including the
superior colliculi at the brain stem; the lateral geniculate nuclei at the
thalamus; the visual areas at the occipital lobe, especially the Visual
Word Form Area (VWFA) at the occipitotemporal area; among others—
before the visual information reaches the frontotemporal areas of the
cortex to arrive at a conscious perception.

By far, the bulk of the information from the retina is discarded
along this journey. But how does the brain select the "thin stream of
data" of 100 bits/sec at the end of the journey to make sure that it pre-
serves the information the reader needs to recognize the word he or
she is looking at? Clearly, these processes of selection and eventual
perception and recognition are based in large part on what the brain
has learned from the many years of training that culture has provided.

To be able to eventually answer this fundamental question about
brain processes more fully, we need to pay special attention to aspects
of various orthographies, perhaps not unlike the early efforts of Eden
(1960) in his formalization of handwriting. For decades, linguists have
made important use of the concept of "distinctive features" in analyzing the sound systems of the spoken languages of the world; see, for
instance, Jakobson, Fant, and Halle (1951). A parallel approach for the
written languages of the world, discovering their distinctive features,
may prove to be equally essential for understanding reading. The recent
work of Changizi and Shimojo (2005) seems to be a useful step pointing
in this direction, as discussed in Dehaene (2009).

The Latin alphabet, for instance, inclines toward curvilinear (or
circular) strokes in the construction of its letters. The first five letters—
a, b, c, d, and e—are all based on modifications of the circle. In contrast,
the strokes of the sinogram are mostly linear.

Compared with the couple dozen or so letters in the Latin alphabet,
there are far more—thousands of—sinograms in use (Cheng, 1988).
Consequently, their graphic complexity is much greater than that of
alphabets, and their discrimination also requires a higher level of visual acuity. In Table I.2, we illustrate some of the distinctive features that
are necessary for a Chinese reader.

The three sinograms in cell 1A in Table I.2 are each made with
two downward strokes. However, the meeting of these two strokes at
the top is distinctive. It is the same case for the three sinograms in cell
1B, in which the last stroke looks like a fishhook that starts on the left
and proceeds downward. Where it actually starts is distinctive in three

Table I.2. Sinogram "distinctive features" necessary for a Chinese reader

	A	B
1	八 人 入	己 已 巳
2	日 曰	土 士 未 末
3	田 由 胃 冑	甲 申 （由 甲）
4	大 太 犬　王 玉 主	哀 衰 衷
5	戋 戊 戌 戍	丐 丏 宮 官
6	束 柬 東	兵 乒 乓

ways. The two sinograms in 2A are interesting because they are distinguished by their proportions: the taller one means "sun," and the wider one means "to speak." The two pairs of sinograms in 2B are distinguished by the relative lengths of the two horizontal strokes. In each pair, the upper stroke is longer in the right sinogram and the lower stroke is longer in the left sinogram. Similarly, we can discover more distinctive features used in written Chinese by examining the remaining four rows of sinograms given previously.

CLOSING REMARKS

We now close this brief overview of the two major writing traditions in the world today. The alphabet tradition is based on speech segments the size of phonemes. Sapir (1933) first raised the issue of the psychological reality of the phoneme almost a century ago; more recently, Read, Zhang, Nie, and Ding (1986) reexamined this question in the context of Chinese society. The study of Justeson and Stephens (1991) seems to suggest that the syllable has more cognitive saliency than the phoneme; systematic experimentation on this important question has only just begun (see Doignon-Camus, Bonnefond, Touzalin-Chretien, & Dufour, 2009). In any case, it is not clear that high GPC is always desirable for an efficient orthography, especially in languages that have extensive morphophonemic alternations, as illustrated previously with English vowels.

The logosyllabic tradition, as represented by the sinogram, has spawned various offshoot writing systems, such as the Japanese kana and the Korean Hankul, each in its own way successfully representing a national language. The sinogram is of special interest because it simultaneously presents semantic and phonetic information, albeit neither very precisely. Thus, the sinogram allows the brain to search for the word along both dimensions simultaneously from the outset, whereas the alphabet word enables only the phonetic dimension.

An optimal writing system depends on numerous factors both internal and external (Wang, 1981). The internal factors include how the system treats morphophonemic alternations; how it deals with stresses and tones; boundaries of syllables, words, and phrases; and other factors. The system must also respond effectively to problems of homonymy, which is present to varying extents in all languages. How successfully a writing system is learned often depends on many cultural intangibles. A history of literacy in China is reviewed in Wang, Tsai, and Wang (2009). The external factors include—among various cultural and sociopolitical considerations—the method by which the writing system is taught and maintained.

Peng, Minett, and Wang (2010) find that subjects differ in their brain responses to real and pseudosinograms, depending on whether they are from Hong Kong or the mainland. Currently, sinograms are taught on mainland China with the initial aid of an alphabetic system called the Hanyu Pinyin; they are taught in Taiwan with a quasi-syllabic system called Zhuyin Fuhao; they are taught in Hong Kong without any auxiliary phonetic system at all. Unfortunately, there does not seem to be any systematic planned curriculum anywhere to explain the structure of the sinogram to help with its instruction.

Hopefully, future research will help us sort out these many internal and external factors and thus enable us to understand the nature of reading and writing more deeply. Such new knowledge should in turn lead to significant improvements in reading education for both the normal and the dyslexic reader, as well as add to our basic understanding of how the brain works in one of the most distinctive of human activities.

REFERENCES

Abercrombie, D. (1981). Extending the Roman alphabet: Some orthographic experiments of the past four centuries. In R.E. Asher & E.J.A. Henderson (Eds.), *Toward a history of phonetics* (pp. 207–224). Edinburgh, Scotland: Edinburgh University Press.

Anderson, M.L. (2010). Neural re-use as a fundamental organizational principle of the brain. *Behavioral and Brain Sciences, 33*, 2245–2313.

Bell, A.M. (1867). *Visible speech: The science of universal alphabetics; or, Self-interpreting physiological letters, for the writing of all languages in one alphabet.* London: Simpkin, Marshall.

Caramazza, A., Chialant, D., Capasso, R., & Miceli, G. (2000). Separable processing of consonants and vowels. *Nature, 403*, 428–430.

Chang, K.C. (1980). *Shang civilization.* Princeton, NJ: Yale University Press.

Changizi, M.A., & Shimojo, S. (2005). Character complexity and redundancy in writing systems over human history.

Proceedings of the Royal Society B, 272, 267–275.

Cheng, C.C. (1988). Quantification for understanding language cognition. In B.K. T'sou, T.B.Y. Lai, S.W.K. Chan & W.S.-Y. Wang (Eds.), *Quantitative and computational studies on the Chinese language* (pp. 15–30). Hong Kong: City University of Hong Kong Press.

Cheung, K.-H., & Bauer, R. (2002). *The representation of Cantonese with Chinese characters.* Journal of Chinese Linguistics Monograph Series (No. 18). Berkeley, CA: Project on Linguistic Analysis.

Cheung, K.-Y. (1983). Recent archeological evidence relating to the origin of Chinese characters. In D.N. Keightley (Ed.), *The origins of Chinese civilization* (pp. 323–391). Berkeley: University of California Press.

Cheung, Y.-S. 張日昇. (1968). 試論上古四聲 (A study of the tones in Archaic Chinese). 香港中文大學中國文化研究所學報, *1*, 113–170.

Crystal, D. (2001). *Language and the Internet.* Cambridge, England: Cambridge University Press.

Daniels, P.T. (1992). The syllabic origin of writing and the segmental origin of the alphabet. In P. Downing, S.D. Lima, & M. Noonan (Eds.), *The linguistics of literacy* (pp. 83–110). Amsterdam: John Benjamins.

Daniels, P.T., & W. Bright (Eds.). (1996). *The world's writing systems.* New York: Oxford University Press.

Darwin, C. (1862). *On the various contrivances by which British and foreign orchids are fertilised by insects, and on the good effects of intercrossing.* London: John Murray.

Davidson, I. (2010). The colonization of Australia and its adjacent islands and the evolution of modern cognition. *Current Anthropology, 51*(1), S177–S189.

DeFrancis, J. (1989). *Visible speech: The diverse oneness of writing systems.* Honolulu: University of Hawaii Press.

Dehaene, S. (2005). Evolution of human cortical circuits for reading and arithmetic: The "neuronal recycling" hypothesis. In S. Dehaene, J.-R. Duhamel, M.D. Hauser, & G. Rizzolatti (Eds.), *From monkey brain to human brain* (pp. 133–158). Cambridge, MA: The MIT Press.

Dehaene, S. (2009). *Reading in the brain.* New York: Penguin Viking.

Doignon-Camus, N., Bonnefond, A., Touzalin-Chretien, P., & Dufour, A. (2009). Early perception of written syllables in French: An event-related potential study. *Brain & Language, 111,* 55–60.

Eden, M. (1960). On the formalization of handwriting: Structure of language and its mathematical aspects. *Proceedings of the Twelfth Symposium in Applied Mathematics, XII,* 83–88.

Ellis, A.W., & Brysbaert, M. (2010). Split fovea theory and the role of the two cerebral hemispheres in reading: A review of the evidence. *Neuropsychologia, 48,* 353–365.

Freedman, D.A., & Wang, W.S.-Y. (1996). Language polygenesis: A probabilistic model. *Anthropological Science, 104*(2), 131–138.

Galilei, G. (1632). *Dialogo di Galileo Galilei (Galileo's Dialogue).*

Gould, S.J. (1991). Exaptation: A crucial tool for evolutionary psychology. *Journal of Social Issues, 47,* 43–65.

Gould, S.J., & Vrba, E.S. (1982). Exaptation: A missing term in the science of form. *Paleobiology, 8,* 4–15.

Hardyck, C., Tzeng, O.J.L., & Wang, W.S.-Y. (1977). Cerebral lateralization effects in visual half-field experiments. *Nature, 269,* 705–707.

Hardyck, C., Tzeng, O.J.L., & Wang, W.S.-Y. (1978). Lateralization of function and bilingual decision processes: Is thinking lateralized? *Brain and Language, 5,* 56–71.

Hsiao, J.H.-W., Shillcock, R., & Lee, C.-Y. (2007). Neural correlates of foveal splitting in reading: Evidence from an ERP study of Chinese character recognition. *Neuropsychologia, 45,* 1280–1292.

Hsu, C.-H., Tsai, J.-L., Lee, C.-Y., & Tzeng, O.J.L. (2009). Orthographic combinability and phonological consistency effects in reading Chinese phonograms: An event-related potential study. *Brain and Language, 108,* 56–66.

Husmann, L.E., & Wang, W.S.-Y. (1991). Ethnolinguistic notes on the Dungan. *Sino-Platonic Papers, 27,* 71–84. University of Pennsylvania: Department of Oriental Studies.

Jacob, F. (1977). "Evolution and Tinkering." *Science, 196*(4295), 1161–1166.

Jakobson, R., Fant, C.G.M., & Halle, M. (1951). *Preliminaries to speech analysis.* Cambridge, MA: MIT Press.

Justeson, J.S., & Stephens, L.D. (1991). The evolution of syllabaries from alphabet: Transmission, language contract, and script typology. *Die Sprache, 35,* 2–46.

Keightley, D.N. (1978). *Sources of Shang history.* Berkeley: University of California Press.

Kuo, W.-J., Yeh, T.-C., Duann, J.-R., Wu, Y.-T., Ho, L.-T., Hung, D.L., et al. (2001). A left-lateralized network for reading Chinese words: A 3T fMRI study. *NeuroReport, 12,* 3997–4001.

Lee, C.-Y., Huang, H.-W., Kuo, W.-J., Tsai, J.-L., & Tzeng, O.J.L. (2010). Cognitive and neural basis of the consistency and lexicality effects in reading Chinese. *Journal of Neurolinguistics, 23*(1), 10–27.

Lee, C.-Y., Tsai, J.-L., Chan, W.-H., Hsu, C.-H., Hung, D.L., & Tzeng, O.J.L. (2007). Temporal dynamics of the consistency effect in reading Chinese: An event-related potentials study. *NeuroReport, 18,* 147–151.

Li, X.-Q., Harbottle, G., Zhang, J., & Wang, C. (2003). The earliest writing? Sign use in the seventh millennium BC at Jiahu, Henan Province, China. *Antiquity, 77*(295), 31–45.

Peng, G., Minett, J.W., & Wang, W.S.-Y. (2010). Cultural background influences the liminal perception of Chinese characters: An ERP study. *Journal of Neurolinguistics, 23,* 416–426.

Raichle, M.E. (2010). The brain's dark energy. *Scientific American* (March), 44–49.

Read, C., Zhang, Y.-F., Nie, H.-Y., & Ding, B.-Q. (1986). The ability to manipulate speech sounds depends on knowing alphabetic writing. *Cognition, 24,* 31–44.

Sapir, E. (1921). *Language.* New York: Harcourt.

Sapir, E. (1933). "La réalité psychologique des phonèmes." *Journal de Psychologie Normale et Pathologique, 30,* 247–265.

Sasanuma, S. (1974). Impairment of written language in Japanese aphasics: Kana versus kanji processing. *Journal of Chinese Linguistics, 2,* 141–158.

Siok, W.T., Kay, P., Wang, W.S.-Y., Chan, A.H.D., Chen, L., Luke, K.-K., et al. (2009). Language regions of brain are operative in color perception. *Proceedings of the National Academy of Sciences, 106*(20), 8140–8145.

Siok, W.T., Perfetti, C.A., Jin, Z., & Tan, L.H. (2004). Biological abnormality of impaired reading is constrained by culture. *Nature, 431,* 71–76.

Tzeng, O.J.L., Hung, D.L., & Wang, W.S.-Y. (1977). Speech recoding in reading Chinese characters. *Journal of Experimental Psychology: Human Learning and Memory, 3,* 621–630.

Wang, F., Tsai, Y.-C., & Wang, W.S.-Y. (2009). Chinese literacy. In D. Olson & N. Torrance (Eds.), *Cambridge handbook on literacy* (pp. 386–417). Cambridge, UK: Cambridge University Press.

Wang, W.S.-Y. (1968). Vowel features, paired variables and the English vowel shift. *Language, 44,* 695–708.

Wang, W.S.-Y. (1971). The basis of speech. In C.E. Reed (Ed.), *The learning of language* (pp. 267–306). New York: National Council of Teachers of English.

Wang, W.S.-Y. (1981). Language structure and optimal orthography. In O.J.L. Tzeng & H. Singer (Eds.), *The perception of print: Reading research in experimental psychology* (pp. 223–236). Hillsdale, NJ: Lawrence Erlbaum Associates.

Wang, W.S.-Y. (1982). *Explorations in language evolution.* Hyderabad, India: Osmania University Press.

Wang, W.S.-Y. (2007). The language mosaic and its biological bases. *Journal of Bio-Education, 2*(1), 8–16.

Xu, S. 許慎. (1965). 說文解字段注 (Duan's annotation of *Shou Wen Jie Zi*). 台北: 藝文印書館.

Zhou, Y.-G. 周有光. (1978). 現代漢字中聲旁的表音功能問題 (The question of how well phonetic components in Chinese characters express sounds). 中國語文, 3, 172–177.

Looking Across Orthographies

跨語言研究

PART I CONTENTS

CHAPTER 1

Reading Processes and Reading Problems

Progress Toward a Universal Reading Science

Charles A. Perfetti

The history of reading science is a narrative of asynchronies. Research on basic reading processes and observations of reading problems have not always been in harmony to the degree that we see today. The year 1908 saw the publication of the groundbreaking volume on reading research by Edmund B. Huey, *The Psychology and Pedagogy of Reading.* This book, written while Huey was building the first Department of Psychology at the University of Pittsburgh, was a tour de force that— more than 100 years later—still rewards the reader's effort with the most impressive observations of basic reading processes. Huey described word identification (including the narrow span of visual attention and the word superiority effect), the role of phonology ("inner speech"), comprehension, the evolution of writing systems and the alphabetic principle, and teaching reading (including a debate about phonics), among other things. If these topics sound familiar, it is because they are the staple issues of reading research 100 years later. And the information presented about some of these issues has stood the test of time and the advent of more sophisticated methods to study reading processes.

Huey, however, ignored a question that eventually became one of the most important in reading science: What goes wrong when children have trouble learning to read? That is, what is the nature of what we now call *reading disability,* or dyslexia? Huey dealt with only one problem associated with reading—eye fatigue and how reading hygiene (e.g., adequate lighting) can combat this problem. Although some publications on dyslexia from contemporaries of Huey existed (e.g., Hinshelwood, 1917), these publications were medical case studies and likely escaped the notice of Huey, an experimental psychologist.

This neglect was revisited in 1925, when Samuel Torey Orton published his groundbreaking article on dyslexia, "Word Blindness in School Children," without reference to any prior observations about normative reading. Orton set forth his ideas about hemispheric specialization and "twisted symbols" in what became the landmark analysis of reading disability. However, one searches in vain for reference to Huey or to any of the research Huey reviewed.

Things have changed. From a disconnect between the study of basic reading and the study of reading disability has come a period of mutual influence and convergence. Multiple factors must have contributed to this shift, but significant credit must go to the handful of researchers such as Max Coltheart (1981), who applied his theory of word reading to dyslexia and to studies of dyslexia that reported subtypes that could be linked to word-reading procedures.

This mutual influence is one important component of a more general progress in reading science—a progress that links reading processes to reading problems and that also fills in more of the pictures painted by Huey and Orton. There has been progress in many subareas of reading: the ability to measure reading while it happens on individual words, the development of computational models of word reading, and the analysis of reading comprehension (and its subparts, word, sentence, and text processes), among other things. In what follows, I sketch just a few of these subareas that I see as especially useful in bringing us toward a universal reading science.

THE DISCOVERY OF A CENTRAL ROLE FOR PHONOLOGY IN READING

Although Huey emphasized that reading involves an "inner voice," the important role of phonology in reading was not widely accepted in later descriptions of reading. Indeed, the idea of the inner voice needed decomposition to be addressed carefully. Is it about implicit speech entrained to a memory for extended sections of text (and if so, is it functional or epiphenomenal?) or is it about a means for identifying words from conversion of letters to phonemes? These issues have been addressed, with conclusions of predictable complexity.

The simple point, however, is that in the 70 years after Huey's writing, reading was viewed as mainly a visual process. As Frank Smith put it in *Reading without Nonsense*, fluent readers of English "recognize words in the same way that fluent Chinese readers recognize words" (1979, p. 89). The unstated assumption here was that Chinese is read visually without phonology, with the assertion that readers of English also read without phonology. The early forms of the dual route model, which argued for discrete routes to word reading, provided convergence for this view because although there was a phonological route, the direct visual (nonphonological) route was dominant for skilled reading. The phonological route was for children.

The idea that phonology is a routine part of word reading in English started its ascendancy in the late 1980s in studies of brief exposure masking (Perfetti & Bell, 1991; Perfetti, Bell, & Delaney, 1988), semantic categorization (Van Orden, 1987), and primed lexical decision (Lukatela, Lukatela, & Turvey, 1993). "Fast priming" eye-tracking studies (Ashby & Clifton, 2005; Rayner, Sereno, Lesch, & Pollatsek, 1995) and recent event-related potential (ERP) studies (e.g., Ashby, Sanders, & Kingston, 2009) have added evidence based on fine-grained online procedures. The evidence became strong enough by 1998 that Frost (1998) could propose the "strong phonological theory" to capture the observation that phonology is an obligatory part of word reading.

The question of the nature of word phonology in reading has been less of an object of study, but recent research using eye tracking suggests that syllabic information is functional in word identification (Ashby & Martin, 2008); a recent ERP study suggests that phonemic features (e.g., voicing) are functional (Ashby, Sanders, & Kingston, 2009). Thus the consensus has shifted from phonology as a minor and optional part of word reading to phonology as a routine or automatic process that is triggered by orthography. The content of this phonology is perhaps not just a string of phonemes, but a relatively rich bundle of phonemic features and syllabic information. The function of all this phonology may be to help stabilize the identity of the word and make it available for other processes that need this identity in comprehension.

THE CAUSES OF DYSLEXIA

The early accounts of reading disability (Hinshelwood, 1917; Morgan, 1896) emphasized visual symptoms and their associated neurological causes. The title of Hinshelwood's book, *A Case of Congenital Word Blindness,* captured the basic idea well, and this phrase can be found in later case studies of reading disability. As a very specific word-reading problem, this core symptom—the inability to read words—continues to be studied as alexia and an even more selective problem, alexia without agraphia. Interestingly, although alexia is usually considered an acquired disorder, its predecessor, word blindness, was applied to children for what we would now call *developmental dyslexia* (Minogue, 1927).

Orton's (1925, 1928) theory emphasized a more complex set of problems: a difficulty associating the visual forms of words with their spoken forms, which was symptomatically linked with word- and letter-perception anomalies, especially letter reversals. These manifestations of "strephosymbolia" and its image of "twisted signs" seemed to dominate the application of Orton's work to children's reading problems. The more interesting and more sustainable idea from Orton's theory was that the cause of these symptoms was a failure of the brain to acquire hemispheric dominance, thus depriving the left hemisphere of its function in the mapping of visual forms to language.

Neuroimaging studies suggest that Orton may have been correct in this hemispheric hypothesis. Guinevere Eden and colleagues (Turkeltaub, Gareau, Flowers, Zeffiro, & Eden, 2003) reported that younger and less skilled readers show right temporal hemisphere activation in an implicit reading task and reduced activation in left temporal and frontal (inferior frontal gyrus) areas that are activated in the brains of older and more skilled readers. A related pattern of high skill associated with the left hemisphere and low skill associated with the right hemisphere was reported by Pugh et al. (2001).

The consensus for the post-Orton period can be loosely characterized as an emphasis on visual symptoms and visual-neurological causes with "subtyping" that recognized different manifestations and causes, always including visual neurological, but usually with subtypes. There were few studies to challenge or confirm this visual picture, but eye-scanning research (Tinker & Goodenough, 1931) seemed to confirm the importance of visual anomalies in reading problems.

Now, the consensus on reading disability parallels that of the role of phonology in reading. Phonology is part of word reading, and problems with phonology are causal in reading disability. The ascendancy of the phonological deficit hypothesis has been unrelenting since the late 1970s. There were many contributions to this rise, including Frank Vellutino's 1981 review, which argued against visual deficits and for verbal-based deficits; Bradley and Bryant's 1978 study that suggested an important role for phonemic awareness in learning to read; and related research (e.g., Liberman & Shankweiler, 1987) that strengthened the argument for phonemic awareness and suggested a general role of phonology in reading skill (Brady, Shankweiler, & Mann, 1983). As studies of dyslexia showed increasing evidence for phonological problems, visual system explanations continued to be offered with specific neurological hypotheses (Lovegrove, Bowling, Badcock, & Blackwood, 1980; Stein & Walsh, 1997).

Reading disability should reflect multiple causes because reading involves interacting neural systems. However, phonological factors are usually instrumental in dyslexia, even when they are not the only factor. Ramus et al. (2003), on the basis of published case studies, found that although a few cases had visual problems and a few had cerebellar problems, all 16 cases had phonological problems. This conclusion, based on published case studies, seems to comport with conclusions based on behavioral and cognitive neuroscience experiments.

The neuroimaging studies provide some convergence. Reading disability is associated with underactivation of both the dorsal (superior-temporal and superior parietal) and ventral pathways of the reading network (Pugh et al., 2001; Shaywitz et al., 1998, 2002). Furthermore, imaging studies show that phonological training for children with low reading skills leads to changes in activation along these left hemisphere pathways (Pugh et al., 2001; Simos et al., 2002; Temple et al., 2003). Similar changes are found for skilled adults who learn to read new artificial words with the help of phonology (Sandak et al., 2004). Figure 1.1 shows the locus of observed effects schematically.

The increased activation of specific areas for word reading may be part of a general picture of the effects of training. Brain areas activated during task performance tend to be more diffuse and more frontal for novices, whereas for experts they are stronger in areas that support performance of the specific tasks (Hill & Schneider, 2006). However, with reading expertise acquired over 15 years of reading, the brain resources needed for a word-reading event may decrease. Pugh et al. (2008) reported that skilled readers show a decrease in activation in word-reading areas

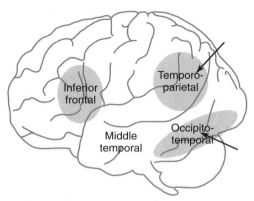

Figure 1.1. Some components of the left hemisphere reading network represented schematically. Arrows indicate posterior areas, including dorsal and ventral "visual word areas," that are affected by training.

when a word is repeated; less skilled readers show an increase. The general picture for reading expertise may be increasing specialization with reduced resources needed within the specialized areas.

Research on dyslexia has progressed in other ways, notably in the genetics of reading disability (e.g., Olson & Byrne, 2004; Smith, Chapter 14, this volume). In addition, an important trend in conceptualizing dyslexia is the distinction between experience deficits and processing deficits. In this conceptualization, "orthographic dyslexia" (or "surface" dyslexia) in English occurs when experience is insufficient to build up orthographically specified word forms (Harm & Seidenberg, 1999; Manis, Seidenberg, Doi, McBride-Chang, & Peterson, 1996). This simplifying move would leave phonological deficits as the main cause of dyslexia.

Reading Problems "Beyond the Word"

The scope of the comprehension problem as a percentage of individuals affected is probably larger than for word-reading disability. In the United States, the 2009 National Assessment of Educational Progress results continued a trend that identifies about 25% of eighth graders and 33% of fourth graders as failing to meet the basic level (the lowest standard) of comprehension.

Understandably, comprehension problems have not been a research priority on par with word reading problems. The research-based consensus on learning to read and on dyslexia is unmatched in comprehension, which is a more complex set of processes. The study of text comprehension can be understood to begin where the study of word-reading leaves off—an assumption that leads to virtually no overlap of the research communities of word reading with those of comprehension.

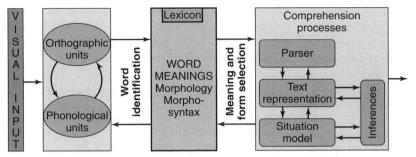

Figure 1.2. The centrality of word meaning in reading. In a feed-forward system, access to word meaning is the output of word identification processes and the input to comprehension processes. In a system that allows direct feedback from comprehension to word identification, the distinction between word identification and comprehension is blurred, but the role of word meaning remains central.

The assumption that text comprehension begins where word reading ends misses the important point that words are pivotal to both. The meaning of a word is the output of word identification and the input to comprehension, which places word meaning squarely in the center of reading. This simple idea is represented in Figure 1.2.

Research on comprehension problems has attended more to the "downstream" comprehension processes that make inferences and monitor comprehension (e.g., Cain & Oakhill, 1999; Nation, 2005; Perfetti, Landi, & Oakhill, 2005). Word comprehension is the neglected middle, despite its pivotal location in comprehension. The role of word meaning is significant in the construction-integration model of Walter Kintsch (1988) in the free-flowing construction phase, in which associations to text elements become activated before the meaning of the word actually read comes to dominate the activation network and provide a meaning link with other text meanings (propositions). The idea that things might go wrong in comprehension precisely at this point does not seem to have attracted much notice in research. Of course, vocabulary has been studied and shows moderately high correlations with reading comprehension. At a more specific level, research by Nation and Snowling (1998, 1999) and Nation (2005) suggests more subtle word semantic deficits (i.e., meaning processing problems) for children with comprehension problems. This suggestion has stimulated other research on the role of word-meaning knowledge in comprehension skill (e.g., Landi & Perfetti, 2007). The lexical quality hypothesis (Perfetti, 2007) is an explicit claim that knowledge of word form and word meaning drives comprehension and that differences in comprehension skill result from differences in this knowledge.

The implication of the semantic deficit hypothesis and the lexical quality hypothesis is that comprehension problems will be observed on a word-by-word basis as readers try to connect the currently read word with the meaning of the text. There is evidence from adult ERP studies suggesting that low-skill comprehenders show less robust word-to-text integration patterns (measured by the N400) when they must understand a word in one sentence as related to the meaning of the preceding sentence (summarized in Perfetti, 2007).

As work on comprehension problems progresses, it is tempting to put forth this parallel: Semantic processing problems are to comprehension failure as phonological problems are to dyslexia. These problems will turn out to be about the number of words a reader knows and a by-product of this knowledge—the ability to retrieve the right features of word meaning to an ongoing understanding of the text.

A MORE UNIVERSAL READING SCIENCE

Has the progress cited been about only progress in reading English? This issue was forcefully expressed by David Share: "The idiosyncrasies of English, an exceptional, indeed, outlier orthography in terms of spelling-sound correspondence, have shaped a contemporary reading science preoccupied with distinctly narrow Anglocentric research issues that have only limited significance for a universal science of reading" (2008, p. 584).

Share's argument causes one to wonder about the status of such things as a nonphonological route to reading, surface (orthographic) dyslexia, and even phonemic awareness in non-English contexts. Indeed, on the one hand, such ideas, which have seemed so central to reading science, may be less than universal. On the other hand, the fact is that reading research by now has a distinctly universal character and its Anglocentrism is on the wane.

First, we have had analyses of writing systems and orthographies that have put reading procedures in a universal perspective for some time. The orthographic depth hypothesis (Katz & Frost, 1992) aimed to explain how variations among orthographies in the transparency of their grapheme-phoneme mappings can affect word reading processes. (One example of a possible ordering from shallow [transparent] to deep is shown in Figure 1.3.)

Figure 1.3. One possible interpretation of orthographic depth, restricted to a very small sample of alphabetic writing. Vowel-less Hebrew and Arabic are deep, but with the vowels included they are shallow.

The universal phonological principle (Perfetti, Zhang, & Berent, 1992) claimed that reading engages phonology at the earliest moment and smallest unit allowed by the writing system. Finally, a refinement of this principle hypothesized that reading procedures assemble phonology according to the grain size of the orthography (Ziegler & Goswami, 2005). Each of these overlapping ideas—orthographic depth, universal phonology, and grain size—has been the object of experimental testing and has guided thinking about what is universal and what is particular across writing systems and orthographies. (I add my usual plea that we distinguish these two, reserving *writing systems* for deep principles of graph-to-phonology mapping and *orthographies* for specific implementation of these principles 'and to keep both apart from *script*, the form details of the graphs.)

It is also useful to note that explicit comparisons across European orthographies have been made and that these comparisons align with the hypothesized differences between English and more shallow orthographies (Aro & Wimmer, 2003).

The Universal Phonological Principle Revisited

Although variation in the implementation of the Greco-Roman alphabets to European languages is interesting, the differences are relatively minor compared with the choices made for writing systems. Chinese provides a high contrast to the set of alphabetic orthographies taken as a whole, so it is this contrast—alphabetic versus logographic (or morphosyllabic)—that has been the real testing ground for the idea of a universal phonology. Whereas alphabets allow letters to activate phonemes, Chinese does not have graphic units that correspond to phonemes. Its graphic units allow connections to syllable-size morphemes.

The universal phonological principle (UPP) claimed that this fact about Chinese mattered only for the details of how phonology came to be activated. The syllable-level phonology, however, was claimed to be a routine or automatic part of character reading. When one considers the fact that a given syllable is associated with many morphemes or words, phonology in Chinese is a nontrivial claim. As illustrated in Figure 1.4, it should be adaptive to go directly from character to meaning because a route from character to syllable does not give much information about meaning. Despite this homophony, the conclusion from a substantial body of research was that phonology is activated anyway.

The details of how phonology is implemented, however, are significantly different. The model proposed by Perfetti, Liu, and Tan (2005) builds an orthographic threshold component to phonology in Chinese. At the point of character identification, this threshold is reached, and activation goes in parallel to the pronunciation of the character and to its meaning. The time course of phonology activation and meaning selection should vary with properties of the character and syllable (number of homophones, character frequency, meaning and phonological consistency

Meaning system

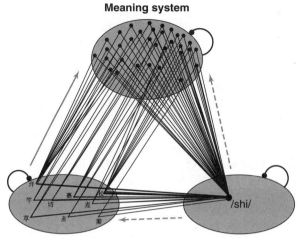

Orthographic system　　　　**Phonological system**

Figure 1.4. Homophony in Chinese. A single syllable can associate with many morphemes. So converting a character to its pronunciation yields many competing morphemes (or words), thus making a pathway from graph to meaning adaptive for reading. (Copyright © 2005 U.S. National Academy of Sciences.) (From Tan, L.H., Spinks, J.A., Eden, G., Perfetti, C.A., & Siok, W.T. [2005]. Reading depends on writing, in Chinese. *Proceedings of the National Academy of Sciences, USA, 102,* 8781–8785; reprinted by permission.)

of radicals), but its phonological activation can sometimes be in evidence prior to semantic activation (Perfetti, Liu, & Tan, 2005; Tan & Perfetti, 1998). Its function, despite the homophony, is the same as in alphabetic writing: not to *mediate* access to meaning but to *stabilize* the word identity.

The Neural Basis of Chinese Reading and Dyslexia

Neuroimaging studies of Chinese show a picture of a partly shared and partly different reading network, compared with alphabetic reading. Many of these studies were carried out by Li-Hai Tan and colleagues (Tan, Feng, Fox, & Gao, 2001; Tan, Liu, et al., 2001). A meta-analysis by Tan, Laird, Li, and Fox (2005) on studies that explicitly tap into phonology led to the picture illustrated in Figure 1.5. (Another meta-analysis of a larger set of studies by Bolger, Schneider, & Perfetti, 2005, led to a slightly different but not incompatible picture.)

We can suggest that the differences shown in Figure 1.5 reflect the recruitment of brain areas in response to two factors: the visual properties of characters (requiring spatial analysis of characters in posterior visual areas) and the mapping principles of characters (involving storage of larger grain phonological units) in parietal (phonological memory) and frontal areas. The left middle frontal gyrus (LMFG) is especially interesting because its function could be one of several that are consistent

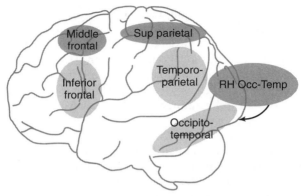

Figure 1.5. Brain networks for alphabetic and Chinese, based on Tan, Laird, Li, and Fox (2005). Chinese involves right hemisphere homologues to the left hemisphere (LH) occipital-temporal area for character identification. Posterior parietal (compared with superior-temporal for alphabetic) and left middle temporal gyrus (compared with inferior frontal gyrus) are involved in phonological and character memory processes. (*Key:* RH; right hemisphere.)

with the demands of Chinese reading. One possibility is that LMFG activity reflects character composition (i.e., stroke sequences) consistent with its location near Exner's area in Broca's area 6, where damage is associated with loss of writing ability. The appeal of this idea is that writing is an integral part of traditional Chinese literacy and may continue to support reading.

A second hypothesis is that the LMFG includes a spatial memory structure that retains an orthographic representation for semantic and phonological processing. The need for such an additional "holding area" beyond the initial orthographic activation in the posterior area comes from the homophony problem. In alphabetic reading, a "release" of spelling information is possible, as phonology is computed rapidly to stabilize identification. Chinese reading, in which phonology is dependent on an orthographic threshold, could benefit from additional access to the character form to verify character identity in the face of phonologically based activation of homophones. This second interpretation of the LMFG may be consistent with a role that extends beyond Chinese to alphabetic reading. LMFG areas near those found in Chinese reading have been reported in studies of English by Binder et al. (2003) and Bolger, Hornickel, Cone, Burman, and Booth (2008) that implicate grapheme-phoneme inconsistency in LMFG activation.

Regardless of how its function is understood in detail, the LMFG seems to be a locus of Chinese reading problems. The LMFG shows less activation (Siok, Perfetti, Jin, & Tan, 2004) and reduced mass (Siok, Niu, Jin, Perfetti, & Tan, 2008) for children with reading problems. This finding certainly suggests that a neuroscientific description of dyslexia will be somewhat different for Chinese reading than for alphabetic reading.

Differences in neuroimaging data across languages or writing systems do not necessarily undermine conclusions about reading processes, including universals and dyslexia, for which there is other evidence, as pointed out by Lee, Hung, and Tzeng (2006) and Ziegler (2006). Indeed, the UPP is a universal claim that stands up to differences produced by writing systems and languages. However, I do not think that a universal account of dyslexia can be embraced unless it is expressed at a comparably abstract level. One possibility is that dyslexia is caused by deficits in the linguistic-graphological components that must be mapped in reading, especially but not limited to phonological components.

Finally, although phonological awareness is a predictor of Chinese reading acquisition (Ho & Bryant, 1997; McBride-Chang & Kail, 2002), it is syllable-level or rime-level awareness rather than phoneme-level awareness that has been demonstrated most clearly. Orthographic knowledge more directly tied to character formation and representation may be more important in Chinese reading (Ho, Chan, Tsang, Lee, & Luan, 2004). This idea is consistent with the observation that the ability to copy characters predicts elementary-grade reading better than measures of phonological awareness (Tan, Spinks, Eden, Perfetti, & Siok, 2005). The relevant writing and language skills also include morphology, as McBride-Chang and colleagues (McBride-Chang & Liu, Chapter 2 of this volume; McBride-Chang, Wagner, Muse, Chow, & Shu, 2005) have emphasized in showing a relation of morphological awareness to reading success.

The behavioral and brain studies show a convergence at a broad level. Phonology is universally involved in reading, but success and failure in Chinese reading involve additional linguistic and writing system factors. This is a generalization that applies also to reading in alphabetic systems.

Learning Across Writing Systems In studies of native English speakers learning Chinese, 1 year of classroom learning produced patterns of brain activation that included two areas shown by native Chinese speakers: right occipital-temporal areas and the left and right middle frontal gyrus (Liu, Dunlap, Fiez, & Perfetti, 2007; Nelson, Liu, Fiez, & Perfetti, 2009; see Figure 1.6). That learners with relatively little experience showed such overlap with native speakers must mean that the writing system itself rather than skill is responsible, although the overlap may increase with skill. Remarkably, Chinese-English bilinguals in the study by Nelson et al. showed the "Chinese pattern," especially bilateral fusiform gyrus and LMFG, when they read English. This assimilation pattern may not apply across all levels of L2 skill, but the result suggests that the brain's reading network developed for a first language can continue to be used in reading a new writing system—provided that the procedures they support continue to be useful. In the case of Chinese readers of English, this result implies that some less analytic processes that operate on letter strings can be functional, even if they are not optimal.

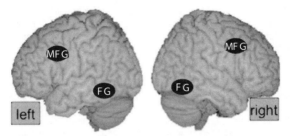

Figure 1.6. Schematic representation of approximate brain areas activated following one year (Nelson et al., 2009) or even a few weeks (Liu et al., 2007) of learning to read Chinese characters by English L1 speakers. The frontal area includes bilateral left middle frontal gyrus (LMFG), and the posterior areas include bilateral fusiform gyrus. (*Key:* MFG; middle frontal gyrus; MFG; middle frontal gyrus FG; fusiform gyrus.)

CONCLUSION

The science of reading has become more integrated and more universal. Unlike their beginnings, basic reading processes and dyslexia research have enjoyed a mutual influence that has made a more solid foundation for both. Progress in reading science can be marked in many ways, and I have mentioned just a few that are most relevant to the goals of this volume. The increased understanding of the role of phonology in stabilizing word identification is one, and its corresponding failure in most cases of alphabetic dyslexia is another. Understanding comprehension problems, which loom large and have a much weaker knowledge base compared with dyslexia, involves a wider range of factors, but a major one is likely to be word meaning processing. The progress in reading was pushed by studies of English, and then by studies of other alphabetic orthographies. Substantial research on nonalphabetic systems, especially Chinese (and Japanese), has made it possible to identify some of the universal components of reading, but it has also made important differences more visible. Reading procedures vary within broad constraints provided by language and writing systems. These constraints cause phonology to be pervasive, but this does not mean that the reading procedures are uniform or that the causes of dyslexia are exactly the same. In fact, they are not.

REFERENCES

Aro, M., & Wimmer, H. (2003). Learning to read: English in comparison to six more regular orthographies. *Applied Psycholinguistics, 24,* 621–635.

Ashby, J., & Clifton, C. (2005). The prosodic property of lexical stress affects eye movements during silent reading. *Cognition, 96*(3), 89–100.

Ashby, J., & Martin, A.E. (2008). Prosodic phonological representations in early visual word recognition. *Journal of Experimental Psychology: Human Perception & Performance, 34,* 224–236.

Ashby, J., Sanders, L.D., & Kingston, J. (2009). Skilled readers begin processing sub-phonemic features by 80 ms during visual word recognition: Evidence from ERPs. *Biological Psychology, 80*(1), 84–94.

Binder, J.R., McKiernan, K.A., Parsons, M.E., Westbury, C.F., Possing, E.T., Kaufman, J.N., et al. (2003). Neural correlates of lexical access during visual word recognition. *Journal of Cognitive Neuroscience, 15,* 372–393.

Bolger, D.J., Hornickel, J., Cone, N.E., Burman, D.D., & Booth, J.R. (2008). Neural correlates of orthographic and phonological consistency effects in children. *Human Brain Mapping, 29,* 1416–1429.

Bolger, D.J., Schneider, W., & Perfetti, C.A. (2005). Cross-cultural effect on the brain revisited: Universal structures plus writing system variation. *Human Brain Mapping, 25*(1), 92–104.

Bradley, L., & Bryant, P.E. (1978). Difficulties in auditory organization as a possible cause of reading backwardness. *Nature, 271,* 285–298.

Brady, S., Shankweiler, D., & Mann, V. (1983). Speech perception and memory coding in relation to reading ability. *Journal of Experimental Child Psychology, 35*(2), 345–367.

Cain, K., & Oakhill, J.V. (1999). Inference making and its relation to comprehension failure. *Reading and Writing, 11,* 489–503.

Coltheart, M. (1981). Disorders of reading and their implications for models of normal reading. Visual cues in word recognition and reading [Special issue]. *Visible Language, 15*(3), 245–286.

Frost, R. (1998). Toward a strong phonological theory of visual word recognition: True issues and false trails. *Psychological Bulletin, 123*(1), 245–286.

Harm, M., & Seidenberg, M. (1999). Phonology, reading acquisition, and dyslexia. Insights from connectionist models. *Psychological Review, 106,* 491–528.

Hill, N.M., & Schneider, W. (2006). Brain changes in the development of expertise: Neurological evidence on skill-based adaptations. In K.A. Ericsson, N. Charness, P. Feltovich, & R. Hoffman (Eds.), *Cambridge handbook of expertise and expert performance* (pp. 653–683). New York: Cambridge University Press.

Hinshelwood, J. (1917). *Congenital word-blindness.* London: H.K. Lewis.

Ho, C.S., & Bryant, P. (1997). Phonological skills are important in learning to read Chinese. *Developmental Psychology, 33*(5), 946–951.

Ho, C.S., Chan, D., Tsang, S.-M., Lee, S.-H., & Luan, V.H. (2004). Cognitive profiling and preliminary subtyping in Chinese developmental dyslexia. *Cognition, 91,* 43–75.

Huey, E.B. (1908). *The psychology and pedagogy of reading,* Macmillan, New York.

Katz, L., & Frost, R. (1992). Reading in different orthographies: The orthographic depth hypothesis. In R. Frost & L. Katz (Eds.), *Orthography, phonology, morphology, and meaning* (pp. 67–84). Amsterdam: Elsevier North Holland Press.

Kintsch, W. (1988). The role of knowledge in discourse comprehension: A construction-integration model. *Psychological Review, 95*(2), 163–182.

Landi, N., & Perfetti, C.A. (2007). An electrophysiological investigation of semantic and phonological processing in skilled and less-skilled comprehenders. *Brain and Language, 102,* 30–45.

Lee, J.R., Hung, D.L., & Tzeng, O. (2006). Cross-linguistic analysis of developmental dyslexia: Does phonology matter in learning to read Chinese? *Language and Linguistics, 7*(3), 573–594.

Liberman, L., & Shankweiler, D. (1987). Phonology and the problems of learning to read and write. *Memory and Learning Disabilities: Advances in Learning and Behavioral Disabilities [Suppl. 2],* 203–224.

Liu, Y., Dunlap, S., Fiez, J., & Perfetti, C.A. (2007). Evidence for neural accommodation to a writing system following learning. *Human Brain Mapping, 28,* 1223–1234.

Lovegrove, W.J., Bowling, A., Badcock, D., & Blackwood, M. (1980). Specific reading disability: Differences in contrast sensitivity as a function of spatial frequency. *Science, 210,* 439–440.

Lukatela, G., Lukatela, K., & Turvey, M.T. (1993). Further evidence for phonological constraints on visual lexical access: TOWED primes FROG. *Perception & Psychophysics, 53,* 461–466.

Manis, F.R., Seidenberg, M.S., Doi, L.M., McBride-Chang, C., & Peterson, A. (1996). On the bases of two subtypes of developmental dyslexia. *Cognition, 58,* 157–195.

McBride-Chang, C., & Kail, R. (2002). Cross-cultural similarities in the predictors of reading acquisition. *Child Development, 73,* 1392–1407.

McBride-Chang, C., Wagner, R.K., Muse, A., Chow, W.Y.B., & Shu, H. (2005). The role of morphological awareness in children's vocabulary acquisition in English. *Applied Psycholinguistics, 26,* 415–435.

Minogue, B.M. (1967). Congenital word blindness: A case study. *Psychiatric Quarterly, 1*(2), 226–230.

Morgan, W.P. (1896). A case of congenital word blindness. *The British Medical Journal, 2,* 1378.

Nation, K. (2005). Reading comprehension difficulties. In. M.J. Snowling & C. Hulme (Eds.), *The science of reading* (pp. 248–265). Oxford, England: Blackwell.

Nation, K., & Snowling, M.J. (1998). Semantic processing and the development of word recognition skills: Evidence from children with reading comprehension difficulties. *Journal of Memory and Language, 39,* 85–101.

Nation, K., & Snowling, M.J. (1999). Developmental differences in sensitivity to semantic relations among good and poor comprehenders: Evidence from semantic priming. *Cognition, 70*(1), B1–B13.

Nelson, J.R., Liu, Y., Fiez, J., & Perfetti, C.A. (2009). Assimilation and accommodation patters in ventral occipitotemporal cortex in learning a second writing system. *Human Brain Mapping, 30,* 810–820.

Olson, R.K., & Byrne, B. (2004). Genetic and environmental influences on reading and language ability and disability. In H. Catts & A. Kamhi (Eds.), *The connections between language and reading disabilities* (pp. 137–200). Mahwah, NJ: Lawrence Erlbaum Associates.

Orton, S. (1925). Word blindness in school children. *Archives of Neurology and Psychiatry, 14,* 581–615.

Orton, S. (1928). Specific reading disability—strephosymbolia. *Journal of the American Medical Association, 90,* 1095–1099.

Perfetti, C.A. (2007). Reading ability: Lexical quality to comprehension. *Scientific Studies of Reading, 11*(4), 357–383.

Perfetti, C.A., & Bell, L. (1991). Phonemic activation during the first 40 ms of word identification: Evidence from backward masking and masked priming. *Journal of Memory and Language, 30,* 473–485.

Perfetti, C.A., Bell, L., & Delaney, S. (1988). Automatic phonetic activation in silent word reading: Evidence from backward masking. *Journal of Memory and Language, 27,* 59–70.

Perfetti, C.A., Landi, N., & Oakhill, J. (2005). The acquisition of reading comprehension skill. In M.J. Snowling & C. Hulme (Eds.), *The science of reading: A handbook* (pp. 227–247). Oxford, England: Blackwell.

Perfetti, C.A., Liu, Y., & Tan, L.H. (2005). The Lexical Constituency Model: Some implications of research on Chinese for general theories of reading. *Psychological Review, 12*(11), 43–59.

Perfetti, C.A., Zhang, S., & Berent, I. (1992). Reading in English and Chinese: Evidence for a "universal" phonological principle. In R. Frost & L. Katz (Eds.), *Orthography, phonology, morphology, and meaning* (pp. 227–248). Amsterdam: North-Holland.

Pugh, K.R., Frost, S.J., Sandak, R., Landi, N., Rueckl, J.G., Constable, R.T., et al. (2008). Effects of stimulus difficulty and repetition on printed word identification: An fMRI comparison of nonimpaired and reading-disabled adolescent cohorts. *Journal of Cognitive Neuroscience, 20*(7), 1146–1160.

Pugh, K.R., Mencl, W.E., Jenner, A.R., Katz, L., Frost, S.J., Lee, J.R., et al. (2001). Neurobiological studies of reading and reading disability. *Journal of Communication Disorders, 39,* 479–492.

Ramus, F., Rosen, S., Dakin, S.C., Day, B.L., Castellote, J.M., White, S., et al. (2003). Theories of developmental dyslexia: Insights from a multiple case study dyslexic adults. *Brain, 126*(4), 841–865.

Rayner, K., Sereno, S.C., Lesch, M.F., & Pollatsek, A. (1995). Phonological codes are automatically activated during reading: Evidence from an eye-movement priming paradigm. *Psychological Science, 6,* 26–32.

Sandak, R., Mencl, W.E., Frost, S.J., Rueckl, J.G., Katz, L., Moore, D., et al. (2004). The neurobiology of adaptive learning in reading: A contrast of different training conditions. *Cognitive, Affective, & Behavioral Neuroscience, 4,* 67–88.

Share, D.L. (2008). On the Anglocentricities of current reading research and practice: The perils of overreliance on an "outlier" orthography. *Psychological Bulletin, 134*(4), 584–615.

Shaywitz, S.E., Shaywitz, B.A., Pugh, K.R., Fulbright, R.K., Constable, R.T., Mencel, W.E., et al. (1998). Functional disruption in the organization of the brain for reading in dyslexia. *Proceedings of the National Academy of Sciences, USA, 95*(5), 2636–2641.

Shaywitz, B., Shaywitz, S., Pugh, K., Mencl, W., Fulbright, R., & Skudlarski, P. (2002). Disruption of posterior brain systems for reading in children with developmental dyslexia. *Biological Psychiatry, 52*(2), 101–110.

Simos, P.G., Fletcher, J.M., Bergman, E., Breier, J.I., Foorman, B.R., Castillo, E.M., et al. (2002). Dyslexia-specific brain activation profile becomes normal following successful remedial training. *Neurology, 58,* 1203–1213.

Siok, W.T., Niu, Z. Jin, Z., Perfetti, C.A., & Tan, L.H. (2008). A structural-functional basis for dyslexia in the cortex of Chinese readers. *Proceedings of the National Academy of Sciences, USA, 105*(14), 5561–5566.

Siok, W.T., Perfetti, C.A., Jin, Z., & Tan, L.H. (2004). Biological abnormality of impaired reading constrained by culture: Evidence from Chinese. *Nature,* September 1, 71–76.

Smith, F. (1979). *Reading without nonsense.* New York: Teachers College Press.

Stein J., & Walsh, V. (1997). To see but not to read; the magnocellular theory of dyslexia. *Trends in Neuroscience, 20,* 147–152.

Tan L.H., Feng C.M, Fox P.T., & Gao J.H. (2001). An fMRI study with written Chinese. *Neuroreport, 12,* 83–88.

Tan, L.H., Laird, A.R., Li, K., & Fox, P.T. (2005). Neuroanatomical correlates of phonological processing of Chinese characters and alphabetic words: A meta-analysis. *Human Brain Mapping, 25,* 83–91.

Tan L.H., Liu H.L., Perfetti C.A., Spinks J.A., Fox P.T., & Gao J.H. (2001). The neural system underlying Chinese logograph reading. *NeuroImage, 13,* 836–846.

Tan, L.H., & Perfetti, C.A. (1998). Phonological codes as early sources of constraint in Chinese word identification: A review of current discoveries and theoretical accounts. *Reading and Writing: An Interdisciplinary Journal, 10,* 165–200.

Tan, L.H., Spinks, J.A., Eden, G., Perfetti, C.A., & Siok, W.T. (2005). Reading depends on writing, in Chinese. *Proceedings of the National Academy of Sciences, USA, 102,* 8781–8785.

Temple, E., Deutsch, G.K., Poldrack, R.A., Miller, S.L., Tallal, P., Merzenich, M.M., et al. (2003). Neural deficits in children with dyslexia ameliorated by behavioral remediation: Evidence from functional MRI. *Proceedings of the National Academy of Sciences, USA, 100,* 2860–2865.

Tinker, M.A., & Goodenough, F.L. (1931). Mirror reading as a method of analyzing factors involved in word perception. *Journal of Educational Psychology, 22*(7), 493–502.

Turkeltaub, P.E., Gareau, L., Flowers, D.L., Zeffiro, T.A., & Eden, G.F. (2003). Development of neural mechanisms for reading. *Nature Neuroscience, 6*(7), 767–773.

Van Orden, G.C. (1987). A ROWS is a ROSE: Spelling, sound, and reading. *Memory & Cognition, 15,* 181–198.

Vellutino, F.R. (1981). *Dyslexia: Theory and research.* Cambridge, MA: The MIT Press.

Ziegler, J.C. (2006). Do differences in brain activation challenge universal theories of dyslexia? *Brain and Language, 98*(3), 341–343.

Ziegler, J., & Goswami, U. (2005). Reading acquisition, developmental dyslexia, and skilled reading across languages: A psycholinguistic grain size theory. *Psychological Bulletin, 131*(1), 3–29.

CHAPTER 2

Fundamentals of Chinese Reading Development and How They Might Affect Concepts of Dyslexia in Chinese

Catherine McBride-Chang and Phil D. Liu

There are at least three fundamental differences between Chinese and alphabetic languages and orthographies in general, which make a comparison between them crucial in exploring the universals and specifics of dyslexia. The first is the relative opacity of consistent phonological information in print in Chinese. The second is the clear distinctiveness of the Chinese syllable in language and literacy. The third is the definite orthographic structures of Chinese characters, some features of which have no analogy in alphabetic reading and writing. In addition, the environment in which Chinese is taught and learned likely affects conceptualization and measurement of dyslexia in Chinese. In this chapter, we overview these characteristics of Chinese in order to tackle an overarching question: What is the best way to characterize dyslexia in Chinese?

The first fundamental difference between Chinese and alphabetic orthographies is the relative unreliability of phonological information in Chinese (Yin & Weekes, 2003). Because Chinese characters themselves are holistic representations of syllables rather than representations using smaller phonological units such as phonemes, the aspects of phonological sensitivity that may explain reading development in Chinese are less clear and systematic as compared with those for alphabetic languages. For example, in only approximately 38% of characters can the pronunciation of the character be predicted directly from its phonetic radical. This lack of generalizability of phonological information from one character to the next makes reliance on phonological sensitivity as the key indicator of reading difficulties less clear in Chinese as compared with alphabetic orthographies.

In the current consensus definition, reading and writing difficulties suffered by those with dyslexia "typically result from a deficit in the phonological component of language that is often unexpected in relation to other cognitive abilities and the provision of effective classroom instruction" (Lyon, Shaywitz, & Shaywitz, 2003, p. 2). This definition stresses phonological processing as key in understanding dyslexia (e.g., Share, 2008; Ziegler, 2006; Ziegler & Goswami, 2005). There is ample evidence for the link between dyslexia in Chinese children and phonological processing, including phonological awareness (Ho, Law, & Ng, 2000), rapid automatized naming (Chan, Ho, Tsang, Lee, & Chung, 2007; Ho & Lai, 1999), and phonological memory (Ho & Lai, 1999). Most researchers agree that there is a "universal phonological principle" across orthographies (Perfetti & Tan, 1998; Perfetti, Zhang, & Berent, 1992) and that phonological sensitivity is a root cause of reading disability in Chinese. Moreover, there are dimensions of phonological sensitivity that are highlighted in Chinese but rare or nonexistent in many alphabetic orthographies. For example, Chinese children's lexical tone sensitivity is uniquely associated with word recognition skills in some studies (McBride-Chang, Tong, et al., 2008) and distinguishes those with and without dyslexia or risk for dyslexia (e.g., Cheung, Chung, et al., 2009; McBride-Chang, Lam, et al., 2008). Moreover, Pinyin and Zhuyin-Fuhao, phonological systems used in mainland China and Taiwan, respectively, serve an alphabetic-like function for learning Chinese. Children formally learn these phonological coding systems by the middle of first grade and make use of them to learn new Chinese characters. These systems systematically code rimes and onsets, and sometimes finals, as well as lexical tone. Thus, such systems are useful in making phonological information explicit, including the dimension of lexical tone, which is important for character recognition. More implicitly, using an oddball paradigm, Meng et al. (2005) compared 11-year-old mainland Chinese children with dyslexia to typically developing children (at an average age of 11 years) on mismatched negativity (MMN) responses using event-related brain potentials. They found that even though the two groups of children did not differ in MMN responses to stimuli that deviated in pure tone frequency and Chinese lexical tones, dyslexic children showed a smaller MMN response to stimuli that deviated in initial consonants or vowels of Chinese syllables, as well as to stimuli that deviated in temporal information of composite tone patterns. Thus, phonological sensitivity distinguishes children with reading difficulties in Chinese from those without such difficulties.

Despite all of these features of Chinese literacy training that highlight the importance of phonological information, however, a strict reliance on phonological coding alone for learning to read Chinese is impossible, both because of the lack of consistency in phonological information and because of the many homophones across Chinese characters. Moreover, whereas a key way to help children with dyslexia in alphabetic languages improve their reading is via phonological awareness training (Schneider, Roth, & Ennemoser, 2000; Schuele & Boudreau, 2008), a focus on phonological awareness by itself seems unlikely to ameliorate reading difficulties in Chinese children with dyslexia. Indeed, of the training studies published on facilitating Chinese character or word reading in Chinese children, relatively few (Ho & Cheung, 1999; Ho & Ma, 1999) have focused exclusively on phonological awareness for this reason.

Moreover, deficits in relation to Chinese dyslexia often go beyond phonological awareness skills (e.g., Ho, Chan, Chung, Lee, & Tsang,

2007; Ho, Chan, Lee, Tsang, & Luan, 2004; Ho, Chan, Tsang, & Lee, 2002; Ho & Lai, 1999; Ho et al., 2000; Shu, McBride-Chang, Wu, & Liu, 2006; Shu, Meng, Chen, Luan, & Cao, 2005). For example, Ho et al. (2002) found that among Hong Kong Chinese children with dyslexia (mean age of 8.7 years), half showed deficits in rapid naming, 38.9% manifested deficits in orthographic processing, and 36.7% showed deficits in visual-perceptual skills. Only 15% of Hong Kong Chinese children with dyslexia had specific problems with phonological sensitivity. Ho et al. (2004) further suggested that deficits in orthographic processing and rapid naming might be the crux of the problem in Chinese developmental dyslexia. In another study of Chinese fifth and sixth graders from Beijing (Shu et al., 2006), morphological awareness, rapid naming, and vocabulary knowledge were the three skills (out of nine tested) that significantly distinguished dyslexic children from typical readers; phonological awareness could not uniquely distinguish across groups.

Beyond the relatively weak phonological awareness–Chinese reading connection, a second major factor in Chinese literacy is the almost perfect correspondence among individual syllables, morphemes, and Chinese characters. This is in stark contrast to alphabetic languages, in which morphemes might be relatively long (e.g., *lettuce* is one morpheme) or short (e.g., the *s* in *boats* is also one morpheme) in sound patterns or letter representations. This connection may facilitate children's understanding that one sound representation corresponds equally to both the morpheme and Chinese character it represents. Indeed, it is common for young Chinese readers to appear to "read" a passage they are assigned simply by 1) memorizing the short text and 2) allotting one character to every spoken syllable as they point, character by character. When young Chinese children are asked to identify a Chinese character in isolation, even on the same page as the one they were just "reading," they often cannot do so in isolation without working through every character before it by pointing.

The morpheme–character connection can be taken further in analyzing Chinese children's reading development. Identifying morphemes in Chinese speech is common, even among adults. For example, in introducing oneself, it is common to explain the character that corresponds with one's name (e.g., Knowing that the morpheme of *Jeou* in Ma Ying Jeou's given name corresponds to the character meaning/ pronounced as 9 in Chinese helps everyone to process its pronunciation and written form). In addition, in Chinese, lexical compounding is prevalent, not just in proper names but in all words. Thus, literally, *computer* can be translated as *electric brain*, and *careful* comprises two morphemes together that mean *small heart*. The extent to which adults and children analyze such words separately into morphemes versus holistically is not absolutely clear. However, it does seem to be the case that Chinese children who understand how morphemes fit together in language (e.g., In English, a new concept of a castle made of chocolate could be called a *chocolate castle* but not a *castle chocolate*) tend to be better readers than those who do not (McBride-Chang, Shu, Zhou, Wat, & Wagner, 2003; McBride-Chang et al., 2005; Tong, McBride-Chang, Shu, & Wong, 2009). This is the case presumably in part because children (and foreign language learners of Chinese) gradually come to recognize certain morphemes as characters across different words and use their knowledge of these to generalize across new words. Along with compounding, the prevalence of homophones, which can often be disambiguated only in the context of such compounding, is important to emphasize. The high percentage of homophones almost by definition requires that children learn to distinguish them in compound words, that is, words composed of two or more morphemes. Sensitivity to homophones is also important in distinguishing dyslexic from non-dyslexic Chinese readers (e.g., Shu et al., 2006) and for explaining growth in Chinese word recognition longitudinally (Tong, McBride-Chang, Wong, et al., 2009).

Several studies have highlighted the fact that morphological awareness, broadly defined to incorporate features of both oral and written language, can facilitate word reading and writing, given the importance of morphological skills for learning to read Chinese (Li, Anderson, Nagy, & Zhang, 2002). For example, at least two studies (Packard et al., 2006; Wu et al., 2009), working with primary school children, demonstrated that a combination of oral and written instruction in Chinese morphology improved children's literacy skills. Another study (Chow, McBride-Chang, Cheung, & Chow, 2008) also found that children of parents who combined oral language homophone and morphological construction games with their kindergartners as training twice per week for 15–20 minutes each time increased in word-reading skills relative to children who participated in parent–child reading activities only over 12 weeks. These studies suggest that targeting morphological skills at different levels might be particularly effective in promoting reading growth in Chinese children of different literacy levels.

A third distinctive aspect of Chinese is the structure within individual characters. Most characters are called *compound characters* because they comprise a combination of a single semantic radical and a phonetic. There are about 200 semantic radicals and 800 phonetics in use in Chinese writing, and their positions within a given character, as well as their functions, are somewhat systematic, cuing certain clues as to meaning and sound within a given character, respectively (Shu, Chen, Anderson, Wu, & Xuan, 2003). For example, in the compound character 坪 (ping2, *level ground*), the right part 平 (ping2) is a phonetic radical and has the same pronunciation as that of the whole character. The left part 土 (tu3) is a semantic radical, indicating that the meaning of the character is related to the meaning of 土 (meaning *earth* or *ground*). Not all characters have such a regular pattern, but many do. Radicals are composed of strokes, that is, smaller written units. There are five basic strokes (the horizontal stroke "一", the vertical stroke "丨", the left-descending stroke "丿", the right-descending stroke "丶", and the bending stroke "乙"), as well as several variants of these different combinations, which constitute all Chinese characters. For example, the Chinese character 木 (mu4, *wood*) consists of the first four basic strokes, and in the Chinese character 永 (yong4, *forever*), there are two variants of the bending stroke. Each character is composed of radicals following one of five spatial structures, including up-down (e.g., 昌), right-left (e.g., 明), surrounded (e.g., 国), semi-surrounded (e.g., 边), and single (e.g., 手), or more complex structures derived from these five basic structures (e.g., 漏, including both left-right and semi-surrounded structures). More than 60% of Chinese characters learned by primary school children have 7–12 strokes (e.g., a 7-stroke character is 作; a 12-stroke character is 寒); moreover, more than 80% of characters have complex, rather than single, orthographic structures (Shu et al., 2003).

The relatively complex orthographic structures of the Chinese writing system make visual-spatial perceptual skills and orthographic processing important for the processing of Chinese characters (e.g., Tong, McBride-Chang, Shu, et al., 2009) because children have to pay attention to strokes, stroke patterns, and spatial orders of radicals in order to correctly recognize specific Chinese characters. This complexity may partly explain why deficits in visual skill and orthographic processing are fairly prevalent in Chinese children with dyslexia (e.g., Ho et al., 2002; Ho et al., 2004; Meng, Tian, Jian, & Zhou, 2007). Moreover, semantic radicals are unique in Chinese, with no clear analogy to alphabetic reading. This is because semantic radicals within compound characters are not pronounced. This feature of Chinese has led some prominent researchers (e.g., Shu & Anderson, 1997) to argue that semantic radicals represent morphological awareness and others (e.g., Cheung et al., 2007; Ho, Ng, & Ng, 2003) to describe these as orthographic processing elements.

Apart from these three striking features of Chinese in relation to alphabetic orthographies, the ways in which literacy skills are taught in Chinese societies must be considered in order to get a full picture of how typical development and reading impairment in Chinese might best be understood (e.g., Cheung & Ng, 2003). There are at least three aspects of Chinese typical learning environments that might have an impact on views about Chinese reading in this respect. First, traditionally, Chinese children learn to read and write Chinese in large measure via copying (Wu, Li, & Anderson, 1999). Writing characters or two- or three-character words 10 or 20 times each is the norm for solidifying and integrating individual character information in most places. In some places, there is an additional analytic focus on the features of the character, such as where the phonetics or semantic radicals are placed, their sounds or meanings vis-à-vis the individual character, and even the different words that include this character in their makeup. Other places engage in relatively little of this analytic instruction. However, Chinese teachers and parents view copying as an essential aspect of learning to read and write Chinese (Tan, Spinks, Eden, Perfetti, & Siok, 2005). Although copying occurs in English and other alphabets as well, its importance is reduced for these orthographies because individual letters occur much more frequently across words than do individual characters (compare approximately 26 individual letters to thousands of characters possible), so they are more often integrated into whatever is being written. Some individual characters, in contrast, might be infrequently used. In addition, there is relatively little emphasis on the precise way in which a given letter should be written, whereas there is always a clear, correct way to write a given character. Our work indicates that when parents are asked to help their children to learn to write characters, they invariably make use of some copying techniques, and their emphasis on higher order information—such as the meaning of the character or its components—is relatively small (Lin et al., 2009). Moreover, almost no Chinese parents ever make reference to any phonological information contained within the character (Lin, McBride-Chang, Aram, & Levin, in press; Lin et al., 2009). In contrast, in alphabetic languages such as Hebrew, such a phonological emphasis tends to be the norm among parents trying to scaffold their young children's writing. Thus the importance of copying and how to supplement copying with other more analytic strategies of learning to read and write Chinese is a primary issue in Chinese literacy teaching.

Given the primacy of copying for learning to write Chinese, coupled with the prevalence of Pinyin—popular in many Chinese societies and buoyed by the Internet age as a phonological coding system for typing Chinese—another potentially important issue for literacy skills learning in Chinese involves the potential dissociation between writing and reading in Chinese. Because using Pinyin is so easy and learning to write Chinese characters fluently is so effortful, it is possible for Chinese children (or adults) to be proficient in reading Chinese and much less so in writing it. This dissociation is also possible in some alphabetic languages—especially those such as English with some tricky (sometimes virtually inexplicable) spellings—but in alphabetic systems, there is still some overlap between reading and writing given the consistency of phonemes to graphemes. The dissociation in Chinese can be far greater.

Given all of these issues, it is important to consider best approaches to diagnosing dyslexia in Chinese. There is strong evidence that dyslexia is heritable (e.g., Grigorenko, Wood, Meyer, & Pauls, 2000; Schumacher et al., 2006; for a review, see Demonet, Taylor, & Chaix, 2004; Wong, Kidd, Ho, & Au, 2010). However, the genetic correlation for reading increases significantly with schooling (e.g., Samuelsson et al., 2007), underscoring the importance of early intervention for children with reading difficulties. Many intervention programs have been developed and successfully conducted in alphabetic languages (e.g., Kast, Meyer, Vogeli, Gross, & Jancke, 2007; Tressoldi, Vio, & Iozzino, 2007; van Otterloo, van der Leij, & Henrichs, 2009). Such interventions can facilitate dyslexic children's cognitive skills and even change brain patterns (e.g., Eden et al., 2004; Meyler, Keller, Cherkassky, Gabrieli, & Just, 2008; Temple et al., 2003; for a review, see Demonet et al., 2004). Unfortunately, it is not necessarily clear what the core deficits in Chinese dyslexia are, at least to the extent that tools to diagnose dyslexia in Chinese children are clearly comprehensive enough to capture these difficulties. In mainland China, there are not yet consistently agreed-on definitions of dyslexia. In Hong Kong and Taiwan, good tools are available, but there is no agreement on the core deficits marking dyslexia in Chinese.

For example, to what extent should dyslexia be defined as a phonological deficit in Chinese? This question focuses less on causal mechanisms in dyslexia and more on practical identification of Chinese children with dyslexia. Although there appears to be relatively universal agreement that phonological difficulties may be the root of reading impairment across orthographies, including Chinese, practically speaking, it may not be the case that older Chinese children with dyslexia can be diagnosed as such with phonological tasks alone for reasons of measurement. The kinds of phonological tasks that tend best to distinguish young Chinese children with dyslexia (e.g., syllable deletion, tone detection) typically show ceiling effects for children ages 6 years and older. Thus, although phonological difficulties may have been the source (or one of the sources) of reading difficulties initially, these particular metalinguistic skills may have been ameliorated by the middle primary years for Chinese children. Regardless of whether such phonological difficulties can be detected, phonological difficulties by themselves do not represent a complete picture of metalinguistic difficulties manifested in Chinese children with reading difficulties.

A second issue on which there are relatively few data is the extent to which dyslexia involves a word-reading versus a word-writing problem in Chinese. The criteria for diagnosing children as dyslexic in Hong Kong are that children must score below a standard score of 70 across the combined tasks of word reading, word writing, and speeded (1-minute) word reading, as well as manifest some other cognitive-linguistic difficulties. It is likely that any child with a word-reading problem will also have difficulties in word writing in Chinese. However, it is less clear whether there are children who have specific word-writing difficulties in Chinese only and whether such children should receive specific treatments for such difficulties. Because Chinese likely involves a broader range of skills for literacy development than those typically identified—at least for young children in English and other alphabetic orthographies—this issue is worth considering. In fact, for children with good phonological awareness who are allowed to use Pinyin on a regular basis on the computer, it is possible to type Chinese compositions well but have limited knowledge of how to write Chinese characters. The extent to which writing difficulties constitute broader language-based (e.g., morphological) difficulties—or even more broadly, visual-orthographic/spatial confusions—may be an important issue to consider in future work.

Finally, in considering how best to recognize and remediate Chinese children with reading difficulties, one must also note that Chinese societies differ substantially in their approaches to literacy development— perhaps more so than for any other orthography in the world. For example, in English, there may be minor differences in spelling (realize/ realise) or pronunciation (H) of words or even letters across English-speaking societies. In some Arabic-speaking countries, there are bigger differences still with words read differently in standard dialectal representations versus other dialectal representations of Arabic (e.g., Wagner, 1993). Thus, it is possible for readers of Arabic from different nations to be able to read the same text but pronounce these words differently— indeed, even mutually unintelligibly. Chinese is similar to this aspect of Arabic (many linguists agree that Mandarin and Cantonese are different languages; see, for example, Cheung & Ng, 2003) but can have still greater print differences than in alphabetic orthographies because simplified and traditional script can differ substantially as well. There is some suggestion from previous research that traditional characters (used in Taiwan and Hong Kong) are easier to read but more difficult to write than simplified characters (used in mainland China and Singapore; see McBride-Chang et al., 2005, for a review). Thus, depending on the extent to which word-and-character reading versus word-and-character writing define dyslexia in Chinese, these issues may differ even across Chinese societies.

To summarize, because of the fairly broad base of skills required to read and write Chinese fluently, some consideration of Chinese specifically for understanding and defining dyslexia is essential at this period in history. There is enough known about expert Chinese reading and Chinese children's reading development now that a number of important questions can be addressed in this aspect. It is likely that although there are a number of "universals" to developmental dyslexia in Chinese, there are a number of specific features of it to be incorporated as well. Thus skills such as copying abilities, pure-visual as well as visual-orthographic sensitivity, and morphological awareness can be combined with more traditional phonological processing abilities to provide a maximally comprehensive analysis of the strengths and weaknesses of Chinese children with difficulties in learning to read and write.

ACKNOWLEDGMENT

We are grateful to the Research Grants Council Grant #2120298 for support in writing this book chapter and for supporting some of the research discussed in it.

REFERENCES

Chan, D., Ho, C.S.-H., Tsang, S.-M., Lee, S.-H., & Chung, K.K.H. (2007). Prevalence, gender ratio and gender differences in reading-related cognitive abilities among Chinese children with dyslexia in Hong Kong. *Educational Studies, 33,* 249–265.

Cheung, H., Chan, M., & Chong, K. (2007). Use of orthographic knowledge in reading by Chinese-English biscriptal children. *Language Learning, 57,* 469–505.

Cheung, H., Chung, K.K., Wong, S.L.W., McBride-Chang, C., Penney, T.B., & Ho, C.S.H. (2009). Perception of tone and aspiration contrasts in Chinese children with dyslexia. *Journal of Child Psychology and Psychiatry, 50,* 726–733.

Cheung, H., & Ng, L. (2003). Chinese reading development in some major Chinese societies: An introduction. In C. McBride-Chang & H.-C. Chen (Eds.), *Reading development in Chinese children* (pp. 3–17). London: Praeger.

Chow, B.W.-Y., McBride-Chang, C., Cheung, H., & Chow, C.S.-L. (2008). Dialogic reading and morphology training in Chinese children: Effects on language and literacy. *Developmental Psychology, 44,* 233–244.

Demonet, J.-F., Taylor, M.J., & Chaix, Y. (2004). Developmental dyslexia. *Lancet, 363,* 1451–1460.

Eden, G.F., Jones, K.M., Cappell, K., Gareau, L., Wood, F.B., Zeffiro, T.A., et al. (2004). Neural changes following remediation in adult developmental dyslexia. *Neuron, 44,* 411–422.

Grigorenko, E.L., Wood, F.B., Meyer, M.S., & Pauls, D.L. (2000). Chromosome 6p influences on different dyslexia-related cognitive processes: Further confirmation. *American Journal of Human Genetics, 66,* 715–723.

Ho, C.S.-H., Chan, D.W.-O., Lee, S.-H., Tsang, S.-M., & Luan, V.H. (2004). Cognitive profiling and preliminary subtyping in Chinese developmental dyslexia. *Cognition, 91,* 43–75.

Ho, C.S.-H., Chan, D.W., Chung, K.K.H., Lee, S.-H., & Tsang, S.-M. (2007). In search of subtypes of Chinese developmental dyslexia. *Journal of Experimental Child Psychology, 97,* 61–83.

Ho, C.S.-H., Chan, D.W.-O., Tsang, S.-M., & Lee, S.-H. (2002). The cognitive profile and multiple-deficit hypothesis in Chinese developmental dyslexia. *Developmental Psychology, 38,* 543–553.

Ho, C.S.-H, & Cheung, C.-K. (1999). Does training in phonological awareness skills improve Chinese dyslexic children's reading performance? *Educational Research Journal, 14,* 209–228.

Ho, C.S.-H., & Lai, D.H.-C. (1999). Naming-speed deficits and phonological memory deficits in Chinese developmental dyslexia. *Learning and Individual Differences, 11,* 173–186.

Ho, C.S.-H., Law, T.P.-S., & Ng, P.M. (2000). The phonological deficit hypothesis in Chinese developmental dyslexia. *Reading and Writing, 13,* 57–79.

Ho, C.S.-H., & Ma, R.N.-L. (1999). Training in phonological strategies improves Chinese dyslexic children's character reading skills. *Journal of Research in Reading, 22,* 131–142.

Ho, C.S., Ng, T.-T., & Ng, W.-K. (2003). A "radical" approach to reading development in Chinese: The role of semantic radicals and phonetic radicals. *Journal of Literacy Research, 35,* 849–878.

Kast, M., Meyer, M., Vogeli, C., Gross, M., & Jancke, L. (2007). Computer-based multisensory learning in children with developmental dyslexia. *Restorative Neurology and Neuroscience, 25,* 355–369.

Li, W., Anderson, R.C., Nagy, W., & Zhang, H. (2002). Facets of metalinguistic awareness that contribute to Chinese literacy. In W. Li, J.S. Gaffiney, & J.L. Packard (Eds.), *Chinese children's reading acquisition: Theoretical and pedagogical issues* (pp. 87–106). Boston: Kluwer Academic.

Lin, D., McBride-Chang, C., Aram, D., & Levin, I. (in press). Mother–child joint writing in Chinese kindergartners: Metalinguistic awareness, maternal mediation, and literacy acquisition. *Journal of Research in Reading.* doi: 10.1111/j.1467-9817.2010.01446.x

Lin, D., McBride-Chang, C., Aram, D., Levin, I., Cheung, R.Y.M., & Chow, Y.Y.Y. (2009). Maternal mediation of writing in Chinese children. *Language and Cognitive Processes, 24,* 1286–1311.

Lyon, G.R., Shaywitz, S.E., & Shaywitz, B.A. (2003). A definition of dyslexia. *Annals of Dyslexia, 53,* 1–14.

McBride-Chang, C., Cho, J.-R., Liu, H., Wagner, R.K., Shu, H., Zhou, A., Cheuk, C.S.-M., et al. (2005). Changing models across cultures: Associations of phonological and morphological awareness to reading in Beijing, Hong Kong, Korea, and America. *Journal of Experimental Child Psychology, 92,* 140–160.

McBride-Chang, C., Lam, F., Lam, C., Doo, S., Wong, S.W.L., & Chow, Y.Y.Y. (2008). Word recognition and cognitive profiles of Chinese pre-school children at risk for dyslexia through language delay or familial history of dyslexia. *Journal of Child Psychology and Psychiatry, 49,* 211–218.

McBride-Chang, C., Shu, H., Zhou, A., Wat, C.P., & Wagner, R.K. (2003). Morphological awareness uniquely predicts young children's Chinese character recognition. *Journal of Educational Psychology, 95,* 743–751.

McBride-Chang, C., Tong, X., Shu, H., Wong, A.M.-Y., Leung, K., & Tardif, T. (2008). Syllable, phoneme, and tone: Psycholinguistic units in early Chinese and English word recognition. *Scientific Studies of Reading, 12,* 171–194.

Meng, X., Sai, X., Wang, C., Wang, J., Sha, S., & Zhou, X. (2005). Auditory and speech processing and reading development in Chinese school children: Behavioural and ERP evidence. *Dyslexia, 11,* 292–310.

Meng, X., Tian, X., Jian, J., & Zhou, X. (2007). Orthographic and phonological processing in Chinese dyslexic children: An ERP study on sentence reading. *Brain Research, 1179,* 119–130.

Meyler, A., Keller, T.A., Cherkassky, V.L., Gabrieli, J.D.E., & Just, M.A. (2008). Modifying the brain activation of poor readers during sentence comprehension with extended remedial instruction: A longitudinal study of neuroplasticity. *Neuropsychologia, 46,* 2580–2592.

Packard, J.L., Chen, X., Li, W., Wu, X., Gaffney, J.S., Li, H., et al. (2006). Explicit instruction in orthographic structure and word morphology helps Chinese children learn to write characters. *Reading and Writing, 19,* 457–487.

Perfetti, C.A., & Tan, L.H. (1998). The time course of graphic, phonological, and semantic activation in visual Chinese character identification. *Journal of Experimental Psychology: Learning, Memory, and Cognition, 24,* 101–118.

Perfetti, C.A., Zhang, S., & Berent, I. (1992). Reading in English and Chinese: Evidence for a "Universal" Phonological Principle. In R. Frost & L. Katz (Eds.),

Orthography, phonology, morphology, and meaning (pp. 227–248). Amsterdam: North-Holland.

Samuelsson, S., Olson, R.K., Wadsworth, S., Corley, R., DeFries, J.C., Willcutt, E., et al. (2007). Genetic and environmental influences on pre-reading skills and early reading and spelling development: A comparison among United States, Australia, and Scandinavia. *Reading and Writing: An Interdisciplinary Journal, 20,* 51–75.

Schneider, W., Roth, E., & Ennemoser, M. (2000). Training phonological skills and letter knowledge in children at risk for dyslexia: A comparison of three kindergarten intervention programs. *Journal of Educational Psychology, 92*(2), 284–295.

Schuele, C.M., & Boudreau, D. (2008). Phonological awareness intervention: Beyond the basics. *Language, Speech, and Hearing Services in Schools, 39*(1), 3–20.

Schumacher, J., Anthoni, H., Dahdouh, F., Konig, I.R., Hillmer, A.M., Kluck, N., et al. (2006). Strong genetic evidence of DCDC2 as a susceptibility gene for dyslexia. *American Journal of Human Genetics, 78,* 52–62.

Share, D.L. (2008). On the Anglocentricities of current reading research and practice: The perils of overreliance on an "outlier" orthography. *Psychological Bulletin, 134,* 584–615.

Shu, H., & Anderson, R.C. (1997). Role of radical awareness in the character and word acquisition of Chinese children. *Reading Research Quarterly, 32,* 78–89.

Shu, H., Chen, X., Anderson, R.C., Wu, N., & Xuan, Y. (2003). Properties of school Chinese: Implications for learning to read. *Child Development, 74,* 27–47.

Shu, H., McBride-Chang, C., Wu, S., & Liu, H. (2006). Understanding Chinese developmental dyslexia: Morphological awareness as a core cognitive construct. *Journal of Educational Psychology, 98,* 122–133.

Shu, H., Meng, X., Chen, X., Luan, H., & Cao, F. (2005). The subtypes of developmental dyslexia in Chinese: Evidence from three cases. *Dyslexia, 11,* 311–329.

Tan, L.H., Spinks, J.A., Eden, G., Perfetti, C.A., & Siok, W.T. (2005). Reading depends on writing, in Chinese. *PNAS, 102,* 8781–8785.

Temple, E., Deutsch, G.K., Poldrack, R.A., Miller, S.L., Tallal, P., Merzenich, M.M., et al. (2003). Neural deficits in children with dyslexia ameliorated by behavioral remediation: Evidence from functional MRI. *PNAS, 100,* 2860–2865.

Tong, X., McBride-Chang, C., Shu, H., & Wong, A.M.-Y. (2009). Morphological awareness, orthographic knowledge, and spelling errors: Keys to understanding early Chinese literacy acquisition. *Scientific Studies of Reading, 13,* 1–27.

Tong, X., McBride-Chang, C., Wong, A.M.-Y., Shu, H., Reitsma, P., & Rispens, J. (2009). Longitudinal predictors of very early Chinese literacy acquisition. *Journal of Research in Reading.* doi: 10.1111/j.1467–9817.2009.01426.x

Tressoldi, P.E., Vio, C., & Iozzino, R. (2007). Efficacy of an intervention to improve fluency in children with developmental dyslexia in a regular orthography. *Journal of Learning Disabilities, 40,* 203–209.

van Otterloo, S.G., van der Leij, A., & Henrichs, L.F. (2009). Early home-based intervention in the Netherlands for children at familial risk of dyslexia. *Dyslexia, 15,* 187–217.

Wagner, D.A. (1993). *Literacy, culture, and development.* New York: Cambridge University Press.

Wong, A.M.-Y., Kidd, J.C., Ho, C.S.-H., & Au, T.K.-F. (2010). Characterizing the overlap between SLI and dyslexia in Chinese: The role of phonology and beyond. *Scientific Studies of Reading, 14,* 30–57.

Wu, X., Anderson, R.C., Li, W., Wu, X., Li, H., Zhang, J., et al. (2009). Morphological awareness and Chinese children's literacy development: An intervention study. *Scientific Studies of Reading, 13,* 26–52.

Wu, X., Li, W., & Anderson, R.C. (1999). Reading instruction in China. *Journal of Curriculum Studies, 31,* 571–586.

Yin, W.G., & Weekes, B.S. (2003). Dyslexia in Chinese: Clues from cognitive neuropsychology. *Annals of Dyslexia, 53,* 255–279.

Ziegler, J.C. (2006). Do differences in brain activation challenge universal theories of dyslexia? *Brain and Language, 98,* 341–343.

Ziegler, J.C., & Goswami, U. (2005). Reading acquisition, developmental dyslexia, and skilled reading across languages: A psycholinguistic grain size theory. *Psychological Bulletin, 131,* 3–29.

CHAPTER 3

The Statistical Learning Perspective on Chinese Reading

Chia-Ying Lee

INTRODUCTION

Research on word recognition has shown that a word's identification is affected by its neighborhood properties, such as orthography-to-phonology consistency (i.e., the degree to which similarly spelled words are pronounced similarly [Taraban & McClelland, 1987]), the orthographic neighborhood size (i.e., the number of words that can be created by changing a single letter in a target word [Andrews, 1989; Coltheart, Davelaar, Jonasson, & Besner, 1977; Grainger, O'Regan, Jacobs, & Segui, 1989]), and the phonological neighborhood density (i.e., the number of words that can be derived by changing one phoneme in a target word [Pylkkanen, Stringfellow, & Marantz, 2002; Vitevitch, Luce, Pisoni, & Auer, 1999]). Various models of visual word recognition have been developed to account for those findings. In one example, the dual-route cascade (DRC) model, which proposed distinct routes for reading aloud (Coltheart, Curtis, Atkins, & Haller, 1993; Coltheart, Rastle, Perry, Langdon, & Ziegler, 2001), posits two routes to lexical access. The lexical route accesses a word's lexical representation and its stored pronunciation by one-to-one direct mapping, whereas the sublexical route assembles a word's meaning or pronunciation via the grapheme-to-phoneme correspondence rules. The connectionist models, such as the triangle model proposed by Seidenberg and McClelland (1989), emphasize the role of statistical learning and posit that knowledge of spelling-to-sound relationships are represented in a distributed fashion. Word recognition is an instantiation of a continuous and dynamic learning process that depends on the interaction among the new input, the current state of the system, and its previous history.

Recently, Grainger and Ziegler (2008) proposed the bimodal interactive activation model (BIAM; see Figure 3.1). This model proposes three essential codes in the architecture similar to the triangle model (Seidenberg & McClelland, 1989): orthography, phonology, and semantics. In addition, the BIAM has added a sublexical and lexical distinction to the framework; this distinction results in the separation of orthographic and phonological codes into two processing pools, one of which corresponds to whole-word representations and the other to orthographic and phonological sequences that are smaller than the whole word (sublexical units, such as single or multiletter combinations and phonemes or combination of phonemes). Most important, BIAM assumes that visual word recognition relies on bidirectional

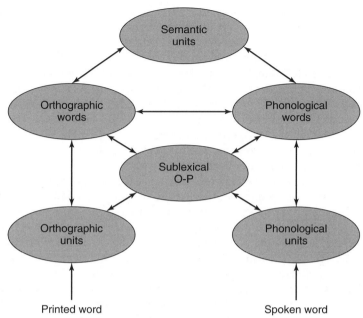

Figure 3.1. The architecture of the bimodal interactive activation model (BIAM) for word recognition. (From Grainger, J., & Ziegler, J.C. [2008]. Cross-code consistency in a functional architecture for word recognition. In E.L. Grigorenko & A.J. Naples [Eds.], *Single-word reading: Behavioral and biological perspectives. New directions in communication disorders research: Integrative approaches* [pp. 129–157]. Mahwah, NJ: Lawrence Erlbaum Associates; adapted by permission.)

coactivation of orthographic, phonological, and semantic units and that cross-code (orthographic, phonology, and semantic) consistency is the major force supporting stable word recognition (Grainger & Ziegler, 2008). Cross-code consistency represents the level of compatibility or coherence of all coactivated representations across the three types of code. To be more specific, consistency refers to the conditional probabilities that describe the mapping of items in one set (i.e., one level of representation or one type of code) onto items in another set, which represents how well the presence of a given item in set A (e.g., orthography) predicts the occurrence of an item in set B (e.g., phonology). The conditional probabilities can be measured bidirectionally (A to B or B to A), which are termed *feed-forward* and *feed-backward consistency,* respectively. These statistical mapping consistencies among orthography, phonology, and semantics can be acquired through learning to read and can affect performance in connectionist models, either by determining the weight strength between units as a function of the learning algorithm or via competitive mechanisms across units in the same set (i.e., within-level inhibition).

Based on the BIAM, when a person reads a word, the actual word and other candidates for the target word will be activated; the activated candidates include orthographic, phonological, and semantic repre-sentations of the target word itself and also representations for other candidate words that share similar neighborhood properties (such as orthographically and phonologically similar words) with the target words. The model's ability to simulate activation of other nontarget rep-resentations lends itself to naturally account for different kinds of neighborhood effects, such as the bidirectional mapping consistency between orthography and phonology, effects of semantic ambiguity (mapping between orthography and semantics or between phonology and semantics), and also orthographic and phonological neighborhood effects (Grainger & Ziegler, 2008).

Indeed, infant studies have demonstrated that statistical properties of speech are acquired through exposure to ambient language (Saffran, Johnson, Aslin, & Newport, 1999); a similar, more domain-general statistical-learning mechanism might also work throughout reading acquisition. The connectionist framework provides a simple but powerful model of how people learn statistical regularities. In the present chapter, we review behavioral and neuroimaging data on the role of mapping consistency between orthography and phonology in Chinese reading and focus on the statistical learning approach to evaluate whether this framework can be applied to explain how Chinese readers learn statis-tical regularities from the linguistic inputs through learning to read.

CHARACTERISTICS OF THE CHINESE WRITING SYSTEM

Chinese is often classified as a logographic writing system. Originally, Chinese characters were mainly designed to resemble the objects that they represent, either literally (pictographs) or metaphorically (ideo-graphs). (See also Wang & Tsai, Introduction in this volume.) However, not all concepts or meanings are concrete enough to be conveyed by pictorial resemblance to physical objects. By the time of the Shang dynasty, a lot of phonograms had been created to solve this problem; these were created by compounding two characters to form a single unit or character (DeFrancis, 1989). One of the component characters pro-vides information on word meaning (the semantic radical) and the other provides information for the pronunciation (the phonetic radical). In modern Chinese, more than 80% of Chinese characters are compound. Often (in around 90% of characters), the semantic radical appears on the left and the phonetic radical on the right (Lo, Hue, & Tsai, 2007). How-ever, the pronunciation and meaning are not always clear from the semantic or phonetic radicals due to changes in the pronunciation or meaning of Chinese characters over time.

Even more problematically, Chinese syllables have a relatively sim-ple form, with the majority being of consonant–vowel structure and with only two consonants that can follow the vowel in Mandarin (the nasal consonants /n/ and /ŋ/; Hua & Dodd, 2000). As a consequence, there are approximately 420 syllables in Mandarin (before consideration of tone)[1] that map onto around 5,000 different characters. On average, 11 characters share a single pronunciation. The pervasive homophony of Chinese implies that a graphic form is important for selecting meaning and escaping homophony in reading Chinese. In addition, unlike English—in which words are composed of letters representing phonemes—Chinese characters map onto single-syllable morphemes rather than onto phonemes in the spoken language. This characteristic leads easily to the assumption that there is a closer connection between graphic form and meaning in Chinese and that phonological knowledge may not be crucial in learning to read.

However, reading is fundamentally a process of learning a set of visual symbols to represent the phonological representations that have been established based on the oral language experience during preliterate childhood. All writing systems represent information about the pronunciation of words, even in Chinese. Studies have suggested that phonology is much involved at several levels of word processing from the character up through the sentence (Perfetti, Liu, & Tan, 2005; Perfetti & Zhang, 1995; Tan & Perfetti, 1999; Tzeng & Hung, 1978; Zhang & Perfetti, 1993), despite the fact that the characteristics of the Chinese writing system seem to disfavor its usage. For example, when asked to decide whether a character is a member of a semantic category, Chinese readers were slower and made more errors in rejecting a homophone of a category instance (Chua, 1999; Xu et al., 1999). The result is parallel to what has been found in English (Van Orden, 1987). In the priming task, the target character was identified faster and more accurately when the prime was a homophone (Perfetti et al., 2005; Perfetti & Tan, 1998; Tan & Perfetti, 1997). This evidence supports the idea that phonological information is activated as part of character identification.

The other way to discuss the role of phonology in Chinese reading is to trace the reading development and the reading difficulty across different writing systems. Learning to read requires children to associate letters and orthographic forms to sounds, and problems in representing or manipulating the units of sound may lead to reading difficulty. Indeed, research has shown that the majority of children with dyslexia perform more poorly than their peers in these tasks, including verbal short-term memory, rapid automatized naming, phonological awareness, or phonological decoding. Here, the representational use of phonological information is seen as critical in the etiology of developmental dyslexia (Snowling, 2000). Those who believe that phonology plays a minimal role in reading Chinese might suggest that there will be no dyslexia in Chinese readers, given that reading Chinese favors direct mappings between characters and meanings (Rozin, Poritsky, & Sotsky, 1971). In fact, the prevalence of reading difficulty among Taiwanese and Japanese is comparable to that for Americans (around 3%–10%), demonstrating that orthography is not the crucial factor determining the incidence of reading difficulty (Stevenson et al., 1982). Although

---

[1]Even when taking the four tones into account, there are no more than 1,700 syllables.

there are studies suggesting that Chinese dyslexia may arise from deficits in visual–spatial analysis (Huang & Hanley, 1995; Siok, Perfetti, Jin, & Tan, 2004; Siok, Spinks, Jin, & Tan, 2009), studies have demonstrated that both rapid automatized naming and phonological awareness performance predict Chinese reading performance, even with statistical controls for their intelligence quotient (IQ), parents' education, and socioeconomic status (Ho & Bryant, 1997a; Ho & Bryant, 1997b; McBride-Chang & Kail, 2002; Shu, Peng, & McBride-Chang, 2008; Siok & Fletcher, 2001). Young readers matched for reading age with students with dyslexia also showed better performance in phonemic awareness than did older readers with dyslexia (Lee & Ko, 2009). This result suggests that despite cross-language variability in the rate at which children acquire phoneme awareness, the differences in phonological sensitivity appear to predict reading and spelling development across languages, even in Chinese.

THE MAPPING PRINCIPLE BETWEEN CHINESE ORTHOGRAPHY AND PHONOLOGY

In Chinese, the phonological relationship between a phonogram and its phonetic radical can be considered in terms of *regularity* or *consistency*. *Regularity* refers to whether the sound of a character is identical with that of its phonetic radical. For example, 楓 (*feng1*) is pronounced the same as its phonetic radical 風 (*feng1*) and is defined as a regular character, whereas 猜 (*tsai1*) is pronounced differently from its phonetic radical 青 (*qing1*) and is thus defined as an irregular character. Previous studies have also demonstrated a frequency by regularity interaction in naming Chinese phonograms: The speed of naming a regular character is much faster than that of naming an irregular character, especially for low-frequency characters (Hue, 1992; Lee, Tsai, Su, Tzeng, & Hung, 2005; Seidenberg, 1985). Those data suggest that Chinese phonograms are not read via a direct association between orthography and phonology, but involve sublexical processes. However, the overall picture is more nuanced.

The phonetic radicals of many phonograms, called *independent phonograms*, are no longer legitimate characters and are thus unpronounceable in modern Chinese. The concept of regularity cannot be applied to independent phonograms; the definition of regularity is based on whether the phonograms and their phonetic radicals sound the same. Alternatively, the phonological relationship between a phonogram and a phonetic radical can be addressed by consistency rather than regularity; consistency indicates whether the pronunciation of a character agrees with those of its orthographic neighbors containing the same phonetic radical. For example, 搖 (pronunciation *yao2*) has six orthographic neighbors, 鷂, 瑤, 遙, 徭, 傜, and 謠. All neighbors are *"friends"* of 搖 because they have the same pronunciation. On the other hand, 流

(*liu2*) also has six orthographic neighbors, only 琉 (*liu2*) and 硫 (*liu2*) are its "friends," but not 梳 (*shu1*), 疏 (*shu1*), and 毓 (*yu4*). Therefore, 搖 and its orthographic neighbors are high-consistency characters (consistency index = 1), and 流, 琉, and 硫 are low-consistency characters (consistency index = 0.33).

It is worth noting that the indices of consistency for English and Chinese are parallel with respect to the representation of the statistical relationship between orthographic forms and their pronunciations. In studies of English, the consistency effect refers to findings which suggest that naming responses are faster and more accurate for words that have orthographic and phonological consistency (e.g., *-ean* in the final position of a monosyllabic word is always pronounced /in/ as in *lean, dean, bean*). In contrast, naming responses are slower and less accurate for words lacking consistency (e.g., *-int* corresponds to /ɪnt/ in *mint* and to /aint/ in *pint*), observed primarily for low-frequency words (Jared, 1997; Jared, 2002; Jared, McRae, & Seidenberg, 1990; Seidenberg & Waters, 1985; Seidenberg, Waters, Barnes, & Tanenhaus, 1984; Taraban & McClelland, 1987). The consistency effect was used to support a single mechanism, such as that proposed in the triangle model (Seidenberg & McClelland, 1989), for converting printed words and pseudowords into speech sounds correlating to the statistical mapping observed between orthography and phonology.

Studies have demonstrated the consistency effect in the naming of Chinese phonograms (Fang, Horng, & Tzeng, 1986; Lee et al., 2005; Tzeng, Lin, Hung, & Lee, 1995). Lee et al. (2005) orthogonally manipulated regularity and consistency and found a significant interaction similar to that in English between these two indices for naming low-frequency characters. This finding suggests that neither consistency nor regularity alone can represent the knowledge of orthography-to-phonology correspondences in Chinese. Furthermore, Lee et al. (2005) also demonstrated consistency effects in naming independent Chinese phonograms irrespective of whether they are high- or low-frequency words. The data support the contentions that 1) Chinese readers learn the statistical mapping between orthography and phonology, and 2) knowledge for the statistical mapping is not restricted to phonograms whose phonetic radicals are legal characters. Performance in naming Chinese phonograms does not depend exclusively on whether the phonology of the phonetic radical is activated; rather, it depends on the impact of orthographic neighbors, with or without consistent pronunciations.

A question remains as to whether the consistency effect originates from competition among the phonological representations associated with the phonetic radical at the sublexical level or is due to competition among the phonograms that share the same phonetic radical at the lexical level. To answer this question, Tsai, Lee, Tzeng, Hung, and Yen (2004) manipulated a character's parafoveal preview benefit to evaluate whether the phonetic consistency effect could be found. Eye movement studies of reading sentences have shown that not only the fixated word, but also words in the parafoveal region can be processed. The parafoveal information extracted from a word could facilitate the word's processing on the subsequent fixation, which is referred to as the *parafoveal preview benefit* (Rayner, 1998). This preview benefit can reflect the early processing of a word that occurs before a word is fixated during reading. Tsai et al. (2004) examined the role of phonological coding in the processing of parafoveal characters by measuring eye movements while reading Chinese sentences; they found that readers were able to benefit more from parafoveal preview for high-consistency targets than for low-consistency targets. This finding suggests that phonological coding from the phonetic radical is activated early, when the character is available for parafoveal preview (Tsai et al., 2004).

Another way to address this question is to take advantage of event-related potentials (ERPs), which provide excellent temporal resolution and the added benefit of distinct ERP components that can index different stages of processes. For example, N170 has been associated with word form analysis, and P200 has been used to index mechanisms related to feature detection (Luck & Hillyard, 1994). Studies have demonstrated the spelling-to-sound regularity effect in the P200 and suggested that this component may be associated with the extraction of the orthographic and phonological features of words in the early stage of lexical processing (Barnea & Breznitz, 1998; Sereno, Rayner, & Posner, 1998). N400 is well known for being associated with lexical semantic processing (Curran, Tucker, Kutas, & Posner, 1993). Current studies have found that sublexical syllable frequency and congruency effects occurred in the P200 time window at the frontal region, whereas the lexicality and lexical frequency effects were seen in the later N400 window (Barber, Vergara, & Carreiras, 2004; Carreiras, Vergara, & Barber, 2005). These findings were used to support the two-stage framework for lexical access by using P200 and N400 to index the sublexical and lexical processing, respectively.

Lee, Tsai, Chiu, Tzeng, and Hung (2006) examined ERP components to trace the time course of extracting phonology while reading Chinese pseudocharacters. In this study, participants were asked to passively attend to a set of pseudocharacters, each paired with a spoken syllable. This syllable had either a predictable or unpredictable pronunciation determined by the constituent phonetic radical of the pseudocharacter. Pseudocharacters paired with unpredictable pronunciations elicited greater P200 and N400 responses. The P200 component could indicate the early extraction of phonology in reading Chinese pseudocharacters; the N400 is likely associated with postlexical processing (Lee et al., 2006). Another ERP study showed that low-consistency characters elicited greater N170 amplitude in the temporal-occipital region and greater P200 amplitude in the frontal region than did high-consistency characters, and that high-consistency characters showed greater negativity of N400 amplitude than low-consistency characters. These findings were interpreted as indicating that low-consistency characters produce greater activation for the initial analysis of the orthographical and phonological representations (indexed by P200) and that high-consistency characters involve a greater lexical competition in the later stage (indexed by N400; Lee et al., 2007; see Figure 3.2).

In addition, a series of event-related functional magnetic resonance imaging (fMRI) studies have used frequency, consistency, and lexicality as markers and identified a set of neural correlates—including the left inferior frontal gyrus, the left temporoparietal region (inferior parietal gyrus and supramarginal gyrus), and the left temporal–occipital junction—as being involved in Chinese orthography-to-phonology transformation (Kuo et al., 2003; Lee, Huang, Kuo, Tsai, & Tzeng, 2010; Lee et al., 2004). These findings are congruent with those of researchers using alphabetic scripts (Devlin, Jamison, Gonnerman, & Matthews, 2006; Dietz, Jones, Gareau, Zeffiro, & Eden, 2005; Pugh et al., 2000) and suggest that the neural circuits involved in the temporoparietal and the ventral occipitotemporal areas for visual word recognition might be language-universal.

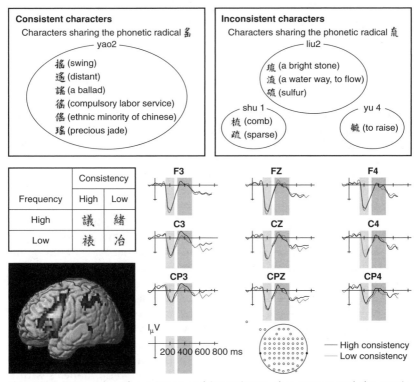

Figure 3.2. Examples of consistent and inconsistent phonograms and the consistency effect demonstrated by the fMRI and ERP studies (Lee et al., 2004; Lee et al., 2007).

STATISTICAL-LEARNING
PERSPECTIVE OF READING ACQUISITION:
NEIGHBORHOOD SIZE AND PHONETIC AWARENESS

For reading acquisition in alphabetic writing systems, written words are learned on the basis of phonological decoding, through which the child translates a printed letter string into its spoken format. This mechanism mainly focuses on the sublexical units, particularly grapheme–phoneme correspondences. Children perceive that the same letter (or grapheme) is often pronounced in the same way. Upon understanding this principle, they can begin to exploit the regularities between graphemic and phonological representations in order to translate unfamiliar printed words into their spoken equivalents, especially in learning to read orthographically consistent writing systems, such as Finish, Greek, or German. However, studies have shown that children learning to read English develop a sublexical strategy at a larger grain size. For example, Barron and Baron (1977) have shown that from the second grade, children apply grapheme-to-phoneme correspondences when reading unfamiliar English words.

Treiman, Goswami, and Bruck (1990) showed that by the end of first grade, children were more accurate at reading nonwords with *rimes*, which are the part of a syllable composed of the vowel and any subsequent consonant(s), shared by many words (e.g., *tain* and *goach*) than they were at reading uncommon rimes (e.g., *goan* and *taich*; Treiman et al., 1990). Coltheart and Leahy (1992) also found that children by the end of first grade read and spell regular words better than irregular words when rime consistency is controlled, and by second and third grade, children increasingly take advantage of larger orthographic correspondences. Similar findings have been reported in several studies (Waters, Seidenberg, & Bruck, 1984; Weekes, Castles, & Davies, 2006). These findings suggest that for learning to read English, the spelling-to-sound relations may not be best described in terms of links between graphemes and phonemes individually. Using letter groups that correspond to rimes might be a better strategy. Learning a writing system requires readers to develop an efficient mapping between orthography and phonology. However, the best strategy may differ for different grain sizes to meet the requirement of the orthography of the language that is being read (Ziegler & Goswami, 2005).

A question that needs to be further addressed is how the best mapping principle or the corresponding rules between orthography and phonology emerge in learning to read different writing systems. Based on the statistical learning perspective, children capture the statistical regularity of linguistic input through repetitive exposure to a language and gradually form metalinguistic knowledge. The redundancies within neighborhoods of similar written forms highlight invariant units that are shared across all words in that neighborhood. The phonological recoding strategy based on this finer orthographic unit can be formed if it repeatedly and consistently maps to a specific phonological pattern. In other words, the system's recognition of orthographic neighborhood similarity facilitates the restructuring of orthographic lexical information and forms the best mapping between orthography and phonology.

Assuming that experience or exposure to similar orthographic forms is key to developing awareness of the common unit within a set of orthographic neighbors, one would postulate there would be more pressure for words in a dense orthographic neighborhood to be restructured than for words in a sparse neighborhood. Phonetic consistency, which indicates whether a character agrees with orthographic neighbors containing the same phonetic radical, has been found to be important in reading Chinese. Therefore, it is important to know whether the size of an orthographic neighborhood affects awareness of phonological information conveyed by phonetic radicals.

In Chinese, the orthographic neighborhood size at the character level has been termed *radical combinability* by Feldman and Siok (1997). It can be further divided into phonetic and semantic combinability, defined as the number of phonograms that share the same phonetic or semantic radical, respectively. They found facilitative effects for combinability of both semantic and phonetic radicals when manipulating the radical combinability and radical position in a character decision task; however, these effects were not reliable within their positions. For the phonetic radicals, the combinability effect was significant in both the left and right positions. However, for the semantic radicals, the combinability effect was significant only when the semantic radical was on the left. These findings suggest that radical function (whether it is phonetic or semantic) should be considered when investigating the radical combinability effect (Feldman & Siok, 1997).

Hsu, Tsai, Lee, and Tzeng (2009) used an ERP technique to examine the statistical learning hypothesis as it applies to how Chinese readers acquire phonetic awareness, by manipulating both phonetic consistency and phonetic combinability. Lee et al. (2007) manipulated the high or low consistency of characters while matching their phonetic combinability and found that low-consistency characters elicit a larger N170 in the temporal-occipital region, more positive P200 in the frontal region, and less negative N400 than do high-consistency characters. High-combinability characters imply larger orthographic neighborhoods. If the statistical learning perspective is accurate, one would expect that phonograms with high phonetic combinability would display a greater consistency effect than those with lower phonetic combinability. Indeed, Hsu et al. (2009) revealed a significant interaction between phonetic combinability and consistency at N170 and consistency and combinability effects at P200 and N400. The phonetic consistency on N170, P200, and N400 was more salient when reading characters with large orthographic neighborhoods than when reading those with small orthographic neighborhoods (Hsu et al., 2009). These findings replicated those of Lee et al. (2007) regarding the consistency effect on different ERP components and further showed that phonograms with high phonetic combinability display a greater consistency effect than do those with lower phonetic combinability. The data support the statistical learning hypothesis and imply that orthographic similarity contributes to awareness of phonetic consistency. It seems that characters with high phonetic combinability seem to exert more pressure toward awareness of phonological validity represented by its phonetic radical than do those with low phonetic combinability. In other words, it is easier for readers to be aware of how a phonetic radical represents phonology when this phonetic radical can be embedded in many different phonograms and thus result in being repeatedly mapped to the same or similar pronunciation.

The other way to address how Chinese readers capture the mapping consistency between orthography and phonology is to examine how children become aware of the function of phonetic radicals. According to the Chinese textbooks from three main publishers that are used in Taiwanese elementary schools, children in Taiwan should be taught approximately 2,678 different characters by the end of 6 years of instruction. In general, more frequent characters and less complex characters are introduced earlier. Pictographs and ideographs are typically taught earlier, although the compound characters are dominant across the six grades. Among the characters learned from the first to the sixth grades were high percentages of compound characters (79%, 85%, 87%, 89%, 90%, and 91%, respectively, for the six grade levels). We analyzed the distribution of the phonetic combinability of these compound characters (see Figure 3.3). In the first grade, 60% of compound characters' phonetic combinability is 1. That means that most of the phonetic radicals are associated with a single compound character, so learning exposures are presumably limited for these compound characters. Only 30% of phonetic radicals appeared twice (phonetic combinability is 2) and 10% occur in at least three characters (phonetic combinability equal to or larger than 3), based on characters taught in the first grade. However, the distribution changes gradually from the first to the sixth grade. After third grade, most of the phonetic radicals that have been taught occur in at least three compound characters.

According to this statistical learning perspective, young Chinese readers should be able to capture the statistical properties of the written language from repeated exposure to the printed characters or words and establish different kinds of metalinguistic knowledge of Chinese characters. Indeed, studies have shown that children appear to become sensitive to the potentially useful information provided by radicals as their reading skills improve. Previous studies have focused on how children develop metalinguistic knowledge of the phonetic radical. This specific metalinguistic knowledge has been termed *phonetic awareness*; that is, a reader's knowledge of the principles governing the orthographic–phonological

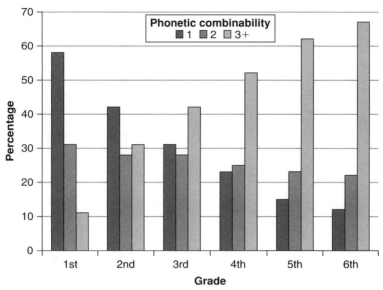

Figure 3.3. The phonetic combinability of the phonograms that children learn from first through sixth grades.

relationship in Chinese characters, such as which component is most likely to represent the clue for pronunciation or its validity in representing phonology (Shu, Anderson, & Wu, 2000). Shu and Anderson (1997) reported that children rated as good readers by their teachers were better at using radical information in reading than their less proficient counterparts. Other studies have consistently shown similar effects—specifically, that both adult and child readers could extract radical information to interpret the meaning and pronunciation of characters and pseudocharacters (Feng, Miller, Shu, & Zhang, 2001; Shu et al., 2000; Shu, Chen, Anderson, Wu, & Xuan, 2003). Lo, Hue, and Tsai (2007) examined how children in the second, fourth, and sixth grades with different vocabulary sizes guess the pronunciation of pseudocharacters. Their data showed that as vocabulary grows, Chinese readers are more likely to adopt the "position strategy" to determine the pronunciation for these pseudocharacters; this strategy indicates that using the right-hand component of the Chinese phonogram will more likely provide reliable clues to the character's pronunciation.

Lee and Tzeng (2008) examined when and how children acquire the knowledge of phonetic consistency and regularity in reading different types of Chinese characters (Lee & Tzeng, 2008). Children in fourth to sixth grades were asked to name a set of phonograms that can be divided into two consistency levels (high and low) and three word types (regular character, irregular character, and independent phonogram); see Figure 3.4. Awareness of phonetic consistency in reading regular characters was seen

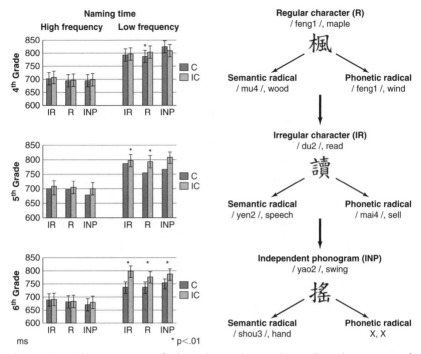

Figure 3.4. The awareness of phonetic consistency in reading three types of characters—regular (R), irregular (IR), and independent phonograms (INP)—in children from fourth to sixth grade. (*Key:* C, consistent characters; IC, inconsistent characters.)

in fourth-grade children; for irregular characters, this awareness developed later (fifth grade). By the end of the first semester of sixth grade, children showed consistency effects in reading all three types of characters. These findings also imply that phonetic awareness in reading Chinese is an emergent property of vocabulary growth, which is congruent with the statistical model for language acquisition. That is, by learning to read a large number of Chinese characters, children gradually realize that some characters with a phonetic radical correspond to the same or similar pronunciations. In English, awareness of rime consistency generally develops by the end of the first grade (Coltheart & Leahy, 1992). The awareness of the mapping consistency from orthography to phonology seems to develop much later in learning Chinese, but the evidence suggests that the development of recoding strategies at multiple grain sizes does not hold back Chinese or English children from developing orthography–phonology recoding strategies.

CONCLUSION

Learning any writing system requires an efficient mapping from orthography to phonology, and beginning readers need to develop efficient phonological recoding strategies. However, languages vary in phonological structure and in the consistency with which that phonology is represented in the orthography. These factors determine cross-language differences in the grain size of lexical representations, the reading strategies developed, and the rate at which children acquire reading skills (Ziegler & Goswami, 2005). For an alphabetic writing system in which orthographic structures correspond to speech units of different sizes and characteristics, it is not surprising to conclude that the phonology is critical for learning to read. However, given that the Chinese writing system represents morphosyllabic rather than phonemic information, how Chinese readers establish the efficient mapping between orthography and phonology and what the functional grain size could be for the efficient phonological recoding in learning to read Chinese are intriguing issues.

This chapter reviews a series of behavioral studies that demonstrate how Chinese readers capture the mapping consistency between character and sound. The neural correlates responsible for the Chinese orthography-to-phonology transformation are similar to what has been suggested for reading alphabetic writing systems. Meanwhile, ERP evidence suggests that the consistency effect in reading Chinese has an impact on early sublexical phonological computation and later lexical semantic competition (Lee et al., 2006; Lee et al., 2007). Most important, the consistency effect was mainly found in phonograms with large orthographic neighborhoods (phonetic combinability), suggesting an interplay between orthographic density and the mapping from orthography to phonology in the different stages of lexical processing (Hsu et al., 2009). Finally, a study with children from the fourth to sixth grades showed the developmental trajectories of when and how the knowledge of phonetic consistency is acquired by children learning to read (Lee & Ko, 2009; Lee & Tzeng, 2008). Taken together, these findings imply that although phonological information is not explicitly expressed in Chinese characters, the coding strategies for different grain sizes emerge for readers from the orthography that is being read. Based on cross-linguistic evidence, it appears that the statistical learning approach holds such that it can account for readers' ability to pick up subtle statistical regularities about orthographic as well as phonological patterns reflected in the early language inputs.

Most important, cross-linguistic comparisons of symbol-sound consistency suggest that there might be a statistical learning mechanism of literacy across orthographies, although the specific properties of a language can make it easier or harder for children to learn the phonology and spell. Based on these findings, Chinese readers do not simply learn the coding based nology of characters as a whole by rote. Phonological coding based on sublexical units, such as radicals, is established when readers learn enough visual forms that share the same sub-units that can be mapped to one or a set of pronunciations or gs. Although inefficient symbol–sound mapping is thought universal hallma-

of dyslexia (Ziegler, 2006), the specific characteristics of languages might lead to a qualitatively different manifestation across languages. More research is needed in order to predict or to explain why some children fail to learn to read Chinese at both the behavioral and neural levels.

REFERENCES

Andrews, S. (1989). Frequency and neighborhood effects on lexical access: Activation or search. *Journal of Experimental Psychology: Learning, Memory, and Cognition, 15,* 802–814.

Barber, H., Vergara, M., & Carreiras, M. (2004). Syllable-frequency effects in visual word recognition: Evidence from ERPs. *Neuroreport, 15,* 545–548.

Barnea, A., & Breznitz, Z. (1998). Phonological and orthographic processing of Hebrew words: Electrophysiological aspects. *Journal of Genetic Psychology, 159,* 492–504.

Barron, R.W., & Baron, J. (1977). How children get meaning from printed words. *Child Development, 48,* 587–594.

Carreiras, M., Vergara, M., & Barber, H. (2005). Early event-related potential effects of syllabic processing during visual word recognition. *Journal of Cognitive Neuroscience, 17,* 1803–1817.

Chua, F.K. (1999). Phonological recoding in Chinese logograph recognition. *Journal of Experimental Psychology: Learning, Memory, and Cognition, 25,* 876–891.

Coltheart, M., Curtis, B., Atkins, P., & Haller, M. (1993). Models of reading aloud: Dual-route and parallel-distributed-processing approaches. *Psychological Review, 100*(4), 589–608.

Coltheart, M., Davelaar, E., Jonasson, J.T., & Besner, D. (1977). Access to the internal lexicon. In S. Domic (Ed.), *Attention and performance* (Vol. VI, pp. 535–555). New York: Academic Press.

Coltheart, V., & Leahy, J. (1992). Children's effects' reading of nonwords: Journal regularity and consistency. *ing, Experimental Psychology, Learning, Coltheart, and Cognition, 18,* 718–729.

Langdon, Rastle, K., Perry, C., A dual ro Ziegler, J. (2001). DRC: word reco ded model of visual Psychological nd reading aloud. Curran, T., Tuc 108, 204–256.

Posner, M.I. (, Kutas, M., & N400: Brain el graphy of the ing semantic ex tivity reflect- ectroenceph-

alography and Clinical Neurophysiology, 88, 188–209.

DeFrancis, J. (1989). *Visible speech: The diverse oneness of writing systems.* Honolulu: University of Hawaii Press.

Devlin, J.T., Jamison, H.L., Gonnerman, L.M., & Matthews, P.M. (2006). The role of the posterior fusiform gyrus in reading. *Journal of Cognitive Neuroscience, 18,* 911–922.

Dietz, N.A., Jones, K.M., Gareau, L., Zeffiro, T.A., & Eden, G.F. (2005). Phonological decoding involves left posterior fusiform gyrus. *Human Brain Mapping, 26,* 81–93.

Fang, S.P., Horng, R.Y., & Tzeng, O.J.L. (1986). Consistency effects in the Chinese character and pseudo-character naming tasks. In H.S.R. Kao & R. Hoosain (Eds.), *Linguistics, psychology, and the Chinese language* (pp. 11–21). Hong Kong: University of Hong Kong, Center of Asian Studies.

Feldman, L.B., & Siok, W.W.T. (1997). The role of component function in visual recognition of Chinese characters. *Journal of Experimental Psychology: Learning, Memory, & Cognition, 23,* 776–781.

Feng, G., Miller, K., Shu, H., & Zhang, H. (2001). Rowed to recovery: The use of phonological and orthographic information in reading Chinese and English. *Journal of Experimental Psychology, Learning, Memory and Cognition, 27,* 1079–1100.

Grainger, J., O'Regan, J.K., Jacobs, A.M., & Segui, J. (1989). On the role of competing word units in visual word recognition: The neighborhood frequency effect. *Perception & Psychophysics, 45,* 189–195.

Grainger, J., & Ziegler, J.C. (2008). Cross-code consistency in a functional architecture for word recognition. In E.L. Grigorenko & A.J. Naples (Eds.), *Single-word reading: Behavioral and biological perspectives. New directions in communication disorders research: Integrative approaches* (pp. 129–157). Mahwah, NJ: Lawrence Erlbaum Associates.

Ho, C.S., & Bryant, P. (1997a). Development of phonological awareness of Chinese children in Hong Kong. *Journal of Psycholinguistic Research, 26,* 109–126.

Ho, C.S., & Bryant, P. (1997b). Phonological skills are important in learning to read Chinese. *Developmental Psychology, 33,* 946–951.

Hsu, C.H., Tsai, J.L., Lee, C.Y., & Tzeng, O.J. (2009). Orthographic combinability and phonological consistency effects in reading Chinese phonograms: An event-related potential study. *Brain and Language, 108,* 56–66.

Hua, Z., & Dodd, B. (2000). The phonological acquisition of Putonghua (Modern Standard Chinese). *Journal of Child Language, 27,* 3–42.

Huang, H.S., & Hanley, J.R. (1995). Phonological awareness and visual skills in learning to read Chinese and English. *Cognition, 54,* 73–98.

Hue, C.-W. (1992). Recognition processes in character naming. In H.-C.E. Chen & O.J.L. Tzeng (Eds.), *Language processing in Chinese: Advances in psychology* (Vol. 90, pp. 93–107). Amsterdam: North-Holland.

Jared, D. (1997). Spelling-sound consistency affects the naming of high-frequency words. *Journal of Memory and Language, 36,* 505–529.

Jared, D. (2002). Spelling-sound consistency and regularity effects in word naming. *Journal of Memory and Language, 46,* 723–750.

Jared, D., McRae, K., & Seidenberg, M.S. (1990). The basis of consistency effects in word naming. *Journal of Memory and Language, 29,* 687–715.

Kuo, W.J., Yeh, T.C., Lee, C.Y., Wu, Y.T., Chou, C.C., Ho, L.T., et al. (2003). Frequency effects of Chinese character processing in the brain: An event-related fMRI study. *Neuroimage, 18,* 720–730.

Lee, C.-Y., Huang, H.-W., Kuo, W.-J., Tsai, J.-L., & Tzeng, O.J.L. (2010). Cognitive and neural basis of the consistency and lexicality effects in reading Chinese. *Journal of Neurolinguistics, 23,* 10–27.

Lee, C.Y., Tsai, J.L., Chan, W.H., Hsu, C.H., Hung, D.L., & Tzeng, O.J.L. (2007). Temporal dynamics of the consistency effect in reading Chinese: An event-related potentials study. *Neuroreport, 18,* 147–151.

Lee, C.Y., Tsai, J.L., Chiu, Y.C., Tzeng, O.J.L., & Hung, D.L. (2006). The early extraction of sublexical phonology in reading Chinese pseudocharacters: An event-related potentials study. *Language and Linguistics, 7,* 619–636.

Lee, C.Y., Tsai, J.L., Kuo, W.J., Yeh, T.C., Wu, Y.T., Ho, L.T., et al. (2004). Neuronal correlates of consistency and frequency effects on Chinese character naming: An event-related fMRI study. *Neuroimage, 23,* 1235–1245.

Lee, C.Y., Tsai, J.L., Su, E.C.I., Tzeng, O.J.L., & Hung, D.L. (2005). Consistency, regularity, and frequency effects in naming Chinese characters. *Language and Linguistics, 6,* 75–107.

Lee, C.Y., & Tzeng, Y.-L. (2008). The awareness of phonetic regularity and consistency in learning to read Chinese. Presented at the Fifteenth Annual Meeting Society for the Scientific Study of Reading, Asheville, North Carolina.

Lee, J.R., & Ko, H. (2009). Phonological representation unit in the phonological awareness task among Taiwanese students. *Bulletin of Educational Psychology, 41*(1), 111–124.

Lo, M., Hue, C.-W., & Tsai, F.-Z. (2007). Chinese readers' knowledge of how Chinese orthography represents phonology. *Chinese Journal of Psychology, 49,* 315–334.

Luck, S.J., & Hillyard, S.A. (1994). Electrophysiological correlates of feature analysis during visual search. *Psychophysiology, 31,* 291–308.

McBride-Chang, C., & Kail, R.V. (2002). Cross-cultural similarities in the predictors of reading acquisition. *Child Development, 73,* 1392–1407.

Perfetti, C.A., Liu, Y., & Tan, L.H. (2005). The lexical constituency model: Some implications of research on Chinese for general theories of reading. *Psychological Review, 112,* 43–59.

Perfetti, C.A., & Tan, L.H. (1998). The time course of graphic, phonological, and semantic activation in Chinese character identification. *Journal of Experimental Psychology: Learning, Memory, and Cognition. 24,* 101–118.

Perfetti, C.A., & Zhang, S.L. (1995). Very early phonological activation in Chinese reading. *Journal of Experimental Psychology: Learning, Memory, and Cognition, 21,* 24–33.

Pugh, K.R., Mencl, W.E., Jenner, A.P Katz, L., Frost, S.J., Lee, J.R., et al Functional neuroimaging reading and reading disab opmental dyslexia). *Mental*

& *Developmental Disabilities Research Reviews, 6,* 207–213.

Pylkkanen, L., Stringfellow, A., & Marantz, A. (2002). Neuromagnetic evidence for the timing of lexical activation: An MEG component sensitive to phonotactic probability but not to neighborhood density. *Brain & Language, 81,* 666–678.

Rayner, K. (1998). Eye movements in reading and information processing: 20 years of research. *Psychological Bulletin, 124,* 372–422.

Rozin, P., Poritsky, S., & Sotsky, R. (1971). American children with reading problems can easily learn to read English represented by Chinese characters. *Science, 171,* 1264–1267.

Saffran, J.R., Johnson, E.K., Aslin, R.N., & Newport, E.L. (1999). Statistical learning of tone sequences by human infants and adults. *Cognition, 70,* 27–52.

Seidenberg, M.S. (1985). The time course of phonological code activation in two writing systems. *Cognition, 19,* 1–30.

Seidenberg, M.S., & McClelland, J.L. (1989). A distributed, developmental model of word recognition and naming. *Psychological Review, 96*(4), 523–568.

Seidenberg, M.S., & Waters, G.S. (1985). Spelling-sound effects in reading: Time-course and decision criteria. *Memory and Cognition, 13,* 557–572.

Seidenberg, M.S., Waters, G.S., Barnes, M.A., & Tanenhaus, M.K. (1984). When does irregular spelling or pronunciation influence word recognition? *Journal of Verbal Learning & Verbal Behavior, 23,* 383–404.

Sereno, S.C., Rayner, K., & Posner, M.I. (1998). Establishing a time-line of word recognition: Evidence from eye movements and event-related potentials. *Neuroreport, 9,* 2195–2200.

Shu, H., & Anderson, R.C. (1997). Role of radical awareness in the character and word acquisition of Chinese children. *Reading Research Quarterly, 32*(1), 78–89.

Shu, H., Anderson, R.C., & Wu, N. (2000). Phonetic awareness: Knowledge of orthography–phonology relationships in the character acquisition of Chinese children. *Journal of Educational Psychology, 92,* 56–62.

Shu, H., Chen, X., Anderson, R.C., Wu, N., & Xuan, Y. (2003). Properties of school Chinese: Implications for learning to read. *Child Development, 74,* 27–47.

Shu, H., Peng, H., & McBride-Chang, C. (2008). Phonological awareness in young Chinese children. *Developmental Science, 11,* 171–181.

Siok, W.T., & Fletcher, P. (2001). The role of phonological awareness and visual-orthographic skills in Chinese reading acquisition. *Developmental Psychology, 37,* 886–899.

Siok, W.T., Perfetti, C.A., Jin, Z., & Tan, L.H. (2004). Biological abnormality of impaired reading is constrained by culture. *Nature, 431,* 71–76.

Siok, W.T., Spinks, J.A., Jin, Z., & Tan, L.H. (2009). Developmental dyslexia is characterized by the co-existence of visuospatial and phonological disorders in Chinese children. *Current Biology, 19,* R890–R892.

Snowling, M.J. (2000). *Dyslexia.* Oxford, England: Blackwell.

Stevenson, H.W., Stigler, J.W., Lee, S.-Y., Lucker, G.W., Kitamura, S., & Hsu, C.-C. (1982). Reading disabilities: The case of Chinese, Japanese, and English. *Child Development, 53,* 1164–1181.

Tan, L.H., & Perfetti, C.A. (1997). Visual Chinese character recognition: Does phonological information mediate access to meaning? *Journal of Memory and Language, 37,* 41–57.

Tan, L.H., & Perfetti, C.A. (1999). Phonological activation in visual identification of Chinese two-character words. *Journal of Experimental Psychology: Learning, Memory, and Cognition, 25,* 382–393.

Taraban, R., & McClelland, J.L. (1987). Conspiracy effects in word pronunciation. *Journal of Memory and Language, 26,* 608–631.

Treiman, R., Goswami, U., & Bruck, M. (1990). Not all nonwords are alike: Implications for reading development and theory. *Memory and Cognition, 18,* 559–567.

Tsai, J.L., Lee, C.Y., Tzeng, O.J.L., Hung, D.L., & Yen, N.S. (2004). Use of phonological codes for Chinese characters: Evidence from processing of parafoveal preview when reading sentences. *Brain & Language, 91,* 235–244.

Tzeng, O.J.L., & Hung, D.L. (1978). Reading the Chinese character: Some basic research. *Acta Psychologica Taiwanica, 20,* 45–49.

Tzeng, O.J.L., Lin, Z.H., Hung, D.L., & Lee, W.L. (1995). Learning to be a conspirator: A tale of becoming a good Chinese reader. In B. de Gelder & J. Morais (Eds.), *Speech and reading: A comparative approach* (pp. 227–246). Hove, England: Erlbaum, Taylor & Francis.

Van Orden, G.C. (1987). A ROWS is a ROSE: Spelling, sound, and reading. *Memory & Cognition, 15,* 181–198.

Vitevitch, M.S., Luce, P.A., Pisoni, D.B., & Auer, E.T. (1999). Phonotactics, neighborhood activation, and lexical access for spoken words. *Brain & Language, 68,* 306–311.

Waters, G.S., Seidenberg, M.S., & Bruck, M. (1984). Children's and adults' use of spelling-sound information in three reading tasks. *Memory and Cognition, 12,* 293–305.

Weekes, B.S., Castles, A.E., & Davies, R.A. (2006). Effects of consistency and age of acquisition on reading and spelling among developing readers. *Reading and Writing, 19,* 133–169.

Xu, Y.D., Pollatsek, A., & Potter, M.C. (1999). The activation of phonology during silent Chinese word reading. *Journal of Experimental Psychology, Learning Memory, and Cognition, 25,* 838–857.

Zhang, S.L., & Perfetti, C.A. (1993). The tongue-twister effect in reading Chinese. *Journal of Experimental Psychology: Learning, Memory, and Cognition, 19,* 1082–1093.

Ziegler, J.C. (2006). Do differences in brain activation challenge universal theories of dyslexia? *Brain & Language, 98,* 341–343.

Ziegler, J.C., & Goswami, U. (2005). Reading acquisition, developmental dyslexia, and skilled reading across languages: A psycholinguistic grain size theory. *Psychological Bulletin, 131,* 3–29.

CHAPTER 4

Prevention of Reading Difficulties in Highly Transparent Finnish

Ulla Richardson, Mikko Aro, and Heikki Lyytinen

INTRODUCTION

In a highly transparent writing system, one has to learn only a few correspondences of small size units between spoken and written language because they are consistently the same in all the contexts in which they occur. In Finnish, which is fully consistent at the grapheme–phoneme level, the child has to learn only a small number of letter–sound connections, as we explain in this chapter. We also describe our efforts to alleviate and possibly prevent problems that even children who are learning an easy-to-acquire writing system may face.

First, we illustrate in detail the Finnish writing system from the perspective of the learner. Then we document how reading problems are still possible, independent of how easy learning should be, and illustrate how indicators of these problems can be detected before children enter school and how this knowledge should be used for helping these children to overcome the hurdles they may have from the beginning of their formal education. We then describe how we have organized prevention for Finnish children. We also introduce our efforts to enhance and broaden use of our preventive technology—which is shown to support efficient reading acquisition of our children—for children with greater challenges, such as English-speaking children who must master a highly nontransparent written language with a huge number of correspondences to be learned. Finally, we illustrate briefly our attempts to help children who do not receive appropriate reading instruction in Africa.

CHALLENGES OF THE FINNISH ORTHOGRAPHY FROM THE POINT OF VIEW OF A BEGINNING READER

A Finnish child needs to learn only 23 letters and one 2-letter grapheme,[1] which represent the 24 Finnish phonemes, in order to have the required foundations for learning to read. The next step is to learn to assemble spoken items according to the sequence of letters, each representing one phoneme. Because of the transparency, the child needs

---

[1] The only two-letter grapheme, *ng*, corresponds to /ŋ/.

nothing else to be able to generate from the letter sequences any pronounceable item correctly. It is for fluency that fast identification of larger units is needed. A syllable is a natural unit for Finnish children because of the trochaic rhythm of the Finnish language, which facilitates appropriate segmentation of words. School teaching also proceeds immediately from the letter sounds to practicing the assembly of syllables and short words; thus children encounter relatively easy experiences that help them to chunk written material appropriately into syllables.

In Finland, children typically learn letter names before school entry. Children encounter letters at an early age in the home environment, and although formal reading instruction does not take place at kindergarten, most of the letters are introduced there as part of the preschool curriculum. Thus, at the time of school entry (first grade), the majority of the children know most of the letter names. When reading instruction begins, explicit attention is paid to letter sounds and phonemic assembly to support independent decoding skills. For most children, learning the associations between letter names and letter sounds does not pose problems because all Finnish letter names also include the letter sound. Because phonemes are represented with single-letter graphemes (with the mentioned exception), and the correspondences are bidirectionally regular and unambiguous, the phonemic structure of the words is visible and explicit for the reader. As mentioned previously, after mastering letter sounds and phonemic assembly skills, tools for pronouncing any written item are available for the beginning reader. Thus the basic skills of literacy usually develop quickly and effortlessly. For many children, learning to read is a rapid off/on transition, and more than one third of the children master basic decoding skills even before school entry and the beginning of reading instruction (Aro, 2006).

To summarize, the features of the Finnish writing system offer most children efficient tools for independent reading and self-teaching from the very early stages of reading instruction and literacy development. Even though the early steps toward reading are usually easy to make for most children, some children need a significant amount of instructional effort to master basic decoding.

Whereas the Finnish writing system is in many of the language child learning the orthographic cipher, there are opment of reading that pose specific challenges for the furthe to be long due to the skills after the initial stages. First, the wo tem, and compounding agglutinative morphology, rich deriva ave hundreds of different that occur in Finnish. Any single morphemes. Minor differences orthographic forms, depending ly change the meaning. Together, words in texts often consist of systematic phonemic assembl in inflectional endings ma these features underlir a strategy of early reading. A child must concentrate on accuracy to be able to detect morphological information, which is coded often with only one or two letters. Despite this seemingly simple encoding, however, there are few short, frequently repeated items that can guide the reader into recognition-based reading. Consequently, repetitions at the level of words accumulate relatively slowly when compared with many other languages with different types of morphological systems. Fluent and automatic reading is probably based on the repetition-induced use of larger units, such as frequent letter combinations, syllables, or morphemes. Achieving fluent reading seems to be a problem for a number of children; poor reading is typically manifested as slow, albeit accurate reading.

It seems that the features of the Finnish orthography might lower the threshold on the first doorstep into reading: phonemic assembly and decoding. The small number of phonemes and graphemes result in repetitions sufficient for most children to master the grapheme–phoneme correspondences and become accurate readers. However, struggling readers often remain slow and dysfluent, unable to use larger-grain-size units to support assembly of long words that they encounter in texts. The dysfluency problem is often amplified because slow and laborious reading affects the motivation for independent reading practice; reading development can thus be frozen at the level of phonemic assembly, whereas peers with more practice have more automatized skills and are able to use different levels of orthographic units as well as other language skills to support their reading development.

The challenges from the point of view of preventing reading problems are twofold: first, how to efficiently support children struggling in the mastery of basic skills required for becoming literate in letter–sound correspondences and phonemic assembly; and second, how to best support the development of fluency after the child has mastered the tools, allowing accurate, independent decoding. To date, the focus of intervention approaches has mostly been on the first mentioned challenge of reading development. However, as noted by Share (2008), more attention needs to be paid to the development and implementation of interventions in reading fluency. In this chapter, we illustrate how we have approached these issues on the basis of the knowledge of reading development in Finnish.

EARLY IDENTIFICATION OF CHILDREN WHO FACE DIFFICULTIES

The Jyväskylä Longitudinal Study of Dyslexia (JLD) reveals that Finnish-speaking children can face difficulties in learning to read, independent of the fact that reading acquisition is easy for most learners of Finnish. Most of those with severe difficulties have a familial background of dyslexia (Lyytinen 2008). Many of these otherwise

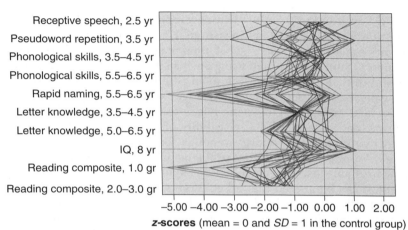

Receptive speech, 2.5 yr
Pseudoword repetition, 3.5 yr
Phonological skills, 3.5–4.5 yr
Phonological skills, 5.5–6.5 yr
Rapid naming, 5.5–6.5 yr
Letter knowledge, 3.5–4.5 yr
Letter knowledge, 5.0–6.5 yr
IQ, 8 yr
Reading composite, 1.0 gr
Reading composite, 2.0–3.0 gr

−5.00 −4.00 −3.00 −2.00 −1.00 0.00 1.00 2.00

z-scores (mean = 0 and *SD* = 1 in the control group)

Figure 4.1. Individual profiles of all JLD children from the familial risk group showing compromised reading.

Note: Reading composite (accuracy and fluency of reading), 2–3. Grade > 1 *SD* below normal, and performance and verbal IQ ≥ 80.

(*Key:* IQ, intelligence quotient; JLD, Jyväskylä Longitudinal Study of Dyslexia; SD, standard deviation. From Lyytinen, H., Erskine, J., Kujala, J., Ojanen, E., & Richardson, U. [2009]. In search of a science-based application: A learning tool for reading acquisition. *Scandinavian Journal of Psychology, 50,* 668–675; reprinted by permission.)

typically developing children find reading acquisition difficult. Such a problem seems surprising, given that more than one third of Finnish first-grade students (who enter school at the age of 7) learn to read without any formal instruction.

The data from the JLD reveal convincingly that Finnish children who fail to acquire letter names from their natural environment have difficulties learning to read. Letter knowledge is a surprisingly strong predictor from the age of 5, as seen in Figure 4.1. In the JLD (for the most recent review of the findings, see Lyytinen et al., 2008), we intensively observed children at familial risk for dyslexia from birth onward. Strong indications of risk could be detected in the first few days of life (see Guttorm, Leppänen, Hämäläinen, Eklund, & Lyytinen, 2009, for review). However, on a more practical level, relatively accurate identification of risk can be made 1–3 years before the child begins school. (For a detailed analysis of the predictors, see Puolakanaho et al., 2007.) The ability to recall letter names appears to be the most predictive practical indicator of reading difficulty and can be used early enough to be the only required tool for identifying children in need of preventive intervention. Figure 4.1 illustrates the individual profiles of the development of skills considered to be predictive of reading acquisition from early childhood to the age when children go to school for all those children who were later diagnosed as dyslexic. Children who faced severe problems could be identified on the basis of compromised letter knowledge prior to school e⁻

Of children in the JLD, 78% had development of letter knowledge in the lowest 20% overall, as measured 1.5 years (at 5.5 years of age) before school entry. Thus a substantial majority in need of preventive support could be identified using such a single simple measure. Note, however, that although most in need could be detected correctly, not all children with poor letter knowledge faced reading problems (i.e., were false positives). Observing false positives is fortunate because it means that there is still the possibility of overcoming the problem if the environment is supportive enough. Based on the fact that about one third of those with initial problems in storing letter names were able to attain close to average reading skills in their ordinary environment, it can be argued that all children showing this type of indication of risk can be helped and should be helped to guarantee their success. One third of those with initial problems in storing letter names were able to attain close to average reading skills in their ordinary environment, it can be argued that all children showing this type of indication of risk can be helped and should be helped to guarantee their success. That is, developing societies should be given the resources to implement preventive practices, even for those children who may end up not needing them. This investment may not need to be great compared with the benefits that it can produce in the well-being of children throughout their lives; early failure usually has long-ranging consequences, such as lowering schooling-related motivation and limiting children's ultimate career potential; thus low-cost interventions that can prevent such results should be viewed as important investments.

GRAPHOGAME: A GAME FOR SUPPORTING CHILDREN'S READING ACQUISITION

Because the data from the JLD project clearly indicated that children who have difficulties in reading acquisition have problems in letter knowledge before they enter school, we sought to assist these children by designing a learning game specifically centered around connecting speech sounds to written symbols. The original version of the computer game, Graphogame,[2] was designed in 2002 at the University of Jyväskylä and has been further developed in collaboration with the Niilo Mäki Foundation. The basic game format looks simple: The learner hears a clearly articulated speech sound through headphones; then, several balls with letters begin to fall from the top of the computer screen. The task is to select the letter ball that corresponds to the presented sound before the ball reaches the bottom of the screen. The goal of the game is to guide learners to correctly associate visual symbols with speech sounds.

---

[2]The game is called *Ekapeli* in Finnish and was also called Literate in some earlier publications.

Behind its simple appearance, the game hides several theoretically, methodologically, and technologically driven principles. These principles have been utilized in various ways over the years as the game has been further refined. The various game versions focus the training on different aspects of literacy skills, starting with grapheme–phoneme associations, moving to larger units, and eventually reaching learning material that transfers the focus from accuracy to fluent sentence reading and comprehension. However, the principles that guide the development of the various game versions are based on a handful of basic concepts that we consider to be important for effective learning. In the following discussion, we briefly present these key features of the game design.

From the outset of playing, the learner is guided to understand the alphabetic principle, connecting letters to speech sounds. In the case of single letters, the corresponding phoneme is presented rather than the letter name. In cases in which a letter or a larger unit can be associated with more than one specific sound, these visual symbols are presented in a context in which only one specific sound or sound sequence is correct. In addition to the grapheme–phoneme consistency principle, frequency of the orthographic symbol or symbol sequence was taken into consideration in the selection of the learning material. We thus aimed for high consistency and frequency levels in the game's learning material, although in the versions that aim at training fluency, the contrast between high and low frequency items is also utilized.

The quality of both the audio and visual presentations is carefully controlled. The role of speech representations in terms of accuracy of phoneme perception (specifically, phonemic length, which is a distinctive feature in Finnish) has been shown to predict literacy skills even after controlling all of the other best known predictors, including phonological skills (Pennala et al., 2010). By providing distinct and prototypical examples of speech material, the game facilitates the formation of specific phoneme categories needed in a given language.

For learning to take place—specifically among those who may have learning difficulties—the same learning material is repeated hundreds of times, but within different contexts. The various contexts are, for example, composed of different game levels and types of tasks, or the targets to be learned are presented within a specific selection of other items (distractors). To promote automatization, the game is designed to require the learner to make quick associations.

The reward mechanism within the game follows two main principles. First, the adaptation procedures provide the child with a sufficient amount of successful experiences. Based on each child's earlier game performance, he or she is expected to achieve 80% correct. This is accomplished as follows: Each game level has a maximum number of trials (usually 28). If the child manages to select a correct visual symbol (letter, syllable, word, and so forth) that corresponds to the sound that was presented, the number of alternatives will increase in the next trial (the maximum is usually seven alternatives). If the child selects an incorrect symbol, the correct symbol is shown on its own (no other symbols are shown) and the child has to select this one in order to continue (each sound will thus be connected to the corresponding sound each time). The next trial will have fewer choices. The game keeps track of all the selections that the child makes (including timings, and so forth), and within the maximum number of trials in each level the game presents items for the child (either with fewer alternatives to choose from and/or presenting the items that the child has known earlier in the game), so that 80% of the selections that the child makes will be correct within a level. Thus the game provides instant feedback to reinforce learning. If a correct selection is made, a short reinforcing sound and a visual effect are presented. By providing the correct response when an error is made, the learner never gets negative feedback; instead, he or she is guided to correct responses.

A significant motivational feature of the game design is online adaptation according to the performance of the player. As noted, progression throughout the game is computationally controlled to facilitate the presentation of appropriate learning material for each individual learner for each game level. To achieve this goal, the game designers have employed mathematical modeling (e.g., Kujala, Richardson, & Lyytinen, 2010). Thus the game is able to provide the appropriate amount of challenge for each learner to motivate further training. In addition, supportive measures for effective training are embedded in the game design by ensuring that the game levels are brief and that no unnecessary stimuli (visual or auditory) are presented. In this way, the learner is encouraged to focus on the material to be learned, and children are rewarded with, for example, virtual stickers as motivation for further training. Through the short but frequent gaming sessions, each child has opportunities for effective learning and receives intensive training. (For more details, see Lyytinen, Erskine, Kujala, Ojanen, & Richardson, 2009.)

All of these key features of the game continue to guide the development work as the game developers attempt to tackle the challenges of making the game work in different languages, for different technological platforms, and for different levels of literacy learning and different types of learners. The developmental work has been encouraged by the numerous research findings on the efficacy of the training, to which we turn next.

In Finnish, for which this game was originally developed, the efficacy of Graphogame training has been shown in several independent studies. Hintikka, Aro, and Lyytinen (2005) showed that poor readers in first grade improved their letter knowledge during Graphogame intervention significantly more than those who received regular reading support. In addition, Lyytinen, Ronimus, Alanko, Poikkeus, and Taanila

(2007) found that letter knowledge and blending sounds on the basis of letter sequences improved after Graphogame intervention for kindergarten and first-grade children. Similar findings arise from a study of preschool children with a familial history of dyslexia (Mönkkönen, Lyytinen, & Richardson, in press). In addition, the results of a longitudinal intervention study (Saine, Lerkkanen, Ahonen, Tolvanen, & Lyytinen, 2011) indicated that children with low prereading skills from first grade through third grade benefited significantly from relatively short Graphogame training (mean playing time just under 5 hours) in comparison to children who received the same reading support at school but did not play the game. The benefits included better performance on letter knowledge, decoding, accuracy, spelling, and fluency measures during the posttests and follow-ups of the 3-year longitudinal study.

Based on these encouraging research findings, Graphogame has been developed for additional languages. A comparatively straightforward starting point was to adapt the game into other languages that have relatively transparent orthographies. In a transparent orthography, the grapheme–phoneme correlations can be drilled in a straightforward manner without complications because the letter–sound correspondences are consistent regardless of context. German is considered to be relatively transparent; therefore, a German version was designed first, and a longitudinal intervention study was conducted in Switzerland with prereading kindergarten children (Brem et al., 2010). After a relatively short training period (average 3 hours, 44 minutes within 8 weeks), children's letter knowledge improved significantly. Reading skills also improved slightly. In addition to behavioral measures, brain activation was investigated. Both event-related potential (ERP) and functional magnetic resonance imaging (fMRI) results indicated that the short training period which focused mainly on grapheme–phoneme correspondences was sufficient to initialize print sensitivity of the occipito-temporal cortex.

To date, Graphogame has been adapted to several languages (Finnish, German, Estonian, Greek, Swedish, Cinyanja, Dutch, and English) and efficacy studies are underway to determine whether the game is an efficient means of facilitating the learning of basic literacy skills in those languages.

Apart from orthographic factors, special challenges arise in situations in which learning occurs in multilingual settings. In Africa, in general, the relatively recently established writing systems are transparent, consequently easier to learn, and known to affect the rate of literacy acquisition positively (Seymour, Aro, & Erskine, 2003). However, several pilot studies conducted in Zambia showed that this is not necessarily the case in multilingual settings where teaching may not be adequate. Matfwali (2005) addresses the case of learners whose native tongue is Cinyanja but are in schools in which the official language is English. Students are expected to learn initial literacy skills in their provincial language in first grade, after which the primary language of instruction is English. However, only 46% of the students in third grade could name the letters of the alphabet and only 29% could relate the given sounds to appropriate letters in Cinyanja. This result was surprising due to the transparency of the language. For instance, normally developing Finnish-speaking children learn to read accurately by the end of their first term at school, as do most children who are learners of other transparent orthographies. In order to facilitate learning in Zambia, a Cinyanja version of Graphogame was developed. After only 2 hours of Graphogame training, first-grade students significantly improved both their spelling and orthographic skills (Chilufya, 2008). This result was as expected when using phonics for training basic literacy skills in a transparent orthography. Therefore, the reason for the poor performance of the learners of Cinyanja who had received basic literacy education in Cinyanja at school is baffling. The game log data from Graphogame playing may shed some light on this issue. For instance, in a study by Ojanen (2007), the Graphogame log data showed that learners of Cinyanja often selected the letter *a* instead of the letter *e* when the sound /e/ was presented, the letter *e* for the sound /i/, and the letter *i* for the sound /a/ (see Figure 4.2 for the illustration). This type of confusion suggests that

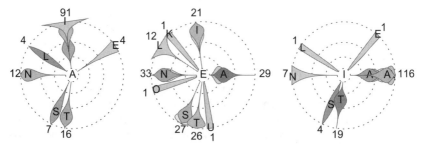

Figure 4.2. An illustration of the Daisygraph of a Zambian subject with target items A, E, and I. The outermost circle represents 100% correct performance and the other circles represent 75%, 50%, and 0% performance. The target (heard sound) item is in the center of the graph, and the letters outside of the circle represent the written distractor (incorrect alternative) items that have been presented visually to the player during the trials of connection building. In the first graph, the letters I, E, L, N, S, and T have been presented as distractors to the target item A. A perfect differentiation of the phonemic space is shown in the graph with the target E and distractor L, showing that the player has answered correctly in all 12 trials with E as a target and L as a distractor. Poor differentiation is seen with the target E and distractor A, where the player's answers are at the 50% performance circle (equivalent of guessing) with 29 trials. With the target A and distractor I, the large number of trials has been divided into 20 subsequent trials with the results of each interval plotted separately so as to indicate the progress in differentiation: in this case, the player has started the game with poor differentiation of the target A and distractor I, but reached 100% correct performance (the outermost circle in the graph) at the end of training. (From Lyytinen, H., Erskine, J., Kujala, J., Ojanen, E., & Richardson, U. [2009]. In search of a science-based application: A learning tool for reading acquisition. *Scandinavian Journal of Psychology, 50,* 668–675; reprinted by permission.)

learners have not learned corresponding phonemes for Cinyanja letters, but instead have learned English letter names (e.g., English letter name for the letter *e* is /i:/, whereas the sound for the corresponding letter in Cinyanja is /e/). It seems obvious that Zambian learners should be instructed to read their own native language by using a phonics-based approach so that they can learn to read accurately relatively quickly. However, due to the influence of the English language and/or an inappropriate method of teaching early literacy skills, even some children in the third and fourth grades do not know grapheme–phoneme correspondences, as reflected in their poor reading skills (Kaoma, 2008). As was suggested with the pilot studies carried out in Zambia, employing Graphogame can have a significant effect on learning basic literacy skills in a transparent orthography and may also contribute to the development of improved teaching methods.

Apart from the efficacy studies on Graphogame training in relatively transparent orthographies, there also exists some evidence of the benefits of such training in the context of a language with a less transparent orthography: English. The English language is a good example of a highly nontransparent orthography in which most of the letters do not have exactly the same corresponding sound in all written contexts. Therefore, as compared with a child learning to read in Finnish, a child learning to read in English will have to learn many more sound–letter correspondences in order to be able to read or spell different words. This difference is reflected in the rate at which the typically developing English-speaking child learns basic literacy skills: It takes about 2 years longer to reach the same reading accuracy level in English as it does in Finnish (Seymour, Aro, & Erskine, 2003). Thus, the lack of transparency of the orthography poses a challenge for the Graphogame type of training. Two approaches for designing the training material for the English versions of Graphogame have been adopted. One of the versions can be defined as a Graphogame phonics approach, although it quickly progresses to introduce common exception words. The other English language version introduces few grapheme–phoneme correspondences at first, which are immediately presented within common rime units. In addition, the training material is presented in such a way that the players are encouraged to use analogy in an attempt to turn attention to the larger units rather than single phonemes. The impetus for the two different approaches derives from theories that support either small or large unit sizes for efficient early learning of literacy skills. The small unit size approach is largely based on Seymour's (1997) foundation literacy theory, which suggests that the smallest units are learned first before moving on to larger units. Contrary to this, Goswami and Bryant (1990) and also later Ziegler and Goswami (2005) suggest that with nontransparent orthographies such as English, it is more effective to learn to pay attention to larger units first before moving on to smaller units and also associating both onsets and rime units of words to strings of letters utilizing analogies between the words already known. Preliminary results using either the phonics or the onset-rime version of the English Graphogame in intervention studies with children with and without recognized reading difficulties indicate greater improvement on standardized tests of reading as compared with children who did not play the game (Kyle, Richardson, Lyytinen, & Goswami, 2009). The longitudinal data collection continues in order to gain appropriate control data from a sufficient number of children (a group that receives regular literacy education at school and a group who receives computerized mathematics intervention), so it remains to be seen whether the current result holds. If the research data show evidence of the effectiveness of Graphogame training, even with a highly nontransparent orthography and with both normally developing and reading challenged children, this effectiveness could have an impact on literacy skills, both for typically developing and for early struggling readers.

So far, the research evidence on the efficacy of using Graphogame methodology for supporting reading acquisition seems promising. However, carefully controlled studies on the use of different language versions need to be conducted before any far-reaching conclusions can be drawn. If a language version is shown to be effective for basic literacy learning, the next challenge is to find ways of distributing this web-based game for all who may benefit from playing. In Finland, where the efficacy of Graphogame training has been shown in several studies, the Ministry of Education (MOE) has provided means for further development as well as maintenance of the Graphogame service (including user support, data retrieval and analysis, and game and server maintenance). In this way, all the children in Finland will be able to access the game free of charge; to date, over 60,000 children have played Graphogame in Finland. Similar arrangements are needed internationally for the game to be distributed globally. One step has already been taken: because all learners may not have access to computers, a mobile phone version of Graphogame has been designed. The preliminary results on the efficacy of the mobile phone version in Finnish indicate that preschool learners' letter knowledge improves significantly after only a few hours of playing in comparison to those of nonplaying children (Richardson et al., forthcoming). These results also indicate that training with the mobile phone version is at least as efficacious as training with the computer version. Apart from distribution, the big challenge is to develop the game further so that training will assist learners to become fluent readers. For this aim, the game content has already been further developed in Finnish, but experimental studies are needed in order to determine whether it is possible to improve fluency with this game approach.

CONCLUSION

Until recently, most of the prevailing literacy acquisition research was based on research concerning English acquisition. These days, due to cross-linguistic research findings (e.g., Seymour, Aro, & Erskine, 2003), the importance of the effect of the orthography has been acknowledged. Here, we sought to demonstrate that learning to read more transparent writing systems than English follows different lines in many respects. If each letter (grapheme) represents only one sound in any given context, children who are language-oriented may learn to read almost spontaneously. But, this is not true if children are instructed in a way that is incompatible with the facts of the language, as seems to occur surprisingly widely in Africa, where the orthographies of the vernacular languages are transparent, yet instruction is influenced by English. Also, attempts to teach children who do not speak English to read English have naturally failed. According to MOE (2006), the percentage of pupils reaching *minimum* or *satisfactory* performance levels in English was 29.2% (according to MOE, 2008, it was 34.6%) and *desirable* level was as low as 6.2%. This level is one reason many African countries have decided to start reading instruction using familial (vernacular) languages. The problem is, however, that the materials available to teachers are based on knowledge associated with instructing reading in English. Thus, as mentioned earlier, instead of sounding the alphabets using the phoneme sounds such as /i/ for the letter *i* as should be done in transparent languages, the English letter names are used (in this case, /ai/). This leads to utter confusion, which is not helped by the fact that even the sound cues in letter names in English are not necessarily appropriate to discover the letter–sound correspondences because they do not inform about the most common sound associated with each particular letter in English.

We indicated earlier that there are both biological and pedagogical factors that may compromise reading acquisition, even in the contexts of a highly transparent writing system. It could be estimated that a relatively small (<10%) proportion of children need preventive intervention, and a small (<1%) proportion of children (who are most likely dyslexic) need more than the preventive intervention available via Graphogame in Finland. On the other hand, in Africa, a substantially high proportion— possibly the majority—of children may benefit from such phonics instruction because of the lack of effective instruction. When we used Graphogame in Lusaka, Zambia, the most common challenge was that children had to relearn letter–sound connections that they had acquired inappropriately on the basis of English letter names, based on instructional practices handed down across generations. Thus, the first challenge we face in our attempts to help children in Africa is to encourage teachers themselves to learn the appropriate letter–sound correspondences for their language. We are currently exploring the efficacy of using Graphogame, which works on inexpensive mobile phones, to help teachers learn the appropriate correspondences.

ACKNOLWEDGEMENTS

The following colleagues have made a substantial contribution in the summarized studies: Timo Ahonen, Kenneth Eklund, Tomi Guttorm, Jarmo Hämäläinen, Paavo H.T. Leppänen, Paula Lyytinen, Anna-Maija Poikkeus, Anne Puolakanaho, Asko Tolvanen and Minna Torppa. The following researchers in connection to the Marie Curie Excellence project "Graphogame" (supported by European Commission's FP6, MEXT-CT-2004-104203) contributed significantly to the development, research and implementation activities associated with Graphogame: Silvia Brem, Jane Erskine, Janne Kujala, Fiona Kyle, Anne Mönkkönen, Marika Peltonen & Gonny Willems, Tuomo Hokkanen, Ville Mönkkönen, Iivo Kapanen, and Miika Pekkarinen have done the programming of our learning games, and Juha-Matti Latvala (co-ordinator) and Ritva Ketonen (clinical services) have worked for the LukiMat www-environment. The Jyväskylä Longitudinal study of Dyslexia (JLD) has belonged to the Finnish Center of Excellence Program for several consecutive periods (#40166 for 1997–1999, and #44858 for 2000–2005 and #213486 for 2006–2011) and is supported by the Academy of Finland, the Niilo Mäki Foundation and the University of Jyväskylä.

REFERENCES

Aro, M. (2006). Learning to read: The effect of orthography. In R.M. Joshi & P.G. Aaron (Eds.), *Handbook of orthography and literacy* (pp. 531–550). Mahwah, NJ: Lawrence Erlbaum Associates.

Brem, S., Bach, S., Kucian, K., Guttorm, T.K., Martin, E., Lyytinen, H., Brandeis, D., & Richardson, U. (2010). Brain sensitivity to print emerges when children learn letter-speech correspondences. *Proceedings of the National Academy of Sciences. 107*(17), 7939–7944.

Chilufya, J. (2008). *The effect of computer-assisted letter-sound correspondence training on learning to read in Zambia.* Unpublished master's thesis. Department of Psychology, University of Jyväskylä, Finland.

Goswami, U., & Bryant, P.E. (1990). *Phonological skills and learning to read.* Hillsdale, NJ: Lawrence Erlbaum Associates.

Guttorm, T.K., Leppänen, P.H.T., Hämäläinen, J., Eklund, K.M., & Lyytinen, H. (2009, November 4). Newborn event-related potentials predict poorer pre-reading skills in children with dyslexia. *Journal of Learning Disabilities, 43*(5), 391–401. doi:10.1177/0022219409345005

Hintikka, S., Aro, M., & Lyytinen, H. (2005). Computerized training of the correspondences between phonological and orthographic units. *Written Language & Literacy, 8,* 155–178.

Kaoma, S. (2008). *Does the Literate game help 3rd and 4th grade Zambian children learn how to read?* Unpublished master's thesis, Department of Psychology, University of Jyväskylä, Finland.

Kujala, J., Richardson, U., & Lyytinen, H. (2010). A Bayesian-optimal principle for learner-friendly adaptation in learning games. *Journal of Mathematical Psychology, 54*(2), 247–255.

Kyle, F., Richardson, U., Lyytinen, H., & Goswami, U. (2009). *A new computerised reading intervention game: Graphogame Rime.* Poster presented at the 16th Annual Meeting of Society for Scientific Study of Reading, Boston.

Lyytinen, H., Erskine, J., Ahonen, T., Aro, M., Eklund, K., Guttorm, T., et al. (2008). Early identification and prevention of dyslexia: Results from a prospective follow-up study of children at familial risk for dyslexia. In G. Reid, A. Fawcett, F. Manis, & L. Siegel (Eds.), *The SAGE*

Handbook of Dyslexia (pp. 121–146). London: Sage Publishers.

Lyytinen, H., Erskine, J., Kujala, J., Ojanen, E., & Richardson, U. (2009). In search of a science-based application: A learning tool for reading acquisition. *Scandinavian Journal of Psychology, 50,* 668–675.

Lyytinen, H., Ronimus, M., Alanko, A., Poikkeus, A., & Taanila, M. (2007). Early identification of dyslexia and the use of computer game–based practice to support reading acquisition. *Nordic Psychology, 59,* 109–126.

Matfwali, B. (2005). *Nature and prevalence of reading difficulties in the third grade: The case of Lusaka.* Unpublished master's dissertation. University of Zambia, Lusaka, Zambia.

Ministry of Education. (2006). *Learning achievements at the middle basic level: Zambia national assessment survey report.* Lusaka, Zambia: Author.

Ministry of Education. (2008). *Learning achievements at the middle basic level: Zambia national assessment survey report.* Lusaka: Zambia Examination Council.

Mönkkönen, A., Lyytinen, H., & Richardson, U. (forthcoming). The effectiveness of computerized Graphogame1-intervention training for Finnish pre-school-aged children.

Ojanen, E. (2007). *Sewero La-ma-u: A phonetic approach to literacy teaching in Zambia.* Master's thesis, Department of Psychology, University of Jyväskylä. Retrieved December 22, 2010, from http://thesis.jyu.fi/07/URN_NBN_fi_jyu-2007702.pdf 107 (17), 7939-7944.

Pennala, R., Eklund, K., Richardson, U., Martin, M., Hämäläinen, J., Leppänen, P.H.T., et al. (2010). Phoneme duration discrimination and its relation to

reading and spelling skills in children at familial risk for dyslexia at the three first grades in school. *Journal of Speech, Language, and Hearing Research, 53,* 710–724.

Puolakanaho, A., Ahonen, T., Aro, M., Eklund, K., Leppänen, P.H.T., Poikkeus, A.-M., et al. (2007). Very early phonological and language skills: Estimating individual risk of reading disability. *Journal of Child Psychology and Psychiatry, 48,* 923–931.

Richardson, U., Salminen, T., Latvala, J., & Lyytinen, H. (forthcoming). Mobile phone as a platform for developing reading skills.

Saine, N.L., Lerkkanen, M.-K., Ahonen, T., Tolvanen, A., & Lyytinen, H. (2011). Computer-assisted remedial reading intervention for school beginners at-risk for reading disability. *Child Development.*

Seymour, P.H.K. (1997). Foundations of orthographic development. In C. Perfetti, L. Rieben, & M. Fayol (Eds.), *Learning to spell* (pp. 319–337). Hillsdale, NJ: Lawrence Erlbaum Associates.

Seymour, P.H.K., Aro, M., & Erskine, J.M. (2003). Foundation literacy acquisition in European orthographies. *British Journal of Psychology, 94,* 143–174.

Share, D.L. (2008). On the Anglocentricities of current reading research and practice: The perils of overreliance on an "outlier" orthography. *Psychological Bulletin, 134*(4), 584–615.

Ziegler, J., & Goswami, U. (2005). Reading acquisition, developmental dyslexia, and skilled reading across languages: A psycholinguistic grain size theory. *Psychological Bulletin, 131*(1), 3–29.

CHAPTER 5

Reading Akshara

Indian Alphasyllabary

Prakash Padakannaya and Nallur B. Ramachandra

Once learned, reading appears spontaneous and effortless. But we all know that reading is not a spontaneous biological skill such as speech. Mere exposure to a speaking community is enough to facilitate the development of speech and language in a typically developing child. Children are wired to learn to speak the language to which they are exposed. However, this fundamental principle is not true for reading and writing. A child will not learn to read and write if he or she is merely surrounded by charts, books, and magazines. Reading and writing need to be taught explicitly. Reading is a product of cultural evolution that needs to be laboriously learned by each generation. Writing was invented relatively recently in the evolutionary history of mankind—about 4,000–5,000 years ago. There are no dedicated neural centers or pathways for reading in the human brain as there are for visual or auditory sensory processing. Reading is possible as a result of "neuronal recycling" (see Dehaene, 2009; Pugh & McCardle, 2009; Wolf, 2007), that is, due to the plasticity of the human brain in employing already existing neuronal architecture to learn new skills (reading, in this case). Reading involves visual language processing; print presents coded symbols that represent spoken language. While reading, one has to decode or phonologically recode these written symbols in order to map them to spoken language. To put it in a simple way, we read something that has been written or printed. However, there is a great diversity in the way different languages are written. All writing systems and orthographies have certain common features (Dehaene, 2009; Pandey, 2007; Perfetti & Dunlap, 2008): all orthographies represent spoken language, and all orthographies have a finite set of primary symbols that could generate or create all the words of the language in question. In spite of these universal properties, orthographies vary widely on some important dimensions, such as level of representation, consistency of phonology–orthography mapping, orthographic layout, and so forth. Therefore, it may be assumed that—everything else being uniform—the specific type of orthography modulates the reading process distinctively. There are orthography-free processes and orthography-specific features involved in reading. For example, text comprehension is more of an orthography-free process, but decoding is more orthography-specific.

Reading is one of the most active fields of interdisciplinary research in cognition. However, our present-day knowledge of reading is largely based on the research reported from alphabetic writing systems, and much of that is research on English, which has a uniquely irregular morphophonemic orthography. As if to address this imbalance, increasing research has been reported in the past decade from the other extreme of the continuum, that is, Chinese morphosyllabic orthography (commonly called a logographic system). Chinese morphosyllables provide an ideal contrast to alphabets in some sense; one may argue that all types of orthographic modulations of reading processes should in principle be derived from comparisons between Chinese and English reading. We, however, believe that a universal theory and its mosaic variations across orthographies can best be achieved by examining the constraints and consequences that different orthographies pose vis-à-vis reading. In light of this background, we attempt to offer a comprehensive account of reading in the Indian alphasyllabary, which is still largely not known well among researchers outside India. We discuss the nature of Indian orthography (alphasyllabary); the concept of the akshara (the alphasyllabic grapheme) in terms of its phonological structure, orthographic layout, transparency, grain size, and other aspects; and then move on to discuss some of the studies, mostly carried out by us, on reading acquisition, skilled reading, and reading disability in Indian alphasyllabary. This discussion will include some recent findings using functional magnetic resonance imaging (fMRI) and genetic analysis of dyslexia. Finally, we briefly indicate some future research possibilities with regard to akshara in a broader cross-linguistic perspective.

INDIAN ORTHOGRAPHY

Graphemes are the building blocks of orthography. They represent the units of language: morphosyllable, syllable, phoneme, and consonant. The morphosyllabic graphemes in Chinese are referred to as characters; in Japanese, these are called Kanji, and in moraic/syllabic Kana, graphemes are known as Moji. However, in English, graphemes need not always refer to a single alphabet or letter because often a grapheme may be a digraph (as /ch/ in chip) representing a phoneme. In Indian writing systems, the graphemes are called akshara. We discuss the salient features of akshara shortly; first, we briefly look into the evolution of writing in India.

The earliest record of written symbols in India dates to the Indus Valley civilization period (3500–2000 B.C.). Due to the limited collections available and the lack of knowledge about the language used, scholars are divided on the question of whether the inscriptions can be called an orthography (Coulmas, 1989; Dani, 1963; Patel, Pandey, & Rajgor, 2007; Shendge, 2010; Sproat, 2006; Taylor & Taylor, 1983). Most recently, Shendge described the Indus Valley writings as a logographic system used to keep accounts. However, the Indus system is believed to have moved into disuse with the extinction of the language used in the period. Modern Indian writing systems do not have any lineage from Indus Valley inscriptions. The second instance of development of a writing system occurred during the period of King Asoka (272–231 B.C.), which is considered the period of origin of the Indic writing system proper. During that time there were two scripts in use, both of Semitic origin: Kharosthi and Brahmi. *Semitic languages* refer to languages spoken in Western Asia, such as Akkadian, Aramaic, Hebrew, Arabic, and other languages of the Middle East.

The term *Kharosthi* is believed to have been derived either from the Aramaic word *haru:tta:* meaning *writing/engraving* or the Persian word *kha:r-usta,* meaning *ass-camel* and implying a caravan of merchants. The term *Brahmi* is derived from *Brahma,* the Hindu god of creation. Both Kharosthi and Brahmi were written from right to left, owing to their Semitic origin, but Brahmi later was written rightward. Kharosthi was in use for about 600 years, from 300 B.C. to 300 A.D. Use of Brahmi became more prevalent as it was used to spread Buddhism by King Asoka (Dani, 1963; Patel, 2010). All the Indic writing systems and those used in Myanmar, Indonesia, and Thailand are evolved from Brahmi (see Coulmas, 1989; Patel, Pandey, & Rajgor, 2007). India is home to more than a thousand languages belonging to four different families, including Indo-Aryan, Dravidian, Astro-Asiatic, and Tibeto-Burman, but all of the orthographies of modern India evolved from a common source—Brahmi—and hence share the same salient features.

The basic features of Brahmi can be summarized as follows (Coulmas, 1989):

- It has symbols for syllabic (initial) vowels: /a/, /i/, /u/, and /e/.
- It has consonant symbols that have an inherent vowel /a/ in them.
- Other vowels in CV combinations are denoted by diacritic marks.
- Consonant clusters are represented by ligatures.
- The inherent /a/ vowel can be muted by a special diacritic called a *halant.*

The written unit in Brahmi script is called the *akshara.* It means *imperishable.* Aksharas represent open syllables, including independently expressed vowels. The concept of the akshara was developed even before the adoption of a writing system by the Indians. They had good phonetic knowledge, as is evident from the spectacular arrangement, or order, of aksharas in the basic chart of letters, which is called *varnamala* (*mala* meaning *string* and *varna* meaning *type or kind of akshara*) or *akasaramala* (*string of letters*). The vowels are separated from consonants and presented first, followed by diphthongs and pure nasalized and aspirated forms of vowels. Consonants, which follow vowels, are arranged in five rows in the order of velars, prepalatals, retroflexes, dentals, and bilabials. Each row has five aksharas: voiceless (nonaspirated and aspirated), voiced (nonaspirated and aspirated), followed by a corresponding nasal consonant. These 25 consonants are taught as *vargeeya vyanjanas* (grouped consonants), which are followed by ungrouped consonants (*avargeeya vyanjanas*), which include semivowels, sibilants, and laterals, in that order. The Kannada *varnamala* is shown in Figure 5.1 (also see Karanth, 2006; Patel, 2004; Prakash & Joshi, 1995; and Sproat, 2006, for more illustrations). Thus Brahmi, though borrowed

THE KANNADA ALPHABET

ಅ	ಆ	ಇ	ಈ	ಉ	ಊ	ಋ	ಎ	ಏ	ಐ
(a)	(a^)	(i)	(i^)	(u)	(u^)	(r^)	(e)	(e^)	(ai)

ಒ	ಓ	ಔ	ಅಂ	ಅಃ
(o)	(o^)	(ou)	(am)	(a^ha)

ಕ	ಖ	ಗ	ಘ	ಙ
(ka)	(kha)	(ga)	(gha)	(n^ga)

ಚ	ಛ	ಜ	ಝ	ಞ
(cha)	(chha)	(ja)	(jha)	(nya)

ಟ	ಠ	ಡ	ಢ	ಣ
(t^a)	(tt^ha)	(d^a)	(d^ha)	(n^a)

ತ	ಥ	ದ	ಧ	ನ
(ta)	(tha)	(da)	(dha)	(na)

ಪ	ಫ	ಬ	ಭ	ಮ
(pa)	(pha)	(ba)	(bha)	(ma)

ಯ	ರ	ಲ	ವ	ಶ	ಷ	ಸ	ಹ	ಳ
(ya)	(ra)	(la)	(va)	(sha)	(ss^ha)	(sa)	(ha)	(l^a)

Figure 5.1. *Kannada varnamala* (basic letters).

originally from the Semitic system, was a scientifically recreated and nativized script of Indians. All the features of Brahmi discussed previously are common features of modern Indic writing systems, which are all alphasyllabaries.

The Indic scripts (except that of Urdu) present a hybrid of pure alphabetic systems and pure syllabic systems. Aksharas stand for open syllables, which are visually analyzable into phonemic constituents, though those component parts cannot stand alone (Bright, 1996). One could argue that it is an alphabetic system or a syllabic system or an intermediate type. Accordingly, it has been called an *alphabet*, a *syllabary*, a *semisyllabary*, a *pseudoalphabet*, a *pseudosyllabary*, and an *alphasyllabary*. However, we prefer the term *alphasyllabary*, not only because it is the term currently in vogue, but also because we believe that the term accurately describes the Indic scripts as a separate category, along with other terms such as *alphabet, syllabary,* and *logography*.

Aksharas, Indian alphasyllabographs (as given in *aksharamala*), have distinct forms for vowels that appear independently and for the consonants with inherent schwa vowel. We call these *primary forms*. Vowels, when combined with consonants, are represented with different glyphs (*matras*). Similarly, when consonants are combined with another consonant (even when a consonant forms a geminated form), they are represented with a different conjunct form. The conjunct forms are often reduced or miniature consonant forms. Thus, both vowels and consonants have two forms: primary (independent) and secondary (in CV and CC combination).

Another feature that differs from alphabets is that there are no letter names for aksharas. The name of an akshara is the same as the sound it stands for. The typical number of entries on a basic akshara chart (*varnamala* or *aksharamala*) is around 47–50 (except Tamil, which has only 32 basic forms), with about 14 vowels and 35 consonants. These basic forms— together with all the possible CV combinations—would total up to 470–480 alphasyllabographs. If one also adds all possible CC combinations, the total number of aksharas in any Indian language may exceed 1,000. However, it should be noted that—unlike Chinese characters or Japanese Kanji—these different CC combinations are never taught in the classrooms. In many schools, not all the CV combinations are explicitly taught, as one can learn these combinations by understanding the akshara principle. The principle of akshara formation follows neither the linear model (which segments word into syllables and syllables into phonemes) nor the hierarchical model (which segments word into syllables and then syllables into onset + rime [nucleus + coda]). An akshara, on the other hand, as mentioned earlier, represents an open syllable. The coda always goes to the next akshara (*anusvara*, a nasal akshara, being the lone exception). In other words, akshara can represent onset (with *halant*), onset plus nucleus, or nucleus alone, but not coda. The coda goes with the next akshara (as the onset). Thus an akshara represents CV, CVV, CCV, CCVV, CCCV, CCCVV, V, and VV (VV = long vowels or diphthongs). The consonant forms are written in line; vowel signs are attached to the consonants on the top, right, below, or even on the left side of them. Because of this nonlinearity of CV combinations as well as of CC combinations in many instances, aksharas present visuospatially complex forms. Individual scripts, however, vary in their specific ways of combining phonemic units within akshara. Aksharas in Tamil and Oriya, for example, are more round in shape; in Devanagari and Bengali, there are more vertical lines. Individual scripts also vary in terms of transparency (e.g., Devanagari is more transparent than Tamil), the extent of merging between vowel and consonant (e.g., aksharas in Kannada are more fused than in Tamil), and explicitness of phonemic units.

As a result, Indian scripts look different from one another, but it is not difficult to decipher an unknown script on the basis of a known script due to the common underlying principle. Patel (2004, 2010) presents an excellent account of a structural analysis of akshara. Sproat (2006) and Sproat and Padakannaya (2008) provide an account of the variations in script layout across Indian languages.

The level of language representation in terms of symbol–sound mapping is one dimension in which orthographies are described. This aspect has been the focus of discussion in previous paragraphs. Aksharas represent the spoken language at the syllable level, though the orthographic syllables do not necessarily correspond to phonological syllables (Sproat & Padakannaya, 2008). The other dimension that is crucial vis-à-vis reading is the transparency or *opacity of orthography*, which refers to the consistency in symbol–sound mapping rules. English orthography is highly opaque, with inconsistent mapping between graphemes and phonemes. As a contrast, Finnish is considered a transparent orthography, with almost perfect correspondence between graphemes and phonemes in either direction. The transparency of orthography in alphabetic writing systems influences the reading acquisition process in two ways (Wimmer & Goswami, 1994): a direct effect would be that a highly transparent orthography facilitates use of the grapheme-phoneme-conversion (g-p-c) strategy and an opaque one hinders it; an indirect implication would be that a phonics method of teaching reading is more suitable for a transparent orthography than for an opaque orthography. Indian alphasyllabary is highly transparent, with almost perfect mapping between letters and sounds. However, the transparency in alphasyllabary does not mean exactly the same thing as it does when discussing alphabets, as the two writing systems cannot be compared directly for orthographic effects (Perfetti & Dunlap, 2008). Some common erroneous generalizations will be mentioned later in the chapter.

Sproat and Padakannaya (2008) and Padakannaya and Mohanty (2004) provide a comprehensive account of how reading Indian languages is different from reading alphabetic scripts. They observed that research from nonalphabetic, nonlogographic languages is scarce and that even testing hypotheses in alphasyllabaries is a challenging task, as basic corpora of information are often lacking for these writing systems. As a consequence, researchers often tend to fit their data into the current Western models uncritically. For instance, even if normal Indian children seem to follow holistic-analytic-synthetic phases (similar to the logographic-alphabetic-orthographic stages envisaged in Frith's 1985 model) while learning to read and write in their native language, the underlying processes could be different from that described in Frith's model. They also observe that most of the knowledge on reading Indian languages has come from indirect studies that tried to validate the hypotheses derived from Western theories rather than probing reading processes in Indian alphasyllabary per se.

Reading Acquisition

We believe that there are universal and orthography-specific processes in reading acquisition. We have observed that children learning to read Kannada (a South Indian language) do show phonological and orthographic knowledge-based phases similar to those observed in alphabetic orthographies. Some studies (Karanth & Prakash, 1996; Nag, 2007; Padakannaya, 2002, 2003) suggest that reading acquisition in an Indian alphasyllabary proceeds from simple to complex forms. This is probably true for any kind of writing system (Dehaene, 2009). However, we failed to observe a logographic stage in our longitudinal study on early reading acquisition (Karanth & Prakash, 1996). We also found no evidence for an orthographic stage. Developmental phases of acquisition observed are linked to the levels of complexities inherent in the script. The typical course of reading acquisition seems to engage the following sequence of mastering akshara: simple basic aksharas → CV aksharas with vowel glyphs → geminated conjunct consonants → complex conjunct consonants.

Role of Phonemic Awareness

According to Western theories and studies of alphabetic languages, phonemic awareness is the most crucial factor in learning to read. Deficient phonemic awareness is often seen as the root cause of developmental dyslexia. However, studies of Indian children and adult literates and illiterates clearly demonstrate that phonemic awareness is not so crucial for reading akshara-based texts (Nag, 2007; Padakannaya, 2000; Prakash, Rekha, Nigam, & Karanth, 1993). Success in phonemic awareness tasks seem to depend on the number of alphabet-like features present in the stimuli, explicit expression of target elements in the test stimuli, and the number of operations one may need to perform on given stimuli in order to arrive at a correct answer (Sproat, 2006; Wali, Sproat, Padakannaya, & Bhuvaneshwari, 2009). Even in remedial teaching for dyslexia, training in phonemic awareness alone was not effective (Padakannaya, Chandana, & Suma, 2001). A recent study (Kritika, 2008), however, has been able to link phonemic awareness with the ability to read conjunct consonant words in Kannada. This is likely attributable to the fact that conjunct consonants in Kannada present a complex pattern that calls for decoding and blending of sounds.

Skilled Reading

There are two basic strategies that readers employ while reading: assembled phonology strategy and addressed phonology strategy. *Assembled phonology* refers to the conversion of orthography to phonology for accessing meaning. It is believed that readers rely on assembled phonology while reading unfamiliar words and nonwords. *Addressed phonology* refers to directly accessing meaning first and then phonology. Readers are believed to rely on such lexical strategies while reading high-frequency words and irregular words. As aksharas present a transparent system, studies suggest that Indians mainly employ assembled phonology while reading. This strategy is reflected in a weak frequency effect and significant word length effect in naming speed (Karanth, 2002; Karanth, Mathew, & Kurien, 2004; Padakannaya & Rao, 2002).

ARE AKSHARAS READ SYLLABICALLY OR ALPHABETICALLY?

Because aksharas exhibit the properties of both alphabetic and syllabic systems, an interesting question is whether the akshara is processed syllabically or alphabetically or both ways. If we go by the available studies, there is no definite answer in favor of either alphabetic processing or syllabic processing. Before citing some relevant studies, let us examine the akshara alphasyllabary from the viewpoint of psycholinguistic grain size theory (PGST; Ziegler & Goswami, 2005). PGST postulates three kinds of problems one has to overcome to achieve success in reading: availability, consistency, and grain size. *Availability* refers to the fact that not all the phonological units are consciously accessible prior to reading. All the available studies suggest that development of syllable awareness is spontaneous (and therefore observed among preliterates, illiterates, and literates in all languages and available before reading instructions begin); awareness at the phonemic level is linked to alphabetic literacy (Morais, Cary, Alegria, & Bertelson, 1979; Padakannaya, 2000). For a typical Indian child, phonological recoding of akshara should not pose a serious problem because aksharas represent open syllables. *Consistency* refers to consistency in mapping between orthographic units and phonology. Again, aksharas show nearly perfect consistency in mapping between orthography and phonology; hence, readers should not have any problems in converting aksharas to corresponding sounds and vice versa. *Grain size* refers to the size of linguistic units represented by orthographic units. The larger the grain size, the greater the number of symbols in the orthography and the number of grapho–phono associations one needs to master. On the one hand, readers can process akshara as an open syllable. On the other hand, the akshara allows processing at the phoneme level, too, as the phonemic components of akshara can be visually analyzable. Thus the Indian alphasyllabary provides dual sublexical routes (one at the syllabic/akshara level and another at the phonemic level). It is interesting to examine this seeming paradox.

Support for the claim that aksharas are processed syllabically comes from the following observations:

- Indians (both children and adults alike) perform poorly on phonemic awareness tasks (e.g., Karanth & Prakash, 1996; Nag, 2007; Padakannaya, 2000), both in longitudinal and cross-sectional as well as cross-language studies. If we were to assume that individuals process aksharas in terms of constituent phonemic components, they ought to have shown good performance in such tasks as phoneme deletion, phoneme oddity, phoneme reversal, and so forth.

- In a singing task of syllabification, the performance reflecting akshara segmentation (e.g., syllabifying /krshna/ as /kr/ and /shna/ in terms of two component aksharas) increased as a function of number of years of schooling in the alphasyllabary (Shruthi, 2003).

- The fact that Indian children take about four years of schooling to master the alphasyllabary also suggests that akshara-based processing is probably the canonical approach for reading the Indian alphasyllabary. Even a recent fMRI study supports this view (Das, Padakannaya, Pugh, & Singh, 2011).

- We have found syllable awareness to be a better predictor of reading in the Indian alphasyllabary than phoneme awareness on several occasions.

However, there is equally convincing evidence to support the view that the Indian alphasyllabary is processed phonemically. The major findings to support this argument are as follows:

- In many of the Indian alphasyllabaries, there are some interesting aksharas for which the spoken order of elements is different from the written order. For instance, /KiTaB/ in Hindi is written as /IkTaB/. Similar features exist in Tamil, Telugu, and Oriya. In simple naming tasks, such nonlinear words and nonwords result in a significantly longer reaction time as compared with naming linear/control stimuli (Vaid & Gupta, 2002). The argument here in favor of phonemic processing is that if aksharas are processed as syllables, the order of phonemic elements should not matter. The fact that the stimuli that had phonemes in the opposite order of speaking elicited significantly longer response times implies that the participants were processing them in terms of phonemic components.

- A recent study (Kritika, 2008) has shown situations where phonemic processing is critical for reading aksharas. The study illustrated that though phonological recoding of simple CV aksharas does not call for processing at the phonemic level, successful processing of CCV aksharas does require processing at the phonemic level.

- Occasionally observed erroneous combinations of consonant and vowel glyphs, even by adults, suggest that readers have distinct internal representations for consonant forms and secondary forms of vowels. One such example in Kannada is combining /ka:/ with diphthong /ai/ to form a single representation with long /ka:/ written in line and adding the secondary form /ai/ below /ka:/.

- Dual representation for vowels in the form of primary and secondary forms raises the interesting question of whether those two allographs have a single mental representation. Though there are no published studies on the issue, it is likely that readers indeed have separate representations for these allographs. If it can be experimentally demonstrated, that would support the phonemic representation and phonemic processing of aksharas.

Thus the Indian alphasyllabary provides a unique system that combines syllabic and alphabetic properties. It needs to be studied more extensively. Akshara processing, its neural underpinning, and the pedagogical implications need to be investigated. There have been a few recent fMRI studies on Devanagari script in this direction.

BRAIN IMAGING STUDIES

Reading, as mentioned in the beginning of this chapter, is a cognitive task that needs to be learned by recycling the existing neural structures that are intended primarily to serve other innate or more biological functions. The reading pathways that a child develops depend in part on the orthographic demands that one is exposed to. For instance, learning to read morphosyllabic Chinese characters may require recruitment of larger areas of visual cortex (possibly bilateral) related to visuospatial processing and lateroparietal areas related to semantic/phonological processing. On the contrary, learning to read a transparent syllabic language such as Japanese Kana or Indian Devanagari may require involvement of such left hemispheric regions as the inferior parietal lobule (IPL), medial temporal gyrus, and inferior temporal gyrus, linked to letter–sound conversions. Thus, although there could be core cortical centers that are universally suitable for reading skill and probably show up in reading any kind of orthography, different orthographies also require some specific neural pathways to develop successful reading.

Neuroimaging studies on reading in Indian languages are still in their infancy. One Indian script for which some imaging studies have been recently initiated is Devanagari. Das, Kumar, Bapi, Padakannaya, and Singh (2009) reported the first fMRI study on reading Hindi alphasyllabary. The task employed was reading Hindi phrases silently. The study found activation in the left insula, fusiform gyrus, and inferior frontal gyrus (IFG), as seen for reading alphabetic scripts, and in the right superior parietal lobule (R-SPL), often associated with reading syllabary. Bilateral activations were also recorded in the middle frontal gyrus, the area believed to be involved in visuospatial processing (Yoon, Cho, Chung, & Park, 2005). More recently, Kumar, Das, Bapi, Padakannaya, and Singh (2009) conducted an fMRI study on phrase reading in Hindi–English late bilinguals, using covert reading of Hindi and English phrases. The results agreed with those of Das et al. (2009). Kumar et al. also observed left putamen activation while reading English, the less fluent language of the participants. Das, Kumar, Bapi, Padakannaya, and Singh (2009) examined the specific cortical activations while reading Hindi words and phrases aloud and found activation of the IPL, superior parietal lobule, and superior/middle temporal gyri in reading the Indian alphasyllabary.

More than 65% of children in the world today are bilingual, and a great majority are also biliterate or working to become biliterate (Singh, Chakravarty, & Padakannaya, 2011). Learning to read two or more distinct orthographies is emerging as an area of major interest because of its theoretical and practical significance. There are some general principles applicable to any kind of writing system (Perfetti, 2003), suggesting a common neuroanatomical network for reading across languages, but there are also orthography-specific pathways that in turn can be seen as suggesting separate processing networks for different orthographies (Meschyan & Hernandez, 2006; Tan et al., 2003). Bolger, Perfetti, and Schneider (2005) suggest that different writing systems may engage the same gross cortical regions, but activation within those regions differs across writing systems. Pugh and McCardle (2009) explain the situation in terms of different weights within a broad universal pathway, while accounting for differences in reading diverse orthographies. A study by Das, Padakannaya, Pugh, and Singh (2011) suggests that reading Devanagari would show up predominantly in the dorsal route, although reading English would follow a more ventral pathway. The same study also suggests that one's early experience with visual input in the form of orthographic codes from two languages may facilitate the development of functional plasticity and distinct neural pathways for reading that endure through adulthood.

Thus these studies illustrate that the complex visuospatial layout of Devanagari, its alphabetic and syllabic nature, and its transparency influence the cortical regions recruited while reading. The visual complexity of aksharas seems to call for participation by larger bilateral regions than does reading other types of orthographies, especially in the parietal, occipital, and frontal regions. The transparency of the orthography seems to have resulted in overreliance on assembled phonology strategies reflected in the activation of the IPL region. Thus there is a need for more studies on akshara processing, as such studies will throw more light on human brain plasticity and the orthography–reading relationship (Singh, Chakravarty, & Padakannaya, 2011).

Developmental dyslexia, characterized by a core deficit in reading, despite normal intelligence and adequate teaching methods, is now regarded as a neurobiological disorder that often runs in families. Singh, Chakravarty, and Padakannaya (2011) present a review of the functional anatomy of reading in different orthographies and subsequent differences in the manifestation of dyslexia. According to Nehru (1997, 2001), script-specific orthographic features determine, at least in part, the clinical expression of dyslexia and dysgraphia. These observations echo the arguments put forth by Karanth (2002, 2003), Gupta and Jamal (2006), and Chengappa, Bhat, and Padakannaya (2004). The next section briefly describes some recent advances in research on the genetics of dyslexia in readers of the Indian alphasyllabary.

GENETICS OF DYSLEXIA IN ALPHASYLLABARY

The tendency of dyslexia to run in families has become clear over past decades; early descriptions and modern family studies indicate that a substantial majority of affected children have affected relatives, with the average risk among first degree relatives being about 30% (Saviour & Ramachandra, 2005). Because reading is a complex cognitive process, multiple genes of relatively small effect are expected to contribute to its variability. Molecular linkage studies have indicated promising candidate loci on chromosomes 1, 2, 3, 6, 15, and 18 (Fisher et al., 2002; Grigorenko et al., 2001; Saviour & Ramachandra, 2006). However, genetic studies of dyslexia have only been done since 2005 in India. We report here some of the early findings of our own ongoing research.

Prevalence of Dyslexia

A group of 179 dyslexic children was selected from different schools in India. The prevalence rate was estimated to be 9.87% in Karnataka, where Kannada is the major language. This rate is similar to the 8.5% reported for Malayalam, in an adjacent state (Bhakta, Hackett, & Hackett, 2002). As in most previous studies (Geschwind & Galaburda, 1985; Pennington et al., 1991; Shaywitz, Shaywitz, Fletcher, & Escobar, 1990; Wolff & Melngailis, 1994), we found that male probands outnumbered females in the ratio 3.7:1; this is similar to the 4:1 ratio usually cited for clinically ascertained samples. The gender ratio of affected relatives was 1.4:1. These observations are consistent with a number of earlier studies (see, e.g., Saviour & Ramachandra, 2005).

Accurate documentation of the family history is an essential part of genetic assessment, and the best method of recording this information is by constructing a family pedigree. In 1950, Hallgren (based on a meta-analysis of earlier studies) reported that 88% of the dyslexic children had at least one first-degree relative with the same reading problems, suggesting an autosomal dominant mode of inheritance; this finding was supported by later research (Pennington et al., 1991; Pennington & Smith, 1983). Our examination of immediate family members (576 first-degree relatives and 1,624 second-degree relatives) of 179 children with dyslexia revealed that 28% of family members were affected (Saviour, 2008; Saviour & Ramachandra, 2005). In a majority of families, at least one first-degree relative was affected. In all, data on 68% of the families pointed to a familial heritability of dyslexia; similarly, 60% of pedigrees showed affected individuals in two, three, four, and in one exceptional case, five generations. This pattern of inheritance suggests a dominant type of inheritance. In some cases, the trait followed family lines but was not present in all generations and was not gender specific; in such cases, the inheritance of the trait was considered to be autosomal recessive. About 7% of the pedigrees demonstrated this condition. The transmission of dyslexia is complex and probably polygenic, influenced by a number of genes (Ellis, 1985; Finucci, Guthrie, Childs, Abbey, & Childs, 1976; Grigorenko et al., 1997; Lewitter et al., 1980; Pennington et al., 1991). This may be the reason for the absence of a uniform pattern of transmission in family pedigrees. However, in about 33% of the families, dyslexia appeared to be nonfamilial, which could be due to extrinsic factors as suggested by Wolff and Melngailis (1994) or to variations in ascertainment. The probands in the above-mentioned study were all diagnosed already and certified by government-approved institutions. These government institutions use similar but not necessarily uniform diagnostic criteria.

Consanguinity

Zahalkova, Vrzal, and Kloboukova (1972) found that consanguinity doesn't have any influence on dyslexia, and none of the earlier studies have reported any association between consanguinity and dyslexia. This lack of association may be due to the low incidence of consanguineous marriages in the Western world. However, in India, consanguineous marriages are common (Bittles, 2002; Smitha & Ramachandra, 2006; Verma & Bijarnia, 2002), and in our study, a significant odds ratio (2.940) was obtained for case-control consanguineous families. In consanguineous families, the affected members were more severely impaired in reading and spelling abilities. We found that about 30% of the families had consanguineous marriages, which could be a factor for the high prevalence of dyslexia in these families. Different types of consanguineous marriages recorded by us include uncle–niece marriages, first-cousin marriages, and marriages between more distantly related individuals. Among the parents' consanguinity, first-cousin marriage was more prevalent (10.06%), followed by uncle–niece marriage, which was about 5.59%. About 4% of the families showed consanguinity among grandparents. A pedigree analysis of these consanguineous families revealed an autosomal dominant pattern of inheritance as the major mode of inheritance.

Biological Markers

We also conducted preliminary studies on biological markers for reading difficulties. Cholesterol is necessary for normal growth and development of the brain and nervous system (Snipes & Suter, 1997) and is the basic building block of vitamin D in the human body (Stryer, 1988). Total cholesterol should normally be in the range of 150 mg/dL to 220 mg/dL. We estimated the cholesterol level in 100 dyslexics and found that in more than 80% of children, serum cholesterol was below normal levels. It was also found that many of the children with dyslexia had brittle nails due to impairment in calcium absorption, which is in turn linked to low levels of cholesterol in the blood.

The importance of certain highly unsaturated fatty acids (HUFA) for brain development and function is well known (Crawford, 1992). HUFA deficiencies can lead to abnormalities of fatty acid and membrane phospholipids metabolism (Richardson et al., 2000). Brain imaging studies also indicate some kind of lipid abnormality of cerebral membrane lipid turnover in dyslexics (Stevens, Zentall, Abate, Kuezek, & Burgess, 1996). Fatty acid abnormalities could plausibly account for the visual magnocellular deficits that have been well documented in dyslexia. We analyzed all 179 children in our study for fatty acid deficiency (FAD) and found that clinical signs of FAD were higher in children with dyslexia than in nondyslexic controls.

It is generally agreed that delayed developmental milestones are linked to dyslexia. In our study, 41.34% of the children had delayed milestones such as crawling, walking, and babbling. Both univariate and multivariate logistic regression showed significant odds ratios in the occurrence of delayed milestones among children with dyslexia.

Genetics of Dyslexia

Genetic theory began when researchers observed that dyslexia seemed to follow family lines. In 1950, Hallgren reported that more than 80% of children with dyslexia had a family member with dyslexia. Family and twin studies indicate a significant role for genetics in the predisposition for dyslexia (DeFries & Alarcon, 1996; Stevenson, 1991; Stevenson, Graham, Fredman, & McLoughlin, 1987). Through linkage analysis, new sampling methods, and modern statistical analyses, geneticists have made substantial progress in mapping genetic factors influencing reading and language-related skills to specific chromosomal loci. Two methods of linkage analysis have been used in studies of dyslexia: logarithm of the odds, or LOD, score and studies of allele sharing between siblings, based on sib-pair analysis. Behavioral and genetic linkage studies can help us establish the true biological nature of dyslexia and enhance our knowledge of its etiology and remediation. Once specific genes are identified, the study of their gene products and areas of the brain in which they are expressed can shed light on the neurobiological foundations of reading skills and dyslexia. If genetic influences are truly specific to reading components, molecular neurogenetic studies might ultimately help us understand the biological nature of reading skills and the relationships among deficits in different reading components.

The major candidate genes for dyslexia reported include *DCDC2, ROBO1, DYX1C1,* and *KIAA0319* (Cope et al., 2005; Fisher et al., 2002; Gibson & Gruen, 2008; Grigorenko et al., 1997, 2001; Meng et al., 2005; Taipale et al., 2003). We have started single-nucleotide polymorphism (SNP) genotyping of the previously mentioned candidate genes and a whole genome scan with 1 million SNP markers in a few selected families in India. Our preliminary analysis of 20 SNPs in 3 candidate genes in 50 probands showed no association with dyslexia (Saviour, Padakannaya, Surendranath, & Ramachandra, 2009). In another study, we found many positive signals—for example, association of SNPs in new genes and copy number variations in new genes of the three families studied. Preliminary results suggest an X chromosome link. The project also looks into interlanguage phenotypic variations in Kannada and English vis-à-vis genotypic variations, bringing in a "biliteracy in distinct orthographies" dimension. This is an ongoing study that seeks to strengthen or disconfirm these findings.

SOME MISLEADING GENERALIZATIONS
IN CROSS-LINGUISTIC STUDIES

In the previous sections, we developed a case for the Indian alphasyl-labary as a distinct writing system that needs more research attention. Because of the nature of the Indian system, it is easy to confuse conceptual terms specifically developed and widely used in an alphabetic writing context and to make erroneous generalizations. Researchers need to be cautious when generalizing across different writing systems. English terms such as *decoding, letter,* and *spelling* may have different connotations with regard to reading aksharas (see Padakannaya & Mohanty, 2004).

Thus the concept of akshara and its phonological/topographical organization as an orthographic unit has important implications that should not be ignored by reading researchers and practitioners. There is considerable variation among the different scripts of India. The situation presents a natural laboratory for language- and literacy-related research. In the final part of this chapter, we list a few features of the Indian orthographic milieu that could be judiciously harvested by well-designed research plans.

INDIAN LANGUAGE/ORTHOGRAPHY AND RESEARCH
Bilingual and Trilingual Education

Children in India learn to read and write two or three languages at various points in their schooling. The situation in India is complex and varied in this regard. There are groups of children who speak one language at home but are educated in a regional language (e.g., tribal children). There is another group of children who speak one language at home but are educated in English from the beginning of schooling (e.g., urban, lower-middle-class children). There are also children who are taught to read in two or three languages simultaneously from the beginning or at different points of time during their primary education. The situation in India therefore provides a good opportunity to study several aspects of literacy: how children learn to read in two (or three) distinct languages (with different orthographies) successively (in different sequences) versus simultaneously; the effect of the native language as a medium on instruction on subsequent literacy learning in all of these language conditions; the impact of learning to read in a different orthography without prior exposure to that orthography; and the influence of culture on all of these learning conditions.

There are various reasons that such studies should be conducted in India:

- *Orthographic variations within the system of the alphasyllabary.* The Indian alphasyllabary presents scripts that vary widely in specific orthographic rules, topography, and transparency. This situation makes it possible to have comparative studies within and across orthographic systems, bringing more power to the analysis.

- **Multiple script–language associations.** India provides instances of the use of one orthography by multiple languages and cases of one language using multiple scripts. For example, several minority languages in a state use the orthography of the state. Similarly, several languages such as Konkani use different scripts in different states. Such situations provide good opportunities to delineate specific orthographic or linguistic effects in research studies. Similarly, Hindi and Urdu provide an interesting, naturally occurring situation. Hindi and Urdu are similar languages with common syntax and vocabulary, to a large extent. Nevertheless, they are written in completely different scripts. Hindi uses Devanagari, an alphasyllabary, and Urdu has a consonantal orthography, written from right to left. This relationship also provides a unique opportunity to probe the mental lexicon.

- **Literacy and language.** India is a developing country with a large illiterate population, thus providing the opportunity to study and compare literate and illiterate brain activity with regard to language processing.

- **Other features.** There are several other akshara features and variations that allow researchers to manipulate specific aspects, such as altered forms of words, aksharas that violate the general rule, linearity of aksharas' components, phonologically guided but erroneous akshara forms, and aksharas that represent single phonemes and their variations across languages, which are useful in designing effective experiments.

Many of these aspects have been exploited by researchers to some extent, but certainly not to the full extent possible. There is great potential for research in the Indian alphasyllabary, which can make significant contributions to understanding universal and orthography-specific aspects of literacy and language processes in terms of underlying cognitive and neurobiological mechanisms.

ACKNOWLEDGMENTS

We thank William Baker from The Dyslexia Foundation, Peggy McCardle from the National Institutes of Health, and Ken Pugh from Haskins Laboratories, for their support.

REFERENCES

Bhakta, P., Hackett, R.J., & Hackett, L. (2002). The prevalence and association of reading difficulties in a population of South Indian children. *Journal of Research in Reading*, 25(2), 191–202.

Bittles, A.H. (2002). The impact of consanguinity on Indian population. *Indian Journal of Human Genetics*, 8, 45–51.

Bright, W. (1996). The Devanagari script. In Peter Daniels & William Bright (Eds.), *The world's writing systems* (pp. 384–390). New York: Oxford University Press.

Bolger, D.J., Perfetti, C.A., & Schneider, W. (2005). Cross-cultural effect on the brain revisited: Universal structures plus writing system variation. *Human Brain Mapping, 25,* 92–104.

Chengappa, S., Bhat S., & Padakannaya, P. (2004). Reading and writing skills in multilingual/multiliterate aphasics: Two case studies. *Reading and Writing* 17(1–2), 121–135.

Cope, N., Harold, D., Hill, G., Moskvina, V., Stevenson, J., Holmans, P., et al. (2005). Strong evidence that KIAA0319 on chromosome 6p is a susceptibility gene for developmental dyslexia. *American Journal of Human Genetics, 76,* 581–591.

Coulmas, F. (1989). *The writing systems of the world.* Oxford: Basil Blackwell.

Crawford, M.A. (1992). *Essential fatty acids and neurodevelopmental disorder.* New York: Plenum Press.

Dani, A.H. (1963). *Indian palaeography.* Oxford: Clarendon Press.

Das, T., Kumar, U., Bapi, R.S., Padakannaya, P., & Singh, N.C. (2009). Neural representation of an alphasyllabary: The story of Devanagari. *Current Science, 97,* 1033–1038.

Das, T., Bapi, R.S., Padakannaya, P., & Singh, N.C. (in press). Cortical reading network for an alphasyllabary. *Reading and Writing.* doi: 10.1007/ s11145-010-9241-3

Das, T., Padakannaya, P., Pugh, K.R., & Singh, N.C. (2011). Functional plasticity in skilled simultaneous learners. *Neuroimage, 54,* 1476–1487.

DeFries, J.C., & Alarcon, M. (1996). Genetics of specific reading disability. *Mental Retardation and Developmental Disabilities Research Reviews, 2,* 39–47.

Dehaene, S. (2009). *Reading in the brain.* New York: Viking.

Ellis, A.W. (1985). The cognitive neurophysiology of developmental (and acquired) dyslexia: A critical survey. *Cognitive Neuropsychology, 26,* 169–205.

Finucci, J., Guthrie, J., Childs, A., Abbey, H., & Childs, B. (1976). Genetics of specific reading disability. *Annals of Human Genetics, 40,* 1–3.

Fisher, S.E., Francks, C., Marlow, A.J., MacPhie, I.L., Newbury, D.F., Cardon, L.R., et al. (2002). Independent genome-wide scans identify a chromosome 18 quantitative-trait locus influencing dyslexia. *Nature Genetics, 30,* 86–91.

Frith, U. (1985). Beyond the surface of developmental dyslexia. In K.E. Patterson, J.C. Marshall, & M. Coltheart

(Eds.). *Surface dyslexia: Neuropsychological and cognitive studies in phonological reading* (pp. 301–310). London: Erbium.

Geschwind, N., & Galaburda, A.M. (1985). Cerebral lateralization: Biological mechanisms, associations, and pathology. *Archives of Neurology, 42,* 428–459.

Gibson, C.J., & Gruen, J.R. (2008). The human lexinome: Genes of language and reading. *Journal of Communication Disorders, 41,* 409–420.

Grigorenko, E.L., Wood, F.B., Meyer, M.S., Hart, L.A., Speed, W.C., Shuster, A., et al. (1997). Susceptibility loci for distinct components of developmental dyslexia on chromosome 6 and 15. *American Journal of Human Genetics, 60,* 27–39.

Grigorenko, E.L., Wood, F.B., Meyer, M.S., Pauls, J.E.D., Hart, L.A., & Pauls, D.L. (2001). Linkage studies suggest a possible locus for developmental dyslexia on chromosome 1p. *American Journal of Medical Genetics, 105,* 120–129.

Gupta, A., & Jamal, G. (2006). An analysis of reading errors of dyslexic readers in Hindi and English. *Asia Pacific Rehabilitation Journal, 17,* 73–86.

Gupta, A., & Jamal, G. (2007). Reading strategies of bilingual normally progressing and dyslexic readers in Hindi and English. *Applied Psycholinguistics, 28,* 45–66.

Hallgren, B. (1950). Specific dyslexia: A clinical and genetic study. *Acta Psychiartrica et Neurologica Scandinavica, Supplementum, 65,* 1–287.

Karanth, P. (2002). Reading into reading research through nonalphabetic lenses: Evidence from the Indian languages. *Topics in Language Disorders, 23,* 16–27.

Karanth, P. (2003). *Cross-linguistic study of acquired reading disorders: Implications for reading models, disorders, acquisition, and teaching.* New York: Kluwer Academic Publishers.

Karanth. P. (2006). The kagunita of Kannada: Learning to read and write an Indian alphasyllabary. In R.M. Joshi & P.G. Aaron (Eds.), *Handbook of orthography and literacy* (pp. 389–404). Hillsdale, NJ: Lawrence Erlbaum Associates.

Karanth, P., Mathew, A., & Kurien, P. (2004). Orthography and reading speed: Data from native readers of Kannada. *Reading and Writing, 17,* 101–120.

Karanth, P., & Prakash, P. (1996). *Developmental investigation on onset, progress, and stages of literacy acquisition: Its implication for instructional processes.* New

Delhi: National Council of Educational Research and Training Report.

Kritika, N. (2008). *Reading conjunct consonants and phonemic awareness in Kannada.* Master's dissertation, University of Mysore, Mysore (India).

Kumar, U., Das, T., Bapi, R.S., Padakannaya, P., Joshi, R.M., & Singh, N.C. (2009). Reading different orthographies: An fMRI study of phrase reading in Hindi-English bilinguals. *Reading & Writing, 23*(2), 239–254.

Lewitter, F.I., DeFries, J.C., & Elston, R.C. (1980). Genetic model of reading disability. *Behavior Genetics, 10,* 9–30.

Meng, H., Smith, S.D., Hager, K., Held, M., Liu, J., Olson, R.K., et al. (2005). DCDC2 is associated with reading disability and modulates neuronal development in the brain. *Proceedings of the National Academy of Sciences, 102*(47), 17053–17058.

Meschyan, G., & Hernandez, A.E. (2006). Impact of language proficiency and orthographic transparency on bilingual word reading: An fMRI investigation. *Neuroimage, 29,* 1135–1140.

Morais, J., Cary, L., Alegria, J., & Bertelson, P. (1979). Does awareness of speech as a sequence of phonemes arise spontaneously? *Cognition, 7,* 323–331.

Nag, S. (2007). Early reading in Kannada: The pace of acquisition of orthographic knowledge and phonemic awareness. *Journal of Research in Reading, 30*(1), 7–22.

Nehru R. (1997). The neural basis of dyslexia. In S. Mohandas & R. Borgohain (Eds.), *Reviews in Neurology* (pp. 26–50). New Delhi: Indian Academy of Neurology.

Nehru, R. (2001, April 18–21). *Distorted grapheme representation: A new hypothesis to explain reading errors.* Fifth British Dyslexia Association International Conference, York, England.

Padakannaya, P. (2000). *Is phonemic awareness an artifact of alphabetic literacy?* ARMADILLO 11, Texas A&M University, College Station.

Padakannaya, P. (2002). *Reading and writing in nonalphabetic and nonideographic orthography: The case of Kannada.* Symposium on "Learning to read and write in nonalphabetic scripts." International Applied Psychology Conference, Singapore.

Padakannaya, P. (2003). Early reading acquisition. In P. Karanth & J. Rozario (Eds.), *Learning disabilities: A multidisci-*

plinary perspective (pp. 62–76). New Delhi: Sage.

Padakannaya, P., Chandana, M.V., & Suma, S. (2001). *Orthographic awareness, phonemic awareness, and developmental dyslexia.* Conference of Society for Scientific Study of Reading, Boulder, Colorado.

Padakannaya, P., & Mohanty, A.K. (2004). Indian orthography and teaching how to read: A psycholinguistic framework. *Psychological Studies, 49,* 262–271.

Padakannaya, P., & Rao, C. (2002). *Effect of word frequency and lexicality on reading speed.* Second International Conference on Neurology, Language, and Cognition. Institute for Communicative and Cognitive Neurosciences, Cochin, India.

Pandey, P. (2007). Phonology-orthography interface in Devanagari for Hindi. *Written Language & Literacy, 10*(2), 139–156.

Patel, P.G. (2004). *Exploring reading acquisition and dyslexia in India.* New Delhi: Sage.

Patel, P.G. (2010). *The Brahmi writing system: Cross fertilizing epigraphy, archaeology, and linguistics.* New Delhi: Black and White.

Patel, P.G., Pandey, P., & Rajgor, D. (Eds.). (2007). *The Indic scripts: Paleographic and linguistic perspectives.* New Delhi: DK Printworld.

Pennington, B.F., Gilger, J., Pauls, D., Smith, S.S., Smith, S.D., & DeFries, J.C. (1991). Evidence for a major gene transmission of developmental dyslexia. *Journal of the American Medical Association, 18,* 1527–1534.

Pennington, B.F., & Smith, S.D. (1983). Genetic influences on learning disabilities and speech and language disorders. *Child Development, 54,* 369–387.

Perfetti, C.A. (2003). The universal grammar of reading. *Scientific Studies of Reading, 8,* 3–24.

Perfetti, C.A., & Dunlap S. (2008). Learning to read: General principles and writing system variations. In K. Koda & A.M. Zehler (Eds.), *Learning to read across language: Cross-linguistic relationships in first- and second-language literacy development.* New York: Routledge.

Prakash, P., & Joshi, R.M. (1995). Orthography and reading in Kannada: A Dravidian language. In I. Taylor and D. Olson (Eds.), *Scripts and reading: Reading and learning to read alphabets, syllabaries, and characters* (pp. 95–108). London: Kluwer Academic.

Prakash, P., Rekha, D., Nigam, R., & Karanth, P. (1993). Phonological awareness, orthography, and literacy. In Robert J. Scholes (Ed.), *Literacy: Linguistic and cognitive perspectives* (pp. 55–70). Hillsdale, NJ: Lawrence Erlbaum Associates.

Pugh, K., & McCardle, P. (Eds.). (2009). *How children learn to read: Current issues and new directions in the integration of cognition, neurobiology and genetics of reading and dyslexia.* New York: Psychology Press.

Richardson, A.J., Calvin, C.M., Clisby, C., Schoenheimer, D.R., Montgomery, P., Hall, J.A., et al. (2000). Fatty acid deficiency signs predict the severity of reading and related problems in dyslexic children. *Prostagladins, Leukotrienes and Essential Fatty Acids, 63,* 69–74.

Saviour, P. (2008). *Genetic analysis of language disorder with reference to developmental dyslexia.* Doctoral thesis, University of Mysore, Mysore, India.

Saviour, P., Padakannaya, P., Nishanimutt, S., & Ramachandra, N.B. (2009). Familial patterns and biological markers of dyslexia. *International Jl, Of Human Genetics, 9*(1), 21–29.

Saviour, P., Padakannaya, P., Surendranath N., & Ramachandra, N.B. (2009). Familial patterns and biological markers of dyslexia. *International Journal of Human Genetics, 9*(1), 21–29.

Saviour, P., & Ramachandra, N.B. (2005). Modes of genetic transmission of dyslexia in south Indian families. *Indian Journal of Human Genetics, 11*(3), 135–140.

Saviour, P., & Ramachandra, N.B. (2006). Biological basis of dyslexia: A maturing perspective. *Current Science, 90,* 168–175.

Scholes, R. (1991). Phoneme deletion and literacy in native and non-native speakers of English. *Journal of Research in Reading,* 130–140.

Scholes, R. (1998). The case against phonemic awareness. *Journal of Research in Reading, 21,* 177–188.

Shaywitz, S.E., Shaywitz, B.A., Fletcher, J.M., & Escobar, M.D. (1990). Prevalence of reading disability in boys and girls. *Journal of American Medical Academy, 264,* 998–1002.

Shendge, M.L. (2010). *Unsealing the Indus script.* New Delhi: Atlantic.

Shruthi, S. (2003). *A study on syllabification in Kannada speaking children.* Unpublished dissertation, Univeristy of Mysore, Mysore, India.

Singh, N.C., Chakravarty, A., & Padakannaya, P. (2011). Dyslexia across orthographies: Insights from neuroimaging. In R.C. Tripathi, N. Srinivasan, & P.N. Tandon (Eds.), *Psychology, Cognitive, and Behavioral Science: Indian Perspective.* New York: Nova Science Publishers.

Smitha, R., & Ramachandra, N.B. (2006). Parental consanguinity increases congenital heart diseases in South India. *Annals of Human Biology, 33*(5/6), 519–528.

Snipes, G.J., & Suter, U. (1997). *Cholesterol: Its functions and metabolism in biology and medicine.* New York: Plenum Press.

Sproat, R. (2006). Brahmi-derived scripts, script layout, and phonological awareness. *Written Language and Literacy, 9*(1), 45–66.

Sproat, R., & Padakannaya, P. (2008). Script indices. In N. Srinivasan., A.K. Gupta., & J. Pandey (Eds.), *Advances in cognitive science* (Vol. 1, pp. 62–70). New Delhi: Sage.

Stevens, L.J., Zentall, S.S., Abate, M.L., Kuezek, T., & Burgess, J.R. (1996). Omega-3 fatty acids in boys with behaviour, learning, and health problems. *Physiology & Behavior, 59,* 915–920.

Stevenson, J. (1991). Which aspects of processing text mediate genetic effects? *Reading and Writing: An Interdisciplinary Journal, 3,* 249–269.

Stevenson, J., Graham, P., Fredman, G., & McLoughlin, V. (1987). A twin study of genetic influences on reading and spelling ability and disability. *Journal of Child Psychology and Psychiatry, 28,* 229–247.

Stryer, L. (1988). *Biochemistry.* New York: W.H. Freeman.

Taipale, M., Kaminen, N., Nopola-Hemmi, J., Haltia, T., Myllyluoma, B., Lyytinen, H., et al. (2003). A candidate gene for developmental dyslexia encodes a nuclear tetratricopeptide repeat domain protein dynamically regulated in brain. *Proceedings of the National Academy of Sciences, USA, 100,* 11553–11558.

Tan, L.H., Spinks, J.A., Feng, C-M., Siok, W.T., Perfetti, C.A., Xiong, J., et al. (2003). Neural systems of second language reading are shaped by native language. *Human Brain Mapping, 18,* 158–166.

Taylor, I., & Taylor, M. (1983). *The psychology of reading.* New York: Academic Press.

Vaid, J., & Gupta, A. (2002). Exploring word recognition in a semi-alphabetic script: The case of Devanagari. *Brain and Language, 81,* 679–690.

Verma, I.C., & Bijarnia, S. (2002). The burden of genetic disorders in India and a framework for community control. *Community Genetics, 5,* 192–196.

Wali, A., Sproat, R., Padakannaya, P., & Bhuvaneshwari, B. (2009). Model for phonemic awareness in readers of Indian script. *Written Language & Literacy, 12*(2), 161–169.

Wimmer, H., & Goswami, U. (1994). The influence of orthographic consistency on reading development: Word recognition in English and German children. *Cognition, 51,* 91–103.

Wolf, M. (2007). *Proust and the squid.* New York: Harper Collins.

Wolff, P.H., & Melngailis, I. (1994). Family patterns of developmental dyslexia:

Clinical findings. *American Journal of Medical Genetics, 54,* 122–131.

Yoon, H.W., Cho, K., Chung, J., & Park, H.W. (2005). Neural mechanisms of Korean word reading: A functional magnetic resonance imaging study. *Neuroscience Letters, 373,* 206–211.

Zahalkova, M., Vrzal, V., & Kloboukova, E. (1972). Genetical investigations in dyslexia. *Journal of Medical Genetics, 9,* 48–51.

Ziegler, J.C., & Goswami, U. (2005). Reading acquisition, developmental dyslexia, and skilled reading across languages: A psycholinguistic grain size theory. *Psychological Bulletin, 131,* 3–29.

Looking Across Orthographies

Ram Frost

Although the main research effort on reading and dyslexia has historically been concerned with the world's lingua franca—English—in recent decades, we have seen an immense expansion of research that examines reading from a cross-linguistic perspective (e.g., Bialystok, Luk, & Kwan, 2005; Seymour, Aro, & Erskin, 2003; Ziegler & Goswami, 2005; see Share, 2008, for a discussion). Reading words involves the processing and recovery of orthographic, phonological, semantic, and morphological information. Because this information is conveyed differently in each language, the question of how the reader's linguistic environment shapes the reading process is of primary theoretical importance. This issue can be explored, however, only by considering in parallel the characteristics of both normal and disabled reading. The chapters in this section follow this approach by focusing on typical achievers and readers with dyslexia in three contrasting languages: English, Chinese, and Finnish.

Finnish is a language that belongs to the Finno-Ugric family. On the one hand, it is highly transparent and consistent at the grapheme–phoneme level; on the other hand, it has an agglutinative morphology with an extremely rich derivational system, allowing for multiple compounding, which makes many Finnish words long. Therefore, to understand reading and reading disorders in Finnish, both of these characteristics need to be considered. In contrast to Finnish, English is an Indo-European language characterized by not only an opaque relationship between graphemes and phonemes, but also by a relatively impoverished morphology that centers on appending prefixes and suffixes to base words. Because a relatively small set of such morphemes modifies the words' meanings in a consistent way, they are highly frequent as phonological or orthographic units. Therefore, the interplay between phonological and morphological information conveyed by the print affects reading and reading disorders in English in a different way. Finally, within this context, the contrast provided by Chinese, a monomorphemic logographic writing system that is not alphabetic and does not convey phonological information reliably, is striking.

In Chapter 4, Richardson, Aro, and Lyytinen provide an illuminating analysis of the Finnish writing system, which is characterized by extreme orthographic consistency. A recent study by Ziegler et al. (2010) computed the relative level of orthographic transparency of European languages using measures of entropy for the initial letter–sound mappings in each language. Transparency in this context considers how equivocal or unequivocal the representation of phonology by the orthographic system is. Using this measure, Finnish was indeed ranked as the most transparent language among all investigated writing systems. Because the 24 letters of the Finnish orthography (23 letters plus one 2-letter grapheme) represent the 24 Finnish phonemes, Finnish has a perfect onset entropy score of 0.0 (see also Seymour et al., 2003, for a similar comparative study across alphabetic languages). The transparency of Finnish predicts minimal difficulties during reading acquisition. However, as Richardson et al. argue, in order to account for reading disabilities in Finnish, one must also consider the agglutinative morphological structure of the language. Struggling readers in Finnish often cannot use large grain-size units in order to recognize long words, which can have 18 letters or more (e.g., see Kuperman, Bertram, & Baayen, 2008). Finnish thus exemplifies the reason any theory of reading disorders needs to consider not only the phonological consistency of letters and graphemes, but also the full linguistic environment of the reader.

In Chapter 2, McBride-Chang and Liu provide an extensive discussion of the fundamental differences between Chinese and alphabetic languages. First and foremost is the lack of systematic transparency between the printed symbol and phonological information. Chinese logographs represent morphemes that are syllabic units, and phonological information cannot be assembled reliably from the print. The full correspondence between Chinese characters and morphemes, which are the base units of the spoken language, emphasizes the role of morphological awareness for successful reading at the expense of phonological skills. More important, McBride-Chang and Liu provide a detailed analysis of the extensive orthographic complexity involved in deciphering Chinese characters; the reading of Chinese logographs requires attention to strokes, to stroke patterns, and to the spatial order of the different radicals included in the character. The main insight regarding reading in Chinese comes from exploring the ways literacy is taught in Chinese society: specifically, the importance of repeated copying toward memorizing the visual structure of the character. The study of dyslexia in Chinese raises interesting questions regarding the universal role of phonological deficits in reading disabilities and the relative importance of phonological versus visual processing in different orthographic systems.

In Chapter 1, Perfetti tackles this issue by first providing a historical perspective of more than 100 years of reading research. By examining the major controversies that have characterized theories of reading since the beginning of the 20th century, Perfetti's review proceeds to point toward a potential universal science of reading by outlining a systematic pattern of convergence of accumulated findings with normal and disabled readers across orthographies. The first such finding is the universal role of phonology in reading any orthography. The second is a consensus regarding a systematic component related to phonological skills that underlies most reading disabilities. Fluent reading naturally concerns text comprehension, which extends beyond the recognition of single words. However, because the recognition of words results in meaning retrieval, which then becomes the input of comprehension, accessing word-by-word meaning is a process that is central to any reasonable theory of reading. The question at hand is whether some universal principle can account for meaning retrieval across orthographies, such as English and Chinese. Perfetti reviews a large corpus of data that examines the neural basis of Chinese reading and dyslexia. These data converge toward one important conclusion: the universal phonological principle is as relevant to reading in Chinese as it is to all alphabetic languages, although normal and disabled reading in Chinese naturally involves additional factors as well.

In Chapter 3, Lee endorses the universal phonological principle by acknowledging that all writing systems—including Chinese—represent, in one way or another, some information about the pronunciation of words. The chapter focuses on the extensive homophony of Chinese, in which, on average, 11 characters share a single pronunciation, as well as on the effects of regularity and consistency of pronunciation. Overall, Lee demonstrates, by reviewing a large corpus of behavioral and evoked response potential (ERP) studies, that Chinese readers are sensitive to the statistical mapping of orthography to phonology in their language and that phonological encoding of the character's phonetic radical is a relatively early process. Lee offers a statistical learning perspective to account for Chinese reading and reading disabilities by considering the distributional properties of phonetic radicals. Overall, the findings reported by Lee seem to suggest that Chinese readers extract from their linguistic environment the information regarding the consistency between character and sound, and use it in the reading process.

Although each of these chapters discusses a different perspective of reading and dyslexia in a variety of languages, the convergence of conclusions is striking. What decades of cross-linguistic studies have taught us is that any reading theory cannot be divorced from the language in which reading occurs. This is the essence of the ecological theory of reading (Frost, 2009). The question at hand is "What relevant aspects of language need to be considered?" All chapters in this section, one way or the other, have begun by describing the various sources of statistical regularities of the language. Not surprisingly, all of the chapters consider morphology as well because morphology modulates the correlations between form and meaning. Implicitly, their key assumption is that our cognitive system is a statistical-structure detecting device (e.g., Endress & Mehler, 2009; Evans, Saffran, & Robe-Torres, 2009; Gebhart, Newport, & Aslin, 2009). Clearly, the patterns of statistical regularities embodied in Finnish, English, and Chinese differ substantially. This difference has immediate consequences for the organization of the reading system in each language in terms of the division of labor between the mapping of orthography to phonology and semantics. The inevitable conclusion is that in order to model reading, reading acquisition, and reading disorders, the full scope of the reader's linguistic environment must be considered rather than simply focusing on the relationships between letters and sounds.

REFERENCES

Bialystok, B., Luk, G., & Kwan, E. (2005). Bilingualism, biliteracy, and learning to read: Interaction among languages and writing systems. *Scientific Studies of Reading, 9,* 43–61.

Endress, A.D., & Mehler, J. (2009). The surprising power of statistical learning: When fragment knowledge leads to false memories of unheard words. *Journal of Memory and Language, 60,* 351–367.

Evans, J.L., Saffran, J.R., & Robe-Torres, K. (2009). Statistical learning in children with Specific Language Impairment. *Journal of Speech and Hearing Research, 52,* 321–335.

Frost, R. (2009). Reading in Hebrew vs. reading in English: Is there a qualitative difference? In K. Pugh & P. McCardle (Eds.), *How children learn to read: Current issues and new directions in the integration of cognition, neurobiology and genetics of reading and dyslexia research and practice* (pp. 235–254). New York: Psychology Press.

Gebhart, A.L., Newport, E.L., & Aslin, R.N. (2009). Statistical learning of adjacent and nonadjacent dependencies among nonlinguistic sounds. *Psychonomic Bulletin & Review, 16,* 486–490.

Kuperman, V., Bertram., R., & Baayen, R.H. (2008). Morphological dynamics in compound processing. *Language and Cognitive Processes, 23,* 1089–1132.

Seymour, P.H.K., Aro, M., & Erskine, J.M. (2003). Foundation literacy acquisition in European orthographies. *British Journal of Psychology, 94,* 143–174.

Share, D.L. (2008). On the Anglocentricities of current reading research and practice: The perils of overreliance on an "outlier" orthography. *Psychological Bulletin, 134,* 584–615.

Ziegler, J.C., Bertrand, D., Tóth, D., Csépe, V., Reis, A., Faísca, L., et al. (2010). Orthographic depth and its impact on universal predictors of reading: A cross-language investigation. *Psychological Science, 21,* 551–559.

Ziegler, J., & Goswami, U.C. (2005). Reading acquisition, developmental dyslexia, and skilled reading across languages: A psycholinguistic grain size theory. *Psychological Bulletin, 13,* 3–29.

Brain Studies—What They Show Across Orthographies

跨語言的腦功能研究

PART II CONTENTS

CHAPTER 6
Reading as Neuronal Recycling
A Universal Brain Organization Underlying Reading Acquisition
Stanislas Dehaene

It took several million years for *Homo sapiens* to evolve out of a branch of the primate family. However it took only a few tens of thousands of years for this new species of primate to develop a vast array of cultural tools. Human languages, societies, cities, writing, art, science, music, and innumerable other aspects of culture emerged at a remarkably fast pace. Why did our species alone manage to get around the spatial, temporal, and intellectual barriers that confine other species to narrow ecological niches? Darwinian evolution did not have the time to adapt our primate brain to the huge variety of existing cultural inventions. The integration of new cultural tools and representations into our brains must therefore involve the reconversion of primitive brain architectures originally destined for other purposes. In the present chapter, the invention and acquisition of reading are analyzed according to this *neuronal recycling* hypothesis (Dehaene, 2005; Dehaene & Cohen, 2007).

It is often thought that our species is radically different from all others in that it possesses an infinite and largely unconstrained capacity for invention, free of architectural constraints. Noam Chomsky summarizes this hypothesis as follows: "[According to a commonly held view,] it is the richness and specificity of instinct of animals that accounts for their remarkable achievements in some domains and lack of ability in others, so the argument runs, whereas humans, lacking such articulated instinctual structure, are free to think, speak, discover and understand without such limits" (1986, pp. 272–273). But Chomsky immediately concludes by saying, "Both the logic of the problem, and what we are now coming to understand, suggest that this is not the correct way to identify the position of humans in the animal world" (1986, pp. 272–273). Human cultures share too many features for us to pretend that our biological heritage does not have a profound influence on human cultural inventions.

Today, brain imaging brings new support to this universalist conclusion that physical anthropology has never ceased to espouse. When we use functional magnetic resonance to test volunteers on reading, a strong regularity is revealed. Cultural activities such as reading and arithmetic, even though they are relatively recent inventions, call on specific brain areas that are exquisitely attuned to their function and are identical from one person to the next and from one culture to another (even if there are minor differences). Similar brain circuits are activated in readers of Japanese, Hebrew, English, and Italian, with peaks only a few millimeters apart (Bolger, Perfetti, & Schneider, 2005). This result is something of an enigma if we consider that nothing in evolution ever prepared our species to learn to read.

The neuronal recycling model solves this paradox by postulating that the human brain is not less specialized than that of other primates. Its evolutionary past has provided it with a myriad of specialized brain circuits, some of which contain a margin of plasticity that allows them to adapt to new circumstances (a capacity to learn that is itself constrained by sophisticated molecular rules). Using this genetic base, cultural evolution—via trial and error—identifies new inventions that invade the space allowed by brain plasticity.

According to the view I defend here, if the human brain did not have enough time to evolve for reading, then reading must have evolved for the human brain. A kind of evolutionary tinkering (Jacob, 1977) or *exaptation* (Gould & Vrba, 1982) took place in the space of only a few generations and turned old into new without any genome change. Cultural objects are constantly perfected so that they become increasingly easy to learn and transmit to future generations. Our cultures cannot escape from the constraints of human nature; they can only sidestep them minimally. Each cultural object must find its ecological niche in the brain in the form of a circuit whose properties are sufficiently close but whose flexibility allows it to adapt to a new use.

In a recent book, *Reading in the Brain* (Dehaene, 2009), I give a lengthy account of the impact of this approach on the relationship between brain and culture. In this chapter, I would like to return to some of the book's predictions concerning the cerebral bases of reading and the way these predictions have recently been put to the test by brain imaging. According to our hypothesis, evolution gave each brain circuit inherent properties that constrain cultural recycling. Cultural objects are thus not infinitely adaptable. From one culture to the next, they share a number of intrinsic universal properties inherited from the primate brain and originally destined for a different use. In some instances, cerebral constraints are such that circuits prove poorly adaptive to a new use. We will see how all these characteristics can explain a number of otherwise puzzling features of reading acquisition.

THE HIERARCHY OF THE WRITTEN WORD

Every time adults read, they activate a small subpart of the overall brain areas involved in visual recognition (see Figure 6.1). In all literate readers, the same subarea of the ventral visual pathway, in the left occipitotemporal sulcus, specializes for words. In all primates, however, visual recognition involves the ventral visual pathway of the cortex. The operation of this area has been thoroughly researched in the macaque monkey, where it is already responsible for object, place, and face recognition.

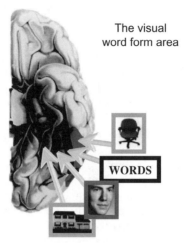

The visual
word form area

WORDS

Figure 6.1. Localization of the visual word form area, a brain region located on the ventral surface of the left hemisphere and systematically activated during written word recognition. This area is part of a patchwork of areas specialized in visual recognition, with focal points responsive to places, faces, and objects, whose layout is the same in all individuals.

In the monkey, electrophysiological investigations have revealed that most of the neurons in the ventral visual pathways of the inferior-temporal cortex respond to visual shapes. A given neuron may discharge maximally for faces, another for hands, stars, chairs, or cats. It should be noted that these complex preferences often come down to a response to one of the most basic elements in the image (Tanaka, 1966). As demonstrated in Keiji Tanaka's research, the neuron that discharges for a hand responds just as well to three rectangles fanning out from one point. By the same token, the neuron that prefers the cat activates at the sight of two superimposed striped discs. Recent recordings confirm that the most complex properties of inferior temporal neurons can be reduced to sensitivity to a hierarchical combination of simple strokes (Baker, Behrmann, & Olson, 2002; Brincat & Connor, 2004). Theoretical models of this neuronal architecture have been successfully developed; these models assume that neurons are organized in a pyramid, where those on the lower levels recognize the most elementary properties of an image (mostly oriented bars) and those further up the scale learn to combine these entries. Through successive combinations of combinations, we arrive at a neuronal architecture for object and face invariant recognition that partially reproduces the performance of the human visual system (Serre, Oliva, & Poggio, 2007;

Ullman, 2007). For example, we recognize a face because specific neurons recognize eyes, a nose, or a mouth, themselves relying on more elementary information gathered further down the scale, all the way to the lowest level of the pyramid.

My colleagues and I propose that this hierarchical visual architecture is recycled for reading, thus explaining our capacity for rapid written word recognition (Dehaene, Cohen, Sigman, & Vinckier, 2005). In cultures around the world, writing of words depends on combinations of combinations of elementary strokes. This is true for alphabetic writing, in which combinations of strokes (curves, or *T*, *L*, or *X* junctions) constitute the letters that make up bigrams (pairs of letters), morphemes (roots, prefixes, suffixes, and endings), and words. This is also the case for Chinese characters, which consist of assemblies of semantic and phonetic radicals, themselves composed of elementary strokes. Considerable data from brain imaging indicate that the architecture of our visual system imposes this kind of universal decomposition on written word recognition. In particular, we have found that the left occipitotemporal region is organized with a posterior-to-anterior gradient in which the most posterior part responds to any strokes and the more anterior sectors respond to letters, pairs of letters, and increasingly complex combinations that eventually form morphemes and small words (see Vinckier et al., 2007). This organization for reading seems to be inherited from the general features of the primate visual recognition system.

THE UNIVERSAL CONFIGURATIONS OF CHARACTERS

It is generally assumed that the shapes of letters are arbitrary and unconstrained by the brain—simply the result of historical accident. In the Egyptian turquoise mines in the Sinai, circa 1800 B.C., speakers of a Semitic language copied the shapes of certain Egyptian characters to denote the first consonant in given words. It would appear that most of the letters in the Phoenician alphabet, transmitted by the Greeks to the Romans, and even the letter names (alpha, beta, gamma, and so on) can be traced back to the scribes. When we turn the letter *A* upside-down, we can still see the head and horns of an ox whose name was roughly pronounced "alf."

Without denying the historical reality of most of our cultural heritage, including the alphabet, this historical viewpoint is not incompatible with the existence of certain cerebral constraints. In fact, there is a striking parallel between the evolution of letters and the degree of shape simplification tolerated by neurons in the inferior temporal cortex, as demonstrated by Tanaka's neurophysiological research. Progressive selection no doubt led to the simplification of signs into abstract symbols made up of only a few strokes. For neurons in the inferior temporal cortex to maintain highly selective and discriminative responses unique to each letter, it was imperative for signs to be whittled down to characteristic and distinct shapes. Although we cannot deny the role played by history, we can no doubt attribute the shape of our letters in part to a need for universal configurations that can be easily recognized by the visual cortex of all primates.

This hypothesis is supported by work carried out by Marc Changizi and Shinsuke Shimojo at the California Institute of Technology (Changizi, Zhang, Ye, & Shimojo, 2006; see also Changizi & Shimojo, 2005). They analyzed the shapes of characters in most of the world's writing systems. Their work focuses solely on the topological organization of the strokes that form characters. *T, L,* or *X* are composed of two strokes; three strokes can make up *F, K, Y, Δ,* and many other shapes. Changizi and Shimojo proposed that these shapes be considered from a purely topological standpoint, barring rotation or distortion. They then counted how many times each of them appeared on a page. This work revealed elegant regularities: In all writing systems, the profile of the frequency with which the different configurations are observed is constant (see Figure 6.2). In particular, *L* and *T* shapes are more frequent than *X; F* appears roughly as often as *X* but is much more frequent than *Y* or *Δ;* and so forth.

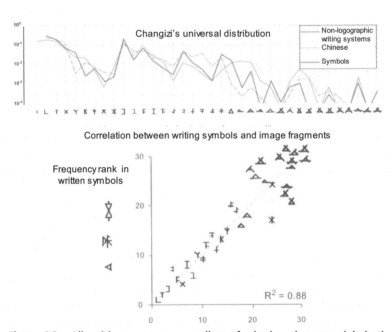

Figure 6.2. All writing systems—regardless of whether they are alphabetic, syllabic, or logographic—rely on a small set of line configurations whose frequency is universal across languages (top). The most frequent configurations are also those that recur most often in natural images (bottom) and that tend to be coded by inferior temporal neurons. (*Source:* Changizi et al., 2006).

What is the reason for this universal distribution of preferred shapes? Chance alone cannot explain it. If we throw sticks on the ground, their intersections do not obey Changizi's frequency law. However, the distribution is replicated when we count how often these shapes are found in the contours of a natural or urban environment. When objects touch each other, are superimposed, or hide one another, their contours frequently arrive at configurations such as T and L. An X is not as frequent, unless a twig crosses a branch or a line. It is even more unusual to find three lines forming a Δ. When the number of configurations is averaged over hundreds of images, their frequency neatly correlates with the universal distribution of written symbols.

Why are these shapes favored over others in writing systems throughout the world? Probably because they are particularly salient and stable indicators of the organization of the visual scene. The letter T, for example, frequently indicates the obliteration of part of one scene by another (the vertical contour of an object disappears behind the horizontal one of another object standing closer to the spectator). This topological configuration resists changes in the viewer's position: it belongs to what are known as the *nonaccidental* properties of the visual scene, or those that cannot be attributed to chance and resist the introduction of noise, distortion, or displacement of either the image or the observer. It is not surprising, then, that the primate visual system pays particular attention to these properties. An alphabet of "protoletters," capable of representing all sorts of visual scenes and objects, is already coded deep in our primate brains. Over time, scribes worldwide have arrived at writing systems composed of the same shapes because they were easily recognizable by our visual system.

THE UNIVERSAL LOCALIZATION OF WRITTEN WORD RECOGNITION

Electrophysiological studies on the macaque monkey have demonstrated that many neurons in the inferior temporal cortex respond to combinations of strokes that constitute nonaccidental properties (Kayaert, Biederman, & Vogels, 2001; Vogels, Biederman, Bar, & Lorincz, 2001). But does this finding apply to humans? Is the response to these properties concentrated in certain areas of the visual system? Could this finding explain why reading always activates a specific area of the cortex?

Szwed, Cohen, Qiao, and I recently used functional magnetic resonance imaging (MRI) to examine responses to combinations of strokes in images and words. Szwed patiently created well-controlled visual stimuli in which a fraction of an image was obliterated (see Figure 6.3). Either the places where strokes meet to form a characteristic configuration, or the more linear area where strokes ran singly in straight lines, were erased. Preceding work by Biederman (1987) had shown that the first type of image is recognized more easily than the second. This

Preserved intersections   Erased intersections

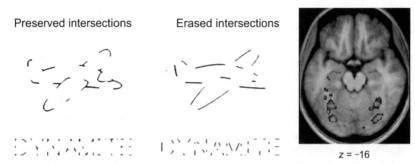

z = –16

Figure 6.3. Objects and words are more easily recognized when characteristic line junctions are preserved than when they are erased (left). Only the most ventral part of the occipitotemporal cortex responds to this property. This observation may explain why reading, which depends largely on intersections of strokes, is housed in this region (see Szwed et al., 2009, 2010).

behavioral observation confirms that line junctions play an essential role in object recognition. We first replicated this result and then extended our study to the written word, whose efficient recognition was also found to be dependent on the preservation of characteristic line configurations (Szwed, Cohen, Qiao, & Dehaene, 2009).

We then moved to neuroimaging (Szwed et al., 2011). Adult expert readers were scanned with functional MRI while they were exposed to these partially deleted written word and picture stimuli. Our results show that the preference for images that contain a characteristic arrangement of strokes originates in the lower ventral part of the visual cortex, a restricted subregion of the general area that reacts to objects. It is precisely in this area and, more specifically, in its lateral section that we find responses to written words—particularly, of course, when they contain numerous stroke junctions.

We thus arrive at a precise hypothesis concerning the origins of the visual word form area (see Figure 6.2) and how it evolved. This area did not have the time to evolve specifically for reading, but it manifests a specialization in all primates for geometric configurations of contour lines such as *L*, *T*, and *X*, whose importance in the recognition of natural objects is demonstrated by Changizi and Biederman. When children learn to read, words migrate automatically to this area because it is already, in some sense, preadapted for words. In no way does this concept of *preadaptation* as used in evolutionary theory imply that evolution foresaw the future use of this region as a reading area. Rather, the invention of writing was possible and took the form that it now has because this area was available in the prereader's brain.

Several other constraints may explain the reproducible position and universal nature of the visual word form area in all readers. First, the lateral part of the ventral visual cortex responds preferentially to the central, high-resolution details of the image, and its mesial part responds to more global and more lateral aspects of the visual scene (Hasson, Levy, Biederman, Hendler, & Malach, 2002). Because reading depends on the recognition of the finer details of characters, it is unsurprising that the lateral inferior temporal cortex should be the key player in this process. Furthermore, the fact that a number of areas in the left hemisphere are specialized for spoken language in most right-handed people explains why reading is systematically lateralized to this hemisphere (Pinel & Dehaene, 2010). The precise location of the visual word form area, deep in the left lateral occipitotemporal gyrus, makes it fall close to the lateral sectors of the temporal lobe that are coding for spoken language, thus minimizing the length of connections needed to bridge from vision to language.

In summary, once we consider the constraints that are placed on the human visual cortex, which we inherit from our primate ancestors, the paradox surrounding the apparent existence of a specific cerebral mechanism for reading, located in the same cortical area for all the world's reading systems, begins to dissolve. In fact, only a limited section of our visual cortex is equipped with the precise combination of shape specialization, resolution, and connectivity necessary for proficient reading. During the process of learning to read, cortical activation rapidly converges on this region (Maurer et al., 2006).

MIRROR SYMMETRY

Our reading systems seem to have evolved to take advantage of our visual system's predisposition for shape recognition and spatial invariance. However, evolution does not imply maximum efficiency. Steven Jay Gould, in books such as *The Panda's Thumb* (1992), has repeatedly underscored the theoretical importance of certain imperfections in evolution such as the panda's sixth finger, which is made out of the elongation of the wrist bone. Such anomalies challenge the finalist view of evolution. A blind and stupid evolutionary process, rather than intelligent design, shaped the panda's thumb.

In the present case, the observation of evolutionary imperfections—both in the reader's brain and in the shapes of written words—could throw considerable light on the origins of writing. It would confirm that we are not dealing with a brain architecture that is free of constraints and is shaped only by repeated practice, but rather with a mechanism that is already equipped with many properties inherited from evolution and must be recycled for the novel task of reading.

Generalization by mirror symmetry could turn out to be the "panda's thumb" of reading—an indication of inefficient cerebral architecture that is poorly adapted to recognizing the written word, but whose existence demonstrates that our reading mechanism was originally intended for a different purpose. Mirror-image recognition is a competence that is deeply rooted in our visual brain, probably because the natural world is largely invariant by the inversion of left and right. The visual system of the primate appears well adapted to this regularity. (For a review, see Dehaene 2009, Chapter 7.) Adults and even children only a few months old immediately recognize a given face or object as being the same when seen from left or right—even when their projections differ radically at the retinal level. Inferior temporal neurons are responsible for mirror invariance. When a monkey is trained to recognize an arbitrary shape in one orientation, neurons that specialize in this particular shape respond immediately regardless of whether the object is presented in the original orientation or in mirror image.

These observations suggest that left–right invariance is rapid, efficient, and deeply rooted in our ventral visual cortex. For young children, however, this predetermined brain organization can have a negative effect on learning to read and write. At the beginning of the learning process, many children write their names indifferently from left to right and from right to left. Furthermore, they have no trouble reading it in mirror image and see nothing strange about it. A simple task readily elicits this mirror behavior in most 6-year-olds. If you ask a child to write his or her name next to the right edge of a sheet of paper, the younger ones do not hesitate to write from right to left. It is as though mirror invariance were perfectly normal at this age. A few years later, this competence vanishes as the child learns to recognize that *p* and *q* and *b* and *d* are different letters.

My claim is that mirror reading is a spontaneous capacity of the primate brain that must be unlearned when learning to read. In a recent neuroimaging experiment, we attempted to define which brain areas are responsible for this adaptation (Dehaene et al., 2009). Using functional MRI, we found that when a written word is repeated, activation decreases in the area that encodes for that word. This phenomenon, called *repetition suppression,* indicates that two strings such as *radio* and *RADIO,* even in different cases (lower or upper) share the same neural code in the left ventral occipitotemporal cortex (Dehaene et al., 2001). Nonetheless, this effect does not occur if the word is preceded by its mirror image (oiʜɒɿ before *radio*). Thus, the visual word form area does not recognize these two shapes as one and the same word: The neural code for written words is *not* invariant by mirror symmetry. On the other hand, when the stimulus is the drawing of an object or an animal, invariance is total: Activation decreases regardless of whether the image is preceded by an identical one or by its mirror image (see Figure 6.4).

In summary, symmetrical images start in the retina as radically different shapes, yet in the end they are encoded by identical groups of neurons in the ventral occipitotemporal cortex. Written words differ radically from images. Our brain imaging results are compatible with the hypothesis that our visual system has to unlearn mirror symmetry in order to read.

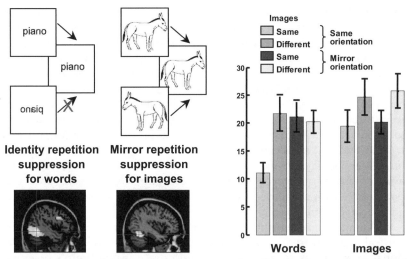

Figure 6.4. The occipitotemporal cortex recognizes that two images are identical or mirror-symmetrical versions of each other. When two images are repeated, either identically or in mirror image, an identical decrease in brain activation (repetition suppression) is observed, indicating that the neural code in this region is largely invariant across mirror symmetry (right graph). However, when a written word is repeated, again identically or in mirror image, the same area of visual cortex no longer reduces its response to the mirror-image presentation. Thus, I suggest that mirror invariance has been unlearned in adult readers, probably because it is important to discriminate mirror letters such as *b* and *d*. Mirror invariance exists in young children and can explain why they experience difficulties with mirror letters (see Dehaene et al. 2009, Chapter 7).

Our work also revealed an unexpected finding: The peak brain area with the greatest mirror invariance for images of objects and animals is located at the precise location of the visual word form area in the left hemisphere (see Figure 6.4). This finding means that we learn to read with a brain area that is highly attuned to the fact that *p* and *q* are identical objects, and is therefore in this sense the least well adapted to reading as far as symmetry is concerned. It is thus hardly surprising that young readers should have difficulty in discriminating letters or words from their mirror images: This discrimination goes against the natural competence of the visual region with which they are learning to read. Mirror errors have nothing to do with dyslexia—all young children can mirror-write, but the capacity vanishes as they learn to read. It is only if this phenomenon extends beyond the age of about 10 that there may be cause for alarm.

THE LITERATE BRAIN

Most of what we know about the cerebral organization of reading comes from experiments with adults. For this reason, we can only infer how the brain of an expert reader has to reorganize itself in order to learn to read. However, my laboratory has recently begun a project aimed at obtaining more direct results. In collaboration with colleagues from Belgium, Brazil, and Portugal,[1] we have started to map the organization of the visual and auditory areas in the brains of illiterates in order to compare them with those of literates and try to understand how education transforms brain circuits (Dehaene et al., 2010).

We recruited adult volunteers, mostly of ages older than 50, who were well integrated in society but simply did not have the opportunity to go to school when they were young. Ten of them had never learned to read and did not even know the names of most letters. Twenty-one others, called *ex-illiterates,* had taken adult reading courses and had attained varying degrees of reading competence. We compared this population with 32 adult readers, including some with matched social and socioeconomic backgrounds.

Our results reveal the vast and unsuspected impact of reading on cortical architecture. From the visual standpoint, as expected, our functional MRI images revealed a major difference in the brain's response to letter strings (see Figure 6.4). Activity in the visual word form area, in the left lateral occipitotemporal gyrus, was directly proportionate to reading scores to such an extent that it was possible to predict over 30% of the variance in reading scores by simply measuring the amount of cortical activity in this region. But this was not the only change. Visual areas higher up the visual stream and all the way up to the primary visual cortex also showed enhanced responses in the literate participants compared with the illiterates, not only in response to words but also to a broad variety of images (faces, houses, tools, checks). In the first cortical stage of vision, area V1, horizontal checkerboards prompted a stronger response than vertical ones in good readers only, suggesting that learning to read increases the precision of visual coding in a specific region of the visual field that is responsible for the extraction of high-spatial-resolution input from horizontal strings of letters.

Although these effects indicate a positive transfer from reading acquisition to the visual recognition of other categories of shapes, the effects of reading were not all positive. For the first time, our study has revealed how the visual word form area functions before reading, and therefore what the likely competitors of visual words are during the acquisition of reading. In illiterates, this area responds most strongly to faces and tools. Learning to read appears to slightly but significantly reduce the visual responses to faces, particularly in the left hemisphere; the right anterior temporal cortex showed an increased response to faces in good readers, in parallel with reading scores. These results are in total agreement with the neuronal recycling model: In order to learn to read, we must reconvert areas that preexist in our primate brain, and we are therefore in danger of losing

---

[1]Notably Lucia Braga, Paulo Ventura, Régine Kolinsky, José Morais, and my colleagues Felipe Pegado, Antoinette Jobert, and Laurent Cohen.

certain capacities that are implemented at the same position in the cortex. Faces and written words enter into competition, such that faces appear to lose cortical ground as reading scores improve. However, it should be noted that the effect is relatively modest and that we do not yet know whether it has a measurable impact on face perception performance.

Higher up in the cortex, within spoken language areas, learning to read has manifestly positive effects. In readers, as opposed to non-readers, activation becomes identical for written and spoken words. This effect is observed in the entire left frontal and temporal cortical network for spoken language. Reading thus provides a novel visual route into a universal language network. But reading also changes this language system. In most areas, responses to spoken language diminish as reading scores increase. This is particularly true in areas associated with cognitive effort, such as the anterior cingulate cortex, where activation decreases notably in expert readers, thus confirming that literacy facilitates sentence comprehension. In the opposite direction, responses to spoken sentences, spoken words, and even to spoken pseudowords *increase* in direct proportion to reading scores in a well-delimited auditory brain area called the *planum temporale,* which is located just posterior to the primary auditory cortex (see Figure 6.5). This area plays a major role in the acquisition of the phonology of the native

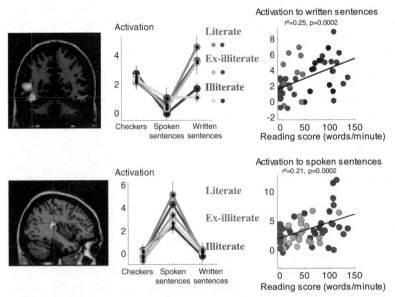

Figure 6.5. The comparison of brain activity in literates and illiterates reveals substantial differences. In this image, two effects are seen: 1) an increased response to written words in the left ventral occipitotemporal area (the visual word form area), closely correlated to reading scores; 2) an increased response to *spoken* language in the left planum temporale, probably linked to refinement in the phonological code (Dehaene et al., 2010).

language (Jacquemot, Pallier, LeBihan, Dehaene, & Dupoux, 2003). Behavioral studies have shown that learning an alphabetic writing system has a distinct effect on phonological competence by providing conscious access to the most basic unit of spoken language, the phoneme (Morais, Cary, Alegria, & Bertelson, 1979). Such phonological awareness is a major positive consequence of literacy on the spoken language system. It appears likely that the left temporal area that we observed, which activates twice as much for spoken language in literates over illiterates, is involved in this key change in language coding. Given the location of this region—early on in the auditory pathway—it might be suggested that literates and illiterates do not even listen to spoken language in the same way.

A final major change in the brain further increases the reader's competence for spoken language: the capacity to activate, in a top-down manner, the areas of the visual cortex that handle orthography in response to spoken words. In an auditory lexical decision task, our imaging study found evidence of activation in the visual word form area in the left occipitotemporal cortex only in literates, not in illiterates. In other words, reading gives us the capacity to enlist an additional visual area to encode spoken language. Here again, earlier behavioral studies demonstrated the considerable influence of orthography on speech processing—for example, English speakers erroneously think that there are more sounds in the word *pitch* than in *rich* and that if we remove the *n* from the spoken word *bind*, we obtain *bid* (the right answer being *bide*) (Ehri & Wilce, 1980; Stuart, 1990; Ziegler & Ferrand, 1998). Learning to read increases our competence by adding an orthographic representation to our existing representations of the spoken word. This increase in the mental space dedicated to language encoding perhaps underlies another major difference between literates and illiterates—learning to read approximately doubles the capacity for short-term verbal memory.

CONCLUSION

Almost everything we think we know about the human brain is based on data from experiments carried out on educated, reading adults. It now appears that these experiments are partially biased because the brains of educated, reading adults have been profoundly transformed by the early and intense schooling that characterizes our society. As we have seen in this brief chapter, learning to read profoundly transforms our brain to the point of specializing a sector of the left ventral visual pathway in order to efficiently handle written symbols, thus turning this region into an entry point in the left-hemispheric language system. At the same time, this recycling process partially competes with areas of our primate brain previously dedicated to face recognition or mirror symmetry.

In the future, it will be important to directly visualize these developmental processes through neuroimaging experiments in young children before and after reading acquisition. Although most current research focuses on the phonological origins of dyslexia, the present results demonstrate that reading acquisition also entails considerable changes to the visual system, and suggest that in a subcategory of dyslexic children, impairments in the speed or efficiency of this visual recycling process might be at the origin of the learning impairment.

REFERENCES

Baker, C., Behrmann, M., & Olson, C. (2002). Impact of learning on representation of parts and wholes in monkey inferotemporal cortex. *Nature Neuroscience, 5*(11), 1210–1216.

Biederman, I. (1987). Recognition-by-components: A theory of human image understanding. *Psychological Review, 94,* 115–147.

Bolger, D.J., Perfetti, C.A., & Schneider, W. (2005). Cross-cultural effect on the brain revisited: Universal structures plus writing system variation. *Human Brain Mapping, 25*(1), 92–104.

Brincat, S.L., & Connor, C.E. (2004). Underlying principles of visual shape selectivity in posterior inferotemporal cortex. *Nature Neuroscience, 7*(8), 880–886.

Changizi, M.A., & Shimojo, S. (2005). Character complexity and redundancy in writing systems over human history. *Proceedings of the Royal Society–Biological Sciences, 272*(1560), 267–275.

Changizi, M.A., Zhang, Q., Ye, H., & Shimojo, S. (2006). The structures of letters and symbols throughout human history are selected to match those found in objects in natural scenes. *American Naturalist, 167*(5), E117–E139.

Chomsky, N. (1986). *Knowledge of language: Its nature, origins, and use.* Westport, CT: Praeger Paperback.

Dehaene, S. (2005). Evolution of human cortical circuits for reading and arithmetic: The "neuronal recycling" hypothesis. In S. Dehaene, J.R. Duhamel, M. Hauser, & G. Rizzolatti (Eds.), *From monkey brain to human brain* (pp. 133–157). Cambridge, MA: The MIT Press.

Dehaene, S. (2009). *Reading in the brain.* New York: Penguin Viking.

Dehaene, S., & Cohen, L. (2007). Cultural recycling of cortical maps. *Neuron, 56*(2), 384–398.

Dehaene, S., Cohen, L., Sigman, M., & Vinckier, F. (2005). The neural code for written words: A proposal. *Trends in Cognitive Science, 9*(7), 335–341.

Dehaene, S., Naccache, L., Cohen, L., Bihan, D.L., Mangin, J.F., Poline, J.B., et al. (2001). Cerebral mechanisms of word masking and unconscious repetition priming. *Nature Neuroscience, 4*(7), 752–758.

Dehaene, S., Nakamura, K., Jobert, A., Kuroki, C., Ogawa, S., & Cohen, L. (2009). Why do children make mirror errors in reading? Neural correlates of mirror invariance in the visual word form area. *NeuroImage, 49*(2), 1837–1848.

Dehaene, S., Pegado, F., Braga, L., Ventura, P., Filho, G., Jobert, A., et al. (2010). How learning to read changes the cortical networks for vision and language. *Science, 330,* 1359–1364.

Ehri, L.C., & Wilce, L.S. (1980). The influence of orthography on readers' conceptualisation of the phonemic structure of words. *Applied Psycholinguistics, 1,* 371–385.

Gould, S.J. (1992). *The panda's thumb: More reflections in natural history.* New York: W.W. Norton.

Gould, S.J., & Vrba, E.S. (1982). Exaptation: A missing term in the science of form. *Paleobiology, 8*(1), 4–15.

Hasson, U., Levy, I., Behrmann, M., Hendler, T., & Malach, R. (2002). Eccentricity bias as an organizing principle for human high-order object areas. *Neuron, 34*(3), 479–490.

Jacob, F. (1977). Evolution and tinkering. *Science, 196*(4295), 1161–1166.

Jacquemot, C., Pallier, C., LeBihan, D., Dehaene, S., & Dupoux, E. (2003). Phonological grammar shapes the auditory cortex: A functional magnetic resonance imaging study. *Journal of Neuroscience, 23*(29), 9541–9546.

Kayaert, G., Biederman, I., & Vogels, R. (2003). Shape tuning in macaque inferior temporal cortex. *Journal of Neuroscience, 23*(7), 3016–3027.

Maurer, U., Brem, S., Kranz, F., Bucher, K., Benz, R., Halder, P., et al. (2006). Coarse neural tuning for print peaks when children learn to read. *NeuroImage,* *33*(2), 749–758.

Morais, J., Cary, L., Alegria, J., & Bertelson, P. (1979). Does awareness of speech as a sequence of phones arise spontaneously? *Cognition, 7,* 323–331.

Pinel, P., & Dehaene, S. (2010). Beyond hemispheric dominance: Brain regions underlying the joint lateralization of language and arithmetic to the left hemisphere. *Journal of Cognitive Neuroscience, 22*(1), 48–66.

Serre, T., Oliva, A., & Poggio, T. (2007). A feedforward architecture accounts for rapid categorization. *Proceedings of the National Academy of Sciences, USA, 104*(15), 6424–6429.

Stuart, M. (1990). Processing strategies in a phoneme deletion task. *Quarterly Journal of Experimental Psychology, 42*(2), 305–327.

Szwed, M., Cohen, L., Qiao, E., & Dehaene, S. (2009). The role of invariant line junctions in object and visual word recognition. *Vision Research, 49*(7), 718–725.

Tanaka, K. (1996). Inferotemporal cortex and object vision. *Annual Review of Neuroscience, 19,* 109–139.

Ullman, S. (2007). Object recognition and segmentation by a fragment-based hierarchy. *Trends in Cognitive Science, 11*(2), 58–64.

Vinckier, F., Dehaene, S., Jobert, A., Dubus, J.P., Sigman, M., & Cohen, L. (2007). Hierarchical coding of letter strings in the ventral stream: Dissecting the inner organization of the visual word-form system. *Neuron, 55*(1), 143–156.

Vogels, R., Biederman, I., Bar, M., & Lorincz, A. (2001). Inferior temporal neurons show greater sensitivity to nonaccidental than to metric shape differences. *Journal of Cognitive Neuroscience, 13*(4), 444–453.

Ziegler, J.C., & Ferrand, L. (1998). Orthography shapes the perception of speech: The consistency effect in auditory word recognition. *Psychonomic Bulletin and Review, 5,* 683–689.

CHAPTER 7

Functional Magnetic Resonance Imaging Studies on Japanese Orthographies
Studies in Reading Development and Reading Difficulties

Ayumi Seki

Functional neuroimaging studies have been used to reveal the neural correlates involved in processing written and spoken language. Recently, large-scale cross-sectional and longitudinal studies have explored the trajectory of brain activation patterns during reading acquisition in both typically and atypically developing readers (e.g., Pugh et al., 2001; Shaywitz et al., 2002). Most of these studies, however, have been conducted in alphabetic orthographies such as English, French, or Italian. This chapter presents a longitudinal functional magnetic resonance imaging (fMRI) study in Japanese, a language with both a phonographic and a logographic writing system, investigating reading acquisition in the first years of school for typical and disabled readers.

In the Japanese writing system, three scripts are used: two phonographic systems that basically represent the phonological basic units of the language (*hiragana* and *katakana*, which together form *kana*) and a logographic writing system (*kanji*) that was imported from China. These systems make Japanese an interesting language for investigating certain types of reading difficulties and examining their neural correlates in brain imaging studies.

THE CHARACTERISTICS OF THE JAPANESE WRITING SYSTEM

An important factor to consider for understanding reading in Japanese is that texts for skilled readers use all three scripts in parallel (Figure 7.1). There are 105 kana graphemes (for each hiragana and katakana), which represent the 105 phonological units of Japanese (mora, described shortly), and there are 2,136 official kanji logographs that are used in everyday life. Kanji is used for most nouns and for the roots of verbs and adjectives. Hiragana is mainly used for suffixes of kanji words and other functional morphemes, and katakana is mainly used for loan words. Hence, Japanese texts cannot be written with only kanji script because—in contrast to Chinese or Vietnamese—Japanese is not a monomorphemic language; it requires phonographic letters, or kana, to denote functional morphemes. In principle, Japanese texts can be written entirely in kana script. However, because the syllabic structure of Japanese is simple (basically CV or V) and most words are short

Figure 7.1.   An example of Japanese script.

(1 to 3 syllables), Japanese has a large number of homophones, and writing entirely in the kana script would result in semantic ambiguity. Kanji characters are used to improve specificity.

In learning to read, Japanese children first learn kana, followed by kanji in the second semester of the first grade (at approximately 7 years of age); at this stage, kana is used to teach children the pronunciation of kanji characters. Therefore, reading kana is a crucial skill for younger school children.

Kana (Hiragana and Katakana)

Although kana is often referred to as *syllabic,* the unit corresponding to a kana grapheme is in fact a phonological unit called a *mora.* Elucidating the exact nature of moras is crucial for understanding some reading difficulties in reading kana.

Mora is a *temporal* unit of oral language: an indicator of how speakers control the length of adjacent word segments and eventually count the length of spoken words. Moras explain various phonological phenomena in Japanese, such as stress positions, vowel epenthesis to foreign words, or speech errors (Kubozono, 2006). Because most Japanese syllables are open syllables (CV or V), spoken Japanese creates monotonous rhythmical sequences (CV-CV-V-CV, and so on); therefore, Japanese speakers produce or assess the length of words with this sense of rhythm. The open syllable (CV or V) is the basic structure of a mora, and, considering these basic moras, the actual length of each mora is more or less the same.

For about two thirds of the graphemes of kana, one kana letter consistently represents one basic mora (CV or V). Because of this transparency between letters and sounds, most children rapidly acquire basic reading proficiency in kana. However, for the remaining one third, there are ambiguities in letter-to-sound mapping. These can come from three sources: 1) a possible discordance between mora and syllabic structure, 2) equivocal mappings between moras and kana letters, and 3) exceptional graphemes requiring subsyllabic analysis for contracted sounds.

The first form of ambiguity, the discordance between moras and syllabic structure, occurs in the few nonopen syllables in Japanese. A good example is a geminate consonant (/Q/),[1] which is counted as an independent mora (e.g., /kitte/ has three moras, as shown by /ki-Q-te/). Phonetically, there is no sound between /ki/ and /te/, but Japanese speakers consider it to have an extra mora (three altogether) because it is "longer" than the word /kite/ (/ki-te/) in which the /t/ is not geminated. Similarly, long vowels such as the /o:/ in /to:fu/ are considered to be composed of two moras (i.e., /to:fu/ has three moras: /to-o-fu/). Another example is CVC syllables with moraic nasal /N/ as the second consonant (e.g., /hoN/). Japanese speakers segment this word as /ho-N/, and treat /N/ as a mora. However, in general speech, the physical duration of /N/ is shorter than the preceding mora (CV, /ho/). From the orthographic perspective, each mora—even the silent period in a geminated consonant word or moraic nasal /N/—is represented by a single grapheme. In that respect, moras can be considered as phono-orthographic units. Because moras are defined as temporal phono-orthographic units, they are abstract entities. Children acquire the sense of moras around the time that they start reading. The segmentation unit for these exceptional (nonopen) syllables shifts from syllable–mora mixture to predominantly mora-based segmentation from ages 4 to 6 along with the improvement of letter-reading skill (Inagaki, Hatano, & Otake, 2000).

The second source of ambiguity concerns more than one possible mapping between moras and kana letters. This ambiguity occurs for a small number of kana letters; some of this ambiguity is modulated by grammatical constraints. For the letter-to-sound mapping, among the 105 graphemes of kana, only two letters can be read in two ways, and the exceptional pronunciations are adopted only when they are used as postpositional particles. For the sound-to-letter mapping, three moras can be written by two different letters (one is a postpositional particle). Among five long vowels (a:, i:, u:, e:, o:), two (o:, e:) can be written in two ways.

The last source of ambiguity stems from the decoding of contracted (palatalized) sounds (CⁱV). There are 33 kana graphemes of this type, written in the combination of a regular size letter and a small letter (see Figure 7.1). The small letter is chosen from three possible kanas (/ya/, /yu/, /yo/), determined by its vowel. Therefore, contracted (palatalized) sounds require subsyllabic segmentation (CⁱV into C + ⁱV).

Whereas reading kana graphemes that represent regular CV moras proceeds without much difficulty, the acquisition of the exceptional kana graphemes is often delayed (Amano, 1986). The decoding accuracy

---

[1]"Q" is a tag that denotes nonlexical lengthening of consonants, used in Corpus of Spontaneous Japanese (CSJ), which is Japanese supported by the Ministry of Education, Culture, Sports, Science and Technology. See http://www.kokken.go.jp/katsudo/seika/corpus/public/.

of kana reaches 89% for regular CV moras by the beginning of the first grade; those of the exceptional moras is much lower: 64% for geminate consonants, 52% for long vowels, and 40% for contracted (palatalized) sounds (C^{j}V; Hotta, 1986). Moreover, Japanese dyslexic children make more errors in reading and writing exceptional kana graphemes (Kassai, Seki, & Koeda, 2006). The graphemes for contracted (palatalized) sounds (C^{j}V) are most difficult for both nonimpaired and dyslexic children and are acquired last.

Kanji

In contrast to kana, kanji is a logographic orthography, as is Chinese. As logographs, both kanji and Chinese characters represent a word or a concept as a whole character. However, most of the characters (both kanji and Chinese characters) also contain phonetic radicals.

In character formation, both Chinese and kanji characters are divided into two main groups: a relatively small number of noncompound characters, and a larger number of compound characters consisting of two or more radicals. Compound characters are either *ideogrammic* compounds (in which two or more characters are combined to suggest a third meaning) or *phonosemantic* compounds (created by the combination of a semantic radical and a phonetic radical). More than 60% of kanji characters used in Japan are phonosemantic compounds, compared with 80%–90% in Chinese. Noncompound characters require holistic mapping from characters to pronunciations, but compound characters allow readers to use analytic mapping.

In addition, kanji characters may be more ambiguous than Chinese characters because of some inherent ambiguity in character-to-sound mapping. Kanji characters often have multiple possible pronunciations. Basically, each kanji character has two types of pronunciations. The *on*-reading is used to represent the original Chinese pronunciation, and the *kun*-reading is used to represent Japanese pronunciations to express native Japanese words and concepts. Some kanji characters have more than one *on*-reading, and some also have more than one *kun*-reading. Therefore, even to read compound characters, the phonemic radicals predict only one *on*-reading among all possible pronunciations.

This phonological ambiguity of kanji reading has been discussed in terms of the competition between holistic (lexical) versus analytic (sublexical) processing similar to alphabetic languages. Previous research has investigated two different levels of consistency, depending on the different definitions of the lexical unit. One is character level consistency, which is consistency between pronunciation of a phonetic radical and a whole character in compound characters (subword validity and radical neighborhood consistency; Masuda & Saito, 2002; Saito, Masuda, & Kawakami, 1999). The other is word level consistency, which is consistency and typicality of pronunciation among two-character

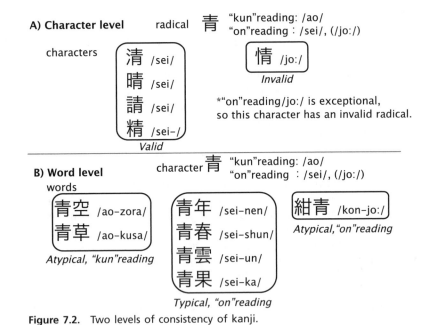

Figure 7.2. Two levels of consistency of kanji.

words (Fushimi, Ijuin, Patterson, & Tatsumi, 1999; Wydell, 1998 [see Figure 7.2]). Generally, for two-character words, the *on*-reading is more typical. The results are equivocal, but in most studies, an interaction of frequency with consistency was observed.

Effects of inconsistency in character-to-sound mapping on performance of children who are learning to read kanji are not simple to establish because of significant differences in the number of characters known to children and because the familiarity of each character needs to be considered as well. The vocabulary size also affects learning kanji. Children are taught kanji in the context of their reading materials, and in most cases—but not always—they begin with more familiar and less complex characters and then move on to less familiar and more complex characters. The rate of noncompound characters is greater in the lower grades. Only semantic radicals are formally taught to children, and different pronunciations of one character are often introduced along with its meaning in reading materials. For noncompound characters with multiple pronunciations, the knowledge of the word is the only means of retrieving the correct pronunciation. For example, 紺青 (/kon-jo/, not /kon-sei/) as seen in Figure 7.2 is an exclusively low-frequency word (an uncommon expression of "deep blue"), and 青 is a noncompound word. Although the character is taught in the first grade, there is no clue regarding how to read the character correctly unless the child knows the word /kon-jo/.

DYSLEXIA IN JAPANESE

The Identification and Prevalence of Dyslexia in Japanese

Since Makita (1968) reported that the prevalence of dyslexia in Japan was 0.9%, it has been believed by researchers that dyslexia in the Japanese language was relatively rare. Recently, the nationwide surveillance by the Ministry of Education, Culture, Sports, Science and Technology (MEXT) reported—based on teachers' assessments—that 2.5% of primary and middle school students had reading difficulties (RD), which included difficulties in both kana and kanji (MEXT, 2004, cited by Seki, Kassai, Uchiyama, & Koeda, 2008).

Given the transparency of kana, accuracy of kana reading is high even for first graders, and it is difficult to identify children who have reading problems in kana (kana RD) simply by monitoring reading errors. Indeed, cross-linguistic studies in European alphabetic languages suggest that reading difficulty in transparent languages is reflected by relatively slow reading speed rather than by reading errors (Ziegler & Goswami, 2005). Similarly, children with kana RD decode individual kana graphemes more slowly, with many inappropriate pauses in words, relative to typical achievers (Kassai et al., 2006; Yamada & Banks, 1994). Although children with kana RD make significantly more errors in exceptional kana graphemes, the most significant measure that differentiated children who were diagnosed with kana RD and nonimpaired children was reading speed (Kassai et al., 2006). Our longitudinal study (from the first to third grades), in which reading speed was used as the screening measure, showed a 1.4% occurrence rate of kana RD (Uchiyama, Seki, & Koeda, 2010).

There is a general consensus that reading difficulties are more prevalent in kanji than in kana. For example, Uno, Wydell, Haruhara, Kaneko, and Shibuya (2009) reported that 6.9% of children scored below -1.5 standard deviation (SD) in accuracy in kanji, which was much higher than those in kana (0.2% in hiragana and 1.4% in katakana). Moreover, they found that reading and writing difficulties in kanji did not always overlap, suggesting that different factors are involved in reading and writing kanji (Uno et al., 2009; Yamada & Banks, 1994).

The Deficits Underlying Dyslexia in Japanese

In English, phonological awareness deficit is the most common predictor of dyslexia, although some recent studies on European languages suggest that phonological awareness may be less important and more time-limited in transparent orthographies (Share 2008; Ziegler et al., 2010). Because the phonological unit corresponding to kana characters is the mora, the awareness of mora is the relevant skill for Japanese children. It was reported that awareness of mora correlated with reading skills of children who begin learning kana (Amano, 1986; Kobayashi, Haynes, Macruso, Hook, & Kato, 2005). However, studies have not successfully proved that preliterate phonological awareness predicts later reading skill in school-age children.

Mora awareness rapidly develops when children begin learning kana (Hara, 2001) because the transparent letter-to-sound relationship gives consistent feedback to learners and shapes their phonological representations (Goswami, 2000; Ziegler & Goswami, 2005). Therefore, phonological awareness of exceptional moras, such as awareness of geminate consonants and contracted sounds, is important to assess in school-age children. Seki et al. (2008) assessed phonological awareness in children with kana RD and nonimpaired children (mean age 9 years) in four types of tasks: mora counting (segmenting real words into moras), mora deletion (deleting moras from real words), word reversal (repeating moras in real words backward), and kana letter rhyming (comparing vowels in presented kana letters). In the first three tasks, half of the target words included exceptional moras. The letter rhyming task was adopted because of comparability of English and because it requires subsyllabic segmentation, which is latent in contracted sounds. In all four tasks, significantly lower performance was demonstrated by the RD group as compared with a control group matched for age, gender, and nonverbal IQ. Even in the simple mora counting task, children with RD made more errors when they were asked to count exceptional moras, such as geminate consonants or long vowels. This outcome suggests that even for transparent scripts such as kana, deficits of phonological awareness or lack of well-specified phonological representations are significant disadvantages in acquiring reading skills.

On the other hand, studies in Hong Kong showed that Chinese-speaking children with RD had deficits in orthographic processing skills (detecting radicals visually) in addition to deficits in phonological skills (Ho, Chan, Lee, Tsang, & Luan 2004). Although the factors causing kanji RD have not been specified, recent studies have suggested that a wide array of cognitive skills may be correlated with reading and writing performance in kanji. Koyama, Hansen, and Stein (2008) assessed multiple cognitive skills as well as auditory/visual sensory processing skills in nonimpaired children. This study revealed that visual memory (especially long-term memory), orthographic awareness (radical position judgment), and phonological short-term memory made significant contributions to both reading and writing kanji. Uno et al. (2009) reported that knowledge of abstract words (vocabulary) contributed to the skill of reading kanji and that both vocabulary and visual memory showed a weaker contribution to writing kanji.

Manifestation of Japanese Dyslexia Across Orthographies

Most children with kana RD also have some difficulty in learning kanji. Because of the greater difficulty in learning kanji in comparison with kana, children who show difficulty only with kanji are not rare. However, we rarely find cases in which children show difficulty reading kana but not kanji. As far as we know, most children with kana RD show severe difficulty in learning English. Cross-linguistic studies among European languages suggest that orthographic consistency is the key factor that determines the manifestation of RD across languages (Seymour, Aro, & Erskine, 2003; Ziegler & Goswami, 2005). However, comparisons of reading difficulties in alphabetic versus nonalphabetic languages, or phonographic versus logographic languages, are few and inconclusive.

Wydell and Butterworth (1999) reported a case study of an English–Japanese bilingual child who showed reading disability in English but not in Japanese (see also Wydell & Kondo, 2003). This case led Wydell to suggest that the prevalence of phonological dyslexia is related to the grain size and transparency of sound-to-letter mapping. By her account, an orthography with highly transparent letter-to-sound mappings (e.g., kana) will not produce a high prevalence of phonological dyslexia, regardless of the grain size of mapping (e.g., phoneme, syllable). Wydell further argued that if the grain size of mapping is large enough to represent a whole morpheme (e.g., kanji) and involves the holistic mapping of a grapheme to its meaning, the incidence of phonological dyslexia would still be low.

Although this suggestion accounts for the case study reported by Wydell, it cannot account for the prevalence of RD in kanji. Learning kanji by simply using holistic mapping would require the mastering of a large number of associations (more than 4,000 for kanji). To overcome or bypass this inherent difficulty, an alternative strategy would be to map subword phonological units to orthographic units; that is, to map the phonological radical of the logograph into sound. Ho et al. (2004) and Koyama et al. (2008) indeed demonstrated that visual processing skills are necessary for such mapping, on top of the reliance on visual memory and vocabulary, which support holistic mapping between logographs and meaning (Koyama et al., 2008; Uno et al., 2009). Because the conjunction of all these skills is required for learning kanji, it is clear why kanji reading is more difficult. Conforming with the case study reported by Wydell, students who show dissociation between English and Japanese reading skills are occasionally found; they exhibit severe reading difficulty with proficient oral communication skills in English and a subtle reading difficulty in Japanese. Children with some phonological deficits, but with strength in other cognitive skills, may display the dissociation of proficiency between English and kanji, showing poor reading in English and adequate kanji reading.

FUNCTIONAL IMAGING STUDIES IN JAPANESE AND OTHER LANGUAGES

Many early functional imaging studies (using positron emission tomography and fMRI) of reading largely compared brain activation between nonimpaired and reading-disabled readers on tasks that involved phonological processing (e.g., pseudoword reading, rhyming tasks). Studies revealed hypoactivation in the left temporoparietal areas—the posterior superior temporal gyrus and the inferior parietal cortex (see Pugh et al., 2001, for a review). A large-scale cross-sectional study also revealed an important role of the left ventral occipitotemporal area (including the fusiform cortex) for skilled reading (Pugh et al., 2001; Shaywitz et al., 2002). Their studies showed that the left temporoparietal area is the region that engages effortful decoding during early reading acquisition and that the left ventral occipitotemporal area is later-developing and associated with fast and fluent word identification (see also Booth et al., 2001; Church, Coalson, Lugar, Petersen, & Schlaggar, 2008). As with the temporoparietal areas, those with reading disabilities also showed functional disruption of the ventral occipitotemporal area; thus, the findings have provided support for a rather pervasive functional disruption of major components of the left hemisphere posterior reading system. The left inferior frontal gyrus and right hemisphere are more strongly activated in those with reading disabilities, especially in older readers, and interpreted as providing compensatory activity.

A cross-linguistic study in alphabetic languages in Europe (English, French, and Italian) also revealed a shared dysfunction in the left posterior areas, including the occipitotemporal area, and suggested a "universal" deficit causing reading disability (Paulesu et al., 2001). However, with regard to nonalphabetic languages, reading Chinese recruits many overlapping—but some distinct—brain areas, mainly the left middle frontal gyrus (BA9). This area has been associated with reading difficulty in Chinese (Bolger, Perfetti, & Schneider, 2005; Siok, Perfetti, Jin, & Tan, 2004; Tan, Laird, Li, & Fox, 2005).

Even before the ventral occipitotemporal area was implicated as a key area for skilled reading in European alphabetic orthographies, the ventral occipitotemporal area had been recognized as the region associated with kanji reading. Lesion studies of acquired alexia suggested that the left angular gyrus (included in the temporoparietal area) lesions caused agraphia for both kanji and kana, with preserved kanji reading, and the left posterior inferior temporal (almost the same area of the ventral occipitotemporal area) lesions caused alexia and agraphia for kanji, with preserved kana function (Iwata, 1986). Functional imaging studies comparing kana and kanji reading (or writing) supported this clinical dissociation. The left temporoparietal region (the angular gyrus and the posterior superior and middle temporal gyrus) and the inferior-to-middle occipital cortex are more strongly activated in kana reading than kanji reading, and the left ventral occipitotemporal area is more strongly related to kanji reading than kana reading (Bolger et al., 2005; Nakamura, Dehaene, Jobert, Bihan, & Koider, 2005; Nakamura, Oga, et al., 2005; Sakurai et al., 2000; and Thuy et al., 2004, for the meta-analysis of five Japanese studies). This dissociation has been discussed in the context of the dual-route models of reading. The phonogram kana requires letter-to-sound rule-based decoding (nonlexical route) and recruits the left temporoparietal dorsal circuit; the logographic kanji can directly access the semantic system (lexical route) and utilizes the ventral occipitotemporal circuit.

Recent fMRI studies have revealed a more detailed differentiation in the fusiform cortex. An fMRI study in French using written letter-strings graded with frequency (false font—symbols, words and rotated letters—to real words) showed that activation becomes more selective for progressively orthographically large units along a plane from posterior to the anterior fusiform cortex. At the same time, left lateralization becomes stronger in the more anterior area (Vinckier et al., 2007). This hierarchical organization in the fusiform cortex was explained in the context of functional specialization, not as regional selectivity; the middle fusiform cortex, which is known as the visual word form area (VWFA), is more specifically tuned to well-learned orthographic patterns. In studies of Japanese scripts, stronger activation in the fusiform cortex for kanji is consistently found among studies, but the coordinate of activation that showed the strongest kanji–kana differences varies among studies (Nakamura, Dehaene, et al., 2005; Sakurai et al., 2000; Thuy et al., 2004). Comparisons across these studies are difficult because stimulus characteristics varied among studies and familiarity of stimuli were not controlled. To describe fine-graded organization in the fusiform cortex reflecting Japanese orthographies, a study using well-controlled stimuli and a within-subjects design will be essential.

Another controversy of kanji reading has been the contribution of the right hemisphere. Comparing to the results in alphabetic languages, most studies have shown more bilateral activation in the fusiform cortex in kanji. Nakamura, Oga, et al. (2005) conducted a direct comparison between the right and left hemispheres. Although the left hemisphere was predominantly activated for both kana and kanji reading, kanji reading involved more areas that showed right-lateralized activation, including the right-middle fusiform cortex. The more bilateral activations in the middle fusiform cortex for logograms were also reported in the comparison of kanji characters and French words (Dehaene et al., 2010), and Chinese characters and English words (Nelson, Liu, Fiez, & Perfetti, 2009). Compared with word reading, object naming shows more bilateral activation of the fusiform. Therefore, the contribution of the right fusiform in kanji reading was explained as a more direct access to semantic knowledge (Nakamura, Oga, et al., 2005), holistic analysis (Nelson et al., 2009), and a remnant of pictographic processing (Dehaene et al., 2010).

FUNCTIONAL IMAGING STUDY IN JAPANESE CHILDREN

Compared with alphabetic languages, neuroimaging studies of developmental reading disability in Japanese are limited. Our ongoing fMRI project aims to describe developmental changes of brain activation along with reading acquisition and attempts to describe different trajectories between nonimpaired children and children with RD.

As reviewed previously, the different contributions of dorsal and ventral circuits to the two scripts (kana versus kanji) has been explained in the context of the simple dual-route model. The phonogram kana requires letter-to-sound rule-based decoding, and the logographic kanji is directly mapped to the semantic system from whole-word identification. However, the contribution of the dorsal and ventral circuits may not be defined only by simple dichotomy of kana and kanji. It must be more dynamic and modified by proficiency of reading skills; note that studies in English show developmental changes in the weightings of the two circuits with both age and proficiency (Shaywitz et al., 2002). To examine dynamic developmental change in neurocircuitry during skill acquisition, a longitudinal neuroimaging study is essential.

As a first report from our longitudinal study, we compared nonimpaired children and children with RD in cross-sections (Uchiyama, Seki, & Koeda, 2010). Children in the second to sixth grades in mainstream education participated in this study. All participants completed the Japanese kana reading tests, which had been recently developed by a research team at the National Center of Neurology and Psychiatry (Kobayashi et al., 2010), and children who scored 2 SDs below the grade average in more than two subtests (either in accuracy or speed) were classified into the RD group. For the task of fMRI, we use a picture–word matching task that was similar to the task used in a recent study of young readers of English (Frost et al., 2009). We hypothesized that even for phonographic kana, highly familiar words must be mapped onto semantics directly from whole-word identification. To test this hypothesis, five categories of stimuli were created by the gradient of visual familiarity (familiar words, unfamiliar words, pseudowords, letter strings, and meaningless marks) to enhance the difference between letter-by-letter decoding and whole-word identification.

In children who were nonimpaired, the left middle fusiform cortex showed stronger activation for familiar words than for letter strings, and the left inferior parietal region (BA40) showed stronger activation for pseudowords than for real words. All children with RD showed hypoactivation in the left fusiform cortex, but the activation of the left inferior parietal region was quite heterogeneous. The results indicate that the fusiform is relevant to reading kana words, when their visual familiarity is high for readers, and the inferior parietal region is more related to effortful decoding. RD children in kana may have a disruption in the left temporoparietal reading-related areas, mainly in the left fusiform cortex. For the most part, these data are quite consistent with previous alphabetic studies.

However, the present cross-sectional analysis cannot determine whether the observed hypoactivation reflects a biological cause or instead is the consequence of low skill levels. At the same time, hyper-activation cannot be interpreted simply as "good" function. A recent study reported that adolescents with RD showed a pattern of increased activity with stimulus repetition in the reading circuit, which suggests the effect of training, and the adolescents who were nonimpaired showed decreased activation with stimulus repetition, which is inter-preted as an increase in efficiency (Pugh et al., 2008). Their results sug-gest that the same degree of activity can indicate a different point in time within learning trajectories. The interpretation of the brain activa-tion will be confirmed by the ongoing longitudinal study coupled with multiple behavioral measures; brain behavior analyses over time can help connect patterns of activation to relevant reading skills or deficits.

The work is ongoing, but at this point we hypothesize that the basic brain circuits in the left hemisphere—the temporoparietal dorsal circuit and the ventral occipitotemporal circuit—are probably universal across orthographies. However, the weightings of the two circuits will differ, not only determined by the characters of each orthography (transpar-ency, phonological and orthographic grain size, visual complexity, etc.), but also modulated by individual difference in reading proficiency and familiarity with written materials. The change in brain activation related to skill acquisition will be observed as 1) functional specialization; that is, differentiation of the cortex into areas which show more specified activation to the well-learned stimuli, and 2) efficiency; that is, increased activation followed by decreased activation (inverted U-shape dynamic change) along with skill acquisition.

FUTURE DIRECTIONS IN RESEARCH FOR JAPANESE DYSLEXIA

Cross-Linguistic and Interlinguistic Studies

Although fluent kana reading is a crucial skill in primary education, difficulty in reading kanji becomes a great barrier in higher education for older children who are dyslexic. However, functional change in the brain during kanji learning for children has never been studied. Kanji and Chinese characters share orthographic features but differ in morpho-logical usage and character–sound mapping. Cross-linguistic studies with Chinese may give us a deeper understanding of both orthographies.

In addition to the cross-linguistic study, the interlinguistic study—the dynamic change of brain function during the second language acquisition—is the main focus of our discussion. The accommodation and assimilation hypothesis suggests that the degree of accommodation and assimilation is greatly influenced by the difference in orthographies (Liu et al., 2007). However, the degree of accommodation and assimila-tion can be modulated by proficiency in both the first and second lan-guages. Similar to the studies on literacy acquisition of a first language, longitudinal studies to investigate intraindividual change, along with proficiency improvement, is essential.

Large-Scale Studies that Include Heterogeneous Participants

The heterogeneity of brain activation in RD is another important issue to be studied. Most fMRI studies, which examine group differences between readers who are nonimpaired and readers who have RD, have excluded children with comorbidities or children who did not fit specific selection criteria. For example, although dyslexia and attention-deficit/hyperactivity disorder (ADHD) are often comorbid, few studies have focused on the functional anatomy underlying RD with or without comorbid ADHD. The underlying mechanism of ADHD is speculated to be a deficit of executive function, which recruits the frontal lobe and the basal ganglia. A deficit in executive function can affect literacy development in many ways, such as problems in sustained attention, efficacy of learning, or working memory, which is crucial for reading comprehension. However, many ADHD children show reading difficulty even after effective medication treatment of the ADHD. The interaction or common mechanisms underlying both conditions need to be studied. To increase our knowledge of the heterogeneity in dyslexia, a large-scale functional imaging study, including a wide range of participants, is crucial.

Studies to Confirm Remediation Effects on the Brain

Brain imaging studies with longitudinal design are also useful to observe functional changes in the brain associated with remediation. Although several larger scale treatment studies have been reported to date in English (Shaywitz et al., 2004; Simos et al., 2002; Temple et al., 2003), this type of study is lacking for Japanese. It is important to know how brain activation patterns are changed after remediation (e.g., normalization of common circuits or utilizing other areas for compensation) and whether these changes differ as a function of age, severity, or script. Moreover, it will be important to begin to explore brain mechanisms underlying individual differences in response to remediation.

CONCLUSION

The Japanese writing system is unique in its use of both phonographic and logographic scripts in parallel. Phonographic kana is basically transparent, but it implies some ambiguity in letter-to-sound mapping as exceptions, which requires phonological awareness as a crucial ability. Logographic kanji is much more ambiguous in character-to-sound mapping, which requires various cognitive skills in addition to phonological processing skills. This contrast deeply affects manifestations of reading difficulty in Japanese. Brain imaging studies have shown that both the dorsal temporoparietal and the occipitotemporal ventral circuits are utilized for reading kanji and kana, but the predominance of each circuit differs by scripts. Furthermore, a study during the acquisition of reading shows that activation of each circuit dynamically changes, along with proficiency. Functional specialization in the left hemisphere reading circuits may be the universal mechanism of the brain for reading acquisition across orthographies and may be an important point of focus for future treatment studies in Japanese.

REFERENCES

Amano, K. (1986). *Kodomono kanamoji no shutoku katei [Process of kana letter learning of children].* Tokyo: Akiyama-shoten.

Bolger, D.J., Perfetti, C.A., & Schneider, W. (2005). Cross-cultural effect on the brain revisited: Universal structures plus writing system variation. *Human Brain Mapping, 25*(1), 92–104.

Booth, J.R., Burman, D.D., Van Santen, F.W., Harasaki, Y., Gitelman, D.R., Parrish, T.B., et al. (2001). The development of specialized brain systems in reading and oral-language. *Child Neuropsychology, 7*(3), 119–141.

Church, J.A., Coalson, R.S., Lugar, H.M., Petersen, S.E., & Schlaggar, B.L. (2008). A developmental fMRI study of reading and repetition reveals changes in phonological and visual mechanisms over age. *Cerebral Cortex, 18*(9), 2054–2065.

Dehaene, S., Nakamura, K., Jobert, A., Kuroki, C., Ogawa, S., & Cohen, L. (2010). Why do children make mirror errors in reading? Neural correlates of mirror invariance in the visual word form area. *NeuroImage, 49*(2), 1837–1848.

Frost, S.J., Landi, N., Mencl, W.E., Sandak, R., Fulbright, R.K., Tejada, E.T., et al. (2009). Phonological awareness predicts activation patterns for print and speech. *Annals of Dyslexia, 59*(1), 78–97.

Fushimi, T., Ijuin, M., Patterson, K., & Tatsumi, I.F. (1999). Consistency, frequency, and lexicality effects in naming Japanese kanji. *Journal of Experimental Psychology: Human Perception and Performance, 5,* 674–691.

Goswami, U. (2000). Phonological representations, reading development, and dyslexia: Towards a cross-linguistic theoretical framework. *Dyslexia, 6*(2), 133–151.

Hara, K. (2001). The development of phonological awareness in Japanese children. *Japanese Journal of Communication Disorders, 18*(1), 10–18.

Ho, C.S., Chan, D.W., Lee, S.H., Tsang, S.M., & Luan, V.H. (2004). Cognitive profiling and preliminary subtyping in Chinese developmental dyslexia. *Cognition, 91*(1), 43–75.

Hotta, O. (1986). *Moji-shido no tame no onsetsu-yomi noryoku chousa [A study of letter reading skill as a basis of reading instruction].* Abstracts for 24th Japanese Association of Educational Psychology, pp. 754–755.

Inagaki, K., Hatano, G., & Otake, T. (2000). The effect of Kana literacy acquisition on the speech segmentation unit used by Japanese young children. *Journal of Experimental Child Psychology, 75*(1), 70–91.

Iwata, M. (1986). Neural mechanism of reading and writing in the Japanese language. *Functional Neurology, 1*(1), 43–52.

Kassai, K., Seki, A., & Koeda, T. (2006). Fundamental deficits of reading sentences in Japanese dyslexia. *Shoni No Seishin To Shinkei, 46*(1), 39–44.

Kobayashi, M.S., Haynes, C.W., Macruso, P., Hook, P.E., & Kato, J. (2005). Effect of mora deletion, nonword repetition, rapid naming, and visual search performance on beginning reading in Japan. *Annals of Dyslexia, 55*(1), 105–128.

Kobayashi, T., Inagaki, M., Gunji, A., Yatabe, K., Kaga, M., Goto, T., et al. (2010). Developmental changes in reading ability of Japanese elementary school children: Analysis of four kana reading tasks. *No to Hattatsu,* 2010, *41*(1), 15–21.

Koyama, M.S., Hansen, P.C., & Stein, J.F. (2008). Logographic Kanji versus honographic Kana in literacy acquisition: How important are visual and phonological skills? *Annals of the New York Academy of Sciences, 1145,* 41–55.

Kuobzono, H. (2006). The phonetic and phonological organization of speech in Japanese. In M. Nakayama, R. Mazuka, and Y. Shirai (Eds.), *The Handbook of East Asian Psycholinguistics* (pp. 191–200). New York: Cambridge University Press.

Liu, Y., Dunlap, S., Fiez, J., & Perfetti, C. (2007). Evidence for neural accommodation to a writing system following learning. *Human Brain Mapping, 28*(11), 1223–1234.

Makita, K. (1968). The reality of reading disability in Japanese children. *American Journal of Orthopsychiatry, 68*, 599–614.

Masuda, H., & Saito, H. (2002). Interactive processing of phonological information in reading Japanese Kanji character words and their phonemic radicals. *Brain and Language, 81*(1–3), 445–453.

Ministry of Education, Culture, Sports, Science and Technology (MEXT). (2004). Strategic promotion of international science and technology activities interim report overview. Retrieved December 28, 2010, from http://www.mext.go.jp/english/news/2004/08/05011301.htm

Nakamura, K., Dehaene, S., Jobert, A., Le Bihan, D., & Kouider, S. (2005). Subliminal convergence of Kanji and Kana words: Further evidence for functional parcellation of the posterior temporal cortex in visual word perception. *Journal of Cognitive Neuroscience, 17*(6), 954–968.

Nakamura, K., Oga, T., Okada, T., Sadato, N., Takayama, Y., Wydell, T., et al. (2005). Hemispheric asymmetry emerges at distinct parts of the occipitotemporal cortex for objects, logograms and phonograms: A functional MRI study. *NeuroImage, 28*(3), 521–528.

Nelson, J.R., Liu, Y., Fiez, J., & Perfetti, C.A. (2009) Assimilation and accommodation patterns in ventral occipitotemporal cortex in learning a second writing system. *Human Brain Mapping, 30*(3), 810–820.

Paulesu, E., Démonet, J.F., Fazio, F., McCrory, E., Chanoine, V., Brunswick, N., et al. (2001). Dyslexia: Cultural diversity and biological unity. *Science, 291*(5511), 2165–2167.

Pugh, K.R., Frost, S.J., Sandak, R., Landi, N., Rueckl, J.G., Constable, R.T., et al. (2008). Effects of stimulus difficulty and repetition on printed word identification: An fMRI comparison of nonimpaired and reading-disabled adolescent cohorts. *Journal of Cognitive Neuroscience, 20*(7), 1146–1160.

Pugh, K.R., Mencl, W.E., Jenner, A.R., Lee, J., Katz, L., Frost, S., et al. (2001). Neurobiological studies of reading development and reading disability. *Journal of Communication Disorders, 34*(6), 240–249.

Saito, H., Masuda, H., & Kawakami, M. (1999). Subword activation in reading Japanese single Kanji character words. *Brain and Language, 68*(1–2), 75–81.

Sakurai, Y., Momose, T., Iwata, M., Sudo, Y., Ohtomo, K., & Kanazawa, I. (2000). Different cortical activity in reading of Kanji words, Kana words, and Kana nonwords. *Cognitive Brain Research, 9*(1), 111–115.

Seki, A., Kassai, K., Uchiyama, H., & Koeda, T. (2008). Reading ability and phonological awareness in Japanese children with dyslexia. *Brain and Development, 30*(3), 179–188.

Seymour, P.H., Aro, M., & Erskine, J.M. (2003). Foundation literacy acquisition in European orthographies. *British Journal Psychology, 94*(2), 143–174.

Share, D.L. (2008). On the Anglocentricities of current reading research and practice: The perils of overreliance on an "outlier" orthography. *Psychological Bulletin, 134*(4), 584–615.

Shaywitz, B.A., Shaywitz, S.E., Blachman, B.A., Pugh, K.R., Fulbright, R.K., Skudlarski, P., et al. (2004). Development of left occipitotemporal systems for skilled reading in children after a phonologically based intervention. *Biological Psychiatry, 55*(9), 926–933.

Shaywitz, B.A., Shaywitz, S.E., Pugh, K.R., Mencl, W.E., Fulbright, R.K., Skudlarski, P., et al. (2002). Disruption of posterior brain systems for reading in children with developmental dyslexia. *Biological Psychiatry, 52*(2), 101–110.

Simos, P.G., Fletcher, J.M., Bergman, E., Breier, J.I., Foorman, B.R., Castillo, E.M., et al. (2002). Dyslexia-specific brain activation profile becomes normal following successful remedial training. *Neurology, 58*(8), 1203–1213.

Siok, W.T., Perfetti, C.A., Jin, Z., & Tan, L.H. (2004). Biological abnormality of impaired reading is constrained by culture. *Nature, 431*, 71–76.

Tan, L.H., Laird, A.R., Li, K., & Fox, P.T. (2005). Neuroanatomical correlates of phonological processing of Chinese characters and alphabetic words: A meta-analysis. *Human Brain Mapping, 25*(1), 83–91.

Temple, E., Deutsch, G.K., Poldrack, R.A., Miller, S.L., Tallal, P., Merzenich, M.M., et al. (2003). Neural deficits in children with dyslexia ameliorated by behavioral remediation: Evidence from functional MRI. *Proceedings of the National Academy of the Sciences, USA, 100*(5), 2860–2865.

Thuy, D.H., Matsuo, K., Nakamura, K., Toma, K., Oga, T., Nakai, T., et al. (2004).

Implicit and explicit processing of kanji and kana words and non-words studied with fMRI. *NeuroImage, 23*(3), 878–889.

Uchiyama, H., Seki, A., & Koeda, T. (2010). A study of the early detection method of dyslexic children using oral sentence reading task [Japanese]. *Psychiatria et Neurologia Paediatrica Japonica, 2010; 50*(4), 399–405.

Uno, A., Wydell T., Haruhara N., Kaneko M., & Shibuya N. (2009). Relationship between reading/writing skills and cognitive abilities among Japanese primary-school children: Normal readers versus poor readers (dyslexics). *Reading and Writing, 22*(7), 755–789.

Vinckier, F., Dehaene, S., Jobert, A., Dubus, J.P., Sigman, M., & Cohen, L. (2007). Hierarchical coding of letter strings in the ventral stream: Dissecting the inner organization of the visual word-form system. *Neuron, 55*(1), 143–156.

Wydell, T. (1998). What matters in kanji word naming: Consistency, regularity, or On/Kun-reading difference? *Reading and Writing, 10*, 359–373.

Wydell, T.N., & Butterworth B.A. (1999). Case study of an English-Japanese bilingual with monolingual dyslexia. *Cognition, 70*(3), 273–305.

Wydell, T.N., & Kondo, T. (2003). Phonological deficit and the reliance on orthographic approximation for reading: A follow-up study on an English-Japanese bilingual with monolingual dyslexia. *Journal of Research in Reading, 26*(1), 33–48.

Yamada, J., & Banks, A. (1994). Evidence for and characteristics of dyslexia among Japanese children. *Annals of Dyslexia, 44*(1), 105–119.

Ziegler, J.C., Bertrand, D., Tóth, D., Csépe, V., Reis, A., Faísca, L., et al. (2010). Orthographic depth and its impact on universal predictors of reading: a cross-language investigation. *Psychological Science, 21*(4), 551–559.

Ziegler, J.C., & Goswami, U. (2005). Reading acquisition, developmental dyslexia, and skilled reading across languages: A psycholinguistic grain size theory. *Psychological Bulletin, 131*(1), 3–29.

CHAPTER 8

Brain Activation Measures in Predicting Reading Skills and Evaluating Intervention Effects in Children at Risk for Dyslexia

Tomi K. Guttorm, Leena Alho-Näveri, Ulla Richardson, and Heikki Lyytinen

One of the possible causes of dyslexia or difficulties in the acquisition of fluent reading is a deficit in phonological processing (Bradley, 1992; Bradley & Bryant, 1978, 1983; Lundberg, Olofsson, & Wall, 1980; Wagner & Torgesen, 1987; Wagner, Torgesen, & Rashotte, 1994). Deficits in phonological processing may in turn result from underlying auditory and/or speech-processing deviations, such as altered perceptual or discrimination processes. Results from neurocognitive brain research in children and adults with dyslexia seem to support this assumption of lower processing-level involvement.

There is strong evidence that dyslexia is genetically transmitted (for a review, see Wood & Grigorenko, 2001). The supposed genetic basis of dyslexia has recently been documented to the single gene level via identification of candidate genes such as *DYX1C1* (Taipale et al., 2003; Wang et al., 2006), *DCDC2* (Meng et al., 2005), *KIAA0319* (Cope et al., 2005; Paracchini et al., 2006), and *ROBO1* (Andrews et al., 2006). Genetic factors can conceivably alter brain development through a large number of different pathways, and the parameters of brain structure affected could be, for example, neuronal number, neuronal migration, and axonal connectivity, all of which are determined—with few exceptions—before birth. Due to these genetic factors, infants born to families with an affected parent or parents (and close relatives) are at elevated risk for the disorder. In the Jyväskylä Longitudinal Study of Dyslexia (see Lyytinen et al., 2001, 2006), one of the goals has been to trace early precursors or markers of dyslexia by following children with and without familial risk of dyslexia from birth to school age. The study of children from shortly after birth allows for the differentiation, for example, between factors present already at birth and those that result from complex gene–environment interaction later on in development.

There are practical limitations regarding the application of behavioral methods in the study of those developmentally early perceptual and discrimination processes which could underlie phenotypic deficits in dyslexia. Event-related potentials (ERPs), however, are suited to the detection of these early processing deviations because the ERP technique does not require behavioral responses from the participants. ERPs are based on electroencephalography (EEG). By averaging multiple time-locked EEG epochs across a stimulus event, it is possible to identify the synchronized ERP pattern that reflects the response of the brain to a given stimulus. ERPs make it possible to follow the time course of the brain's activity with a precision of tens of milliseconds and to thus obtain knowledge of the sequence, timing, and stages of specific processes.

ERPs have thus been utilized to study at-risk populations in infancy, including infants or even newborns at risk for dyslexia (Guttorm, Leppänen, Hämäläinen, Eklund, & Lyytinen, in press; Guttorm et al., 2005; Guttorm, Leppänen, Richardson, & Lyytinen, 2001; Guttorm, Leppänen, Tolvanen, & Lyytinen, 2003; Leppänen, Pihko, Eklund, & Lyytinen, 1999; Leppänen et al., 2002; Molfese, 2000; Molfese & Molfese, 1985, 1997; Pihko et al., 1999). In our earlier ERP studies in the Jyväskylä Longitudinal Study of Dyslexia project, we found significant hemispheric differences between newborns with familial risk of dyslexia ($n=26$) and without familial risk ($n=23$) in their response to speech stimuli presented with equal probability and with long inter-stimulus intervals (Guttorm et al., 2001, 2003). The processing of stop consonant–vowel (CV) syllables /ba/, /da/, and /ga/ was different between the groups in several latency ranges, with the clearest hemispheric differences being obtained at 540–630 milliseconds (ms). At this latency, the responses to /ga/ elicited a larger and more prolonged positive response in the right hemisphere in the at-risk group as compared with the infants in the control group. We speculated that these differences in brain response could reflect atypically enhanced right-hemispheric processing of speech cues such as CV transitions (/ga/ with the longest CV transition).

Evidence of enhanced right-hemisphere involvement in speech processing can also be found in other infant studies within the Jyväskylä Longitudinal Study of Dyslexia. By using a mismatch negativity (MMN; see Näätänen, 1992) paradigm involving vowel duration change (deviant /ka/ versus standard /kaa/), Leppänen et al. (1999) found that the newborn ERPs to deviant and standard stimuli were differentiated from each other in the at-risk group ($n=12$) more consistently in the right hemisphere (central and parietal locations). In the control group ($n=11$), however, this pattern occurred in the left hemisphere (frontal and parietal electrode sites). Furthermore, in a study by Pihko et al. (1999) with 6-month-olds (at-risk group, $n=28$; control group, $n=23$) using the same stimuli, the hemispheric pattern of ERPs (deviant /ka/ versus standard /kaa/) in the at-risk group showed similar tendencies toward right-hemispheric predominance. Evidence of enhanced right-hemispheric speech processing in older individuals with dyslexia has also been obtained in other brain activation studies such as positron emission tomography (Gross-Glenn et al., 1991; Rumsey et al., 1997), functional magnetic resonance imaging (fMRI; Shaywitz et al., 1998, 2004; Temple et al., 2003), and magnetoencephalography (MEG; Simos et al., 2002).

In our subsequent studies, we further tested whether these new-born ERPs could be used to predict later language skills in children with and without familial risk of dyslexia (Guttorm et al., 2005). Our results showed that the enhanced and prolonged predominantly right-hemispheric processing of the speech cues that was typical of at-risk newborns was associated with poorer receptive language skills at 2.5 and 5 years of age. These results suggest that in the infants at risk, the processing of speech cues in the right hemisphere—which is not typically specialized for language processing to the same extent as the left hemisphere—later manifests as problems for tasks that require accurate discrimination of complex speech sounds (receptive language skills). This processing pattern with atypical use of the right hemisphere could affect speech perception as well as the formation of accurate speech sound representations and thus have cascading effects on subsequent language development.

We also examined whether the atypically enhanced and prolonged pattern of right-hemispheric speech processing could also predict poorer prereading skills, such as phonological skills, rapid naming, and acquisition of letter knowledge, at the age of 6.5 years (half a year before the start of formal education in elementary schools in Finland). These skills have been shown to be associated with later reading performance. Our results showed that the infants who were at risk with atypical right-hemispheric speech processing scored significantly lower than the children in the control group without such a pattern in these later prereading measures. Furthermore, those infants who were at risk and who did not show enhanced right-hemispheric speech processing did not differ from the controls (Guttorm et al., in press). These results are interesting because it is widely accepted that appropriate development of phonological sensitivity (the skills to separate words into smaller units and the ability to attend to them as segmented entities) is necessary for the acquisition of the alphabetic principle in preliterate children (see, e.g., Byrne & Fielding-Barnsley, 1990; Ziegler & Goswami, 2005). Our latest results further show that children who are at risk with atypical enhanced and prolonged ERPs in the right hemisphere had lower scores on reading measures, especially in reading fluency, between the first and second grades. These combined results indicate that newborn ERPs can improve the identification accuracy of the children who were diagnosed as dyslexics (based on the second-grade criteria).

In summary, it is thus conceivable that newborn ERPs can be used in the future for the early identification of children at risk for developmental reading problems. Success in these efforts would further facilitate well-directed interventions even before reading problems are typically diagnosed.

One of the possible intervention methods for children with familial risk for dyslexia is studied in the Graphogame project (Lyytinen, Ronimus, Alanko, Poikkeus, & Taanila, 2007) with Finnish, German, Dutch, and

English children. The study followed preschool-age children (6.5 years; Finnish children enter school at age 6 years) who participated in training on grapheme–phoneme correspondences (as well as larger units such as syllables, words, pseudowords, rhymes, and so forth) with a computerized game (Lyytinen et al., 2007; see also Richardson, Aro, & Lyytinen, Chapter 4, this volume). These children were nonreaders and had poor representations of speech sounds and weak initial connections between letters and corresponding sounds. In Finland, the children with and without familial risk of dyslexia started either with the Graphogame or with the nonlinguistic number-knowledge control game training. After the 6 weeks, they switched games to counterbalance the order of the games. These children were measured before and after the first training (pre- and midmeasurements) and after the second training (postmeasurements). The children who did not play (both with and without risk of dyslexia) did not participate in the intervention. All of these groups also had follow-up measurements 1 year later (after first grade).

One of the basic principles of Graphogame is that the first steps in learning to read include matching distinctive visual symbols to units of sounds. Beginning readers have to develop a metalinguistic awareness that spoken words consist of sounds and that letters in written words represent those distinct sounds. The second principle of Graphogame is that in order to alleviate problems in reading acquisition, a sufficiently accurate, intensive, and long-lasting exposure to the phonemes and corresponding letters is needed. Finally, the game should also be enjoyable and allow children an opportunity for success and an appropriate level of challenge in order to keep them fully engaged and involved. Therefore, the Graphogame optimally adapts the training on an individualized basis.

We evaluated the effects of interventions by using both behavioral and brain activation measures (ERPs in Finnish and Swiss children and fMRI in Swiss children). In brain measurements, one of the regions of interest was the visual word form area (VWFA). The functional impairment in this language-specific brain area is associated with deficits in phonological skills and reading. The VWFA consists of the left occipito-temporal regions, especially the left posterior fusiform gyrus, and is specialized for visual word form representations (Cohen et al., 2000; Devlin, Jamison, Gonnerman, & Matthews, 2006; McCandliss, Cohen, & Dehaene, 2003; see also Price & Devlin, 2003, 2004). The activation of the area is atypical in people with dyslexia (Helenius, Tarkiainen, Cornelissen, Hansen, & Salmelin, 1999; Salmelin & Helenius, 2004; Temple et al., 2003).

In visual word recognition studies using ERP methodology, one of the most studied components is called N170. This component is clearest in the left inferior temporal cortex, which is known to be part of the VWFA (Helenius et al., 1999; Tarkiainen, Helenius, Hansen, Cornelissen, & Salmelin, 1999). Various studies have shown that the N170 component is elicited by words, letter strings, and faces around 150–200 ms after stimulus onset (Bentin, Mouchetant-Rostaing, Giard, Echallier, & Pernier, 1999; Cornelissen, Tarkiainen, Helenius, & Salmelin, 2003; Maurer, Brandeis, & McCandliss, 2005; Maurer, Brem, Bucher, & Brandeis, 2005; Rossion, Joyce, Cotrell, & Tarr 2003; Tarkiainen et al., 1999). Words have been shown to elicit larger negativities than symbol strings (Maurer, Brandeis, et al., 2005) and the N170 is larger for orthographic stimuli than for nonorthographic stimuli in the left hemisphere (Bentin et al., 1999). Furthermore, words and pseudowords have been shown to differ from nonwords at posterior sites of the left hemisphere, whereas words have been shown to differ from pseudowords and nonwords at anterior sites of the left hemisphere (Ziegler, Besson, Jacobs, Nazir, & Carr, 1997).

Similar to most other ERP components, N170 has been shown to differ between children and adults (Brem et al., 2006; Maurer, Brem, et al., 2005). Children's N170 component emerged on the right occipitotemporal sites and appeared more in the midoccipital area compared with the brain areas shown by adults. Furthermore, Maurer, Brem, et al. (2005) reported that the children's N170 component, which is often called N240 due to a later and slower appearance, had larger amplitudes, smaller latencies, and different topography than the component detected in adults. This component is highly relevant in the studies of early reading development because it has been shown to be associated with letter knowledge in nonreading children (Maurer, Brandeis, et al., 2005).

The results from the Swiss Graphogame project (Brem et al., in press) showed that print-sensitivity in the VWFA emerges rapidly during acquisition of the grapheme–phoneme correspondences. Words and false fonts activated a bilateral and predominantly ventral posterior occipitotemporal network before the training. Interestingly, print-sensitive activation was enhanced after the training, mainly in the posterior VWFA, with corresponding fMRI results and ERP effects at around 200 ms. These results indicate that specific brain regions in the emerging VWFA are tuned for print and adopt print-specific functions when phonological mapping of graphemes becomes feasible. Because the children with and without familial risk of dyslexia were pooled together due to the small sample sizes in the Swiss data, we still need further research on the print sensitivity differences between these groups. In the Finnish data, our unpublished behavioral and ERP results (with both MMN and N170) indicate that Graphogame is an effective intervention method, especially for children at risk of dyslexia. Similar brain activation results across Swiss and Finnish study sites suggest that reading acquisition shows some universal features, even in languages that differ in the depth of their orthography (see, e.g., Seymour, Aro, & Erskine, 2003).

In summary, our results show that event-related potentials can be used in early identification of children who would later have problems in reading. Our results also suggest that brain activation methodology is a useful tool in evaluating the training effects in children with and without familial risk of dyslexia.

REFERENCES

Andrews, W., Liapi, A., Plachez, C., Camurri, L., Zhang, J.Y., Mori, S., et al. (2006). Robo1 regulates the development of major axon tracts and interneuron migration in the forebrain. *Development, 133,* 2243–2252.

Bentin, S., Mouchetant-Rostaing, Y., Giard, M.H., Echallier, J.F., & Pernier, J. (1999). ERP manifestations of processing printed words at different psycholinguistic levels: Time course and scalp distribution. *Journal of Cognitive Neuroscience, 11,* 235–260.

Bradley, L. (1992). Rhymes, rimes, and learning to read and spell. In C.A. Ferguson, L. Menn, & C. Stoel-Gammon (Eds.), *Phonological development: Models, research, and implications* (pp. 553–562). Timonium, MD: York Press.

Bradley, L., & Bryant, P. (1978). Difficulties in auditory organization as a possible cause of reading backwardness. *Nature, 271,* 746–747.

Bradley, L., & Bryant, P. (1983). Categorizing sounds and learning to read: A causal connection. *Nature, 301,* 419–421.

Brem, S., Bach, S., Kucian, K., Guttorm, T.K., Martin, E., Lyytinen, H., et al. (2010). Brain sensitivity to print emerges when children learn letter-speech sound correspondences. *Proceedings of the National Academy of Sciences, USA, 107*(17), 7939–7944.

Brem, S., Bucher, K., Halder P., Summers P., Dietrich, T., Martin, E., et al. (2006). Evidence for developmental changes in the visual word processing network beyond adolescence. *NeuroImage, 29,* 822–837.

Byrne, B., & Fielding-Barnsley, R. (1990). Acquiring the alphabetic principle: A case for teaching recognition of phoneme identity. *Journal of Educational Psychology, 82,* 805–812.

Cohen, L., Dehaene, S., Naccache, L., Lehéricy, S., Dehaene-Lambertz, G., Hénaff, M., et al. (2000). The visual word form area: Spatial and temporal characterization of an initial stage of reading in normal subjects and posterior split-brain patients. *Brain: A Journal of Neurology, 123,* 291–307.

Cope, N., Harold, D., Hill, G., Moskvina, V., Stevenson, J., Holmans, P., et al. (2005). Strong evidence that KIAA0319 on chromosome 6p is a susceptibility gene for developmental dyslexia.

American Journal of Human Genetics, 76, 581–591.

Cornelissen, P., Tarkiainen, A., Helenius, P., & Salmelin, R. (2003). Cortical effects of shifting letter position in letter strings of varying length. *Journal of Cognitive Neuroscience, 15,* 731–746.

Devlin, J.T., Jamison, H.L., Gonnerman, L.M., & Matthews, P.M. (2006). The role of the posterior fusiform gyrus in reading. *Journal of Cognitive Neuroscience, 18,* 911–922.

Gross-Glenn, K., Duara, R., Barker, W.W., Loewenstein, D., Chang, J.Y., Yoshii, F., et al. (1991). Positron emission tomographic studies during serial word-reading by normal and dyslexic adults. *Journal of Clinical and Experimental Neuropsychology, 13,* 531–544.

Guttorm, T.K., Leppänen, P.H.T., Hämäläinen, J.A., Eklund, K.M., & Lyytinen, H. (2009). Newborn event-related potentials predict poorer pre-reading skills in children at-risk for dyslexia. *Journal of Learning Disabilities, 43*(5), 391–401.

Guttorm, T.K., Leppänen, P.H.T., Poikkeus, A.-M., Eklund, K.M., Lyytinen, P., & Lyytinen, H. (2005). Brain event-related potentials (ERPs) measured at birth predict later language development in children with and without familial risk for dyslexia. *Cortex, 41,* 291–303.

Guttorm, T.K., Leppänen, P.H.T., Richardson, U., & Lyytinen, H. (2001). Event-related potentials and consonant differentiation in newborns with familial risk for dyslexia. *Journal of Learning Disabilities, 34,* 534–544.

Guttorm, T.K., Leppänen, P.H.T., Tolvanen, A., & Lyytinen, H. (2003). Event-related potential in newborns with and without familial risk for dyslexia: Principal component analysis reveals differences between the groups. *Journal of Neural Transmission, 110,* 1059–1074.

Helenius, P., Tarkiainen, A., Cornelissen, P., Hansen, P.C., & Salmelin, R. (1999). Dissociation of normal feature analysis and deficient processing of letter-strings in dyslexic adults. *Cerebral Cortex, 9,* 476–483.

Leppänen, P.H.T., Pihko, E., Eklund, K.M., & Lyytinen, H. (1999). Cortical responses of infants with and without a genetic risk for dyslexia: II. Group effects. *NeuroReport, 10,* 969–973.

Leppänen, P.H.T., Richardson, U., Pihko, E., Eklund, K.M., Guttorm, T.K., Aro, M., et al. (2002). Brain responses to changes in speech sound durations differ between infants with and without familial risk for dyslexia. *Developmental Neuropsychology, 22,* 407–422.

Lundberg, I., Olofsson, Å., & Wall, S. (1980). Reading and spelling skills in the first school years predicted from phonemic awareness skills in kindergarten. *Scandinavian Journal of Psychology, 21,* 159–173.

Lyytinen, H., Ahonen, T., Eklund, K., Guttorm, T.K., Laakso, M.-L., Leinonen, S., et al. (2001). Developmental pathways of children with and without familial risk for dyslexia during the first years of life. *Developmental Neuropsychology, 20,* 535–554.

Lyytinen, H., Erskine, J., Tolvanen, A., Torppa, M., Poikkeus, A., & Lyytinen, P. (2006). Trajectories of reading development: A follow-up from birth to school age of children with and without risk for dyslexia. *Merrill-Palmer Quarterly, 52,* 514–546.

Lyytinen, H., Ronimus, M., Alanko, A., Poikkeus, A., & Taanila, M. (2007). Early identification of dyslexia and the use of computer game-based practice to support reading acquisition. *Nordic Psychology, 59,* 109–126.

Maurer, U., Brandeis, D., & McCandliss, B.D. (2005). Fast, visual specialization for reading in English revealed by the topography of the N170 ERP response. *Behavioral and Brain Functions, 1,* 13.

Maurer, U., Brem, S., Bucher, K., & Brandeis, D. (2005). Emerging neurophysiological specialization for letter strings. *Journal of Cognitive Neuroscience, 17,* 1532–1552.

McCandliss, B.D., Cohen, L., & Dehaene, S. (2003). The visual word form area: Expertise for reading in the fusiform gyrus. *Trends in Cognitive Sciences, 7,* 293–299.

Meng, H., Smith, S.D., Hager, K., Held, M., Liu, J., Olson, R.K., et al. (2005). DCDC2 is associated with reading disability and modulates neuronal development in the brain. *Proceedings of the National Academy of Sciences, USA, 102,* 17053–17058.

Molfese, D.L. (2000). Predicting dyslexia at 8 years of age using neonatal brain responses. *Brain and Language, 72,* 238–245.

Molfese, D.L., & Molfese, V.J. (1985). Electrophysiological indices of auditory discrimination in newborn infants: The bases for predicting later language development? *Infant Behavior and Development, 8,* 197–211.

Molfese, D.L., & Molfese, V.J. (1997). Discrimination of language skills at five years of age using event-related potentials recorded at birth. *Developmental Neuropsychology, 13,* 135–156.

Näätänen, R. (1992). *Attention and brain function.* Hillsdale, NJ: Lawrence Erlbaum Associates.

Paracchini, S., Thomas, A., Castro, S., Lai, C., Paramasivam, M., Wang, Y., et al. (2006). The chromosome 6p22 haplotype associated with dyslexia reduces the expression of KIAA0319, a novel gene involved in neuronal migration. *Human Molecular Genetics, 15,* 1659–1666.

Pihko, E., Leppänen, P.H.T., Eklund, K.M., Cheour, M., Guttorm, T.K., & Lyytinen, H. (1999). Cortical responses of infants with and without a genetic risk for dyslexia: I. Age effects. *NeuroReport, 10,* 901–905.

Price, C.J., & Devlin, J.T. (2003). The myth of the visual word form area. *NeuroImage, 19,* 473–481.

Price, C.J., & Devlin, J.T. (2004). The pro and cons labeling a left occipitotemporal region: "The visual word form area." *NeuroImage, 22,* 477–479.

Rossion, B., Joyce, C.A., Cotrell., G.W., & Tarr., M.J. (2003). Early lateralization and tuning for face, word, and object processing in the visual cortex. *NeuroImage, 20,* 1609–1624.

Rumsey, J.M., Nace, K., Donohue, B., Wise, D., Maisog, J.M., & Andreason, P. (1997). A positron emission tomographic study of impaired word recognition and phonological processing in dyslexic men. *Archives of Neurology, 54,* 562–573.

Salmelin, R., & Helenius, P. (2004). Functional neuroanatomy of impaired reading in dyslexia. *Scientific Studies of Reading, 8,* 257–272.

Seymour, P.H.K., Aro M., & Erskine, J.M. (2003). Foundation literacy acquisition in European orthographies. *British Journal of Psychology, 94,* 143–174.

Shaywitz, B.A., Shaywitz, S.E., Blachman, B.A., Pugh, K.R., Fulbright, R.K., Skudlarski, P., et al. (2004). Development of left occipitotemporal systems for skilled reading in children after a phonologically based intervention. *Biological Psychiatry, 55,* 926–933.

Shaywitz, S.E., Shaywitz, B.A., Pugh, K.R., Fulbright, R.K., Constable, R.T., Mencl, W.E., et al. (1998). Functional disruption in the organization of the brain for reading in dyslexia. *Proceedings of the National Academy of Sciences, USA, 95,* 2636–2641.

Simos, P.G., Fletcher, J.M., Bergman, E., Breier, J.I., Foorman, B.R., Castillo, E.M., et al. (2002). Dyslexia-specific brain activation profile becomes normal following successful remedial training. *Neurology, 58,* 1203–1213.

Taipale, M., Kaminen, N., Nopola-Hemmi, J., Haltia, T., Myllyluoma, B., Lyytinen, H., et al. (2003). A candidate gene for developmental dyslexia encodes a nuclear tetratricopeptide repeat domain protein dynamically regulated in brain. *Proceedings of the National Academy of Sciences, USA, 100,* 11553–11558.

Tarkiainen, A., Helenius, P., Hansen, P.C., Cornelissen, P.L., & Salmelin, R. (1999). Dynamics of letter string perception in the human occipitotemporal cortex. *Brain: A Journal of Neurology, 122,* 2119–2132.

Temple, E., Deutsch, G., Poldrack, R., Miller, S., Tallal, P., Merzenich, M., et al. (2003). Neural deficits in children with dyslexia ameliorated by behavioral remediation: Evidence from functional MRI. *Proceedings of the National Academy of Sciences, USA, 100,* 2860–2865.

Wagner, R.K., & Torgesen, J.K. (1987). The nature of phonological processing and its causal role in the acquisition of reading skills. *Psychological Bulletin, 101,* 192–212.

Wagner, R.K., Torgesen, J.K., & Rashotte, C.A. (1994). Development of reading-related phonological processing abilities: New evidence of bidirectional causality from a latent variable longitudinal study. *Developmental Psychology, 30,* 73–87.

Wang, Y., Paramasivam, M., Thomas, A., Bai, J., Kaminen-Ahola, N., Kere, J., et al. (2006). DYX1C1 functions in neuronal migration in developing neocortex. *Neuroscience, 143,* 515–522.

Wood, F.B., & Grigorenko, E.L. (2001). Emerging issues in the genetics of dyslexia: A methodological preview. *Journal of Learning Disabilities, 34,* 503–511.

Ziegler, J.C., Besson, M., Jacobs, A.M., Nazir, T.A., & Carr, T.H. (1997). Word, pseudoword, and nonword processing: A multitask comparison using event-related brain potentials. *Journal of Cognitive Neuroscience, 9,* 758–775.

Ziegler, J.C., & Goswami, U. (2005). Reading acquisition, developmental dyslexia, and skilled reading across languages: A psycholinguistic grain size theory. *Psychological Bulletin, 131,* 3–29.

Brain Studies—What They Show Across Orthographies

Kenneth R. Pugh

C ognitive neuroscience holds the promise of informing the study of language, reading, and writing (and their disorders). This approach should accomplish three major goals for the study of language and literacy: 1) to support the development of neurobiologically plausible theories of typical versus atypical development that can guide research and practice; 2) to increase sensitivity to individual differences on neurocognitive factors that affect reading acquisition (and that might eventually serve as targets for remediation); and 3) to benefit our efforts to facilitate early identification of risk for language and prereading difficulties with an eye toward prevention. The extant cognitive neuroscience literature on language and reading is fast growing and exciting, but much more research is needed before gene–brain–behavior accounts of dyslexia are within our grasp.

Despite the need for ongoing research, there has been significant progress. Several candidate genes have been proposed that appear to be associated with language and reading difficulties (see Section IV, "Genetics and Neurobiology," in this volume); at the level of brain systems, structural and functional imaging studies have identified critical left-hemisphere (LH) "neurocircuits" associated with individual differences in language and reading skills, and treatment studies conducted to date suggest that effective remediation can have at least a partially normalizing effect on these LH reading systems (see Frost et al., 2009, for a review).

The Dyslexia Foundation conference in Taiwan brought together leading researchers from various countries to review and discuss what researchers know, what they do not know, and what is needed to move the scientific study of dyslexia forward. Chapters in this section focus on cognitive neuroscience (with major emphasis on functional neuroimaging) and what it can tell us about reading across orthographies. The discussions focus in part on how diverse imaging methods (e.g., electroencephalography [EEG], functional magnetic resonance imaging [fMRI], structural MRI, and magnetoencephalography [MEG]) can be brought to bear to inform our understanding of dyslexia and how we can use these methods synergistically. But at the core of the discussions during the conference and in the chapters herein is the call for greater emphasis on cross-language comparative (and bilingual) brain research. Such research, conducted with comparable (and state of the art) methods, should allow us to identify those neurocognitive markers that are universal in dyslexia (as well as those that may be unique to a given orthography). Chapters 6 through 8 provide a clear starting point for this enterprise; each chapter charts what is known about the brain and dyslexia in different orthographies, as well as what kinds of new research designs might be developed in order to move toward universal accounts of typical and atypical reading development.

In Chapter 6, Dehaene, for example, takes a "neuroevolutionary" perspective on reading. He argues cogently that specific computational (processing) characteristics of ventral visual pathways in the brain will constrain the design choices made when inventing new writing systems and will ensure the development of at least partial language-invariant neuronal circuits to support reading at the level of the individual. Thus, in this account, biology promotes universality even in a cultural invention such as writing systems, which provides an interesting contrast to linguistically motivated universality arguments made by others (see Perfetti, Chapter 1 of this volume). Dehaene describes a neuronal recycling framework for understanding how reading develops, why there must be universals at the level of neurocircuits even for diverse writing systems, and why some aspects of literacy acquisition might be particularly challenging to emergent readers because of the processing characteristics of key regions in the LH. He summarizes provocative imaging studies in laying out this account and considers the kinds of new research that will help move us closer to a universal brain-based account of reading and its disorders, grounded in a deeper understanding of computational properties of neurocircuits.

Tan, in a conference presentation partially summarized in Chapter 1 of this volume by Perfetti, summarizes results from an impressive program of research on both typically and atypically developing readers in Chinese (Siok, Niu, Jin, Perfetti, & Tan, 2008). Studies to date from Tan's team provide only limited support for universality accounts. He presents evidence of largely overlapping, but partially distinct, neurocircuits in Chinese relative to reading in alphabetic orthographies. It is important that for one region which appears to have an increased role in Chinese reading—the LH middle frontal gyrus—both functional and structural imaging data reveal significant differences between typically developing and dyslexic readers. Despite the partially separable neurocircuits in Chinese versus those invoked when reading alphabetic orthographies, Tan's work does indicate some overlap in dyslexia findings with alphabetic languages, particularly those LH ventral regions discussed by Dehaene in Chapter 6 and Seki in Chapter 7. Thus, a nuanced account emerges in Tan's discussion of language-invariant versus language-specific neuronal factors and how they could guide development, constrain second language learning, and inform effective treatments.

In Chapter 7, Seki provides a succinct and clear overview for the reader on the fascinating complexities of the Kana and Kanji scripts in Japanese. She goes on to discuss behavioral evidence for critical differences between dyslexic and typically developing readers in phonological and cognitive skills that have complex effects on the learning and mastery of these two scripts, one of which is orthographically to phonologically transparent (kana) and the other of which is highly opaque (kanji). This within-language orthographic depth (transparency) contrast opens fascinating avenues for research in dyslexia that drive her ongoing program of research. Seki also presents provocative new fMRI results from an ongoing sample of dyslexic readers that converge well with findings from alphabetic orthographies (anomalous activation in left ventral and temporoparietal regions). Seki concludes by considering next steps concerning universals in learning, remediation, and second language acquisition.

In Chapter 8, Guttorm, Alho-Näveri, Richardson, and Lyytinen add to this section in several important ways. They present a clear rationale for taking advantage of the unique features of EEG technology as a way of understanding brain development. They demonstrate how the fine-grained temporal resolution of EEG and its applicability to studying young children can be fruitfully used to inform research on reading development and developmental disabilities. Indeed, this team has led the way in this arena by conducting large-scale longitudinal studies of risk for reading disability. This chapter also shows the importance of studying a language such as Finnish (which has an exceedingly transparent orthography wherein letter-to-phoneme correspondences are completely regular) in cross-linguistic dyslexia research. Given the relative ease of learning letter/phoneme mappings in Finnish in contrast with irregular languages such as English, the behavioral phenotype for dyslexia for readers of this language might be somewhat different. The extensive data reviewed shows some overlap with findings from less transparent languages such as English, but some important differences as well. In English, dyslexic readers are both slow and inaccurate in word decoding, but in Finnish, dyslexic readers are slow but not inaccurate, which makes sense, given the transparency of this language. Phonological impairments appear to be a key factor in Finnish and in other alphabetic orthographies as seen in EEG studies that reveal clearly that early speech perception competencies presage later language and reading difficulties. Whether this predictive relation holds in all written languages promises to be a hot topic in the coming years. Finally, Guttorm et al. also present evidence that EEG can yield exquisitely sensitive indices of response to intervention—perhaps a level of sensitivity that might reveal effects even before they are evident in reading performance.

Padakannaya and Ramachandra, in Chapter 5 in the previous section of this volume, present a scholarly overview of the writing systems associated with Indic languages such as Hindi and Tamil. Although research on the neurobiology of dyslexia in these highly transparent, alphasyllabic languages is not yet available, they introduce some preliminary normative fMRI data on Hindi readers and Hindi–English bilinguals that in broad terms reinforce the themes raised by other chapters, suggesting largely overlapping neurocircuits for the vastly different orthographies. The promise of brain imaging studies in a country with such a large number and variety of languages in which so many individuals are multilingual is exciting. Padakannaya and Ramachandra provide a conceptual foundation for this type of future neurocognitive work.

In summary, each of these chapters deals with questions about how the brain reorganizes itself in learning to read in different orthographies and how this process may go awry in dyslexia. Although there are many unknowns at present, these chapters do suggest, at the brain circuitry level, similarities across languages that appear to outweigh differences. Thus, LH ventral regions appear to support skilled reading and discriminate good from poor readers in both alphabetic and nonalphabetic orthographies (though as suggested by Siok et al. [2008], there are important differences in other brain regions that need to be taken into account). We must also note, however, that even though the same brain pathways develop reading specialization in distinct orthographies, this fact does not necessarily imply that the kind of information being processed by these common pathways is identical. For instance, the same brain regions may code for fine-grained phonological features in alphabetic languages (wherein phonemes are represented) and coarser grained phonological features in languages such as Chinese that do not code for phonemes. Thus, universality in brain pathways across diverse writing systems does not necessarily imply that the teaching of reading or its remediation must be somehow universal; such a relationship is an open research question, and brain research alone will not provide definitive answers. However, the extant neuroimaging data showing largely overlapping neural substrates does point to neurobiological "end states" that successful teaching and remediation programs in any language must move the learner toward. All of these questions are fertile ground for future studies aimed at developing brain-based theories of typical or atypical reading that can seamlessly account for both language-invariant and noninvariant characteristics of literacy acquisition and its disorders. Next steps, we suggest, must include the promotion of a new generation of cross-linguistic neurocognitive studies with comparable tasks and measures, with well-matched samples of readers, and when feasible, longitudinal designs that track typical and atypical development at both the brain and behavioral levels of analysis. The strong conclusion that can be taken away from both the symposium lectures and these excellent chapters is that these next steps are not only desirable but also feasible, given the technical and experimental tools now available. In aggregate, these chapters help to form a conceptual and methodological starting point for cross-linguistic gene–brain–behavior research in dyslexia.

REFERENCES

Frost, S.J., Sandak, R., Mencl, W.E., Landi, N., Rueckl, J.G., Katz, L., et al. (2009). Mapping the word reading circuitry in skilled and disabled readers. In K. Pugh & P. McCardle (Eds.), *How children learn to read: Current issues and new directions in the integration of cognition, neurobiology, and genetics of reading and* *dyslexia research and practice* (pp. 3–20). New York: Psychology Press.

Siok, W.T., Niu, Z., Jin, Z., Perfetti, C.A., & Tan, L.H. (2008). A structural-functional basis for dyslexia in the cortex of Chinese readers. *Proceedings of the National Academy of Sciences, USA, 105,* 5561–5566.

Additional Approaches to the Study of Dyslexia Across Languages: Modeling

跨語言閱讀障礙研究的另一種方式：電腦模擬

PART III CONTENTS

CHAPTER 9

Reading in Different Writing Systems

One Architecture, Multiple Solutions

Mark S. Seidenberg

C omputational models can be useful tools for exploring how writing systems influence learning to read, skilled reading, and the neural representation of reading. Although I am invited to conferences such as the (lovely) one that inspired this volume on the basis of my computational modeling work, my real interest is in language—not models—and in reading as a particular realization of language. We usually emphasize the differences between language and reading: one evolved in the species, the other was invented (via writing); one is learned through immersion and exposure, the other through instruction and feedback; one is universal, the other is not; and so forth. Yet despite these differences, the same principles govern most aspects of both. For example, whatever the biological predispositions for spoken language turn out to be (e.g., whether they are specific to language, or language takes advantage of many enabling capacities), children still have to learn the language to which they are exposed. The procedures that underlie this learning are, apparently, the same as those that govern learning to read. Thus, the same computational architectures and learning procedures are being used to explain *statistical learning* in language acquisition and the child's later transition into reading (Saffran, 2009; Seidenberg, 2007). For such reasons, I see more similarities across reading and language than are usually acknowledged. One can study reading qua reading, which is interesting enough, but also because it sheds light on language more broadly.

WHAT ARE COMPUTATIONAL MODELS FOR?

In my view, the main goal of reading research is to develop theories of the essential characteristics of reading and to understand how these characteristics are determined by the other capacities out of which reading arose: language, vision, hearing, learning, memory, perception, reasoning, and so forth. We also want to understand the neural structures and circuits that support reading, and how they develop, under genetic and environmental control. Our models are tools in the service of developing such theories, used in conjunction with tools for gathering and evaluating data. Why such models are useful has been described elsewhere (e.g., Seidenberg & Plaut, 2006). Here, I will mention three ways. First, the models are based on a small number of principles concerning knowledge representation, learning, and processing. We do not fully understand all of the relevant principles, and they are modified as necessary in response to new findings and insights. However, the appeal to these general principles reflects both a strong theoretical claim—that the same general principles underlie most aspects of cognition—and an attempt to avoid the circularity that afflicts much theorizing in psychology and cognitive neuroscience, insofar as the candidate principles are independent of reading rather than developed in response to particular findings or *effects*. In fact, our models were initially developed both because of an interest in reading and because reading happened to provide a domain in which to explore these general principles.

Second, the models provide a unique method for testing hypotheses and establishing closer causal relations. For example, most studies of the bases of dyslexia are correlational: dyslexics exhibit an impairment X (e.g., in phonemic awareness) that is thought to have an impact on aspects Y and Z of reading (e.g., learning spelling–sound correspondences, developing fluency). Often it is hard to tell if the deficit is a cause or effect of poor reading. Models provide strong tests of etiological hypotheses: Does the introduction of the candidate impairment in a model that simulates learning basic reading skills give rise to disordered behavior that corresponds to that which is seen in dyslexic children—or to some other pattern (Harm & Seidenberg, 1999)? Sometimes these simulations corroborate existing views in a new way; sometimes they provide new insights (e.g., about why the effectiveness of a given type of intervention depends on the timing of its introduction; Harm, McCandliss, & Seidenberg, 2003).

Third, although our models were initially developed as frankly cognitive accounts of reading behavior (acquisition and skilled performance; normal and disordered performance), they can also be viewed as providing links between behavior and its brain bases. The latter goal is becoming more realistic, with advances in the understanding of the brain circuits that support reading and the growing use of neural network models and related pattern classifier techniques in the analysis of neuroimaging data. For example, as data about the putative visual word form area (VWFA) accumulate (see Dehaene, Chapter 6 of this volume), the models can be used to address why the VWFA exhibits particular characteristics, why it is organized in the observed way, and other questions, as well as to develop predictions that distinguish between competing theories (e.g., as to whether it is strictly visual and whether it represents *word forms*).

The goal of my own work is to contribute to the development of a theory that identifies fundamental principles which underlie reading, abstracting away from details of individual experiments or models. It is definitely *not* the goal to develop a single enormous model that simulates all aspects of reading. My view contrasts with the "bigger is better" school associated with Coltheart and his students and followers (e.g., Coltheart, Rastle, Perry, & Langdon, 2001; Perry, Ziegler, & Zorzi, 2007), in which the explicit goal is to account for as many behaviors as possible within a single computational model. The principal criterion for evaluating a model, on this view, is how many phenomena it addresses. Problems with this approach are discussed elsewhere (Seidenberg & Plaut, 2006; Seidenberg, Zevin, Sibley, Woollams, & Plaut, submitted). We provide evidence that it leads to models that have the undesirable characteristics that create skepticism, for many, about the value of modeling: components that are introduced in response to the specific data they are intended to explain; model performance that is highly sensitive to the settings of large numbers of parameters whose values have no interpretation; models that are brittle insofar as they recreate the results seen in some studies but not the patterns observed across studies; a level of complexity that makes it difficult to tell not only how the model works but whether it works in the sense of accounting for any phenomena.

An Alternative Approach

According to our alternative approach, which might be called *more is better*, there are many models, not one, each of which draws from the same pool of computational principles, with different models focused on identifying basic properties of components of the reading system (e.g., how different tasks are performed; how different codes are represented; learning; bases of dyslexia). Each model implements only part of the broader theoretical framework, incorporating computational principles thought to be relevant to understanding particular phenomena. Each implementation is necessarily limited in scope and lags behind what we think is really true (because building, testing, and interpreting models is hard; also, sometimes implementing something in a model does not add a great deal to what has been discovered by other means). Each model differs from every other model in detail; experiments with a given model and comparisons across models allow one to determine which aspects of the models are critical to their performance and which are not (because they are mere implementational necessities). Models are similar to experiments in this regard. We do not conduct one giant experiment to understand reading either.

What has emerged from this work is not a model per se, but a theoretical framework (see Figure 9.1). The framework reflects experiences with specific models that were tied to various empirical phenomena in conjunction with the development of the connectionist or parallel distributed processing framework, which provides most of the underlying principles. There is considerable skepticism about the utility of these models, some of which surfaced at the Taiwan meeting on which this volume is based. The models are too powerful and can simulate any pattern of results; the models are too weak because they cannot, in principle, account for important characteristics of behavior (e.g., language). The models never work correctly; even when they do, it is too hard to understand why they produce the behavior they do. The models are unnecessary because we can understand reading by

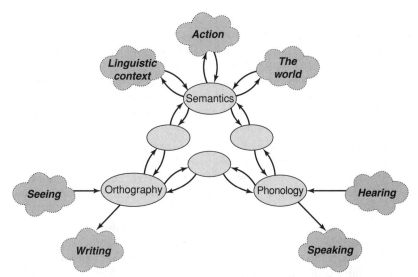

Figure 9.1. General framework for word reading. In contrast to Seidenberg and McClelland's original framework, we now explicitly emphasize the view that the *orthographic, phonological,* and *semantic* representations are themselves learned on the basis of perception, action, interaction with the world, and so on. Thus they too are like hidden unit representations, insofar as their functions are not determined in advanced but rather shaped by their inputs and outputs and participation in different tasks (e.g., reading aloud, comprehending speech).

directly investigating the neural systems that underlie it. Finally, all the models are missing this or that (e.g., serial aspects of processing; impact of explicit instruction).

Addressing these concerns is a topic for another chapter. The short answers are that facts about people (e.g., their perceptual, memory, and learning capacities) and about the world (e.g., the structure of language) impose severe constraints on model behavior. Models tend to fail to learn under conditions that also cause people to fail. Every model is false in detail but can nonetheless contribute to understanding. It is easy to overestimate the difficulty of analyzing model behavior; as with other empirical research, studies of the brain have to be guided by theories in order to know what questions to ask. Brain images do not come with labeled circuits and functions; given the complexity of the system in question (e.g., reading as behavior, brain bases of reading), it takes a computational model to generate hypotheses that overcome the limits of intuition and analogy, and the illusion that understanding can be achieved by just doing enough experiments. Finally, all of the computational models of reading taken together leave most of reading unaddressed. There is a great deal about how words and nonwords are pronounced and much less about how people comprehend phrases, sentences, and texts. It's easy to create a long list of things the models do not incorporate because that would include most of reading. What is the alternative? Theorizing at the level of the box-and-arrow models of the past?[1]

In this chapter, I focus on one area that illustrates how the models can be useful. This focus is relevant to a central theme of the Taiwan conference: reading in different writing systems. I will assume the framework illustrated in Figure 9.1, from which a variety of models can be derived. For this discussion, three properties of this framework are particularly relevant (see Harm & Seidenberg, 1999, 2004, for fuller explanations):

1. *Lexical computations are statistical rather than categorical.* The mappings between different types of information (e.g., spelling, sound, meaning) are better characterized in terms of the statistical relations between them than by other types of knowledge representation, such as rules.

2. *Constraint satisfaction.* The output that a model produces is determined by combining bits of information that are not highly constraining when taken independently. The nonlinear effects of combining disparate sources of information are an important mechanism underlying human intelligence.

3. *Division of labor.* A complex, multicomponent system (e.g., a triangle model of reading; the brain) that is given a task to solve (e.g., computing the meaning of a word from print) does so by converging on an efficient division of labor among its components. In models employing distributed representations (another basic principle) an output pattern (e.g., a meaning) is built out of and subject to constraints from multiple sources: spelling, phonology, context, beliefs and expectations, and so forth. This model contrasts with the either/ or approach inherent in models that emphasize different *routes* to meaning (e.g., visual versus phonological). I sketched how this concept might play out with respect to different writing systems in Seidenberg (1992) and will revisit the issue later in this chapter.

---

[1]Actually, box-and-arrow theorizing is already back. As occurred in Taiwan, concerns about the limitations of computational models are usually raised by researchers who do not employ modeling in their own work, preferring a kind of quasi-computational description of the "logic" of a problem such as word identification or language acquisition. A diagram such as Figure 1 in Dehaene, Cohen, Sigman, and Vinckier (2005) is missing the boxes and arrows but is otherwise similar in character to the famous precomputational neuropsychological models of the 1980s (see, e.g., chapters in Patterson, Marshall, & Coltheart, 1985). The same type of informal argumentation from data to theoretical conclusions that was utilized in the neuropsychological work is seen in the interpretation of contemporary neuroimaging studies (e.g., Glezer, Jiang, & Riesenhuber, 2009). This intuitive approach to data interpretation, widely used in studies of brain-injured patients, was strongly called into question by subsequent computational modeling (e.g., Plaut, 1995; Woollams, Lambon Ralph, Plaut, & Patterson, 2007). Repeatedly, such models have shown that behavior which seems to have an intuitively obvious basis can be explained by other mechanisms familiar from computational modeling. The interpretation of neuroimaging studies is largely still at the box-and-arrow level, raising similar concerns.

WRITING SYSTEMS AND SKILLED READING

Many types of writing systems exist, and people manage to learn and use them every day. The wide variation in how writing systems are organized raises an obvious question: Do people read different types of writing systems in the same way, or differently? This question invites other queries such as: Are some writing systems easier to learn than others? Do they make use of the same neural circuits? Does dyslexia have a universal basis, or does it vary depending on the writing system? All of these questions are the focus of extensive research, with rapid progress being made—even if we have not yet converged on definitive answers.

At the conference, I suggested two "obvious" answers to whether people read different types of writing systems in the same way or differently:

- *Same way.* The brains of the readers of these writing systems are essentially identical; reading involves the same types of capacities (perceptual, learning, conceptual, etc.) regardless of the writing system, and reading is universally the process of deriving meanings from print by using visual, phonological, semantic, and other types of information.

- *Differently.* Writing systems differ in how they are organized; the person/brain responds to these differences, yielding different ways of accomplishing the reading task. Some writing systems are easier to learn than others; dyslexia does not have a universal basis, but rather depends on how anomalies in brain organization relate to the demands of the orthography to which a person is exposed.

Therefore, is the glass half empty or half full? There is an extensive literature in this area, relying mainly on behavioral data and logical analyses of how the reading system must work, given properties of a writing system; there is also a growing body of relevant neuroimaging data. I will review some of this work, identify some questions that seem to be unresolved, and then consider how the issues can be viewed within our computational modeling framework and some new questions that arise.[2]

The Real Significance of My Bar Mitzvah

The first interesting and deservedly influential hypothesis about writing systems and reading was the Orthographic Depth Hypothesis (ODH; Frost, Katz, & Bentin, 1987; Katz & Feldman, 1981). Building on the earlier concept of independent visual versus phonological processing

---

[2]To save space and avoid repetition, the following abbreviations are used: orth, orthography; phon, phonology; sem, semantics. Orth-sem refers to a computation linking orthographic and semantic representations; orth-phon-sem, a computation from orthography to phonology to semantics; and so forth.

systems (Baron & Strawson, 1976; Rubenstein, Lewis, & Rubenstein, 1971), the ODH held that the degree of reliance on each of the pathways would depend on properties of the writing system—specifically, how transparently it encoded phonology. Thus shallower orthographies (the much-studied example was Serbo-Croatian) afford greater reliance on phonological reading, whereas deeper orthographies (Chinese perhaps) rely more on the visual pathway. Baron and Strawson (1976) coined the terms *Chinese* and *Phoenecian* to refer to readers of English who differed in the analogous way (although *Chinese* turns out to be a particularly inapt epithet for *visual reader*, as discussed shortly). English could be seen as requiring a mix of the two, depending on whether a written word had a regular or irregular pronunciation. The ODH was an elegant, original idea—it was an early *division of labor* theory—and it greatly stimulated the science of reading, particularly cross-orthography research. On this view, different writing systems afford different reading mechanisms or strategies.

Two types of findings presented challenges for this account:

1. *Computational evidence.* The ODH was developed at a time when people used rules to characterize spelling–sound regularities. Exceptions to the rules, which seem rife in English, require a second mechanism. Early on, there were two proposals. One proposal assumed a *dual-route* model in which there are visual (orth→sem) and phonological (orth→phon→sem) routes to meaning (Baron & Strawson, 1976; Rubenstein et al., 1971). Exception words could be pronounced by first computing from orth to sem, and then using the sem→phon pathway known from speech production. Other "dual-route" models (Marshall & Newcombe, 1973; Coltheart, Davelaar, Jonasson, & Besner, 1977) split the orth→phon computation into two pathways, a rule-based procedure (for pronouncing nonwords) and a lexical procedure (for pronouncing exceptions such as PINT). The third, orth→sem→phonology procedure was considered relevant only to brain-injured "semantic" readers (e.g., Friedman, 1996).

   For Coltheart et al. (2001), the conclusion that reading aloud in English required two pronunciation mechanisms was "inescapable." However, our first connectionist model (Seidenberg & McClelland, 1989) showed that "rule-governed" and "irregular" words did not demand separate naming mechanisms. Using a single mechanism captured the fact that the pronunciations of irregular words are not arbitrary (PINT is not pronounced "glorph"), but rather overlap with putative regulars (PINT overlaps with PINE, PUNT, and other words). The model could then account for some important additional facts; namely, effects of spelling–sound consistency (Jared, McRae, & Seidenberg, 1990) that remain seriously problematic for traditional dual-route models (see Seidenberg et al., submitted).

   The important implication for the ODH was that the computational mechanisms underlying pronunciation can cope with different degrees of spelling–sound consistency. Therefore, different orthographies might be processed more similarly than the ODH assumed.

2. *Phonology all the way down.* If most words (except perhaps some highly irregular, low-frequency ones) can be pronounced via orth-phon in English as in our models, and a person already knows the spoken language, the orth-phon-sem mechanism might carry more of the burden than usually assumed in comparisons with shallow orthographies. A large body of behavioral evidence eventually showed that people use phonology in reading writing systems that differ greatly with respect to the nature of the mappings between written and spoken forms. Van Orden (1987) showed that people rely heavily on phonology in reading English—an effect that replicates in other writing systems. Xu, Pollatsek, and Potter (1999) showed that phonology is activated in silent word reading in Chinese (see also Zhang & Perfetti, 1993). Phonological properties of words and sentences affect silent reading, as measured by eye fixations (e.g., Pollatsek, Lesch, Morris, & Rayner, 1992; Yates, Friend, & Ploetz, 2008). This body of findings was synthesized by the Ziegler and Goswami (2005) theory, according to which readers use phonological information at whatever grain size their writing system affords: graphemes in alphabetic writing systems, syllables in Japanese kana, phonetics or whole words in Chinese. English makes use of orthographic units that vary in size and complexity: single letters, digraphs, trigraphs, subsyllabic units such as onsets and rimes, idiosyncratic units such as noncontiguous contingencies between letters (the silent *e* rule is an obvious example, but there are other, more subtle statistical regularities hidden there). These facts seem to imply that phonological mediation is pervasive and not highly dependent on writing system.

Are we all Phoenicians then? The role of phonology in skilled reading is established beyond question. What is at issue is whether other mechanisms and types of knowledge contribute as well. The answer is not yet fully known. One problem is that whereas there now are several excellent methods for diagnosing the use of phonology in the computation of meaning from print, there are no corresponding methods for diagnosing the use of orth-sem. The model developed by Harm and myself (Harm & Seidenberg, 2004) instantiated the division-of-labor concept with respect to English: The meaning of a word developed out of input from both arms of the triangle (orth-sem, orth-phon-sem), with context assumed to provide additional input (but not implemented). Evidence that phonology has been activated does not rule out a contribution from orth-sem, but there is no obvious way to assess this possibility using behavioral methods. In the Van Orden (1987) paradigm, false positives are taken as evidence of phonological activation, but correct rejections are not taken as evidence that phonology was deactivated. Rather, they are taken as evidence that participants made the correct answer using a hypothetical spelling check. Thus, unless participants made no false positives at all, the data were taken as implicating phonology regardless of the actual response. This interpretation exemplifies a situation in which neuroimaging may provide more decisive evidence than strictly behavioral studies.

A second problem is that other facts about writing systems, languages, and people seem to militate against a strictly phonological reading strategy. Consider again Serbo-Croatian, the quintessential *shallow* orthography. (The languages are now treated as separate; I will focus on Serbian.) The Serbian alphabet follows the principle that each letter corresponds to one and only one sound. Serbian is an example of what I call Bar Mitzvah languages. Jewish young people participate in a rite of passage called the Bar or Bat Mitzvah, which includes reading aloud a section of the Torah, the holy text. Many 13-year-olds manage this feat even though they do not know the Hebrew language. They can do so because written Hebrew is shallow in pointed form. Thus even mildly observant children can learn to read Hebrew aloud quickly and participate in the ceremony (I am proof of this). There would be many fewer Bar/Bat Mitzvahs if the holy text were written in hieratic glyphs.

Serbian is a fine Bar Mitzvah language insofar as learning the letter–sound correspondences is simple. Then, if one knows the spoken language, it should be easy to compute the meanings of words exclusively via orth-phon-sem. However, I am skeptical. First, correct computation of phonology in Serbian involves more than just grapheme–phoneme correspondences. Suprasegmental information not represented in the writing system is critical to disambiguating words. Thus there are minimal pairs that differ only with respect to stress, such as *zatvori* (first syllable stress, "prisons"; second syllable stress, "to shut," as in "shut the door!"); *proizvodi* (first syllable stress, "products"; second syllable stress, "to produce," as in "it produces nice graphs"). Similarly, *riba* is either "fish" or "to scrub," depending on pitch accent; *luk* is either "onion" or "arch." I do not know of any data about the frequencies of such words, but they are not occasional oddities, according to one native speaker informant. How much these ambiguities in orth-phon would limit reading by this pathway is not clear, but it is a concern. Second, leaving the shallowness of orth-phon conversion aside, what prevents the reader from developing orth-sem? Given enough pairings of spellings with meanings, as occurs every time the reader uses orth-phon-sem, how would a person fail to develop direct orth-sem connections? That is how orth-sem developed in the Harm and Seidenberg (2004) division of labor model of English (discussed later in this chapter). Take-home assignment: Reimplement the Harm and Seidenberg model; train it exactly as before, but treat English as though it were shallow. In Shallow English, *pint* will be pronounced to rhyme with *mint* and so on for the other irregular words. Will the model still develop a division of labor in which both pathways contribute?

My prediction is yes. In the published model, the orth-sem pathway developed for two reasons: 1) to disambiguate homophones such as *pair* and *pare,* and 2) speed: the orth-sem pathway, once trained, operated more rapidly than orth-phon-sem (intuitively, orth-phon-sem is slower because the phonological code has to settle sufficiently to drive the phon-sem mapping). Both considerations would continue to hold in Shallow English. Thus, shallowness is not itself a barrier to the development of orth-sem on this analysis.

What about Hebrew, the actual "Bar Mitzvah language"? I am not prepared to assess the complexity of syllabic stress assignment in Hebrew, except to observe that it has some interesting 5,000-year-old wrinkles. The more important point is that although the vowels are retained for learning purposes, they are deleted in texts for skilled readers. In fact, including the vowels interferes with skilled reading (Bentin & Frost, 1987). Fr smn wh rds nglsh, t's pzzlng hw ppl mng t rd th lngg n ths trnctd, ntrpc frmt. (For someone who reads English, it's puzzling how people manage to read the language in this truncated, entropic format.) Surely the reader relies on context (semantic input) to constrain the meaning of an otherwise ambiguous string of consonants. Ironically, then, even in a writing system that *could* be shallow, the deep form is preferred, suggesting that reading that does not wholly depend on orth-phon-sem can be highly efficient.[3]

In short, simple spelling–sound correspondences are a fine property, but may be either insufficient to support orth-phon-sem or less efficient than other processes (e.g., the full triangle—a system that also incorporates contextual influences).

DIVISION OF LABOR AND ORTHOGRAPHIC DEPTH

At this point, it is still not clear whether the glass is half empty or half full, making this a good time to look again at the models. Assume for the moment that there is a single architecture that supports reading— one that involves computations among orthography, phonology, and semantics, for all writing systems (ignoring context for the moment). If this assumption proves to be wrong, so be it: The goal is discovering what is true, not defending a particular model. Applying this framework to different writing systems requires two additional steps. First, we modify the model's input and output representations to reflect properties of the writing system and spoken language. In a more ambitious model, these representations would themselves be learned, based on relevant sensory (visual, auditory) and motor (writing, speaking)

---

[3]Ram Frost has drawn my attention to the fact that Hebrew was originally unpointed, functioning as a vowel-less writing system for about 2,000 years. Vowels were introduced to maintain standard pronunciations of the holy text, the Torah, during the Jewish diaspora.

information. However, a reasonable first step is to create plausible orthographic and phonological representations that reflect properties specific to a writing system or language (e.g., representations of characters in Chinese versus letters in alphabets). The second step is to find roughly comparable training corpora for the different writing systems and languages. Such corpora are now available for many languages. Doing the job right also requires reasonable estimates of the relative frequencies of words.

Now train two models—say, Chinese and English (because the writing systems are interestingly different)—to compute pronunciations and/or meanings from orthographic input. (We can approximate meaning using featural semantic representations employed in previous research—see, for example, Harm & Seidenberg, 2004—even if they do not fully capture everything about conceptual knowledge. We are not yet looking at cross-linguistic differences in meaning, so the representations will be adequate if they capture some basic facts about semantic similarity and dissimilarity.) The question "Do people read English and Chinese in the same way or differently?" can now be cast as "Do these models solve the tasks we give them in the same way or differently?" Division of labor is not stipulated in advance. The models converge on efficient ways to perform tasks (e.g., computing pronunciations or meanings), given the architecture, training corpus, and learning procedure.

These modeling experiments have begun to be conducted, and some important results are in. In English, people compute pronunciations of words mainly relying on the orth-phon component of the triangle, because the writing system is alphabetic and the codes are correlated (if imperfectly). Input from the orth-sem-phon part of the triangle is mainly needed for lower-frequency, irregularly pronounced words, as seen in both behavioral (Strain, Patterson, & Seidenberg, 1995) and neuroimaging (Frost et al., 2005; Graves, Desai, Humphries, Seidenberg & Binder, 2010) studies. These effects may be modulated by reading skill and perhaps by individual difference factors that strengthen or weaken the contributions from different components. It is also possible to bias reliance on one or the other part of the system through manipulations of stimuli, instructions, and other aspects of an experimental design. The story is similar with respect to the computation of meaning: initially, the system depends mainly on the orth-phon-sem pathway, given that phon→sem is already known for many words from speech, and orth-phon are correlated (Van Orden, Pennington, & Stone, 1990). With additional practice, the more arbitrary orth-sem part of the network begins to come online. At high levels of performance, the computation of meaning relies on input from both parts of the triangle, with the balance between them depending on factors such as type of word (homophone, irregular spelling or pronunciation, frequency). Again, there may be individual difference variables, poorly understood, that create somewhat different divisions of labor for different readers.[4]

The corresponding Chinese models have been developed by Yang, McCandliss, Shu, and Zevin (2008, 2009).[5] These researchers met the challenge of developing an orthographic representation for Chinese, which must include strokes and the spatial relations among components in complex characters. Similarly, their phonological representation is similar to English but also includes tone. Compared with English, there are similarities and differences in the resulting division of labor. In computing pronunciations, the Chinese model picks up on the statistical properties of the mapping in the same way as in English. The systematicity of these correspondences is often underestimated by Western observers. With regard to meaning, Yang et al.'s model (which simulated semantic input using the approach developed by Plaut, McClelland, Seidenberg, & Patterson, 1996) converged on a division of labor that relied more heavily on the orth-sem leg of the triangle and less on the orth-phon-sem leg than in English. Still, the results suggested that both components are implicated in reading most words.

Chinese is particularly interesting when viewed in terms of the division of labor and constraint satisfaction concepts. The most common type of character contains two components: a phonetic (clue to sound) and a radical (clue to meaning; Shu, Chen, Anderson, Wu, & Xuan, 2003). Such characters instantiate the concept of orth-sem and orth-phon-sem processing—both of the pathways are present *in the writing itself*. Moreover, these complex characters richly illustrate the concept of constraint satisfaction. At first these characters seem to present a computational problem: One needs to know the meaning of the whole (character) in order to understand the identities and functions of the parts (radical, phonetic) and vice versa. These component elements are typically ambiguous: 户 is a phonetic in 驴 (donkey) but a radical in 房 (house). Each component provides only partial information about sound or

---

[4]Like every other model, Harm and Seidenberg's (2004) model implemented only part of the lexical system. One simplification was that we did not implement the feedback connections that are envisioned in the full-triangle system, which are also a prominent feature of neural systems. Harm and Seidenberg (1999) emphasized how orthographic knowledge shapes phonological representations, but in a system that implemented feedback loops from phon to orth, the converse would occur: *Orthography* would be shaped by phonological knowledge. Thus the representations we labeled *orthography* are more like hidden units shaped by relations between different codes, yielding a more abstract, mixed code rather than a strictly orthographic one. This does not change the basic division of labor account: The mapping to semantics from this code is still more arbitrary than the mapping to phonology. However, it does predict that representations in the putative visual word form area should be shaped by phonological and possibly other influences, rather than be strictly orthographic.

[5]Perfetti, Liu, and Tan (2005) also developed a model of reading in Chinese. It has a different character, so to speak, insofar as it is not a learning model and cannot develop division of labor. However, such models are useful for illustrating an existing idea or hypothesis.

meaning, respectively; however, the conjunction of the two is highly constraining, allowing the character's meaning to be computed. This is the classic kind of problem that interactive models (e.g., McClelland & Rumelhart, 1981) solve beautifully.

The same type of constraint satisfaction process also applies at a different level of structure: the combination of morphemes to form complex words in Chinese (McBride-Chang & Liu, Chapter 2 of this volume). As McBride-Chang and Liu note, many Chinese words are similar to compound words in English, insofar as they consist of two (or more) morphemes, each of which is itself a word. The morphemes are related to the meaning of the whole, but in different ways and degrees. For example, 鸣 (chirp) = 口 (mouth) + 鸟 (bird) is seemingly transparent, but even here the meanings of the components underdetermine the meaning of the whole. In 问 (ask) = 門 (door) + 口 (mouth), the relations between parts and the whole are even more abstract. Post hoc, it is easy to imagine how 明 (bright) is related to 日 (sun) + 月 (moon), but the meaning could as well have been *celestial body* or *bowl of milk* (Henkes, 2004). English has *boathouse,* a structure where boats are stored, and *lighthouse,* a structure with a big light, but also *ranch house,* which is a type of dwelling (as were some lighthouses). Thus, both the Chinese and English examples vary in how the meanings of the parts (morphemes) relate to the meaning of the whole (word). The same kind of constraint satisfaction process, operating over different types of units, occurs at different structural levels (combining phonetic and radical elements to form complex characters, combining morphemes to form complex words).

The similarities between Chinese and English may extend well beyond the ones that McBride-Chang and Liu discuss in Chapter 2 of this volume. They emphasize the fact that there are more compounds in Chinese than in English, which is true. However, English is full of noun phrases (or nounphrases) with the same modifier–head construction as English compounds, and there is no strong distinction between them (Seidenberg & Gonnerman, 2000). *Boathouse* is, conventionally, a compound word, but does it differ in any way except typographically from *ranch house?* The ability to manage the varying relations between morphemes is relevant to many other kinds of words in English as well. For example, the language has suffixes such as *-er* that attach to nouns. The meaning of the suffixed word is not a simple combinatorial function of the meanings of the parts. A *baker* bakes and a *runner* runs, but a *locker* is a metal compartment, not a person who locks; a *hanger* is used to hang clothing on (unless you are a wallpaper hanger); and—in the right context—*bangers* are food. In each case, the reader must provide additional information about the relations between the morphemes. Better readers are better at doing this (e.g., Singson, Mahony, & Mann, 2000).

Given such findings, what about our glass? perhaps the question isn't whether the glass is half empty or half full, but rather what is in the water. There is one glass, and we all need the same amount to drink. The glass can contain only certain liquids, but the proportions of the liquids vary. That is, there is a single architecture that develops via the same learning procedures, solving the same tasks, under the same pressures (efficiency, accuracy), but converges on different solutions (divisions of labor among the components). These models are clearly first steps, and the account of what happens in various writing systems will undoubtedly change as a broader range of phenomena are addressed.[6] We know that existing models will not turn out to be correct in all details. This is unimportant. The goal is not defending a particular model; we known in advance that every model is false at some level. The more important point is that the models provide a productive, openended framework for investigating the issues. The theory that there is one common architecture (at both cognitive and neural levels) could be wrong; see, for example, the Perfetti, Liu, and Tan (2005) evidence that Chinese involves brain regions not seen in reading English. Say that the spatial relations among the written components are more relevant in Chinese than in English, and that there are brain circuits that are particularly well-suited to encoding these relations. The modeling framework might explain why spatial relations are more important in one case than the other (because, e.g., given the properties of written Chinese, encoding the spatial information creates a more efficient solution to the problem of computing meanings from print). Better understanding of the brain might also explain why a particular region or circuit picks up on this information and how it is combined with other constraints. The conjunction of facts about brain organization and behavior might then explain why a writing system with this structure could exist and be functional, whereas others could not. All this seems promising and very normal science to me.

In summary, the one architecture–multiple solutions theory is, at a minimum, a useful way to frame hypotheses about effects of writing systems on skilled reading. The point is not to ask if the glass is half empty versus half full, but rather how division of labor varies and why.[7]

---

[6]Our models emphasize gradual, implicit, statistical learning, which accounts for a great deal. However, humans learn in other ways as well—in particular through explicit instruction. Writing systems may differ with respect to the amount of explicit instruction they require in order to be learned within a given amount of time (Hutzler, Ziegler, Perry, Wimmer, & Zorzi, 2004); the same may be true of the spoken languages they represent. It would certainly be a useful goal for future models to integrate these different types of experiences. However, this integration would require a better understanding of how explicit and implicit knowledge are integrated, behaviorally and neurally.

[7]Consistent with this analysis, Bolger, Perfetti, and Schneider (2005) concluded from a meta-analysis of neuroimaging studies that reading involves core neural circuitry with some orthography-specific variation. Division of labor concerns a further question: how the contributions of different parts of this system vary as a function of reader skill, writing system, reading strategies, and other factors.

WRITING SYSTEMS AND READING ACQUISITION

To this point, I have focused on skilled reading, but how do differences between writing systems affect learning to read? The general consensus seems to be that shallower orthographies are easier to learn than deeper ones. The logic seems obvious: The child's problem is to learn how to map written symbols onto phonological forms known from speech. This task is easier if units in the written language reliably correspond to units in the spoken language. I'm not prepared to evaluate the relative difficulty of learning to read all the world's many writing systems. I would note that something seems to be going on in Chinese, given two modern developments apparently intended to make the language easier to learn to read: the simplification of characters in China and the introduction of secondary alphabetic scripts in China (pinyin) and Taiwan (zhuyin). Keyboarding demands are also creating much greater reliance on the secondary alphabetic scripts. Japanese children learn kana quickly and easily, but there are the joyo kanji to conquer. All this manages to work out, but there could be differences in the trajectories toward becoming a skilled reader.

Instead, I will examine a narrower question: Are there differences in ease of acquisition among alphabetic writing systems, in particular, as a function of orthographic depth? Again, my reading of the literature is that most people think the issue is settled, based on converging evidence from studies of many languages. Again however, it may be that a different picture emerges if we consider a broader range of considerations.

The evidence is clear that it is easier to learn to pronounce words and nonwords in shallow alphabetic orthographies. For reviews, see Share (2008) and several chapters in Snowling and Hulme (2005) and in Joshi and Aaron (2006). My concern is that there is a tendency to conflate *reading* with *reading aloud*. Reading aloud is a task that many researchers (including me) have used as a way of gaining data about some parts of the reading system. The task isn't otherwise very interesting: people's goal in reading words is computing meanings, not pronunciations; reading aloud is highly relevant to learning to read, but mostly irrelevant to adult life unless you have young children, you like to read poetry (which should always be read aloud), or your job requirements include reading speeches from a teleprompter. The task has been useful, but let's not pretend that it is "reading," which is mainly the task of comprehending written language. In the rest of this chapter, I reserve the term *reading* for comprehending words or texts.

Most of the studies to have examined learning to read from a comparative rather than Anglocentric perspective have focused on decoding (assessed by reading aloud; see the references cited previously). All of these studies show advantages for shallower orthographies over English with respect to pronunciation accuracy, in individuals of varying ages. But reading involves other skills—in particular, knowledge of the spoken language represented by the written code. Thus we should ask, Are children who are better decoders also better readers? This question requires data from other tasks. For example, does earlier decoding skill entail earlier comprehension skill? Do the children who are early good decoders also understand what they read? Does their decoding skill promote better understanding of the grammar of the language such that they comprehend a broader range of sentence structures? Do they also comprehend texts at a younger age? If reading only involved pronunciation, we would conclude from existing research that it is easier to learn to read in some writing systems than others. One could also imagine that, other factors aside, ease in acquiring decoding skills leads to better reading. Reading is not just pronunciation, and learners cannot just put other factors aside.

To my knowledge, the cross-orthography studies on this topic have all investigated word and/or nonword naming and have varied with respect to which other tasks were included. With younger children, there usually are measures of phonological awareness and vocabulary; studies with older children or adults may include an assessment of story or expository text comprehension. In some studies, the identification of reading with reading aloud is complete. For example, Ellis and Hooper (2001) compared three writing systems—English, Welsh, and Albanian—which range from deep to shallow to extremely shallow. The main result is given in the title, "Learning to Read Words in Albanian: A Skill Easily Acquired." The main finding was that "the rate of reading acquisition is faster the shallower the orthography" (2001, p. 163). However, the tasks were reading words and nonwords aloud. Comprehension was not assessed. Were the children reading or barking at print or some of both? In Spencer and Hanley's (2003) study of learning to read in Welsh and English, the primary data concerned differences in *word recognition*. The *word recognition* task was reading aloud; comprehension was not tested. In a follow-up study, Hanley, Masterson, Spencer, and Evan's (2004) title asked, "How Long Do the Advantages of Learning to Read a Transparent Orthography Last?" where the advantages in question are, again, in reading aloud. The study yielded a fascinating pattern of results. In the earlier study of 5-year-olds, children learning to read Welsh outperformed those learning English in reading aloud. The later study examined 10-year-olds. Not surprisingly, much of the decoding gap was eliminated by 10 years of age, although the poorest English readers were worse than the poorest Welsh readers, and the English readers as a group continued to show difficulty with some lower frequency, irregularly pronounced words. The most striking result, however, was that English children performed significantly better on a test of story comprehension. As the authors noted, "This result suggests that a transparent orthography does not confer any advantages as far as reading comprehension is concerned. As comprehension is clearly the goal of reading, this finding is potentially reassuring for teachers of English" (p. 1408). It is also reassuring for theories in which ability to pronounce words is not the only determinant of reading skill.

The Hanley et al. comprehension result is not without precedent. Consider Ellis and Hooper (2001), a careful study of children learning to read in English and in Welsh. The contrast (here as in other studies of these languages) seems nearly ideal, insofar as the writing systems differ in depth, but other potentially confounding cultural and socioeconomic factors are largely moot (the major remaining factor is that whereas English learners are monolingual, the Welsh learners have considerable knowledge of English). The stimuli were carefully developed to allow direct comparisons between the reader groups. The main finding was that the Welsh readers performed substantially better than the English readers on tests of word and nonword pronunciation. Again, however, the English children performed better on a test of comprehension. More interesting still, English children comprehend words that they do not pronounce correctly. This last finding strongly argues against equating pronunciation accuracy with level of understanding.

The most recent study of this type is Ziegler et al. (2010), which again compared reading aloud in English with shallow orthographies, replicating the pattern established in the earlier studies. Although the researchers provided interesting data about participants' performance on several other tasks, comprehension was not assessed.

Some studies in languages other than English have examined relations between reading aloud and comprehension in greater detail. I would single out Durgunoğlu's studies of Turkish, which provide a wealth of data. After reviewing studies of word and nonword naming in Turkish, Durgunoğlu noted, "Phonological awareness and decoding develop rapidly in both young and adult readers of Turkish because of the transparent orthography and the special characteristics of phonology and morphology. However, reading comprehension is still a problem" (2006, p. 226). She then goes on to discuss some of the challenges presented by the spoken language, which has agglutinative morphology (a system in which words can include many affixes) and vowel harmony, and consistent findings that comprehension lags substantially behind word pronunciation.

In summary, whereas it is well established that spelling–sound correspondences are learned more easily in shallow orthographies, the consequences for developing the ability to read with comprehension are by no means clear. Here is a purely speculative conjecture: Most of the studies establishing the importance of decoding in learning to read examined English. The evidence that mastery of spelling–sound correspondences is critical in learning to read English is unassailable (see, for example, the review of the National Reading Panel, 2002). Moreover, there are large individual differences in how difficult children find this initial step in English, and how they are taught has a major impact on success. Perhaps it is the case that in the shallow orthographies, mastery of spelling–sound knowledge is less predictive of the development of true reading skill and associated with smaller individual differences because the task is easier. After all, even dyslexics can learn to pronounce nonwords in shallow orthographies, accurately, if slowly (Mann & Wimmer, 2002). If this is correct, proficiency in reading aloud is not an appropriate metric for assessing ease of learning to read across writing systems.

THE GRAPHOLINGUISTIC EQUILIBRIUM HYPOTHESIS

In 1990, Hoover and Gough proposed a *Simple View of Reading* whereby comprehension is determined by decoding skills and spoken language comprehension. With the hindsight provided by subsequent research, it is easy to fault the theory in detail; for example, whereas Hoover and Gough emphasized the dependence of reading on spoken language, we now known that learning to read affects knowledge of spoken language in ways ranging from effects of alphabetic knowledge on the development of phonemic representations to the acquisition of vocabulary and knowledge of sentence structures that rarely occur in speech. Moreover, some properties of texts relevant to reading are not fully replicated in speech (e.g., writing styles, punctuation). Still, their essential insight was correct: A person's comprehension depends a great deal, if not exclusively, on knowledge of spoken language, modulo level of decoding skill (Braze, Tabor, Shankweiler, & Mencl, 2007). It is worth considering how this relation might play out across languages and orthographies.

For several years now, I've been tracking a tantalizing observation: Certain types of writing systems are used with certain types of languages. In particular, shallow orthographies are associated with languages with complex inflectional morphology (e.g., Serbo-Croatian, Finnish, German, Russian, Italian, Turkish), whereas the deeper orthographies are associated with relatively simple morphology (e.g., Chinese, English). I do not know of any systematic study of the relations between language typology and writing systems. I have probed for counterexamples to this generalization in many talks and have failed to uncover a convincing one. (French is the most frequently cited counterexample, insofar as the spelling–sound mappings are highly consistent and the inflectional morphology less complicated than in many European languages. However, the relevant metric is simplicity compared with English, which has minimal inflectional morphology, and Chinese, which has none. Also, it is the sound–spelling correspondences that are *très compliqué* in French.)

Perhaps the better way to state the generalization is that *if* a language has complex inflectional morphology, then it will have a shallow orthography. This correlation might be expected under an extension of the Simple View of Reading: Reading comprehension is a constant that is maintained via trade-offs between orthographic complexity (depth) and spoken language complexity (mainly realized in morphology, though other properties of languages probably also matter). For example, as the decoding difficulty term gets small (shallow orthography), the spoken language term gets large. I call this the Grapholinguistic Equilibrium Hypothesis. In exchange for getting spelling–sound correspondences for free, you, the reader, will also receive, at no extra charge, inflectional morphology that encodes number (2 levels), gender (3), and case (7). That would be Serbian. In English, you will have to suffer with irregularly pronounced words, but they will be mainly a) high-frequency words and b) shorter than you are used to because c) the inflectional system is trivial (mainly, number on nouns and tense on verbs, although Huddleston & Pullum, 2002, include a couple of other minor types). According to the Grapholinguistic Equilibrium Hypothesis, language typology and orthographic typology are linked with respect to reading comprehension. In essence, spoken languages get the writing systems they deserve.

Because spoken languages develop in advance of their written forms, how would this dependence between writing and speech come about? Clearly, flexibility is on the writing-system side. Consider again Serbo-Croatian, our quintessential shallow orthography. Serbo-Croatian has a complex inflectional system, no doubt. The system is so complex that it is difficult to merely state as a set of rules. Traditional grammars on this topic (e.g., Mirković & Vukadinović, 1991) run to hundreds of pages. There are often several-way contingencies that determine the overt form of a word, making it difficult to describe the system by using rules. For example, a representative rule is: the vocative singular form of singular nouns will have the suffix -e unless the stem ends in /ʃ/, /ʒ/, /tʃ/, /tɕ/, /dʒ/, /dʑ/, /j/, /λ/, or /ɲ/ when it will have -u; some of these nouns will also have variants ending in -e, as will some nouns with stems ending in /ar/ or /ir/.

We have developed connectionist models that learn parts of this system, treating it as statistical rather than rule-governed (Mirković, MacDonald, & Seidenberg, 2004; Mirković, Seidenberg, & Joanisse, in press). What we learned was that the inflections were not the only or even the principal source of learning difficulty; rather, it was deformations of the stem (base) morpheme conditioned on phonological properties of the inflection that were beastly. Consider the examples in Table 9.1: words that are morphologically related to the base form *savetnik* (masculine, *advisor*). The /k/ in the base form is either realized as a /k/ (in the genitive singular *savetnika* and the accusative plural *savetnike*), as /ts/ (nominative plural, *savetnici*), or as /tʃ/ (vocative singular, *savetniče*). In addition, the inflection -e is either preceded by /k/ (*savetnike*) or /tʃ/ (*savetniče*). Thus, it is not sufficient to merely learn the inflections associated with a given word in given gender, case, and number; the inflections and the base morphemes to which they attach are contingent on each other. Here is a clue as to why Serbian could not tolerate a deeper writing system: Imagine writing the language with the letters for vowels functioning as they do in English, each corresponding to several phonemes (e.g., *pop, pope, pond, port*). Or toss in a few random consonants with two pronunciations, such as the English *c* (as in *cap* or *cent*) and *g* (*goat, gin*). The complexity created by the inflectional system, including deformations of the stem morpheme, is high; adding ambiguity in the pronunciations of the written letters, might well create a writing

Table 9.1. Interdependence of morphological stem and inflection in Serbian

Word	Case and number	Inflection
SAVETNIK	Nominative singular	Zero inflected
SAVETNICI	Nominative plural	-I
SAVETNIKA	Genitive singular	-A
SAVETNIČE	Vocative singular	-E
SAVETNIKE	Accusative plural	-E

Note: All forms are masculine gender. K, = /k/ as in "Kevin," č = /tʃ/ as in "church," C = /ts/ as in "pizza."

system that is unreadable. There would be further problems if the full development of one's knowledge of the morphological system depended on instruction that itself involves reading.

These observations are speculative but seem to be worth pursuing further. What they suggest is that how reading occurs in different writing systems does not just depend on properties of the writing system; it also depends on properties of the language that the writing system represents, and the two appear to be closely interdependent. The hypothesis is that writing systems have to be adapted to the spoken language under functional constraints such as ease of learning and processing. Similarly, progress in learning to read depends in part on spoken language acquisition. Written Finnish is shallow, but Finnish children do not start formal education until they are age 6 or 7. Perhaps they need the extra time to work on their morphology.[8]

CONCLUSION

Our models provide a useful way to explore similarities and differences in how writing systems are read. The important concept concerns division of labor in a system that maps between different codes. The solution is driven by the need to compute meanings quickly and accurately and is modulated by properties of a writing system and the language it represents. Different balances between components of the reading model (including context) therefore result.

Most of the comparative research on reading that has been conducted to date has focused on one component of reading—orthography–phonology conversion—which underlies reading aloud. English is definitely deeper than other alphabetic writing systems, making reading aloud more difficult for young readers. I have cautioned against equating *reading aloud* with *reading*, and suggested that researchers begin looking beyond pronunciation to comprehension, which also reflects knowledge of a spoken language. Just as there are differences

---

[8]I say this in jest. Onset of formal schooling could well be determined by cultural rather than linguistic factors. It would be nice if whatever they are doing in Finland (which scores very high on Organization for Economic Cooperation and Development (OECD) cross-national comparisons of reading) could be exported to the United States, but per my analysis, it cannot because the writing systems and languages are so different.

across writing systems with respect to depth, there are differences across spoken languages with respect to the depth of components such as inflectional morphology. Conclusions about ease of learning to read, as opposed to ease of reading aloud, will depend on taking these spoken language differences into account.

ACKNOWLEDGMENTS

I am very grateful to Aydin Durgunoğlu, Marketa Caravolas, Maryellen MacDonald, Leonard Katz, Ram Frost, Cammie McBride, and Jason Zevin for comments and discussion, and especially to Tianlin Wang, Yaling Hsaio, and Jelena Mirković for sharing their knowledge of Chinese and Serbian. It should not be assumed that they necessarily endorse all of the content, however, and all errors that remain are my own.

REFERENCES

Baron, J., & Strawson, C. (1976). Use of orthographic and word-specific knowledge in reading words aloud. *Journal of Experimental Psychology: Human Perception and Performance, 4,* 207–214.

Bentin S., & Frost, R. (1987). Processing lexical ambiguity and visual word recognition in a deep orthography. *Memory and Cognition, 15*(1), 13–23.

Bolger, D., Perfetti, C., & Schneider, W. (2005). Cross-cultural effect on the brain revisited: Universal structures plus writing system variation. *Human Brain Mapping, 25,* 92–104.

Braze, D., Tabor, W., Shankweiler, D., & Mencl, E. (2007). Speaking up for vocabulary: Reading skill differences in young adults. *Journal of Learning Disabilities, 40,* 226–243.

Coltheart, M., Davelaar, E., Jonasson, J., & Besner, D. (1977). Access to the internal lexicon. In S. Dornic (Ed.), *Attention and Performance VI* (pp. 535–555). Hillsdale, NJ: Lawrence Erlbaum Associates.

Coltheart, M., Rastle, K., & Perry, C., & Langdon, R. (2001). DRC: A dual-route cascaded model of visual word recognition and reading aloud. *Psychological Review, 108,* 204–256.

Dehaene, S., Cohen, L., Sigman, M., & Vinckier, F. (2005). The neural code for written words: A proposal. *Trends in Cognitive Sciences, 9,* 335–341.

Durgunoğlu, A.Y. (2006). How the language's characteristics influence Turkish literacy development. In M. Joshi & P.G. Aaron (Eds.), *Handbook of orthography and literacy* (pp. 219–230). Mahwah, NJ: Lawrence Erlbaum Associates.

Ellis, N., & Hooper, M. (2001). Why learning to read is easier in Welsh than in English: Orthographic transparency effects evinced with frequency-matched tests. *Applied Psycholinguistics, 22,* 571–599.

Friedman, R. B. (1996). Recovery from deep alexia to phonological alexia. *Brain and Language, 52,* 114–128.

Frost, R., Katz, L., & Bentin, S. (1987). Strategies for visual word recognition and orthographical depth: A multilingual comparison. *Journal of Experimental Psychology: Human Perception and Performance, 13,* 104–115.

Frost, S., Mencl, W., Sandak, R., Moore, D., Rueckl, J., Katz, L., et al. (2005). A functional magnetic resonance study of the tradeoff between semantics and phonology in reading aloud. *Neuroreport, 16,* 621–626.

Glezer, L.S., Jiang, X., & Riesenhuber, M. (2009). Evidence for highly selective neuronal tuning to whole words in the "visual word form area." *Neuron, 62,* 199–204.

Graves, W.W., Desai, R., Humphries, C., Seidenberg, M.S., & Binder, J.R. (2010). Neural systems for reading aloud: A multiparametric approach. *Cerebral Cortex, 20,* 1799–1815.

Hanley, J.R., Masterson, J., Spencer, L., & Evans, D. (2004). How long do the advantages of learning to read a transparent orthography last? An investigation of the reading skills and reading impairment of Welsh children at 10 years of age. *Quarterly Journal of Experimental Psychology, 57,* 1393–1410.

Harm, M., McCandliss, B., & Seidenberg, M.S. (2003). Modeling the successes and failures of interventions for disabled readers. *Journal of the Society for the Scientific Study of Reading, 7,* 155–182.

Harm, M., & Seidenberg, M.S. (1999). Reading acquisition, phonology, and dyslexia: Insights from a connectionist model. *Psychological Review, 106,* 491–528.

Harm, M., & Seidenberg, M.S. (2004). Computing the meanings of words in reading: Division of labor between visual and phonological processes. *Psychological Review, 111,* 662–720.

Henkes, K. (2004). *Kitten's first full moon.* New York: Greenwillow Publishers.

Hoover, W.A., and Gough, P.B. (1990). The simple view of reading. *Reading and Writing, 2,* 127–160.

Huddleston, R., & Pullum, G. (2002). *The Cambridge grammar of the English language.* Cambridge, England Cambridge University Press.

Hutzler, F., Ziegler, J.C., Perry, C., Wimmer, H., & Zorzi, M. (2004). Do current connectionist learning models account for reading development in different languages? *Cognition, 91,* 273–296.

Jared, D., McRae, K., & Seidenberg, M. (1990). The basis of consistency effects in word naming. *Journal of Memory and Language, 29,* 687–715.

Joshi, M., & Aaron, P.G. (Eds.). (2006). *Handbook of orthography and literacy.* Mahwah, NJ: Lawrence Erlbaum Associates.

Katz, L., & Feldman, L.B. (1981). Linguistic coding in word recognition: Comparisons between a deep and a shallow orthography. In A. Lesgold & C. Perfetti, *Interactive processes in reading* (pp. 85–99). Hillsdale, NJ: Lawrence Erlbaum Associates.

Mann, V., & Wimmer, H. (2002). Phoneme awareness and pathways into literacy: A comparison of German and American children. *Reading & Writing, 15,* 653–682.

Marshall, J., & Newcombe, F. (1973). Patterns of paralexia: A psycholinguistic approach. *Journal of Psycholinguistic Research, 2,* 175–199.

McClelland, J.L., & Rumelhart, D.E. (1981). An interactive activation model of context effects in letter perception: Part 1. *Psychological Review, 88,* 375–407.

Mrazović, J., MacDonald, M.C., & Seidenberg, M.S. (2004). Where does gender come from? Evidence from a complex inflectional system. *Language and Cognitive Processes, 20,* 139–168.

Mrazović, J., Seidenberg, M.S., & Joanisse, M.F. (in press). Probabilistic nature of inflectional structure: Insights from a highly inflected language. *Cognitive Science.*

Mrazović, P., & Vukadinović, Z. (1991). *Serbo-Croatian grammar for foreigners.* Sremski Karlovci: Izdavačka knjižarnica Zorana Stojanović.

National Reading Panel. (2002). *Report.* Retrieved December 28, 2010, from http://www.nationalreadingpanel.org

Patterson, K.E., Marshall, J.C., & Coltheart, M. (Eds.). (1985). *Surface dyslexia: Neuropsychological and cognitive studies of phonological reading.* London: Lawrence Erlbaum Associates.

Perfetti, C.A., Liu, Y., & Tan, L.H. (2005). The lexical constituency model: Some implications of research on Chinese for general theories of reading. *Psychological Review, 112,* 43–59.

Perry, C., Ziegler, J.C, & Zorzi, M. (2007). Nested incremental modeling in the development of computational theories: The CDP+ model of reading aloud. *Psychological Review, 114,* 273–315.

Plaut, D.C. (1995). Double dissociation without modularity: Evidence from connectionist neuropsychology. *Journal of Clinical and Experimental Neuropsychology, 17,* 291–321.

Plaut, D.C., McClelland, J.L., Seidenberg, M.S., & Patterson, K.E. (1996). Understanding normal and impaired word reading: Computational principles in quasiregular domains. *Psychological Review, 103,* 56–115.

Pollatsek, A., Lesch, M., Morris, R., & Rayner, K. (1992). Phonological codes are used in integrating information across saccades in word identification and reading. *Journal of Experimental Psychology: Human Perception and Performance, 18,* 148–162.

Rubenstein, H., Lewis, H., & Rubenstein, M.A. (1971). Evidence for phonemic recoding in visual word recognition. *Journal of Verbal Learning and Verbal Behavior, 10,* 645–657.

Saffran, J.R. (2009). Learning is not a four-letter word: Changing views of infant language acquisition. In M. Gunnar and D. Cicchetti (Eds.),

Minnesota Symposia on Child Psychology: Meeting the Challenges of Translational Research in Child Psychology (pp. 159–187). New York: Wiley.

Seidenberg, M.S. (1992). Beyond orthographic depth: Equitable division of labor. In R. Frost & L. Katz (Eds.), *Orthography, phonology, morphology, and meaning* (pp. 85–118). Amsterdam: Springer-Verlag.

Seidenberg, M.S. (2007). Connectionist models of word reading. In G. Gaskell (Ed.), *Oxford handbook of psycholinguistics* (pp. 235–250). New York: Oxford University Press.

Seidenberg, M.S., & Gonnerman, L.M. (2000). Explaining derivational morphology as the convergence of codes. *Trends in Cognitive Sciences, 4,* 353–361.

Seidenberg, M.S., & McClelland, J.L. (1989). A distributed, developmental model of visual word recognition and naming. *Psychological Review, 96,* 523–568.

Seidenberg, M.S., & Plaut, D.C. (2006). Progress in understanding word reading: Data fitting vs. theory building. In S. Andrews (Ed.), *From ink marks to ideas: Current issues in lexical processing.* Hove, UK: Psychology Press.

Seidenberg, M.S., Zevin, J.D., Sibley, D., Woollams, A., & Plaut, D.C. (submitted). What are computational models of reading for? A comparison of dual-route and parallel distributed processing approaches.

Share, D. (2008). On the Anglocentricities of current reading research and practice: The perils of overreliance on an "outlier" orthography. *Psychological Bulletin, 134,* 584–615.

Shu, H., Chen, X., Anderson, R.C., Wu, N., & Xuan, Y. (2003). Properties of school Chinese: Implications for learning to read. *Child Development, 74*(1), 27–47.

Singson, M., Mahony, D., & Mann, V. (2000). The relation between reading ability and morphological skills. *Reading and Writing, 12,* 219–252.

Snowling, M., & Hulme, C. (2005). *The science of reading.* Oxford, England: Blackwell.

Spencer, L.H., & Hanley, J.R. (2003). Effects of orthographic transparency on reading and phoneme awareness in children learning to reading in Wales. *British Journal of Psychology, 94,* 1–28.

Strain, E., Patterson, K.E., & Seidenberg, M.S. (1995). Semantic effects on word naming. *Journal of Experimental Psychology: Learning, Memory, and Cognition, 21,* 1140–1152.

Van Orden, G.C. (1987). A ROWS is a ROSE: Spelling, sound, and reading. *Memory and Cognition, 15,* 181–198.

Van Orden, G.C., Pennington, B.F., & Stone, G.O. (1990). Word identification in reading and the promise of a subsymbolic psycholinguistics. *Psychological Review, 97,* 488–522.

Woollams, A., Lambon Ralph, M.A., Plaut, D.C., & Patterson, K. (2007). SD-squared: On the association between semantic dementia and surface dyslexia. *Psychological Review, 114,* 316–339.

Xu, Y., Pollatsek, A., & Potter, M.C. (1999). The activation of phonology during silent Chinese word reading. *Journal of Experimental Psychology: Learning, Memory, and Cognition, 25,* 838–857.

Yang, J.F., McCandliss, B.D., Shu, H., & Zevin, J.D. (2008). Division of labor between semantics and phonology in normal and disordered reading development across languages. *Proceedings of the 13th Annual Conference of the Cognitive Science Society.* Mahwah, NJ: Lawrence Erlbaum Associates.

Yang, J.F., McCandliss, B.D., Shu, H., & Zevin, J.D. (2009). Simulating language-specific and language-general effects in a statistical learning model of Chinese reading. *Journal of Memory and Language, 61,* 238–257.

Yates, M., Friend, J., & Ploetz, D.M. (2008). The effect of phonological neighborhood density on eye movements during reading. *Cognition, 107,* 685–692.

Zhang, S., & Perfetti, C.A. (1993). The tongue-twister effect in reading Chinese. *Journal of Experimental Psychology: Learning, Memory, and Cognition, 19,* 1082–1093.

Ziegler, J.C., Bertrand, D., Tóth, D., Csépe, V., Reis, A., Faísca, L., et al. (2010). Orthographic depth and its impact on universal predictors of reading: A cross-language investigation. *Psychological Science, 21,* 551–559.

Ziegler, J.C., & Goswami, U. (2005). Reading acquisition, developmental dyslexia, and skilled reading across languages: A psycholinguistic grain size theory. *Psychological Bulletin, 131,* 3–29.

CHAPTER 10

Understanding Developmental Dyslexia Through Computational Modeling

An Individual Deficit-Based Simulation Approach

Johannes C. Ziegler

R eading is a highly complex task that relies on the integration of visual, orthographic, phonological, and semantic information. The complexity of the reading task is clearly reflected in current computational models of reading (Coltheart, Rastle, Perry, Langdon, & Ziegler, 2001; Harm & Seidenberg, 1999; Perry, Ziegler, & Zorzi, 2007, 2010; Plaut, McClelland, Seidenberg, & Patterson, 1996; Zorzi, Houghton, & Butterworth, 1998). These models specify the ingredients of the reading process in a precise and detailed fashion, thus allowing researchers to simulate normal and impaired reading. Though models of skilled reading have become increasingly complex and detailed (Perry et al., 2007), theories of dyslexia have remained remarkably simple in the sense that most researchers in the field are committed to finding *single* deficits that would explain the abnormal reading performance of children with dyslexia, such as deficits in forming perceptual anchors (Ahissar, 2007), visual-attentional deficits (Vidyasagar & Pammer, 2010), cerebellar deficits (Nicolson, Fawcett, & Dean, 2001), rapid temporal processing deficits (Tallal & Piercy, 1973), or magnocellular deficits (Stein & Walsh, 1997).

A few dyslexia studies moved away from the single-deficit tradition by comparing competing accounts of dyslexia within the same participants—so-called *multiple-case studies* of dyslexia. For example, White et al. (2006) obtained data from 23 English-speaking children with dyslexia, ages 8–12 years, on a variety of tasks (phonology, visual motion, visual stress, auditory, and motor tasks) in order to contrast different theories of dyslexia. Though most of the participants with dyslexia showed severe phonological deficits, no evidence was obtained for visual deficits (although five dyslexics suffered from visual stress symptoms), a minority of children showed auditory deficits (4 out of 23), and a small group of dyslexics showed motor/cerebellar deficits (5 out of 23). In a similar study, Menghini et al. (2010) tested 60 Italian children with dyslexia and age-matched normally reading children on tests of phonological abilities, visual processing, selective and sustained attention, implicit learning, and executive functions. Although most of the dyslexics had phonological deficits (85% had deficits in phonological awareness and 75% had deficits in nonword repetition), there were other deficits noted: 16% of the dyslexics had deficits in visual-spatial attention, about 30% had deficits in executive functions, 43% had deficits in sustained attention, approximately 20% had deficits in visual-spatial perception, and only 10% had deficits in motion perception. No significant deficits were found for implicit memory learning tasks. Interestingly, most of the children with dyslexia with phonological deficits also showed deficits in other domains in combination with a primary phonological deficit, supporting the multiple deficit model of developmental dyslexia (Pennington, 2006).

Thus far, few studies have tried to investigate how deficits in different component skills of reading would impair the reading process itself. In this chapter, I outline an approach that provides a relatively complete model-based description of developmental dyslexia by investigating all component processes of reading as specified in an implemented computational model of skilled reading. For the present purpose, I will focus on the dual-route cascaded (DRC) model of reading aloud (Coltheart et al., 2001), but the same approach can be used in the context of different models, such as connectionist dual process (CDP+) (Perry et al., 2007, 2010). The main idea of the modeling approach is to obtain individual data on the subcomponents of reading and to impair individual models in a way that directly reflects the underlying deficits of each dyslexic. That is, reading performance of each child with dyslexia is simulated by adding noise to those component processes that were found to be impaired in a given individual. Although such an individual-based simulation approach has been used in aphasia research (Dell, Schwartz, Martin, Saffran, & Gagnon, 1997), this approach is fairly novel to the field of developmental dyslexia. This approach may have useful applications for computer-based diagnosis, assessments of children at risk of reading failure, and outcome predictions for dyslexia.

MODEL-BASED ASSESSMENT OF THE COMPONENT SKILLS OF READING

In the DRC model, which has been implemented for English (Coltheart et al., 2001) and for other alphabetic languages such as German (Ziegler, Perry, & Coltheart, 2000) and French (Ziegler, Perry, & Coltheart, 2003), the reading process is fully specified as a series of interacting stages going from feature and letter identification to phonological output processes (see Figure 10.1). Reading aloud is achieved via two routes: the lexical orthographic route and the nonlexical phonological route. The lexical route is necessary for the correct pronunciation of irregular words, and the nonlexical route is necessary for the pronunciation of novel words and nonwords. Accurate attentional, visual, and low-level orthographic processing is necessary for normal reading via either route.

Reading impairments (dyslexia) within the dual-route framework can stem from deficits in either lexical or nonlexical processes or a combination of the two. To investigate potential deficits at each representational level of the model, it is important to assess the functioning

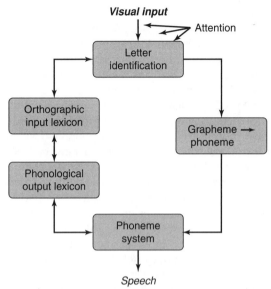

Visual input

Figure 10.1. Subcomponents and basic architecture of the dual-route cascaded (DRC) model of reading aloud.

of each level with tests that do not rely on irregular-word or nonword reading because word and nonword reading always involve more than one processing level (e.g., nonword reading requires not only phonological processes but also letter perception). Thus, in the first step of this research, tasks were designed that tapped the core processing subcomponents: sustained attention, letter processing, orthographic lexicon, phonological lexicon, and grapheme–phoneme mapping. The following study was done with French dyslexics.

Sustained and focused spatial attention is supposedly necessary to integrate features and identify letters. Although this process is currently not implemented in the DRC model, it was useful to measure sustained attention capacities as recent theories of dyslexia put a lot of weight on attentional deficits (Vidyasagar & Pammer, 2010; also see Ziegler, Pech-Georgel, Dufau, & Grainger, 2010). Accurate letter perception is, of course, fundamental for reading. To investigate position-specific letter processing in French, a letter-search task was used in which participants had to identify whether a prespecified target letter was present in an unpronounceable consonant string (e.g., FXVRN). Letter search performance in unpronounceable consonants makes it possible to test the efficiency of letter processing without any lexical activation. The next process on the lexical route is access to the orthographic lexicon. The efficiency of access to the orthographic lexicon was measured by the size of the *word superiority effect;* that is, the difference in letter identification performance when a target letter is embedded in a real word as opposed to a nonword (Ziegler & Jacobs, 1995; Ziegler, Van Orden, & Jacobs, 1997). Previous research has shown that this task is a good measure to assess whether lexical information in the orthographic lexicon can be accessed in order to help letter perception in a top-down fashion (Grainger, Bouttevin, Truc, Bastien, & Ziegler, 2003). Efficient access to the phonological lexicon was measured using a computer-controlled picture-naming task in which participants were asked to produce the names of five objects that were repeatedly displayed on the computer screen. This task required rapid access to phonological representations (Glaser, 1992; Swan & Goswami, 1997; Wolf & Bowers, 1999), while obviously not requiring orthographic processes or grapheme-to-phoneme conversion (GPC). Finally, the efficiency of the nonlexical route was tested in a phoneme-matching task, in which participants had to analyze the phonological similarity of phonemes either at the beginning or the end of spoken words. This task measures the capacity to detect and manipulate phonemes without requiring orthographic or visual-attentional processes. Although phoneme matching does not directly measure the GPC procedure, the claim is that metalinguistic awareness of individual phonemes is necessary to create grapheme–phoneme mappings (Hulme, Caravolas, Malkova, & Brigstocke, 2005).

Twenty-four French-speaking children with dyslexia, ages 8–11 years, were assessed with the previously described test battery, and their performance was compared with that of twenty-four age-matched controls. Figure 10.2 presents the performance of each child in each of the component tasks. In order to compare the size of the deficits across the tasks, the performance was standardized by computing z-scores with respect to the mean and standard deviation (SD) of the control sample. For example, a z-score of -2 for a child with dyslexia means that the child is 2 SDs below the mean of the control sample. This way of presenting the results has two major advantages. First, it allows us to appreciate the severity of the deficit, and second, it allows us to see how many children are deficient on a particular subcomponent. (Note that 1 SD below the mean was used as a cutoff in Figure 10.2.)

The results can be summarized as follows. No deficits were obtained for the sustained attention task (for which only three children were below the 1 SD cutoff). A significant deficit was obtained for letter-in-string perception, which affected about 40% of the children with dyslexia. No significant deficit was obtained for the word superiority effect (only five children had a smaller-than-normal word superiority effect). A robust deficit was obtained for rapid object naming (70% of the children with dyslexia exhibited deficits in this task). Finally, more than 80% of the children with dyslexia showed deficits in the phoneme matching task.

These results are interesting for several reasons. First, they show that deficits in sustained attention are fairly minor in dyslexia, although it should be noted that a more attention-demanding task might have revealed larger deficits. Second, they show that phonological deficits

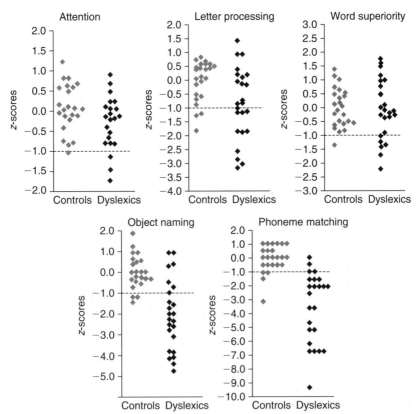

Figure 10.2. Individual patterns of performance of dyslexics (black) and controls (gray) in the five component tasks of reading: sustained attention, letter-in-string perception, word superiority effect, rapid object naming, and phoneme matching.

(object naming, phoneme matching) clearly outweigh the attentional and orthographic deficits in alphabetic languages, both in terms of the size of the deficit and in terms of the percentage of affected children. Third, they highlight the multifactorial nature of dyslexia, as many children were deficient in more than one component task (nine children had a triple deficit, seven had a double deficit, and eight had a single deficit). Finally, the size of the deficits varied substantially from small deficits around −1 SD up to large deficits around −7 SD. In summary, the present data highlight two important facts about dyslexia that seem universal, at least across alphabetic orthographies. First, there is remarkable commonality across participants (and studies) as most participants with dyslexia show phonological deficits; second, there is remarkable heterogeneity in dyslexia because impairment in our study was found to be associated with a variety of different deficits and combinations of deficits. This finding was true of the English and Italian studies of White et al. (2006) and Menghini et al. (2010) as well.

INDIVIDUAL-BASED SIMULATION APPROACH

As can be seen in Figure 10.2, children with dyslexia show deficits in letter processing, deficits in access to lexical phonology (object naming), and deficits in sublexical phonology (phoneme processing). About one third of the children have deficits in these three areas, one third have deficits in two areas, and one third have a deficit in only one area. However, the size of the deficits and the combinations of deficits vary substantially across individuals. The multifactorial nature of the individual deficit data provides the basis for the individual deficit-based simulation approach. This approach is highlighted in Figure 10.3.

The main idea is rather straightforward. Because each component task taps one component of the DRC model, impaired reading of a child with dyslexia can be simulated by disturbing the model proportional to the underlying deficit of a given child. For example, consider a child with dyslexia who has a deficit in phoneme processing of −3, a deficit in lexical phonology of −2, and a deficit in letter processing of −1 (see Figure 10.3). In order to simulate impaired reading of this child, one can add noise to the respective components of the DRC model proportional to the underlying deficit; that is, a noise level of, say, 0.3 is added for phoneme processing, one of 0.2 is added for lexical phonology, and one of 0.1 is added for letter processing. This procedure was applied for each of the 24 children with dyslexia (for details, see Ziegler et al., 2008). In the next step, 24 DRC simulations were performed, one for each child, using the individually established "noisy" parameter sets. One simulation was performed with the normal parameter set (control model). Simulations were obtained for a list of regular and irregular words and nonwords that were also read by the 24 children. The results of the participants and the model (averaged across the 24 participants and the 24 simulations) are presented in Figure 10.4.

As expected, children with dyslexia exhibited major deficits in reading aloud. They made significantly more errors than the controls made

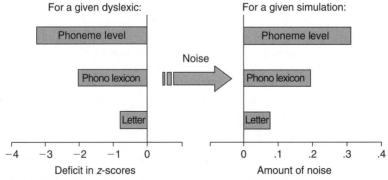

Figure 10.3. Schematic representation of the individual deficit-based simulation approach, in which noise is added to the model proportionally to the underlying deficits.

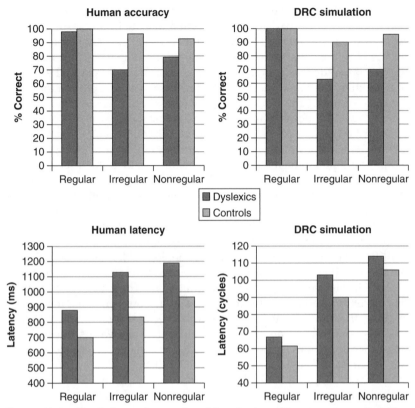

Figure 10.4. Simulations of normal and impaired reading accuracy and reading speed with the dual-route cascaded (DRC) model. Impaired reading was simulated by using the individual deficits to determine the noise levels of each of DRC's component processes.

when reading irregular words and nonwords, and it took them significantly longer to read the three classes of stimuli. Interestingly, accuracy was close to a 100% correct for regular-word reading, but the children with dyslexia still showed a robust speed deficit for regular words. As can be seen in Figure 10.4, the "impaired" model (average of the 24 deficit-based simulations) mirrored the impaired reading data almost perfectly. In terms of accuracy, the model showed a ceiling effect for regular words and significantly higher error rates for the dyslexic model than the normal model for irregular words and nonwords (all $ps < .05$). In terms of reading speed, the model showed significant speed deficits for the three classes of stimuli (all $ps < .05$), as do the human data. Although the model seems to predict somewhat smaller latency deficits than are seen in the human data, it should be noted that the SDs of the model are much smaller. Thus, in terms of effect sizes, the model closely captures the speed deficit seen in the human data. In sum, the models that were impaired on the basis of the deficits in the component tasks exhibited the same reading deficits as did the children with dyslexia.

The novelty of the present approach was to simulate impaired performance on the basis of the individual deficits in the ancillary tasks. Two questions seem crucial at this point: 1) How good are the individual fits? 2) How can alternative noise manipulations that are not based on the individual deficits produce similar results? With regard to the quality of the individual fits, we performed a linear regression between the accuracy rate of the 24 dyslexics on regular words, irregular words, and nonwords (72 data points) and the predictions of the model for these 24 dyslexics (72 data points). The model accounted for 48% of the variance ($p < .0001$). As a comparison, using z-score deficits on letter search, picture naming, and phoneme matching as predictor variables, the three predictor variables together accounted for only 15% of the variance. With regard to the issue of whether alternative noise manipulations would produce similar results, we ran 24 new simulations (one for each dyslexic), but instead of adding noise as a function of each dyslexic's deficit, we added noise randomly to the three levels that were degraded in our previous simulations (letter level, phoneme level, and phonological lexicon). For each dyslexic and each level, the noise level was picked randomly within the range of noise levels used in the previous simulations. The random noise simulations reproduced the correct overall pattern. However, when the predictions of the random noise model were regressed onto the dyslexics' reading performance on regular, irregular, and nonwords, the random noise model accounted for only 8.5% of the variance ($p < .05$), whereas the deficit-based model accounted for 48% of the variance. Thus, clearly, the strength of the individual-deficit approach is striking in its ability to predict the reading performance of individual participants.

SUBTYPES OF DYSLEXIA

Previous research has identified two prominent subtypes of dyslexics who have relatively selective deficits when reading irregular words and nonwords (Castles & Coltheart, 1993; Manis, Seidenberg, Doi, McBride-Chang, & Petersen, 1996; Sprenger-Charolles, Cole, Lacert, & Serniclaes, 2000; also see Griffiths & Snowling, 2002). In particular, surface dyslexics are poor at irregular-word reading but relatively normal at nonword reading. In contrast, phonological dyslexics are poor at nonword reading but relatively normal at irregular-word reading. It was of interest to us to investigate whether the previously identified subtypes could be given a coherent conceptual interpretation based on the ancillary component tasks (for a similar approach, see Griffiths & Snowling, 2002). According to dual-route hypotheses, those with surface dyslexia should show larger deficits on the lexical route (access to the orthographic and phonological lexicons), whereas those with phonological dyslexia should show larger deficits on the nonlexical route.

The 24 dyslexics from the study described earlier were classified using Castles and Coltheart's (1993) regression procedure, wherein pseudoword performance was plotted against irregular-word performance (and vice versa), and the 90% confidence intervals around the regression line are determined from the control group. A child was considered a phonological dyslexic if he or she was below the 90% confidence interval when pseudowords were plotted against irregular words, but within the 90% confidence interval when irregular words were plotted against pseudowords. Surface dyslexics were defined conversely. Note that the classification was based on accuracy data only. Latency data were not used for the classification because many dyslexics had error rates well above 50%. Due to the small number of items, such high error rates make the RT means somewhat unreliable (too few data points per cell) for the purpose of subtyping. According to this procedure, 29% of the sample were surface dyslexics (7 out of 24 individuals) and 19% were phonological dyslexics (4 out of 24 individuals).

In the second step, we simulated the reading performance of these surface and phonological dyslexics using the deficit-based simulation approach described previously. The performance of the impaired model and the average underlying deficits in the subcomponent tasks are presented in Figure 10.5.

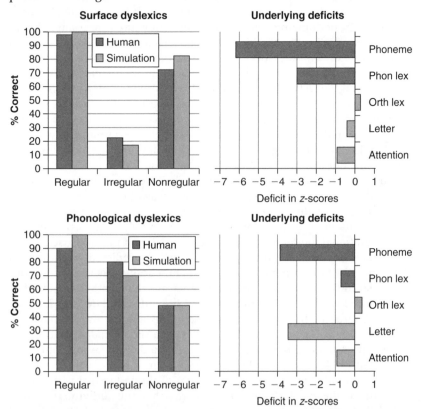

Figure 10.5. Simulations of individuals with surface and phonological dyslexia (left panel) and underlying deficits associated with the dissociated profiles (right panel). (*Key:* Phon lex, phonological lexicon; Orth lex, orthographic lexicon.)

As can be seen in Figure 10.5, the model captures the dissociation between surface and phonological dyslexia surprisingly well. For the surface dyslexics, the model reads only 20% of the irregular words correctly, even though it reads 80% of the nonwords correctly. For the phonological dyslexics, the model reads only 50% of the nonwords correctly, even though it reads 70% of the irregular words correctly. This double dissociation is close to the human data. These results show that continuous noise manipulations can reproduce the major subtypes defined in the literature. According to the analysis of the underlying deficits (Figure 10.5, right panels), the surface dyslexics in this sample had, on average, strong deficits in phoneme matching (sublexical phonology) and object naming (lexical phonology). In contrast, phonological dyslexics had strong deficits in phoneme matching and also in letter processing.

DISCUSSION

The present research highlights two facets of developmental dyslexia. On the one hand, there is a considerable amount of heterogeneity across developmental dyslexics because most of them exhibit a variety of deficits across different domains (letter processing, phoneme processing, phonological lexicon). It is the combination of deficits and their relative size that seems to determine the specific nature of the reading impairment. This finding corroborates the claim that dyslexia is multifactorial in nature (e.g., Pennington, 2006; Smith, Chapter 14 of this volume), which is hardly surprising given the complexity of the reading task. On the other hand, there is a reasonable amount of stability across participants in the sense that almost all dyslexics show phonological deficits—a finding that is consistent with the phonological deficit theory of developmental dyslexia (for review, see Snowling, 2000; Ziegler & Goswami, 2005).

In response to the heterogeneity of developmental dyslexia, I have outlined a new modeling approach that consists of simulating individual differences in reading different kinds of words on the basis of underlying deficits in core components of the reading system as specified by a computational model of reading. The originality of this approach is that individual deficits in reading performance are predicted by individual differences in subcomponents of reading. Practically, this is done by adding noise to those model components that are deficient. The amount of noise added is proportional to the size of the individual deficit. This simulation approach showed a striking match between the human data and the model both for accuracy and latency. The model did a good job in predicting individual performance. Indeed, the deficit-based simulations accounted for 48% of the individual variance in reading, whereas a random noise model accounted for only 8.5% of the individual variance.

One of the most striking results was that the individual deficit-based simulations reproduced the patterns of surface and phonological dyslexia found in the sample. This result is noteworthy because previous accounts of dissociated profiles within the context of the dual-route model (Castles & Coltheart, 1993) assumed that surface dyslexia was due to a lesion of the orthographic lexical route, whereas phonological dyslexia was due to a lesion of the nonlexical phonological route. The present results tell a different story. In the human data, there was no clear-cut dissociation between impaired lexical processing versus impaired nonlexical processing associated with surface and phonological dyslexia. Rather, different combinations of lexical and nonlexical deficits were associated with the two profiles. It is important that the model was able to simulate these dissociated profiles on the basis of multiple underlying deficits without any a priori assumptions about the deficiency of one or the other route.

In particular, in our sample, surface dyslexia was not associated with visual-orthographic deficits but rather with phonological deficits; namely, deficits in picture naming and phoneme matching. The severe picture-naming deficit of our surface dyslexics gives an interesting explanation for how irregular-word reading can be impaired in the absence of a strong deficit to the orthographic lexicon. That is, in order to read irregular words via the lexical route, readers need the ability to access not only their orthographic lexicon but also their phonological lexicon. If access to the phonological lexicon is impaired, as suggested in our picture naming data, a dyslexic reader would show a deficit on irregular-word reading (for a similar suggestion, see Zorzi et al., 1998). Indeed, the picture-naming deficit was significantly larger in surface dyslexics compared with phonological dyslexics, which underscores the possibility that irregular-word reading deficits might be due to poor phonological lexical representations.

Interestingly, phonological dyslexia in the present sample was associated with poor letter perception. The present simulations also supported this interpretation by showing that adding noise to the letter level was particularly damaging for nonword reading. The finding that noise to the letter level affected nonword reading is clearly consistent with recent evidence from spatial attention tasks, which suggests that the phonological dyslexics (but not the surface dyslexics) suffer from the spatial attention problems that have their most disturbing effect on nonword reading (Facoetti et al., 2006). Note that recent developments of the dual-route model of reading include an attentional window that operates on the input to the nonlexical route (Perry et al., 2007). Such a model clearly predicts that deficits in focused visual attention would affect nonword more than irregular-word reading.

The present work on subtypes of dyslexia has important practical implications. First of all, it shows that it is overly simplistic and potentially dangerous to assume that all developmental surface dyslexics must have deficits in the orthographic system(s), whereas all developmental phonological dyslexics must have deficits in the phonological system(s). The present data show that surface dyslexia can result from a phonological deficit (i.e., access to the phonological lexicon), whereas phonological dyslexia can result from a visual-orthographic deficit (i.e., impaired letter processing). More generally, different underlying deficits can give rise to either surface or phonological dyslexia, and the mere observation of a deficit in irregular-word or nonword reading is not sufficient to deduce the underlying causes. These issues are important because once children are classified as either surface or phonological dyslexics, it is rather common that surface dyslexics receive specific orthographic training, whereas phonological dyslexics receive specific phonological training. There is risk in that approach in that the present data suggest that phonological dyslexics might benefit a great deal from orthographic training, whereas surface dyslexics might benefit from phonological training. Consequently, without the kind of background check of component skills advocated here, the exclusive consideration of reading data for the purpose of subtyping might lead to incorrect conclusions about the underlying causes, and therefore the improper treatment, of specific reading problems.

LIMITATIONS AND FUTURE DIRECTIONS

An obvious limitation of the present research is the fact that developmental dyslexia is a developmental disorder, whereas current dual-route models such as DRC or CDP+ are not developmental models (see also Goswami, 2003; Goswami & Ziegler, 2006). It is entirely possible that there are single developmental causes of dyslexia, such as deficits in low-level auditory processing (Goswami et al., 2002; Muneaux, Ziegler, Truc, Thomson, & Goswami, 2004), deficits in categorical perception of speech (e.g., Serniclaes, Van Heghe, Mousty, Carre, & Sprenger-Charolles, 2004; Ziegler, Pech-Georgel, George, & Lorenzi, 2009), or deficits in letter–sound integration (Blau et al., 2010; Blau, van Atteveldt, Ekkebus, Goebel, & Blomert, 2009) that have cascading effects on the developing reading system and that affect various subcomponents of the reading system differently depending on the severity of the initial deficit and individual factors, such as compensatory strategies, training, teaching methods, oral language skills, socioeconomic background, and so forth. For example, one can imagine that a deficit in the categorical perception of speech will not only cause poor phonological development of words (lexical) and phonemes (sublexical), but will also hamper orthographic development because learning to process letters efficiently depends on a child's ability to map the visual code onto a phonological code (Goswami & Ziegler, 2006). Thus, what looks like a triple deficit at the age of 10 might well have been a single deficit at the age of 5. This example actually shows that simulating the reading data of children at the age of 10 with a model of skilled reading is rather appropriate because we are already dealing with an almost fully developed reading system, even if some of its components might be impaired.

To overcome the limitations mentioned previously, what is needed is a real developmental model and real developmental data, such as those of the Jyväskylä Longitudinal Study of Dyslexia (Lyytinen et al., 2001; see also Chapter 4 by Richardson, Aro, & Lyytinen in this volume). A convincing developmental model of reading in alphabetic languages needs to start out with a phonological system that is not yet fully specified in terms of phonemes (Goswami, Ziegler, & Richardson, 2005). The system needs to incorporate explicit teaching of letter–sound correspondences (Hutzler, Ziegler, Perry, Wimmer, & Zorzi, 2004), and it needs to have a self-teaching mechanism that allows orthographic development via successful phonological decoding (Share, 1995). Such a system would indeed allow an individual to study the cascading effects of a deficit that might affect the initial conditions (e.g., poor phonological development) or subsequent learning. It would be extremely interesting to do similar work in nonalphabetic languages.

ACKNOWLEDGMENTS

Preparation of this chapter was supported by an Alexander von Humboldt Fellowship. The research reported in this article was funded by the Agence Nationale de la Recherche (Grant JCJC05_0057). The simulations have been done in collaboration with Conrad Perry.

REFERENCES

Ahissar, M. (2007). Dyslexia and the anchoring-deficit hypothesis. *Trends in Cognitive Sciences, 11*(11), 458–465.

Blau, V., Reithler, J., van Atteveldt, N., Seitz, J., Gerretsen, P., Goebel, R., et al. (2010). Deviant processing of letters and speech sounds as proximate cause of reading failure: A functional magnetic resonance imaging study of dyslexic children. *Brain, 133,* 868–879.

Blau, V., van Atteveldt, N., Ekkebus, M., Goebel, R., & Blomert, L. (2009). Reduced neural integration of letters and speech sounds links phonological and reading deficits in adult dyslexia. *Current Biology, 19*(6), 503–508.

Castles, A., & Coltheart, M. (1993). Varieties of developmental dyslexia. *Cognition, 47*(2), 149–180.

Coltheart, M., Rastle, K., Perry, C., Langdon, R., & Ziegler, J.C. (2001). DRC: A dual route cascaded model of visual word recognition and reading aloud. *Psychological Review, 108*(1), 204–256.

Dell, G.S., Schwartz, M.F., Martin, N., Saffran, E.M., & Gagnon, D.A. (1997). Lexical access in aphasic and nonaphasic speakers. *Psychological Review, 104*(4), 801–838.

Facoetti, A., Zorzi, M., Cestnick, L., Lorusso, M.L., Moltenia, M., Paganoni, P., et al. (2006). The relationship between visuospatial attention and nonword reading in developmental dyslexia. *Cognitive Neuropsychology, 23,* 841–855.

Glaser, W.R. (1992). Picture naming. *Cognition, 42*(1–3), 61–105.

Goswami, U. (2003). Why theories about developmental dyslexia require developmental designs. *Trends in Cognitive Sciences, 7*(12), 534–540.

Goswami, U., Thomson, J., Richardson, U., Stainthorp, R., Hughes, D., Rosen, S., et al. (2002). Amplitude envelope onsets and developmental dyslexia: A new hypothesis. *Proceedings of the National Academy of Sciences, USA, 99*(16), 10911–10916.

Goswami, U., & Ziegler, J.C. (2006). A developmental perspective on the neural code for written words. *Trends in Cognitive Sciences, 10*(4), 142–143.

Goswami, U., Ziegler, J.C., & Richardson, U. (2005). The effects of spelling consistency on phonological awareness: A comparison of English and German. *Journal of Experimental Child Psychology, 92*(4), 345–365.

Grainger, J., Bouttevin, S., Truc, C., Bastien, M., & Ziegler, J. (2003). Word superiority, pseudoword superiority, and learning to read: A comparison of dyslexic and normal readers. *Brain and Language, 87*(3), 432–440.

Griffiths, Y.M., & Snowling, M. (2002). Predictors of exception word and nonword reading in dyslexic children: The severity hypothesis. *Journal of Educational Psychology, 94*(1), 34–43.

Harm, M.W., & Seidenberg, M.S. (1999). Phonology, reading acquisition, and dyslexia: Insights from connectionist models. *Psychological Review, 106*(3), 491–528.

Hulme, C., Caravolas, M., Malkova, G., & Brigstocke, S. (2005). Phoneme isolation ability is not simply a consequence of letter-sound knowledge. *Cognition, 97*(1), B1–B11.

Hutzler, F., Ziegler, J.C., Perry, C., Wimmer, H., & Zorzi, M. (2004). Do current connectionist learning models account for reading development in different languages? *Cognition, 91*(3), 273–296.

Lyytinen, H., Ahonen, T., Eklund, K., Guttorm, T.K., Laakso, M.L., Leinonen, S., et al. (2001). Developmental pathways of children with and without familial risk for dyslexia during the first years of life. *Developmental Neuropsychology, 20*(2), 535–554.

Manis, F.R., Seidenberg, M.S., Doi, L.M., McBride-Chang, C., & Petersen, A. (1996). On the bases of two subtypes of developmental dyslexia. *Cognition, 58*(2), 157–195.

Menghini, D., Finzi, A., Benassi, M., Bolzani, R., Facoetti, A., Giovagnoli, S., et al. (2010). Different underlying neurocognitive deficits in developmental dyslexia: A comparative study. *Neuropsychologia, 48*(4), 863–872.

Muneaux, M., Ziegler, J.C., Truc, C., Thomson, J., & Goswami, U. (2004). Deficits in beat perception and dyslexia: Evidence from French. *NeuroReport, 15*(8), 1255–1259.

Nicolson, R.I., Fawcett, A.J., & Dean, P. (2001). Developmental dyslexia: The cerebellar deficit hypothesis. *Trends in Neurosciences, 24*(9), 508–511.

Pennington, B.F. (2006). From single to multiple deficit models of developmental disorders. *Cognition, 101*(2), 385–413.

Perry, C., Ziegler, J.C., & Zorzi, M. (2007). Nested incremental modeling in the development of computational theories: The CDP+ model of reading aloud. *Psychological Review, 114*(2), 273–315.

Perry, C., Ziegler, J.C., & Zorzi, M. (2010). Beyond single syllables: Large-scale modeling of reading aloud with the Connectionist Dual Process (CDP++) model. *Cognitive Psychology.* doi:10.1016/j.cogpsych.2010.04.001

Plaut, D.C., McClelland, J.L., Seidenberg, M.S., & Patterson, K. (1996). Understanding normal and impaired word reading: Computational principles in quasi-regular domains. *Psychological Review, 103*(1), 56–115.

Serniclaes, W., Van Heghe, S., Mousty, P., Carre, R., & Sprenger-Charolles, L. (2004). Allophonic mode of speech perception in dyslexia. *Journal of Experimental Child Psychology, 87*(4), 336–361.

Share, D.L. (1995). Phonological recoding and self-teaching: Sine qua non of reading acquisition. *Cognition, 55*(2), 151–218.

Snowling, M.J. (2000). *Dyslexia.* Oxford: Blackwell.

Sprenger-Charolles, L., Cole, P., Lacert, P., & Serniclaes, W. (2000). On subtypes of developmental dyslexia: Evidence from processing time and accuracy scores. *Canadian Journal of Experimental Psychology, 54*(2), 87–104.

Stein, J., & Walsh, V. (1997). To see but not to read; The magnocellular theory of dyslexia. *Trends in Neurosciences, 20*(4), 147–152.

Swan, D., & Goswami, U. (1997). Picture naming deficits in developmental dyslexia: The phonological representations hypothesis. *Brain & Language, 56*(3), 334–353.

Tallal, P., & Piercy, M. (1973). Defects of non-verbal auditory perception in children with developmental aphasia. *Nature, 241*(5390), 468–469.

Vidyasagar, T.R., & Pammer, K. (2010). Dyslexia: A deficit in visuo-spatial attention, not in phonological processing. *Trends in Cognitive Sciences, 14*(2), 57–63.

White, S., Milne, E., Rosen, S., Hansen, P., Swettenham, J., Frith, U., et al. (2006). The role of sensorimotor impairments in dyslexia: A multiple case study of dyslexic children. *Developmental Science, 9*(3), 237–255.

Wolf, M., & Bowers, P.G. (1999). The double-deficit hypothesis for the developmental dyslexias. *Journal of Educational Psychology, 91*(3), 415–438.

Ziegler, J.C., Castel, C., Pech-Georgel, C., George, F., Alario, F.X., & Perry, C.

(2008). Developmental dyslexia and the dual route model of reading: Simulating individual differences and subtypes. *Cognition, 107,* 151–178.

Ziegler, J.C., & Goswami, U. (2005). Reading acquisition, developmental dyslexia, and skilled reading across languages: A psycholinguistic grain size theory. *Psychological Bulletin, 131*(1), 3–29.

Ziegler, J.C., & Jacobs, A.M. (1995). Phonological information provides early sources of constraint in the processing of letter strings. *Journal of Memory & Language, 34*(5), 567–593.

Ziegler, J.C., Pech-Georgel, C., Dufau, S., & Grainger, J. (2010). Rapid processing of letters, digits, and symbols: What purely visual-attentional deficit in developmental dyslexia? *Developmental Science.* doi:10.1111/j.1467-7687.2010.00983.x

Ziegler, J.C., Pech-Georgel, C., George, F., & Lorenzi, C. (2009). Speech-perception-in-noise deficits in dyslexia. *Developmental Science, 12*(5), 732–745.

Ziegler, J.C., Perry, C., & Coltheart, M. (2000). The DRC model of visual word recognition and reading aloud: An extension to German. *European Journal of Cognitive Psychology, 12*(3), 413–430.

Ziegler, J.C., Perry, C., & Coltheart, M. (2003). Speed of lexical and nonlexical processing in French: The case of the regularity effect. *Psychonomic Bulletin & Review, 10*(4), 947–953.

Ziegler, J.C., Van Orden, G.C., & Jacobs, A.M. (1997). Phonology can help or hurt the perception of print. *Journal of Experimental Psychology: Human Perception & Performance, 23*(3), 845–860.

Zorzi, M., Houghton, G., & Butterworth, B. (1998). Two routes or one in reading aloud? A connectionist dual-process model. *Journal of Experimental Psychology: Human Perception & Performance, 24*(4), 1131–1161.

CHAPTER 11

Phonological Instability in Young Adult Poor Readers

Time Course Measures and Computational Modeling

James S. Magnuson, Anuenue Kukona, David Braze,
Clinton L. Johns, Julie A. Van Dyke, Whitney Tabor,
W. Einar Mencl, Kenneth R. Pugh, and Donald P. Shankweiler

INTRODUCTION

A fundamental principle shared by nearly all theories of reading is that phonology plays a key role in mediating the mapping from print to meaning (Harm & Seidenberg, 2004; Shankweiler, Liberman, Mark, Fowler, & Fischer, 1979; Snowling & Hulme, 2005; Ziegler & Goswami, 2005). For virtually all individuals, acquiring reading skill—a cultural innovation that builds directly on extant linguistic abilities—is more difficult than spoken language acquisition (Liberman, Shankweiler, & Liberman, 1989). Moreover, many findings link specific reading disability (dyslexia) to impairments in phonological abilities (e.g., Snowling, 1981), or sensory impairments likely to reduce phonological abilities (Tallal, 1980). Although these theories vary in important ways, they share the key postulation of a *phonological deficit hypothesis*. However, phonological deficits have primarily been observed in children, given that most research on reading development and reading disability has focused on this population. Much less attention has been devoted to the adult endpoint of atypical reading development.

In this chapter, we briefly review our recent work with a community-based sample of young adults with a high proportion of poor readers. There are two crucial reasons why this population merits attention. First, though other chapters in this volume make a compelling case for the importance of early detection and intervention for reading disability, thousands reach adulthood each year without achieving a functional level of reading competence. Some may have been genetically predisposed to dyslexia. Others may represent failures of instruction; for example, individuals with the potential to become competent, fluent readers had they been given appropriate experience. Understanding the distribution of these cases will provide the necessary foundation for addressing urgent public health questions: How might reading interventions be best designed for adults? Are there subgroups of adult poor readers for whom different interventions may be most appropriate? Second, examining the endpoint of atypical development may provide new insight into neurobiological and cognitive bases for typical reading and provide constraints on theories of reading development and disability. To that end, we have been carefully characterizing the linguistic and nonlinguistic abilities of our community sample and examining both the functional neural architecture underlying spoken and written language ability and how individual differences in reading relate to other abilities. We briefly review our progress in the project so far.

We then report preliminary results from new experiments with this population, examining the time course of spoken-word recognition and learning. These experiments are motivated by the goal of better understanding potential differences in phonological ability in poor and good readers. They are also pertinent to recent work by Ramus and Szenkovits (2008), who revived and extended a specific sort of phonological deficit hypothesis. Ramus and Szenkovits reviewed three primary dimensions to phonological deficits in dyslexia: reduced phonological awareness, reduced verbal short-term memory, and slowed lexical retrieval. They pointed out that the tasks used to assess these dimensions impose time pressure demands (in the case of rapid naming tasks used to assess lexical access) or require storage or manipulation of phonological representations. They then reviewed unpublished evidence suggesting that adults with dyslexia may have intact phonological representations (e.g., their sample of adult dyslexics showed a phonological similarity effect comparable to that of typical readers in a nonword discrimination task, contra Shankweiler et al., 1979). Ramus and Szenkovits propose therefore that dyslexics may not have degraded phonological representations; rather, the basis for their phonological deficits may be an impairment of phonological access (compare the processing limitation hypothesis of Shankweiler & Crain, 1986), which manifests only (or most prominently) under particularly challenging task demands.

However, the data motivating this phonological access hypothesis come from tasks in which the response reflects a late, possibly postperceptual stage of processing. Measures of the time course of phonological processing could provide greater insight into whether and how phonology might be different in low-ability readers.

In the rest of this chapter, we briefly review our work with our community sample, then report two new experiments that impose minimal task demands and employ fine-grained measures that have been used previously to investigate the time course of language processing and learning in typical adults. We also report simulations using a computational model and then discuss the implications of the experiments and simulations for phonological deficit hypotheses.

THE PROJECT SO FAR

The overarching goal of this project is to examine the linguistic and nonlinguistic abilities and the underlying functional neural architecture supporting linguistic abilities of a broad community sample of young adults. We recruit from high-school equivalency (General Educational

Development, or GED) programs and community colleges in the greater New Haven, Connecticut, region. Participants tend to be from relatively low socioeconomic strata and ethnic minorities. They exhibit a wide range of performance abilities, although a greater proportion of low-ability individuals are found in comparison with more typical (in reading research) samples of college students at research universities.

By sampling from these settings, we achieve important goals. First, though we are able to oversample at the low end of ability ranges in comparison with a university sample, we obtain a wide range of abilities suitable for assessing individual differences. Second, because of the relative socioeconomic homogeneity of this sample, our high- and low-ability participants tend to be well matched demographically. Third, we are able to extend reading research to two strata of the population that have historically been underrepresented: adults with low reading ability and low-socioeconomic-status adults from ethnic minorities. Finally, we note that because our participants are nearly all enrolled in some form of continuing education, we assume that they are generally motivated; indeed, they tend to be diligent, compliant research participants.

Braze, Tabor, Shankweiler, and Mencl (2007) conducted comprehensive linguistic, cognitive, and neuropsychological assessments of a sample of 44 young adults from this community sample. The results were assessed from the perspective of the simple view of reading (Gough & Tunmer, 1986), which states that reading ability is the product of decoding skill and general language comprehension capacity. To oversimplify slightly, the idea is that ability to read text should be predicted by print decoding (pseudoword naming) and listening comprehension abilities. In other words, the chief additional complexity imposed by reading in comparison with listening is the ability to map print to phonology. The simple view failed to fully explain individual differences in the assessments of Braze et al.: Measures of oral vocabulary knowledge explained significant variance above and beyond that explained by decoding and auditory comprehension.

Braze et al. (2007) suggested that this finding, when considered within the framework of the *triangle model* of visual word recognition (Harm & Seidenberg, 2004; Seidenberg & McClelland, 1989; see Figure 11.1), is consistent with the lexical quality hypothesis (Perfetti, 2007; Perfetti & Hart, 2002). The logic is that poor performance on vocabulary measures does not reflect the mere presence or absence of a form or concept in memory. Rather, poor performance reflects relatively slow and noisy activation of representations as a function of less detailed or refined knowledge associated with lexical items in memory. In the triangle model, the representation of a lexical item is distributed in weighted connections linking orthographic and phonological forms and semantic knowledge. When input arrives on any of those banks of interface nodes, activation flows in every direction through the entire system in a gradual fashion. In a well-trained system, coherent covariation in

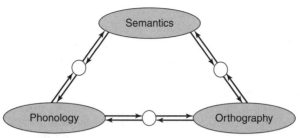

Figure 11.1. Schematic of the triangle model. Each interface level (phonology, orthography, semantics) is a bank of a large number of nodes (which could represent, for example, specific phonological or semantic features, though more abstract, distributed codes are possible as well). Small, empty ovals indicate banks of hidden nodes that do not themselves correspond to a discrete level of representation but afford a larger number of weighted connections between interfaces. Arrows indicate full connectivity (a connection from every node at the origin to every node at the destination). The model is trained to settle to a stable state where a pattern on one interface level (e.g., phonology) leads to correct patterns at the other levels (i.e., orthography and semantics) by adjusting the connection weights in small increments based on how far the model state is from the desired state. (*Sources:* Harm & Seidenberg, 2004; Seidenberg & McClelland, 1989.)

orthography, phonology, and semantics allows the system to settle into distinct states despite similarities between items in any of those dimensions. The system can settle quickly onto a correct phonological form, given the orthographic form of an English word with regular, high-frequency orthographic–phonological mappings based on oft-used orthography–phonology connections. However, given an irregular pattern, it will take the system longer to settle, and connections along the orthography-semantics-phonology sides of the triangle will play a larger role in arriving at the correct stable state. Braze et al. therefore suggested that lexical quality suffers when readers do not have the opportunity to sufficiently tune connections along the orthography–phonology, orthography–semantics, and semantics–phonology pathways (including orthographically conditioned changes in the semantics–phonology pathways observed in well-tuned models) in response to print. Absent such tuning, the system may take longer to settle (analogous to retrieval time in a more conventional memory model), and lexical representations may be less stable or distinctive than in a highly practiced, fluent reader. Phonology–semantics pathways are presumed to be well practiced and therefore well tuned in poor readers who are competent speakers; in contrast, orthographic pathways and orthographic contingencies are presumed to be relatively weak in poor readers. This set of assumptions leads to a prediction that vocabulary should differentially explain variance in poor readers for speech and print. This result is exactly what they found: Vocabulary accounted for significant variance in print comprehension but not in speech comprehension.

Van Dyke, Johns, and Kukona (2010) found additional support for the lexical quality hypothesis in our sample. They examined susceptibility to proactive interference during sentence processing (see also Van Dyke & McElree, 2006). Challenging object-cleft sentences in which a direct object is displaced from its verb (e.g., *It was the boat that the man who lived by the sea fixed*) were presented in a self-paced reading paradigm. Immediately prior to reading these sentences, participants were asked to remember a list of words that included items that were all plausible objects of the verb *fixed* (e.g., table, sink, truck). These researchers looked for individual differences in sensitivity to interference from the memory words by comparing this condition with a noninterference condition identical to the interference condition, except that the memory words could not serve as the direct object of the verb (e.g., the verb *fixed* was substituted for *sailed*, as in *It was the boat that the man who lived by the sea sailed*). The performance of individuals from our community sample on this task was compared with performance on a battery of 25 measures of various cognitive abilities (both linguistic and nonlinguistic). The only factor that explained significant variance in participants' sensitivity to interference was receptive vocabulary (and crucially, not working memory span). Van Dyke et al. (2010) interpreted this result as consistent with the lexical quality hypothesis, assuming that poor-quality lexical representations result in faulty retrieval of the direct object when the direct object must be integrated with its verb.

The functional magnetic resonance imaging (fMRI) results of Shankweiler et al. (2008) further imply that phonology is an important locus of difference between good and poor readers. They used anomalous written and spoken sentences to localize brain regions selectively activated for print and speech in 36 individuals from our community sample. Individuals varied in the degree to which the areas recruited for the two modalities overlapped. Regressions with reading skill measures revealed that the amount of overlap increased with reading skill, suggesting that overlap in the neural substrates of speech and reading is a hallmark of the endpoint of a successful reading development trajectory.

Collectively, these studies are highly consistent with the view that reading difficulties have specific phonological bases. However, these results do not reveal the way(s) in which good and poor readers' phonological processes differ, suggesting that further direct examination of phonological abilities in our community sample is warranted. The experimental results we present here are in a preliminary report on new tasks that we are using to assess the time course of phonological processing and learning in our sample, with the goal of arriving at a better understanding of how phonological skills differ in naturalistic tasks as a function of reading skill.

EXPERIMENT 1

In Experiment 1, we used the paradigm of Dahan, Magnuson, Tanenhaus, and Hogan (2001) because it provides a test of the time course for processing fine-grained phonological detail, but in a task that minimizes cognitive demands. Dahan et al. investigated the impact of misleading coarticulation (subphonemic/subcategorical mismatches). They achieved misleading coarticulation by cross-splicing recordings of words. For example, they took the initial consonant-vowel (CV) from *neck*, cut as late as possible before the final stop consonant, and spliced it together with the final consonant of *net*. The result sounds like *net*, but the vowel includes coarticulation consistent with /k/. They labeled this sort of item *w2w1* (word 2 spliced to word 1). They also had cases in which the initial CV came from a nonword (*nep* + *net* → n3w1). Finally, they included cross-spliced items without misleading coarticulation by splicing together two recordings of a target word such as *net* (w1w1). Dahan et al. presented these items with displays similar to the one shown in Figure 11.2, using the visual world paradigm (VWP; Tanenhaus, Spivey-Knowlton, Eberhard, & Sedivy, 1995). Eye movements were recorded as participants followed spoken instructions such as "point to the net."

The motivation for their study was the apparent deficiency in the TRACE model (McClelland & Elman, 1986) identified by Marslen-Wilson and Warren (1994). Specifically, human lexical decision reaction times appeared inconsistent with the time course of activation in TRACE. However, the time course measure provided by the VWP (Figure 11.2, right) showed that the TRACE predictions (Figure 11.2, center) were remarkably accurate. Crucially, participants fixated the competitor, *neck*, most when there was misleading coarticulation consistent with that

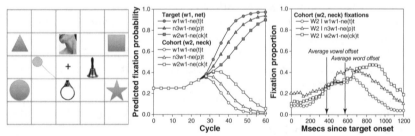

Figure 11.2. Sample display (left). TRACE predictions (center). Each pair of shapes (e.g., closed and open circles) represent the activations of the target word (closed symbols) and the competitor word (open symbols) when each cross-spliced stimulus is presented to the model. The key predictions are greater competitor activation given coarticulation consistent with the competitor (w2w1) and least given coarticulation consistent with the target (w1w1) due to bottom-up fit to lexical items. Given coarticulation consistent with a nonword (n3w1), an intermediate level of competitor activation is predicted because neither the target nor the competitor has an advantage based on the bottom-up stimulus. Competitor fixations over time (right) from Dahan et al. (2001).

word (w2w1) and least when the coarticulation was fully consistent with the target (w1w1). Fixation proportions were intermediate when misleading coarticulation did not map onto a word (n3w1). TRACE predicts the w1w1 and w2w1 patterns transparently; the word with best bottom-up match is initially activated most strongly. The n3w1 results follow because neither *net* nor *neck* has an advantage as the nonword coarticulation is heard; thus, both reach a relatively high level of activation before the disambiguating final consonant.

What might we predict for our sample? If linguistic difficulties arise from sensory or phonological impairments, such that research participants have "fuzzy" (e.g., under the phonological quality hypothesis of Joanisse, 2004) or slow-to-activate phonological representations (compare the generalized slowing hypothesis of Kail, 1994), we might expect them to be less affected by misleading coarticulation and to show weaker competition effects. On the phonological access hypothesis (Ramus & Szenkovits, 2008), if the task minimizes processing demands, our sample ought to look no different from a typical college sample. Although one might argue that demands remain substantial in this task, note that there is no time pressure, and the task is extremely naturalistic (for a laboratory task); participants simply follow spoken instructions to interact with items in a display. Thus, differences in our (on average) lower ability readers may reveal more details about the ways in which their phonology may differ from that of typical readers.

Methods

Participants   The participants were 32 college-age adults (mean age of 21) recruited from community colleges and GED programs in the New Haven area. A subset of the 25-test assessment battery is summarized in Table 11.1, which makes it apparent that this population tends to lag in language and other cognitive domains. Our approach with samples from this population is to employ a continuum method of analysis, including nonlinguistic abilities in regression models rather than partitioning the sample based on ability and/or excluding participants based on thresholds. For the current report, because we have a fairly small sample, we will compare our sample with typical college students. The results we report do not differ if we remove, for example, participants with low approximated intelligence quotients (IQs) (< 75), so the full sample is included.

Materials   The auditory materials were those used by Dahan et al. (2001) and consisted of 15 *word 1, word 2, nonword 3* triplets (w1,w2,n3), such as *net, neck,* and *nep* (for the full set, see Appendix B of Dahan et al., 2001). The visual materials were similar to those used by Dahan et al., except that we used photographs instead of line drawings.

Procedure   The procedure was identical to that of Dahan et al. except that we used color photographs of real objects rather than line

Table 11.1. Sample characteristics

Standardized ($M = 100$, $SD = 15$)		Age-equivalent scores	
Assessment	Mean (SD)	Assessment	Mean (SD)
WASI general IQ approximation	89 (15)	Chronological age	21 (2)
PPVT picture vocabulary	89 (13)	WJ3 word identification	14 (3)
CTOPP phonological awareness	79 (16)	WJ3 word attack	12 (4)
CTOPP phonological memory	91 (10)		

Key: M, mean; *SD,* standard deviation; WASI, Wechsler Abbreviated Scale of Intelligence (Wechsler, 1999); PPVT, Peabody Picture Vocabulary Test–Third Edition (Dunn & Dunn, 1997); CTOPP, Comprehensive Test of Phonological Processing (Wagner, Torgesen, & Rashotte, 1999; WJ3, Woodcock-Johnson III Test of Achievement (Woodcock, McGrew, & Mather, 2000).

drawings. There were three lists, with five items assigned to each condition (w1w1 [consistent coarticulation], w2w1 [misleading cohort coarticulation], and n3w1 [misleading nonword coarticulation]) in each list. Participants were randomly assigned to lists. On each trial, four pictures of objects and four simple geometrical shapes appeared when the participant clicked on a central fixation cross (see Figure 11.2). On critical trials, these included the target (e.g., *net*) and a cohort competitor (e.g., *neck*). A spoken instruction was presented over speakers, such as "Point to the net; now click on it and put it below the circle." We tracked eye movements using an SR Research EyeLink II head-mounted eye tracker. The measure of interest was the probability of fixating each item over time from the onset of the target word. (See Dahan et al., 2001, for full details on the makeup of critical and filler trials.)

Results

Eye movements were parsed into saccades and fixations. Saccade time was attributed to the following fixation because the initiation of a saccade is the earliest indicator of the choice to fixate the next gaze position. Figure 11.3 shows competitor fixations (target fixations are essentially complementary) from our sample, with competitor fixations from Dahan and colleagues' *presumed typical* sample for qualitative comparison. There is a striking difference between the groups: The fixation proportions to competitors are relatively elevated in each condition in the community sample. The typical sample had cohort peaks of approximately 0.5 for w2w1, 0.45 for n3w1, and 0.3 for w1w1. Our sample had peaks of 0.6, 0.4, and 0.4, respectively. Competitor proportions also remain elevated for a more extended time. There is also a striking similarity with the typical college sample: There is no apparent delay in the response to the bottom-up signal.

An analysis of variance comparing mean fixation proportion in the window from 200 to 1200 milliseconds (ms) suffices to quantify the obvious pattern in the figure for our sample. (We are currently collecting data from a new sample of college students along with formal language ability assessments to afford more direct investigation of individual differences.)

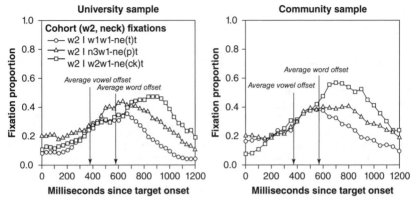

Figure 11.3. Competitor effects in Dahan and colleagues' presumed typical sample (left) and our community sample that included many poor readers (right). The arrows indicate mean vowel offset and word offset. There is notably greater and more sustained competition in the community sample.

The main effect of condition was significant ($F[2, 62] = 12.3$, $p < .001$). Planned comparisons revealed that mean fixation proportions were reliably higher in the w2w1 condition (0.53) than in the n3w1 condition (0.42; $F[1, 31] = 8.0$, $p = .008$) and marginally higher in the n3w1 condition than in the w1w1 condition (0.33; $F[1, 31] = 3.8$, $p = .06$).

Together, these patterns rule out all of the predictions discussed previously. Generalized slowing does not apply because there is no apparent delay in bottom-up response. Delayed, weak, or absent competitor effects that might be predicted on phonological quality hypotheses were not observed. Instead, our sample appeared to be *more* sensitive to subtle phonetic detail than typical participants, showing greater lexical competition effects. This may be compatible with the phonological access hypothesis of Ramus and Szenkovits (2008) in that initial lexical contact appears to proceed with similar timing in lower ability readers, but differences emerge in subtle details of lexical activation and competition.

Computational Modeling

To help make sense of this unexpected result, we turned to the jTRACE reimplementation of TRACE (Strauss, Harris, & Magnuson, 2007), which includes several additional features, such as a graphical user interface and plotting and scripting utilities. TRACE is an interactive network (i.e., a neural network with recurrent [feed-forward, feed-back, and inhibitory] connections with fixed parameter settings rather than connection weights changeable via online learning; see Figure 11.4). Although TRACE has well-known limitations (as discussed in McClelland & Elman, 1986), it still has the deepest and broadest empirical coverage

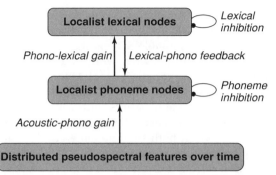

Figure 11.4. Schematic of the TRACE interactive-activation model of speech perception and spoken word recognition. Each level represents a bank of many nodes. At the phoneme and lexical levels, a localist representation is used (i.e., with one node per phoneme and one node per word). Arrows stand for partial connectivity between levels; phonemes have feed-forward connections to each word containing them, with reciprocal feedback connections. The loops with round connectors on the phoneme and lexical levels indicate lateral inhibition within levels, such that active nodes send inhibitory signals to other nodes within the same layer. Lateral inhibition governs activation, allowing a single node to tend to dominate within each level at the time scale of phonemes and words. Each of these connection types has associated gain parameters. Changing these parameters changes the behavior of the entire system but tends to have the largest impact at the level where the parameter is changed (e.g., Changing phoneme inhibition changes phonological stability but also has repercussions at the lexical level). (In the full model, phoneme and lexical nodes are temporal-spatial templates reduplicated many times so that there are many copies of each phoneme node aligned with long stretches of the potential input window, which is what allows the model to handle over-time input. See McClelland & Elman, 1986, for details.)

of any model of spoken-word recognition, while compactly embodying the core principles shared by most current theories (see Magnuson, Mirman, & Harris, in press).

Our strategy was simple. Starting with the default parameters used by Dahan et al. (2001) to obtain the simulations shown in the middle panel of Figure 11.2, we explored a wide range of changes to several parameters in TRACE, changing them one at a time. The goal was to determine whether any parameter could be changed to produce the observed pattern: increased competition effects without any slowing of initial lexical access. Although we tried many parameters, only reducing lateral inhibition at the phoneme or lexical level could produce this pattern. We will summarize the results with a few theoretically motivated parameter explorations.

Generalized slowing (turning down feedforward gain at any level of the model) does not work; it slows initial activations and damps competition effects. "Fuzzing" phonology by adding noise to the input or to any level within the model does not work; it also damps competition effects. Lexical decay—the parameter that McMurray, Samelson, Lee, and Tomblin (2010) claim best fits individual differences in a lexical competition in a group of adolescents with a range of language and cognitive abilities—influences activations too late and weakly. Reducing lateral inhibition works, at both the phoneme and lexical levels, when lateral inhibition is reduced by approximately 50% from default levels. Reducing inhibition does not affect initial activation rates, but it allows larger competition effects because it delays the impact of late-arriving bottom-up disambiguation.

Summary

In Experiment 1 we found that a sample with a high proportion of poor readers exhibited larger competition effects in response to misleading coarticulation than do typical college students, without any evidence that processing is generally slowed or delayed (because they respond equally quickly to word-initial information). Simulations with TRACE suggest that the only way to achieve larger competition effects in this paradigm without slowing initial processing is by reducing lateral inhibition at the phoneme or lexical level. There is a potentially interesting connection to the notion that poor readers have difficulties in suppression of irrelevant details or representations at multiple levels (Gernsbacher, 1993).

EXPERIMENT 2

In Experiment 2, we continued our exploration of our sample's phonological abilities by examining lexical competition in the context of an artificial lexicon learning task, modeled after a study by Magnuson, Tanenhaus, Aslin, and Dahan (2003). This examination allowed us to simultaneously study phonological competition effects in word recognition (How strongly do "cohorts" such as /pibo/ and /pibu/ compete? How strongly do rhymes such as /pibo/ and /dibo/ compete?) and word learning ability in this population. Magnuson et al. (2003) were motivated in part by the goal of precisely controlling lexical characteristics such as phonological similarity, frequency, and neighborhood density. This approach has an added advantage for our sample. To the degree that our sample diverges from the performance of typical participants using real words, it is difficult to determine the locus of the difference. There may be deep reasons, such as differential organization of processing mechanisms, or shallow ones, such as simple differences in vocabulary size. An artificial lexicon paradigm allows us to put participants on maximally similar footing. Although they arrive with individual differences in linguistic and cognitive abilities, the items are equally unfamiliar to all.

On a sensory, phonological, or cognitive theory of the etiology of reading disability, one might expect our sample to perform worse than one of typical college students. There are two precedents using familiar, real words in the visual world eye tracking paradigm that suggest possible outcomes. Desroches, Joanisse, and Robertson (2006) examined cohort and rhyme competition effects in children with dyslexia and found that—unlike typically developing peers—these children did not exhibit rhyme competition effects. In contrast, McMurray et al. (2010) reported that adolescents meeting criteria for specific language impairment (SLI) showed stronger cohort *and* rhyme effects, though only in the late time course (a result that is potentially consistent with the elevated and persistent onset competition effects we observed in Experiment 1).

Methods

Participants   There were two groups of participants. One group, the community sample (CS) group, was a subset of 22 participants from our community sample in Experiment 1. The other was a group of unassessed but presumed typically developing (TD) college students from the University of Connecticut (the TD group, $n = 14$).

Materials   The auditory materials were eight artificial words constructed such that each item had one cohort (onset) competitor in the artificial lexicon and one rhyme. The words were /pibo/, /pibu/, /dibo/, /dibu/, /tupa/, /tupi/, /bupa/, and /bupi/. The visual materials were photos of eight unusual animals from other continents unlikely to be familiar to Americans. Names were mapped randomly to pictures for each participant.

Procedure   Each trial had identical structure. A fixation cross appeared in the center of the screen. When the participant clicked the cross, the trial began. Two pictures appeared, at left and right; 500 ms later, an instruction was played, such as "Find the pibo." At first, participants could only guess. If they clicked on the incorrect object, they heard, "Try again." When they clicked on the correct object, they heard feedback, such as, "That's right, that's the pibo!" The experiment consisted of 8 blocks of 24 trials. Each item appeared as the target 3 times per block, paired with its cohort, its rhyme, and an unrelated item. Thus, each block had eight cohort, rhyme, and unrelated trials. There was no formal test; instead, we measured behavior continuously over learning.

Results and Discussion

Accuracy and response time (for accurate trials) are shown in Figure 11.5 for the two groups. Growth-curve analysis was used to assess change over time for the two groups, using orthogonal power polynomials, following the methods described by Mirman, Dixon, and Magnuson (2008). In this

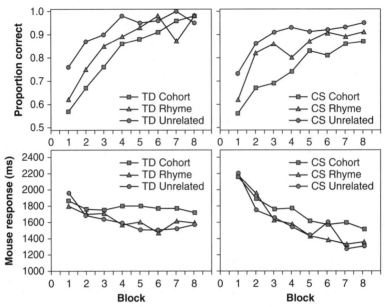

Figure 11.5. Mean accuracy (top row) and mouse-click response time (bottom row) in Experiment 2 for the assumed typically developing (TD) group (left column) and the community sample (CS) group with many poor readers (right).

approach, polynomial curves are fit to individual data and analyses are conducted on curve parameters. A conceptual benefit of this approach is that the intercept is recentered such that it is analogous to mean fixation proportion. In accuracy, collapsing over groups, the intercept was reliably lower for cohort than rhyme trials, and for rhyme versus unrelated trials. In reaction time, cohort trials had higher intercept than the other two trial types, which did not differ from each other. Notably, the TD and CS groups did not differ in intercept for accuracy or RT. But they did differ in slope, as is clear from Figure 11.5. Interestingly, both groups show strong effects of competitor type in accuracy.

Fixation proportions over time are presented compactly in Figure 11.6 by showing target fixations (competitor fixations are essentially complementary) averaged over all correct trials (as the patterns did not change substantially with training). Qualitatively, there is a striking result. There are clear effects of both cohort and rhyme for the TD group sample. The cohort effect is stronger and earlier, as with real words (Allopenna, Magnuson, & Tanenhaus, 1998; Desroches et al., 2006), and the rhyme effect emerges later. Growth curve analysis reveals reliable intercept differences for the TD group (unrelated > rhyme > cohort) analogous to differences in mean proportion over the analysis window. In contrast, the CS group shows a strong cohort effect, but not even a hint of a rhyme effect. This pattern is confirmed by assessing intercepts (unrelated ≈ rhyme > cohort).

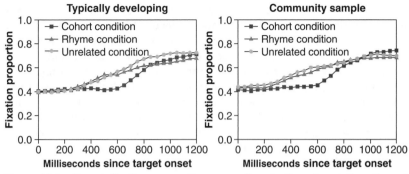

Figure 11.6. Target fixation proportions over time in Experiment 2, collapsed across block and only including correct trials, averaged over all 8 blocks. (Left) Typically developing (TD) group; (right) community sample (CS) group. These patterns of results were apparent from the first training/testing block.

Our results are consistent with those of Desroches et al. (2006), who reported an absence of rhyme effects in children with dyslexia using a similar eye tracking paradigm with familiar, real words. They are not consistent with the recent report of McMurray et al. (2010) that indicates that adolescents with SLI show larger but later competition effects than typically developing peers. We again turned to the model in order to explore possible bases for such a pattern.

Computational Modeling

As with Experiment 1, we explored the pattern of results using the jTRACE model. Because TRACE is not a learning model (although see the Hebbian version of TRACE developed by Mirman, McClelland, & Holt, 2006), we treated TRACE as a model of the stabilized system at the end of learning. Again, we changed one parameter at a time, looking for a change that would leave the magnitude and timing of the cohort effect intact, ideally while wiping out the rhyme effect. We again tried several parameters. Here we summarize the most theoretically interesting ones.

Generalized slowing (feed-forward gain) does not work; it changes timing but does not wipe out rhyme effects. Fuzzing phonology by adding input or internal noise tends to boost both competition effects. Lexical decay does not selectively affect rhyme effects. Reducing lexical lateral inhibition does not work; it actually boosts rhyme effects. *Reducing phoneme lateral inhibition does work* and is the only parameter that can induce the correct change in model performance. It does not completely wipe out rhyme effects, but comes close, while leaving the cohort time course intact. This is a counterintuitive outcome, but it follows from what happens to phonemes other than the initial phoneme of the target word. In general, with inhibition reduced, similar phonemes get much more active because they receive less inhibition from phonemes with bottom-up or top-down support. The result is that even though the phoneme inhibition parameter is lower, there is actually greater inhibitory flow at the phoneme level—because so many more phonemes remain active, the total inhibition in the system increases. This greater total inhibition puts rhymes at even greater disadvantage than under the standard phoneme inhibition parameter setting.

Interestingly, lateral inhibition at the phoneme level was one of two parameters that could achieve the correct pattern to fit the CS group behavior in Experiment 1. The other was lexical inhibition, but this cannot capture the pattern of Experiment 2. We return to this in the general discussion section following the summary of this experiment.

Summary

In Experiment 2, we found that a sample with a high proportion of poor readers achieved final accuracy levels similar to a TD comparison group. However, the time course of learning was substantially different, with slower learning in early trials. A comparison of phonological competition effects using fixation proportions over time revealed that the poor readers showed similar onset (cohort) competition effects to the TD comparison group, but failed to exhibit an effect of rhyme competition. This result replicates a report that children with dyslexia did not exhibit rhyme effects in a similar study (Desroches et al., 2006). In computational modeling with TRACE, the only way to substantially reduce rhyme effects without perturbing cohort (onset) effects was to reduce lateral inhibition at the phoneme level, which was one of the parameter manipulations that allowed the model to capture the enhanced subcategorical mismatch effects observed in Experiment 1.

GENERAL DISCUSSION

We found clear evidence that low-ability adult readers continue to differ from typical peers in phonological processing. Our sample with a high proportion of poor readers showed substantially *larger* sensitivity to misleading coarticulation than typical peers in Experiment 1. The sample learned new words with a different trajectory than typical peers in Experiment 2 and failed to exhibit rhyme competition effects. At the same time, they did not appear to differ in the timing of initial lexical access (e.g., signal driven differences in fixation proportions emerge for university and community samples at virtually identical lags relative to target onsets in Figures 11.3 and 11.6).

The two primary patterns of differences—enhanced competition due to misleading coarticulation and absence of rhyme effects—can be modeled in TRACE in only one way: reduced lateral inhibition at the phoneme level. What conclusions can be drawn from this convergence of modeling results? First, we do not wish to imply that we believe that discrete representations of phonemes in the brain necessarily exist, let alone that there is a discrete parameter controlling lateral inhibition at that level. The ability of TRACE to simulate differences based on reduced phoneme inhibition instead points to the level of phonological organization in the dynamical system it is meant to simulate; that is, the mechanisms underlying human word recognition.

It is crucial to note that although adding noise (for example) to TRACE did not succeed in simulating the correct patterns, this result does not mean that adding noise would not succeed in another modeling framework. Instead, our simulations identify the organizational level of the system—sublexical phonological organization—that appears to be crucially different in poor readers. It is also important to note that our results are potentially consistent with any form of the phonological deficit hypothesis, although they somewhat favor accounts that assume typical phonetic resolution (that is, their phonological representations allow at least equal sensitivity to subphonemic phonetic detail, given the results of Experiment 1) and differences in the stability of phonological representations.

In particular, our results may be compatible with the phonological access hypothesis proposed by Ramus and Szenkovits (2008). Direct manipulations of representational quality in the TRACE model (e.g., adding noise) did not capture the subtle differences in the (millisecond-scale) time course of lexical activation and competition we observed in our lower ability readers in both experiments. Instead, we were able to simulate the patterns observed in Experiments 1 and 2 by changing the dynamics and stability of the phoneme level in TRACE (via reduced inhibition). The convergence on phoneme inhibition in the simulations of Experiments 1 and 2 increases our confidence that we may be on the right track. One next step will be to use the reparameterized model to generate predictions for the community sample in other tasks.

One could easily construe reduction of phoneme inhibition as a change in the dynamics of phonological access and therefore as consistent with the phonological access hypothesis. However, our results also suggest that differences in phonological access may be more subtle than suggested by Ramus and Szenkovits (2008), who emphasize the (specifically verbal) executive demands implied by difficulties in tasks tapping into phonological awareness, verbal short-term memory, and speed of lexical access. The fact that we observed differences in the time course of lexical activation, competition, and learning in poor adult readers in minimally demanding, naturalistic tasks suggests that the locus of the phonological deficit may be a low-level property of the system that requires either difficult or sensitive tasks to be detected. This possibility requires further testing. Our next step will be to use an individual-differences approach to examine these issues in both a larger community sample and samples of university students, both in conventional statistical modeling of individual differences and computational modeling (finding specific model parameterizations for each participant and then generating individual-specific predictions for other tasks. Compare the participant-based modeling approach of Ziegler et al., 2008).

ACKNOWLEDGMENTS

We thank Will Baker, Peggy McCardle, Ovid Sing, and Jun Ren Lee for organizing an outstanding workshop. We thank Mark Seidenberg and Johannes Ziegler for helpful discussions of computational modeling. This work was supported by the NIH Grant HD-40353 to Haskins Laboratories.

REFERENCES

Allopenna, P.D., Magnuson, J.S., and Tanenhaus, M.K. (1998). Tracking the time course of spoken word recognition using eye movements: Evidence for continuous mapping models. *Journal of Memory and Language, 38,* 419–439.

Braze, D., Tabor, W., Shankweiler, D.P., & Mencl, W.E. (2007). Speaking up for vocabulary: Reading skill differences in young adults. *Journal of Learning Disabilities, 40*(3), 226–243.

Dahan, D., Magnuson, J.S., Tanenhaus, M.K., & Hogan, E.M. (2001). Subcategorical mismatches and the time course of lexical access: Evidence for lexical competition. *Language and Cognitive Processes, 16,* 507–534.

Desroches, A.S, Joanisse, M.F., & Robertson, E.K. (2006). Specific phonological impairments in dyslexia revealed by eye tracking. *Cognition, 100,* B32–B42.

Dunn, L.M., & Dunn, L.M. (1997). *Peabody Picture Vocabulary Test–3rd ed.* Circle Pines, MN: American Guidance Service.

Gernsbacher, M.A. (1993). Less skilled readers have less efficient suppression mechanisms. *Psychological Science, 4,* 294–298.

Gough, P.B., & Tunmer, W.E. (1986). Decoding, reading, and reading disability. *Remedial and Special Education, 7,* 6–10.

Harm, M.W., & Seidenberg, M.S. (2004). Computing the meanings of words in reading: Cooperative division of labor between visual and phonological processes. *Psychological Review, 111,* 662–720.

Joanisse, M.F. (2004). Specific language impairments in children: Phonology, semantics and the English past tense. *Current Directions in Psychological Science, 13,* 156–160.

Kail, R. (1994). A method for studying the generalized slowing hypothesis in children with specific language impairment. *Journal of Speech & Hearing Research, 37,* 418–421.

Liberman, I.Y., Shankweiler, D., & Liberman, A.M. (1989). The alphabetic principle and learning to read. In D. Shankweiler & I.Y. Liberman (Eds.), *Phonology and reading disability: Solving the reading puzzle* (pp. 1–33). Ann Arbor: University of Michigan Press.

Magnuson, J.S., Mirman, D., & Harris, H.D. (in press). Computational models of spoken word recognition. In M. Spivey, K. McRae, & M. Joanisse (Eds.), *The Cambridge handbook of psycholinguistics.* New York: Cambridge University Press.

Magnuson, J.S., Tanenhaus, M.K., Aslin, R.N., and Dahan, D. (2003). The time course of spoken word recognition and learning: Studies with artificial lexicons. *Journal Experimental Psychology: General, 132*(2), 202–227.

Marslen-Wilson, W.D., & Warren, P. (1994). Levels of perceptual representation and process in lexical access: Words, phonemes, and features. *Psychological Review, 101,* 653–675.

McClelland, J.L., & Elman, J.L. (1986). The TRACE model of speech perception. *Cognitive Psychology, 18,* 1–86.

McMurray, B., Samelson, V.M., Lee, S.H., & Tomblin, J.B. (2010). Individual differences in online spoken word recognition: Implications for SLI. *Cognitive Psychology, 60,* 1–39.

Mirman, D., Dixon, J.A., & Magnuson, J.S. (2008). Statistical and computational models of the visual world paradigm: Growth curves and individual differences. *Journal of Memory & Language, 59*(4), 475–494.

Mirman, D., McClelland, J.L., & Holt, L.L. (2006). An interactive Hebbian account of lexically guided tuning of speech perception. *Psychonomic Bulletin & Review, 13*(6), 958–965.

Perfetti, C. (2007). Reading ability: Lexical quality to comprehension. *Scientific Studies of Reading, 11*(4), 357–383.

Perfetti, C.A., & Hart, L. (2002). The lexical quality hypothesis. In L. Verhoeven, C. Elbro, & P. Reitsma (Eds.), *Precursors of functional literacy* (pp. 189–213). Amsterdam/Philadelphia: John Benjamins.

Ramus, F., & Szenkovits, G. (2008). What phonological deficit? *Quarterly Journal of Experimental Psychology, 61*, 129–141.

Seidenberg, M.S., & McClelland, J.L. (1989). A distributed, developmental model of word recognition and naming. *Psychological Review, 96*, 523–568.

Shankweiler, D., & Crain, S. (1986). Language mechanisms and reading disorder: A modular approach. *Cognition, 24*, 139–168.

Shankweiler, D., Liberman, I.Y., Mark, L.S., Fowler, C.A., & Fischer, F.W. (1979). The speech code and learning to read. *Journal of Experimental Psychology: Human Learning and Memory, 5*, 531–545.

Shankweiler, D.P., Mencl, W.E., Braze, D., Tabor, W., Pugh, K.R., & Fulbright, R.K. (2008). Reading differences and brain: Cortical integration of speech and print in sentence processing varies with reader skill. *Developmental Neuropsychology, 33*(6), 745–776.

Snowling, M.J. (1981). Phonemic deficits in developmental dyslexia. *Psychological Research, 43*, 219–234.

Snowling, M.J., & Hulme, C. (2005). *The science of reading: A handbook.* West Sussex, England: Blackwell.

Strauss, T.J., Harris, H.D., & Magnuson, J.S. (2007). jTRACE: A reimplementation and extension of the TRACE model of speech perception and spoken word recognition. *Behavior Research Methods, 39*, 19–30.

Tallal, P. (1980). Auditory temporal perception, phonics, and reading disabilities in children. *Brain and Language, 9*, 182–198.

Tanenhaus, M.K., Spivey-Knowlton, M., Eberhard, K., & Sedivy, J.C. (1995). Integration of visual and linguistic information is spoken-language comprehension. *Science, 268*, 1632–1634.

Van Dyke, J.A., Johns, C.L., & Kukona, A. (2010, March). *Individual differences in sentence comprehension: A retrieval interference approach.* Talk presented at the 2010 CUNY Human Sentence Processing Conference, New York City.

Van Dyke, J.A., & McElree, B. (2006). Retrieval interference in sentence comprehension. *Journal of Memory and Language, 55*, 157–166.

Wagner, R.K., Torgesen, J.K., & Rashotte, C. (1999). *Comprehensive Test of Phonological Processing (CTOPP).* Austin, TX: PRO-ED.

Wechsler, D. (1999). *Wechsler Abbreviated Scale of Intelligence (WASI).* San Antonio, TX: Harcourt Assessment.

Woodcock, R.W., McGrew, K.S., & Mather, N. (2000). *Woodcock-Johnson III Tests of Achievement.* Itasca, IL: Riverside.

Ziegler, J., Castel, C., Pech-Georgel, C., George, F., Alario, F-X., & Perry, C. (2008). Developmental dyslexia and the dual route model of reading: Simulating individual differences and subtypes. *Cognition, 107*, 151–178.

Ziegler, J., & Goswami, U. (2005). Reading acquisition, developmental dyslexia, and skilled reading across languages: A psycholinguistic grain size theory. *Psychological Bulletin, 131*, 3–29.

CHAPTER 12

Using Response to Intervention for Identification and Classification

Richard K. Wagner, Jessica Brown Waesche,
Christopher Schatschneider, Jon K. Maner, and Yusra Ahmed

Regardless of the discipline, identification and classification are among the most fundamental aspects of science. Biologists identify and classify specimens, creating and revising taxonomies in the process. Physicists identify and classify subatomic particles that are produced when high-voltage streams of protons are smashed into each other in giant subterranean particle accelerators. Clinical psychologists and psychiatrists identify clusters of symptoms and use them to classify clients into categories described in the latest version of the *Diagnostic and Statistical Manual of Mental Disorders, Fourth Edition (DSM-IV-TR;* American Psychiatric Association, 2000).

Identification and classification are critical features of scientific research and many areas of practice, regardless of whether the phenomena in question are genuinely categorical or continuous. Although we talk about most conditions as though they are categorical—as in deciding that someone "has" attention deficit disorder, developmental dyslexia, or depression—only in rare cases that follow simple Mendelian inheritance are conditions strictly categorical. For example, diagnoses of hypertension, many forms of heart disease, kidney failure, and liver disorders are made on the basis of test results that have continuous distributions. Making a diagnosis often requires imposing a categorical determination on continuous data, and nearly all conditions occur at varying degrees of severity. This is typical for developmental dyslexia as well.

Presently, there are several competing views about how to identify individuals with developmental dyslexia. In the present chapter, we 1) briefly review these competing views, 2) consider how to examine agreement among methods of identification based on the competing views, 3) introduce a new agreement statistic, and 4) review the results of empirical studies of agreement among alternative identification procedures.

DEVELOPMENTAL DYSLEXIA

Developmental dyslexia refers to unexpected poor reading that cannot be attributed to sensory impairments, motor impairments, emotional impairments, mental deficiency, economic or cultural disadvantage, or inadequate reading instruction (Adams & Bruck, 1993; Bruck, 1990; Gough & Tunmer, 1986; Lyon, Shaywitz, & Shaywitz, 2003; Perfetti, 1985, 1986; Siegel, 2003; Stanovich, 1994). Most individuals with developmental dyslexia show impaired word-level reading (e.g., see Adams, 1990;

National Research Council, 1998; Stanovich, 1982; Vellutino, 1979). Although many individuals with dyslexia also are impaired in reading comprehension, the impaired comprehension often results from the impairment in word-level reading (Aaron, 1989; Stanovich & Siegel, 1994) or as a consequence of language impairments. Additional support for the primacy of deficits in word-level reading comes from the fact that adults who have compensated for their reading difficulty and no longer are impaired at reading comprehension nevertheless continue to struggle with word recognition (Bruck, 1990, 1993; Scarborough, 1984).

Most individuals with developmental dyslexia perform poorly on measures of phonological awareness and phonological decoding and have fewer words that can be decoded by sight (Ehri, 1998; Fox, 1994; Rack, Snowling, & Olson, 1992; Siegel & Faux, 1989). *Phonological awareness* refers to an individual's awareness and access to the sound structure of his or her oral language (Wagner & Torgesen, 1987). *Phonological decoding* refers to decoding words by sounding them out, as when one is asked to decode nonwords such as *brep.*

Traditionally, the operational definition of *unexpected poor reading* involves classifying people based on severe discrepancy between aptitude, as measured by intelligence or achievement tests outside the realm of reading (e.g., mathematics) and reading skill. However, most research-based definitions of developmental dyslexia now omit a discrepancy requirement, largely because young poor readers display similar profiles of skills and instructional needs regardless of whether their poor reading is discrepant from their intelligence quotient (IQ; see Fletcher, Lyon, Fuchs, & Barnes, 2007, for a recent review of this literature). Based in part on this research literature, professional practice is beginning to change in the United States and throughout the world. In the United States, the most recent reauthorization of the Individuals with Disabilities Education Act (IDEA)—the Individuals with Disabilities Education Improvement Act of 2004 (IDEA 2004; PL 108-446)—no longer requires that people display a discrepancy between aptitude and achievement to be eligible to receive special education services.

IDEA specifically identifies response to intervention (RTI) as an alternative eligibility determination for specific learning disabilities, including reading disability. RTI models are being implemented in Taiwan and Hong Kong, as well as in many countries. Fuchs, Mock, Morgan, and Young (2003) provide a prototypical RTI model consisting of five steps:

1. Students receive effective instruction in their general education classrooms.

2. Progress is monitored, and children who are not responding to effective instruction are identified.

3. Nonresponders are provided with additional, more intensive instruction or intervention such as small-group or individual tutoring.

4. Progress monitoring continues.

5. Students who still are not responsive to intervention are either provided with more intensive intervention or referred for special education services, depending on the specific RTI model being implemented.

Although a growing number of studies of the RTI model are now available (e.g., Case, Speece, & Malloy, 2003; Fletcher, Lyon, Fuchs, & Barnes, 2007; Fuchs & Fuchs, 1998; Fuchs, Mock, Morgan, & Young, 2003), many important questions remain unanswered (Fuchs, Deshler, & Reschly, 2004; Reynolds & Shaywitz, 2009). Perhaps the most important unanswered question regarding the implementation of an RTI model is, What is an effective operational definition of inadequate RTI?

Vellutino et al. (1996) proposed a "median split" operational definition. Poor readers are identified initially, perhaps on the basis of teacher nomination. Intervention is provided, and progress is monitored and quantified in terms of slope of growth over repeated measures. Students whose slopes are below the median are considered to be nonresponders. Alternatively, Fuchs, Fuchs, and Compton (2004) proposed a "slope-discrepancy model" in which nonresponders are identified not by reference to a median split but rather in reference to classroom, school, district, state, or national norms. A concern about using slopes to quantify RTI, however, is that individual differences in slopes tend to be less reliable than individual differences in status or relative achievement at a given point in time and may not make a contribution to prediction of RTI that is independent of measures of achievement status (Schatschneider, Wagner, & Crawford, 2008).

An alternative to relying on slope is to make decisions in an RTI model on the basis of a one-time assessment of achievement status (i.e., relative position). For example, the *final benchmark* approach (Good, Simmons, & Kame'enui, 2001) identifies nonresponders as those whose achievement falls below a benchmark score that is based on prior longitudinal studies of reading. A *normalization* model (Torgesen et al., 2001) is similar, but rather than compare raw scores on an assessment to a benchmark score, standard scores are used and students who score below a standard score of 90 after intervention are considered to be nonresponders. Finally, a *dual-discrepancy* (Fuchs & Fuchs, 1998; Speece & Case, 2001) model requires below-average scores on both slope and final achievement level or status.

Given these different approaches to classification, a critical issue is whether the alternative operational definitions of RTI converge by identifying the same group of students who are poor readers (versus different groups of poor readers). If largely overlapping groups of poor readers are identified using alternative operational definitions of RTI, it may not matter which definition is adopted. On the other hand, if alternative operational definitions identify largely different groups of poor readers, determining which definition to use becomes critical.

RECENT STUDIES THAT COMPARED ALTERNATIVE APPROACHES WITH IDENTIFYING NONRESPONDERS

Two studies have compared alternative definitions of RTI in RTI models. The Fuchs, Fuchs, and Compton (2004) study compared alternative definitions of RTI in samples of first- and second-grade students. The data were analyzed retrospectively from completed reading intervention studies. Students who were at risk were identified on the basis of screening measures given at the beginning of the year. The teachers implemented Peer-Assisted Learning Strategies (PALS; Fuchs, Fuchs, Mathes, & Simmons, 1997), and responsiveness to PALS was monitored. Students whose performance remained substantially below that of classroom peers were considered to be nonresponders. Alternative RTI-based approaches were used to gauge responsiveness to PALS, including using a median split of growth in Dolch sight word reading in first grade and a median split of growth in oral reading fluency in second grade. The key result for present purposes is that the alternative RTI-based predictors generated largely different groups of poor readers. No specific agreement statistics were provided, however, and data that would permit calculating agreement statistics after the fact were not reported.

The Barth et al. (2008) study was carried out on a sample of 399 first-grade students. The purpose was to compare alternative RTI-based methods, cut points, and measures to determine the extent to which alternative operationalizations of RTI models overlap and agree in identifying adequate and inadequate responders. The alternative operationalizations included measures of RTI based on slope, final status, or dual discrepancy (i.e., low on both slope and final status). The different cut points included scoring 0.5, 1.0, and 1.5 standard deviations (SDs) below the mean of typically achieving students. The measures included the Test of Word Reading Efficiency (Torgesen, Wagner, & Rashotte, 1999) and the Continuous Monitoring of Early Reading Skills (CMERS; Mathes, Torgesen, & Herron, in press), a computer-based progress monitoring assessment. They identified kappa as the best overall index of agreement because it controls for chance levels of agreement.

Overall, agreement across methods, cut points, and measures was generally poor. Roughly 85% of kappas did not reach the minimal level of agreement of .40. Further, most of the minimal level of agreement that was found was agreement that individuals were not poor readers, as opposed to agreement that individuals were poor readers. Before presenting the results of a recent study that we carried out examining agreement among alternative approaches to identifying nonresponders, it is important to consider how best to quantify agreement between alternative methods.

QUANTIFYING AGREEMENT BETWEEN TWO METHODS OF CLASSIFICATION

To what extent do two methods agree on whether an individual has developmental dyslexia? Answering this important and straightforward

Table 12.1. Hypothetical comparison between two methods of classification

	Method A	Method B	
Developmental dyslexia	(a) 6	(b) 2	8
Adequate reading	(c) 4	(d) 88	92
Totals	10	90	100

question has been more difficult than one might imagine. Consider the hypothetical situation portrayed in Table 12.1. This is a two-by-two table that describes agreement between two methods of classifying 100 individuals as either having developmental dyslexia or being adequate readers. Both methods agree that 6 individuals have developmental dyslexia (cell a) and that 88 do not (cell d). There is disagreement about the status of 6 individuals: 2 are considered to have developmental dyslexia by method B but not by method A (cell b); 4 are considered to have developmental dyslexia by method A but not by method B (cell c). What is the best way to describe the degree to which the two methods agree about whether individuals have developmental dyslexia?

Overall Proportion of Agreement

Perhaps the simplest measure of agreement is overall proportion of agreement. Methods A and B agree that 6 individuals have developmental dyslexia and 88 do not. Thus, they agree on 94 (cell a plus cell d) out of the 100 cases, for an overall proportion of agreement of .94.

Although straightforward, overall proportion of agreement is inflated by chance. Imagine two people simultaneously tossing coins in the air and calling out "developmental dyslexia" if their coin lands heads up and "adequate reader" if their coin lands tails up. If they each toss their coins 100 times, the expected distribution of agreement is presented in Table 12.2. Obviously, there is no true relation between the diagnoses proclaimed by the two individuals. Each of their diagnoses depends completely on chance. For Table 12.2, the overall proportion of agreement is .5, which reflects the level of chance agreement expected between two coin tosses. The problem, then, for overall proportion of agreement, is that the value of .94 obtained for the data presented in Table 12.1 is inflated by chance agreement. Fortunately, kappa was developed to handle this problem, and you may recall that Barth et al. (2008) featured kappa in reporting the results of their study because it corrects for chance agreement.

Table 12.2. Comparison between two methods of classification based completely on coin tosses

	Method A	Method B	
Developmental dyslexia	(a) 25	(b) 25	50
Adequate reading	(c) 25	(d) 25	50
Totals	50	50	100

Kappa

Cohen's kappa provides an index of the overall proportion of agreement corrected for chance. It is an index of the extent to which observed agreement exceeds that expected on the basis of chance. For the classification data presented in Table 12.1, the obtained value of kappa is .634.

That kappa indeed represents the overall proportion of agreement corrected for chance can be confirmed by applying kappa to the coin-tossing data presented in Table 12.2. Because the data were created by hypothetical coin tosses, agreement has to be due to chance. If you toss two coins, half the time they will agree on heads or tails. The value of kappa for the data in Table 12.2 is 0. There is no agreement beyond chance, which is what would be expected if we make diagnoses by tossing coins!

An advantage of kappa over the overall proportion of agreement, beyond the desirable fact that it corrects for chance agreement, is that its mathematical sampling distribution is known. This means that values of kappa have associated standard errors and confidence intervals. The formula for calculating the standard error of kappa is complex, although in practice it is largely determined by the size of kappa and by the proportion of agreement expected on the basis of chance (Hanley, 1987). For the data presented in Table 12.1 that yielded a kappa of .634, the standard error is .137, and the 95% confidence interval ranges from .365 to .903. Because the confidence interval does not include 0, we know that our value of kappa is significantly greater than 0, and consequently that our two methods agree significantly above chance.

There is an important limitation of kappa for its use as an index of agreement between two methods of classification. The limitation is that it overestimates the actual level of agreement between alternative methods of diagnosing developmental dyslexia. Kappa represents an average of 1) agreement above chance that individuals have developmental dyslexia and 2) agreement above chance that individuals do not have developmental dyslexia (i.e., are adequate readers). Under normal conditions, agreement that individuals do not have developmental dyslexia is higher than is agreement that they do.

The reason why agreement that individuals are adequate readers is higher than agreement that individuals have developmental dyslexia can be understood by referring to Figure 12.1. Measurement error causes observed scores to vary about an individual's underlying true score. In Figure 12.1, measurement error is represented by error bars. For individuals with true scores that are in the vicinity of a cut point, measurement error can cause their observed scores to be on one side of the cut point on one assessment and on the opposite side of the cut point on a second assessment. As can be seen in Figure 12.1, for categories with relatively low base rates, such as developmental dyslexia, most of the individuals with developmental dyslexia necessarily will score near the cut point: There simply is not much room in the distribution to get away from the cut point if you have developmental dyslexia. In contrast,

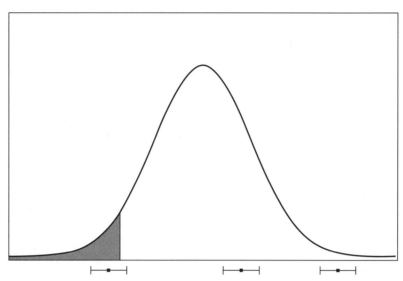

Figure 12.1. The effects of measurement error on scores near a cut point.

individuals who do not have developmental dyslexia can be far away from the cut point in the distribution. Measurement error therefore is less likely to cause fluctuation in categorization for individuals who do not have developmental dyslexia compared with individuals who do. Because kappa is an average of agreement about both individuals who have developmental dyslexia and individuals who do not, kappa *overestimates* agreement above chance that individuals have developmental dyslexia and *underestimates* agreement above chance that individuals do not. In sum, although kappa has important advantages as a strategy for assessing agreement (e.g., it controls for chance agreement), it also has some disadvantages (e.g., it overestimates agreement for low-base rate categories).

Affected-Status Agreement Statistic

To measure agreement in a way that is not inflated by agreement that individuals are not affected by developmental dyslexia, Waesche, Schatschneider, Maner, Ahmed, and Wagner (2011) developed the affected status agreement statistic to overcome the previously noted limitation of kappa. For this statistic, affected-status agreement is calculated as the proportion of students classified as having developmental dyslexia, by both definitions being compared, out of the group of students classified as reading disabled by either definition. For example, suppose that 100 students were identified as having developmental dyslexia by two different definitions, and that 75 of these 100 students were identified by both definitions. The affected-status agreement would then be 75 divided by 100, or .75. Referring again to Table 12.1, affected-status agreement would be calculated by dividing cell a by the sum of cells a, b, and c. For the current example, the affected-status agreement would be 6 divided by the sum of 6 + 2 + 4, or .50.

Table 12.3. Calculating proportion agreement expected due to chance

	Method A	Method B	
Developmental dyslexia	(a) .10(.08) = .008	(b) .90(.08) = .072	.08
Adequate reading	(c) .10(.92) = .092	(d) .90(.92) = .828	.92
Proportions	.10	.90	1.00

As with kappa, the affected-status agreement can provide an index of proportion agreement beyond chance. To find the chance-corrected affected-status agreement, the first step is to find the proportion of agreement expected due to chance. For the data presented in Table 12.1, finding the proportion agreement expected due to chance for each cell requires multiplying the corresponding base rates for each cell. These calculations are presented in Table 12.3. Because the affected-status agreement statistic is calculated by dividing cell a by the sum of cells a, b, and c, the following formula is used to calculate how much of affected-status agreement would be due to chance:

$$Pr(e) = \frac{.008}{.008 + .092 + .072} = .047$$

To calculate chance-corrected affected-status agreement, the obtained values are substituted into the following equation:

$$p(a) = \frac{Pr(a) - Pr(e)}{1 - Pr(e)} = \frac{.5 - .047}{1 - .047} = \frac{.453}{.953} = .48$$

Notice that there is little difference between affected-status agreement (.5) and chance-corrected affected-status agreement (.48). Recall that when kappa was used to correct overall agreement for agreement due to chance, the difference was considerable. For the present example, overall agreement was .94 and kappa was .634, a drop of one third. The reason for the difference in effects of correcting for chance in affected-status agreement and overall agreement is that overall agreement includes the cell representing agreement that individuals are not affected by developmental dyslexia. When base rates are low for a target condition, most individuals are not affected. Under these conditions, chance agreement is high that individuals are not affected. This accounts for the large difference between overall agreement and kappa. Because affected-status agreement does not include the cell representing agreement that individuals are not affected, there is relatively little difference between the original and chance-corrected versions of the affected-status agreement statistic. This characteristic thus reflects an advantage of the affected-status agreement statistic over kappa. Waesche et al. (2011) used the affected-status agreement statistic to study agreement among alternative definitions of dyslexia.

The large-scale Waesche et al. (2011) study of 288,114 students in first through third grades compared rates of agreement among alternative definitions of reading disability and their 1- and 2-year stabilities. The available reading measures were Dynamic Indicators of Basic Early Literacy Skills (DIBELS), Oral Reading Fluency (ORF) and Nonsense Word Fluency (NWF; Good, Kaminski, Smith, Laimon, & Dill, 2001). Six levels of severity of poor reading were examined (25th, 20th, 15th, 10th, 5th, and 3rd percentile ranks) to determine whether agreement increased with increasing severity of the reading problem. Four operational definitions were compared, including traditional unexpected low achievement and three RTI-based definitions: low achievement, low growth, and dual discrepancy. Agreement was measured using the affected-status agreement statistic described earlier.

Beginning with agreement among alternative operational definitions, the agreement between the traditional unexpected low achievement and the three RTI-based definitions of low growth, low achievement, and dual discrepancy was poor. For example, at the 3rd percentile, the median affected-status agreement rates between unexpected low-achievement definition and the three RTI-based definitions were .25, .23, and .25 percent for the low-achievement, low-growth, and dual-discrepancy definitions, respectively. With decreasing severity of the reading problem, the agreement rates increased; affected-status agreement rates at the 25th percentile were roughly double in magnitude of those at the 3rd percentile. Thus, the results did not support the idea that the alternative definitions would converge on the same group of poor readers as severity of the reading problem increased. We believe the phenomenon of increasing rates of agreement with decreasing severity of the reading problem is largely attributable to the fact that the larger area of affected scores made it possible for more of them to be further away from the cutoff score and therefore less likely to change categories as a result of measurement error (Francis et al., 2005). Referring to Figure 12.1, a less stringent criterion for qualifying as having impaired reading corresponds to expanding the shaded area. This criterion makes it possible for affected individuals to be further away from the cutoff score.

Turning to the three RTI-based definitions, the median affected-status agreement between the low-achievement and low-growth definitions was .51 at the 3rd percentile level of severity, increasing to .72 at the 25th percentile. This level of agreement was higher than that just described between the traditional unexpected low-achievement definitions and the RTI-based definitions, although relatively low nonetheless. Higher levels of agreement were found between the dual-discrepancy definition and both the low-achievement and low-growth definitions, with median affected-status agreements around .70 at the 3rd percentile, increasing to .80 at the 25th percentile. These higher rates of agreement are likely to be artifacts of the part–whole relations between the dual-discrepancy definition and both low-achievement and low-growth definitions. Identification by the dual-discrepancy definition required meeting the low-achievement and low-growth definitions.

Turning to 1-year and 2-year stability, the longitudinal stability was low for all of the definitions. The affected-status agreement rates were largely below .50. The poorest performer in terms of stability was the low-growth definition, likely due to the lessened reliability of measures of growth relative to measures of status under typical conditions (Schatschneider, Wagner, & Crawford, 2008).

CONCLUSION

In summary, all three studies suggest low agreement among alternative operational definitions of RTI. Some, but not all, of the lack of agreement between alternative operational definitions can be attributed to a lessened precision using cut scores in relatively continuous distributions due to measurement error affecting categorization of individuals near the cutoff score (Francis et al., 2005). The substantial remaining lack of agreement is troublesome.

We offer several recommendations for moving forward. First, we think it is essential to have separate operational definitions of developmental dyslexia to be used for research purposes and of learning disabilities to be used for determining eligibility for special education services. Doing so will avoid inherent conflicts between scientific and political realities. For example, a student with an IQ of 140 and with achievement in math at a commensurate level, but whose reading is below average with a standard score of 88, is likely to have developmental dyslexia and would make a valuable participant in a study. However, because the level of reading achievement is not substantially below grade level, it is unlikely that special education services of any sort would be made available to this student in the United States. Federal and state policy limit special education services to students whose reading performance is poor relative to one's grade-level peers. This policy is based on economic considerations rather than scientific ones.

Second, we think it is important to look cross-culturally for universal aspects of an affected phenotype or phenotypes. The candidate with the most evidence cross-culturally is impaired phonological processing, which appears to be an early aspect of impaired reading regardless of the nature of the script an individual must learn to read (Goulandris, 2003). Other possibilities also should be explored. One is *late-emerging* developmental dyslexia, which may or may not turn out to be a separate kind of developmental dyslexia. Another possible phenotype worth exploring is impaired reading comprehension with adequate word-level decoding. A key question here is whether the comprehension problems of individuals who are adequate at word-level decoding are in any way specific to reading rather than to general to oral language.

We think it is critical for scientific studies of developmental dyslexia to be based on a rigorously validated phenotype that may require multiple assessments of phonological processing and reading. We also recommend that constructs be represented with latent variables and that serious effort be made to avoid apparent differences that derive from measurement artifacts. For example, students with reading problems who are attempting to learn to read transparent languages such as Finnish or German tend to be relatively accurate but slow. In contrast, poor readers who are attempting to learn to read opaque languages such as English make errors and also are slow. Does being accurate but slow in reading Finnish represent the same underlying problem in reading skill that being inaccurate and slow in reading English represents? Careful experimental designs coupled with new agreement statistics that focus more clearly on affected individuals is one way to begin to answer this and related questions.

REFERENCES

Aaron, P.G. (1989). Qualitative and quantitative differences among dyslexic, normal, and nondyslexic poor readers. *Reading & Writing, 1,* 291–308.

Adams, M.J. (1990). *Beginning to read: Thinking and learning about print.* Cambridge, MA: The MIT Press

Adams, M.J., & Bruck, M. (1993). Word recognition: The interface of educational policies and scientific research. *Reading & Writing, 5,* 113–139.

American Psychiatric Association. (2000). *Diagnostic and statistical manual of mental disorders* (4th ed., text revision). Washington, DC: Author.

Barth, A.E., Stuebing, K.K., Anthony, J.L., Denton, C.A., Mathes, P.G., Fletcher, J.M., et al. (2008). Agreement among response to intervention criteria for identifying responder status. *Learning and Individual Differences, 18,* 296–307.

Bruck, M. (1990). Word-recognition skills of adults with childhood diagnoses of dyslexia. *Developmental Psychology, 26,* 439–454.

Bruck, M. (1993). Word recognition and component phonological processing skills of adults with childhood diagnosis of dyslexia. *Developmental Review, 13,* 258–268.

Case, L.P., Speece, D.L., & Molloy, D.E. (2003). The validity of a response-to-instruction paradigm to identify reading disabilities: A longitudinal analysis of individual difference and contextual factors. *School Psychology Review, 32,* 557–582.

Ehri, L.C. (1998). Grapheme–phoneme knowledge is essential to learning to read words in English. In J.L. Metsala & L.C. Ehri (Eds.), *Word recognition in beginning literacy* (pp. 3–40). Mahwah, NJ: Lawrence Erlbaum Associates.

Fletcher, J.M., Lyon, G.R., Fuchs, L., & Barnes, M.A. (2007). *Learning disabilities: From identification to intervention.* New York: Guilford.

Fox, E. (1994). Grapheme–phoneme correspondence in dyslexic and matched control readers. *British Journal of Psychology, 85,* 41–53.

Francis, D.J., Fletcher, J.M., Stuebing, K.K., Lyon, G.R., Shaywitz, B.A., & Shaywitz, S.E. (2005). Psychometric approaches to the identification of LD: IQ and achievement scores are not sufficient. *Journal of Learning Disabilities, 38,* 98–108.

Fuchs, D., Deshler, D.D., & Reschly, D.J. (2004). National Research Center on Learning Disabilities: Multimethod Studies of Identification and Classification Issues. *Learning Disability Quarterly, 27*(4), 189–195.

Fuchs, D., Fuchs, L.S., & Compton, D. (2004). Identifying reading disabilities by responsiveness-to-instruction: Specifying measures and criteria. *Learning Disability Quarterly, 27,* 216–227.

Fuchs, D., Fuchs, L.S., Mathes, P., & Simmons, D. (1997). Peer-Assisted Learning Strategies: Making classrooms more responsive to student diversity. *American Educational Research Journal, 34,* 174–206.

Fuchs, D., Mock, D., Morgan, P.L., & Young, C.L. (2003). Responsiveness-to-intervention: Definitions, evidence, and implications for the learning disabilities construct. *Learning Disabilities Research & Practice, 18,* 157–171.

Fuchs, L.S., & Fuchs, D. (1998). Treatment validity: A unifying concept for reconceptualizing the identification of learning disabilities. *Learning Disabilities Research & Practice, 13,* 204–219.

Good, R.H., Kaminski, R.A., Smith, S., Laimon, D., & Dill, S. (2001). *Dynamic* indicators of basic early literacy skills (5th ed.). Eugene: University of Oregon.

Good, R.H., Simmons, D.C., & Kame'enui, E.J. (2001). The importance and decision-making utility of a continuum of fluency-based indicators of foundational reading skills for third-grade high-stakes outcomes. *Scientific Studies of Reading, 5*, 257–288.

Gough, P.B., & Tunmer, W.E. (1986). Decoding, reading, and reading disability. *Remedial and Special Education, 7*, 6–10.

Goulandris, N. (Ed.). (2003). *Dyslexia in different languages: Cross-linguistic comparisons.* London: Whurr Publishers.

Hanely, J.A. (1987). Standard error of the Kappa statistic. *Psychological Bulletin, 102*, 315–321.

Lyon, G.R., Shaywitz, S.E., & Shaywitz, B.A. (2003). A definition of dyslexia. *Annals of Dyslexia, 53*, 1–14.

Mathes, P.G., Torgesen, J.K., & Herron, J. Continuous Monitoring of Early Reading Skills (CMERS) (In press) [Computer software]. San Rafael, CA: Talking Fingers, Inc

National Research Council. (1998). *Preventing reading difficulties in young children.* Washington, DC: National Academy Press.

Perfetti, C.A. (1985). *Reading ability.* New York: Oxford University Press.

Perfetti, C.A. (1986). Continuities in reading acquisition, reading skill, and reading disability. *Remedial & Special Education, 7*, 11–21.

Rack, J.P., Snowling, M.J., & Olson, R.K. (1992). The nonword reading deficit in developmental dyslexia: A review. *Reading Research Quarterly, 27*, 28–53.

Reynolds, C.R., & Shaywitz, S.E. (2009). Response to intervention: Ready or not? From wait-to-fail to watch-them-fail. *School Psychology Review, 24*, 130–145.

Scarborough, H.S. (1984). Continuity between childhood dyslexia and adult reading. *British Journal of Psychology, 75*, 329–348.

Schatschneider, C.L., Wagner, R.K., & Crawford, E. (2008). The importance of measuring growth in response to intervention models: Testing a core assumption. *Learning and Individual Differences, 18*, 308–315.

Siegel, L.S. (2003). Basic cognitive processes and reading disabilities. In H.L. Swanson & K.R. Harris (Eds.), *Handbook of learning disabilities* (pp. 158–181). New York: Guilford Press.

Siegel, L.S., & Faux, D. (1989). Acquisition of certain grapheme–phoneme correspondences in normally achieving and disabled readers. *Reading & Writing, 1*, 37–52.

Speece, D.L., & Case, L.P. (2001). Classification in context: An alternative approach to identifying early reading disability. *Journal of Educational Psychology, 93*, 735–749.

Stanovich, K.E. (1982). Individual differences in the cognitive processes of reading: I. Word decoding. *Journal of Learning Disabilities, 15*, 485–493.

Stanovich, K.E. (1994). Does dyslexia exist? *Journal of Child Psychology & Psychiatry & Allied Disciplines, 35*, 579–595.

Stanovich, K.E., & Siegel, L.S. (1994). Phenotypic performance profile of children with reading disabilities: A regression-based test of the phonological-core variable-difference model. *Journal of Educational Psychology, 86*, 24–53.

Torgesen, J.K., Alexander, A.W., Wagner, R.K., Rashotte, C.A., Voeller, K.K.S., & Conway, T. (2001). Intensive remedial instruction for children with severe reading disabilities: Immediate and long-term outcomes from two instructional approaches. *Journal of Learning Disabilities, 34*, 33–58.

Torgesen, J.K., Wagner, R.K., & Rashotte, C.A. (1999). *Test of Word Reading Efficiency.* Austin, TX: PRO-ED.

Vellutino, F.R. (1979). *Dyslexia: Theory and research.* Cambridge, MA: The MIT Press.

Vellutino, F.R., Scanlon, D.M., Sipay, E.R., Small, S.G., Chen, R., Pratt, A., et al. (1996). Cognitive profiles of difficult-to-remediate and readily remediated poor readers: Early intervention as a vehicle for distinguishing between cognitive and experiential deficits as basic causes of specific reading disability. *Journal of Educational Psychology, 88*, 601–638.

Waesche, J.B., Schatschneider, C., Maner, J.K., Ahmed, Y., & Wagner, R.K. (2011). Examining Agreement and Longitudinal Stability Among Traditional and RTI-Based Definitions of Reading Disability Using the Affected-Status Agreement Statistic. *Journal of Learning Disabilities, 44*, 296–307.

Wagner, R.K., & Torgesen, J.K. (1987). The nature of phonological processing and its causal role in the acquisition of reading skills. *Psychological Bulletin, 101*, 192–212.

Reflections on Additional Approaches to the Study of Dyslexia

Brett Miller, Peggy McCardle, and Jun Ren Lee

M odel development, conceptual development, and their testing and evaluation refine our understanding of the underlying mechanisms involved in normal and impaired reading development. The expanded use of computational models forces a level of specificity that previous primarily cognitive or developmental accounts of reading did not require. To build and test a computational model, modelers generally need to develop a conceptual framework for a particular phenomenon—in this case, reading—and make difficult decisions about *what* to implement within the model and, critically, *how* to implement that conceptual model. This specificity brings the benefit of potentially providing insights not only when a model successfully accounts for general patterns of empirical data, but also in its failures; these failures provide insight into what the actual underlying structure in children or adults might be. Although one can debate how accurately particular theoretical or conceptual accounts of reading—particularly computational models—might reflect children's or adults' actual reading or word reading, their impact on conceptual and empirically focused research has been remarkable. The chapters in this section argue for and help to demonstrate the value of modeling in helping us move toward a firmer understanding of reading disability in children and adults.

In Chapter 9, Seidenberg argues for the value of computational modeling to help elucidate the underlying structure or cognitive architecture involved in reading. Compared with other approaches to theoretical model development, computational models often build on fewer, more general principles of how people represent knowledge and learn. Seidenberg argues for the value of models for hypothesis testing and establishing closer causal relations. The value is sometimes underemphasized outside of the community of researchers who are developing and working with these models. However, models provide a unique opportunity to test specific assumptions and see where the models fail to account for patterns of data observed in the field. This can also aid in interpretation or allow differentiation between possible accounts for why one might observe a certain pattern of data.

Although currently not fully realized, Seidenberg points out that computational accounts may move us closer to providing a specified link between brain and behavior and to enriching our understanding of the relationship between structure and function as it relates to reading or language tasks. Making this linkage will be exceedingly complex;

however, increased meaningful interaction between model developers and neurobiological researchers might not only help to refine our conceptual understanding of the function of architecture in the brain, but it might also help the field progress from identification of neurophenotypes of dyslexia toward models of how and why brain differences affect reading skill development (Pugh & McCardle, 2009). Seidenberg argues for an approach that incorporates three properties in particular: statistical rather than categorical relationships, constraint satisfaction (or the idea that a particular outcome is derived by the combination of information sources that by themselves may not significantly constrain the solution), and division of labor in a model. This type of account, as advocated by Seidenberg and others, demonstrates that rule-governed approaches to modeling reading are unnecessary to generate normal word reading; instead, the author points out that patterns of reading performance—such as reading regular and irregular words—can be produced accurately by building a model sensitive to words' statistical regularities. This demonstration shows the potential utility of using computational approaches to examine possible underlying mechanisms involved in reading.

Despite the potential of these approaches, relatively little work has been completed using a computational modeling framework examining cross-linguistic similarities or differences (although some exceptions exist, such as German and English using a single underlying model structure [Ziegler, Chapter 10, this volume]). The need for increased attention to cross-linguistic research is noted throughout this volume, and in this section Seidenberg (Chapter 9) and Wagner et al. (Chapter 12, this volume) further highlight phonology as a possible primary, but not exclusive, candidate for investigation in cross-linguistic studies. For instance, Seidenberg presents a nice illustration of how other information beyond spelling-to-sound correspondences can provide critical constraints for modeling efforts. In this illustration, he chose to highlight some modeling efforts using Serbian, a transparent language. In this case, syllabic stress provided an important constraint to help identify the word being referred to; interestingly, this is information that is not overtly represented in the written form.

Finally, we would like to highlight the ortholinguistic equilibrium hypothesis posited in Chapter 9 by Seidenberg. This hypothesis predicts that languages with higher degrees of complexity at one level (e.g., transparency of orthography) tend to have less complexity at other levels (e.g., morphology). Seidenberg uses modeling work in Serbian (Mirković, MacDonald, & Seidenberg, 2004) to illustrate both the extent of the morphological complexity in Serbian and how models can serve as experiments to build a better understanding of what needs to be accounted for to produce skilled reading. More generally, the Serbian case illustrates the import of adjusting models for specific aspects of a language or writing system. Remember the argument here is that models are not designed to reflect *truth* as much as they are used as a means of understanding, predicting, and investigating a phenomenon (in our examples, reading; Seidenberg, Chapter 9).

In Chapter 10, Ziegler discusses his current efforts to model individual rather than group-level data. He demonstrates the potential of using an individual differences approach to the problem of reading and reading disability and, along with it, the potential power of using modeling as an experiment to help elucidate the underlying structure of reading disability.

Ziegler collected performance data on tasks related to word reading (e.g., tasks focused on attention, letter processing, grapheme–phoneme mapping) and used the data to model word reading performance in a sample of French-speaking children, ages 8–11, with dyslexia. The general approach taken was to gather reading subcomponent data on each child, then use the data to inform how to "impair" the models of an individual child's performance to directly reflect each child's underlying impairments. To do this, Ziegler used the dual-route cascading (DRC) model of reading aloud (a computational model of word reading; for one example, see Coltheart, Rastle, Perry, Langdon, & Ziegler, 2001). Tasks were strategically chosen to link to components of the DRC model and to facilitate examination of the model's performance by perturbing the model (adding noise) in relation to an individual's performance. The data from these behavioral tasks showed an impairment in letter-in-string perception for about 40% of the children in Ziegler's sample, a more widespread difficulty in rapid object naming (approximately 70% of the sample), and phoneme-matching difficulties in more than 80% of the children. As Ziegler points out, these data highlight the multidimensional nature of the difficulties faced by dyslexics.

With these tasks guiding decisions about how to perturb the DRC model for each individual-level simulation, Ziegler's model simulated word reading (regular and irregularly pronounced words) for each of the 24 participants. It is important to note that additional data were then collected from each of these individuals on their reading of these words. Of specific interest was how well the model overall could account for data at the individual level across the 24 simulations (one data set per participant). In the simulation, the model accounted for an average of about 48% of the variance in word reading across the 24 simulations that constitute the model for children with reading disabilities. To account for this variance, Ziegler adjusted the level of perturbation for each of the aspects of the model that corresponded to the factors that proved to be significantly more difficult on the component tasks discussed previously, but not on the word reading task that is being modeled, which is an important detail.

In contrast, one might argue that random perturbations could show the general behavioral pattern seen in the word reading; however, in this case, Ziegler and colleagues could account for only about 8.5% of the variance, significantly less than the simulations adjusted based on the *extent* of difficulty that individuals had in the component tasks. The success of modeling at the individual level is particularly noteworthy for investigations of individual differences, and at a group level, this modeling effort reflects that one can show patterns of deficits consistent with surface or phonological dyslexia without assuming the standard underlying deficit in the model; this feature highlights the need for researchers to assess skills more broadly rather than skills narrowly focused on word reading. Finally, although the DRC model—which is a model based on adult word reading—showed strong potential to model differences in children's performance, we are still left with the need for a true developmental model.

Consistent with the need to view reading through a developmental lens, Magnuson et al. (Chapter 11) examine both the linguistic and nonlinguistic skills in a struggling young adult population. This particular population has received increased public attention in the U.S. of late with the national interest in adolescent transitions and the needs of adult learners (e.g., Achieve, 2010; ACT, 2006; Alliance for Excellent Education, 2010; Klekotka, 2005). Despite this interest and the clear societal impact, both economically and in terms of health, of not addressing the needs of these struggling learners, as Magnuson et al. point out, we know far less than is optimal to understand the underlying difficulties and strengths these individuals possess, as well as how to most effectively address their needs. Adolescents and adults—to an even greater extent than the younger children who struggle with reading or have a learning disability—represent a heterogeneous group in terms of learning and the presence of learning disabilities. The group includes individuals with learning disabilities (identified or not) who may have been unsuccessfully remediated with multiple intervention approaches or who may have received lower quality instruction that limited their learning.

Magnuson et al. report findings from examining the time course of spoken word recognition and learning in a community sample. Their experiments serve as a nice means of examining the phonological skills of these struggling readers. In their experiments, they take advantage of the visual world paradigm (VWP; e.g., see Cooper, 1974; Tanenhaus, Spivey-Knowlton, Eberhard, & Sedivy, 1995), developed for use with eye-tracking systems to examine the time course of processing spoken text. For those less familiar with this approach, the idea of using eye-movement data to examine spoken-word recognition may seem surprising. In fact, this approach has been shown to be highly sensitive to precisely the type of phonological attributes that Magnuson et al. are investigating (e.g., Dahan, Magnuson, Tanenhaus, & Hogan, 2001).

In this paradigm, listeners are typically shown a display with a number of pictures of objects and asked to respond to what they hear over headphones, such as *Click on the pickle*, while their eye movements and the object they select are recorded. On the screen, there is typically an array of four objects, one or more of which serve as distracters. For example, the participant might see *pickle* and *pie* on different parts of the screen; the input, *click on the pickle,* unfolds over time, and the participant must be able to recognize the difference between the sounds in *pickle* and *pie* to reliably select the right object. Data have accumulated showing that individuals' eye movements during this task are temporally sensitive to the unfolding information that a participant hears (e.g., Cooper, 1974; Dahan, Magnuson, & Tanenhaus, 2001; Dahan, Magnuson, Tanenhaus, & Hogan, 2001; Huettig & Altmann, 2005; Tanenhaus et al., 1995); essentially, gazes to the target object, such as *pickle,* reflect the underlying cognitive processing occurring. The benefit of this approach is that it gives you fine temporal resolution (often 250 to 1,000 samples a second), which can be invaluable in the types of modeling that Magnuson et al. conduct using an implementation of the TRACE model (McClelland & Elman, 1986), jTRACE (Strauss, Harris, & Magnuson, 2007), a model of speech perception.

Magnuson et al. present findings from two VWP studies and subsequent modeling in TRACE to help distinguish between two possible conceptual accounts. Perfetti and Hart (2002) and Ramus and Szenkovits (2008) propose accounts of the difficulties learners face in learning to read. Magnuson et al. use modeling to help elucidate the underlying structure of how these struggling adult readers process phonological information. In the first experiment, the participants listen to sentences with embedded target words (e.g., *pickle* from our earlier example), which may (or may not) have misleading coarticulatory information. For instance, the target word *neck* could be produced by splicing *neck* and *net* together such that the listener would hear an incorrect coarticulation in the formant transition from the vowel to the following consonant cluster; in previous work, Dahan, Magnuson, Tanenhaus, and Hogan (2001) showed that college-age listeners are sensitive to this inaccurate coarticulation. The findings from Magnuson et al. demonstrated that listeners showed stronger competitor effects across conditions in the struggling adult sample; that is, they had a higher proportion of fixations to target competitors than college-age adults, and this overall pattern of increased proportions of fixations to competitors lasted for a longer latency in relation to the temporal unfolding of the auditory presentation of the target word than when compared with the skilled reading data from the college sample. It is important that there was no apparent delay in the response (eye movement to target or competitor) as compared with the college sample.

In the second experiment, participants listen to "words" created using an artificial lexicon. The benefits of using artificial stimuli of this type are that the stimuli allow for fine-grained stimulus control that is simply impossible with real words, and the researcher can control for experience and exposure to this particular language because it will be new for all participants (the community sample and a college sample in this case). In the words formed from the artificial lexicon, some have onset competitors or rhyme competitors. In our discussion here, we focus on the performance results from the community sample. The overall pattern showed differences in the time course of processing, but not in accuracy of their responses when compared with the skilled readers. The community-sample participants on average showed a strong "word" cohort effect similar to the skilled readers but did not show a rhyme effect; the latter finding is consistent with reports of a similar lack of a rhyme effect for children with reading disabilities.

For both experiments, Magnuson et al. modeled the data using jTRACE (Strauss, Harris, & Magnuson, 2007). Essentially, this effort helps elucidate possible mechanisms that might explain the obtained data set. Across the two studies, only one solution within jTRACE was found that could accommodate both sets of data: reduction of the lateral inhibition at the phoneme level. The differences found may have origins in the representation and organization of phonology. The findings are also potentially consistent with the phonological access hypothesis of Ramus and Szenkovits (2008), suggesting that the impairment is at the level of phonological access, but with the important caveat that impairments are most likely to appear under more taxing and sensitive tasks.

The final chapter in this section (Wagner, Waesche, Schatschneider, Maner, & Ahmed, Chapter 12) focuses on issues of classification and identification of individuals with reading disability. In contrast to the other articles in the section, this article addresses how one thinks about identification and classification and the challenges of using various approaches to identify responses in a response to intervention (RTI) framework. RTI provides a service delivery framework that allows for escalation in services (e.g., more intensive instruction, closer progress monitoring) in response to difficulties experienced by the learner. As part of the system, information accumulates about the learner's *response*—or in some cases, inadequate response—to high-quality, evidence-based instruction. This information can form a key part in determining whether a person has a reading disability. As this framework continues to be scaled up, the issue of how one determines responsiveness to instruction becomes increasingly critical if we are to effectively address the needs of all learners, particularly those who struggle.

Wagner et al. begin by describing some of the approaches that have been used to determine whether a learner is responding adequately to instruction. The various approaches that have been proposed have known limitations. For instance, Vellutino et al. (1996) and Fuchs, Fuchs, and Compton (2004) propose using the slope of growth over repeated measures; in the case of Fuchs et al., the slopes are compared with norms—which could be local, district, statewide, or national—to determine whether the response is adequate. However, estimates of slopes are generally less reliable than measurement of status or achievement, and its added benefit over achievement status has been questioned (Schatschneider, Wagner, & Crawford, 2010). Other approaches highlighted here include using achievement status and the reader's performance (raw or standard scores) as compared with a proposed benchmark (e.g., Good, Simmons, & Kame'enui, 2001; Torgesen et al., 2001), or using a combination of achievement status and slope (e.g., Fuchs & Fuchs, 1998; Speece & Case, 2001). All of these approaches are attempting to ascertain, at some level, the appropriate model of response within an RTI framework.

Wagner et al. ask the important question of whether these approaches generate similar or disparate categorizations for individuals and highlight the previous work of Fuchs et al. (2004) and Barth et al. (2008). Both papers conclude that agreement between different conceptualizations of response is relatively poor; the approach of Barth et al. has the added benefit of using kappa as a formal measure of agreement. Kappa reflects the overall proportion of agreement corrected for chance and gives us a formal indicator of the degree of the agreement between different conceptualizations of how student growth should be modeled; unfortunately, kappa also overestimates agreement for low base-rate conditions, such as dyslexia.

Having the most accurate estimate possible of the agreement between different conceptualizations of growth has great import for both scientists and practitioners. Practitioners need to be able to use information about how different approaches to defining growth affect difficult choices in the classroom, such as to decide the recipients of more frequent progress monitoring or more intensive intervention. Scientific conceptualizations of learning disabilities that include whether a person is responsive to evidence-based interventions that one would expect to be effective in developing literacy skills provide us with critical information about the convergence of information about growth in learning. Such information is a key part of determining this broader idea of "responsiveness." We need models of what constitutes responsiveness in order to guide practitioners' implementation of RTI in the field.

In response to this need, Waesche, Schatschneider, Maner, Ahmed, and Wagner (in press; as cited in Wagner et al., Chapter 12) developed an alternative statistic termed the *affected-status agreement statistic*. This statistic relates to kappa in that it can index the proportion of agreement beyond chance; in the chance-corrected affected-status agreement, the mathematical correction that is applied to adjust for chance results in smaller adjustments to agreement estimates between approaches to growth. For conditions with low base rates such as dyslexia, the statistic is an important benefit. Waesche et al. used this statistic to examine agreement; taking advantage of the Florida Progress Monitoring and Reporting Network, they were able to model different classification approaches to reading disability on an exceptionally large number of individuals (almost 300,000). When comparing traditional discrepancy-based formulations and three RTI-based conceptualizations, they found poor agreement between approaches (approximately 25% for identification of individuals at the third percentile). The agreement estimates improved when comparing various RTI definitions; however, substantive disagreement occurred across a range of percentile groups, and agreement was lowest for the most stringent grouping (third percentile).

Wagner et al. argue that the lower agreement at the lowest percentile grouping is likely an artifact of the reduced range for individuals identified with reading disability using the third percentile; a larger range of scores increases the probability that a score will fall further from the cut point and be less likely to change categories between different classifications. It is important to note that the authors are not arguing that the underlying distribution of scores is categorical, but instead that in real-world settings, this type of a categorization is based on data that are likely continuous in nature. They argue that some of the lack of agreement between classification approaches could be attributed to measurement error around cut scores in relatively continuous distributions; this lack of agreement puts pressure on our decision rules for this choice and can affect which children are identified as having learning disabilities and which children receive services.

Overall, the collection of chapters in this section emphasizes the value of modeling, either computational or statistical modeling, both to help solve conceptual and theoretical issues and to address more practical issues of immediate import to practitioners. Model development and testing is key to furthering our understanding of the underlying factors that have an impact on reading and reading disability and can inform and motivate both empirical research and the next generation of interventions. Modeling can also help to elucidate the strengths, challenges, and limitations of current approaches to fundamental problems such as classification and identification of reading disability. Its value to the overall effort to understand and thereby develop more effective prevention and intervention approaches is clear, and the integration of this information in a volume such as this is an example of the integration across scientific approaches that should underlie future research into the neurobiology, genetics, and behavioral aspects of reading development and reading disabilities.

REFERENCES

Achieve. (2010). *Closing the expectations gap*. Washington, DC: Author. Retrieved December 28, 2010, from http://achieve.org/files/AchieveClosingtheExpectationsGap2010.pdf

ACT (2006). *Ready for college and ready for work: Same or different?* Iowa City, IA: Author. Retrieved December 28, 2010, from http://www.all4ed.org/files/PolicyBriefReinventingFedRoleEd.pdf

Alliance for Excellent Education. (2010). *Reinventing the federal role in education: Supporting the goal of college and career readiness for all students.* Washington, DC: Author. Retrieved December 28, 2010, from http://www.all4ed.org/files/PolicyBriefReinventingFedRole Ed.pdf

Barth, A.E., Stuebing, K.K., Anthony, J.L., Denton, C.A., Mathes, P.G., Fletcher, J.M., et al. (2008). Agreement among response to intervention criteria for identifying responder status. *Learning and Individual Differences, 18,* 296–307.

Coltheart, M., Rastle, K., Perry, C., Langdon, R., & Ziegler, J. (2001). DRC: A dual route cascaded model of visual word recognition and reading aloud. *Psychological Review, 108,* 204–256.

Cooper, R. (1974). The control of eye fixation by the meaning of spoken language: A new methodology for the real-time investigation of speech perception, memory, and language processing. *Cognitive Psychology, 6,* 84–107.

Dahan, D., Magnuson, J., & Tanenhaus, M. (2001). Time course of frequency effects in spoken word recognition: Evidence from eye movements. *Cognitive Psychology, 42,* 317–367.

Dahan, D., Magnuson, J., Tanenhaus, M., & Hogan, E. (2001). Subcategorical mismatches and the time course of lexical access: Evidence for lexical competition. *Language and Cognitive Processes, 16,* 507–534.

Fuchs, D., Fuchs, L.S., & Compton, D.L. (2004). Identifying reading disabilities by responsiveness to instruction: Specifying measures and criteria. *Learning Disability Quarterly, 27*(4), 216–228.

Fuchs, L.S., & Fuchs, D. (1998). Treatment validity: A unifying concept for reconceptualizing the identification of learning disabilities. *Learning Disabilities Research and Practice, 13,* 204–219.

Good, R.H., Simmons, D.C., & Kame'enui, E.J. (2001). The importance and decision-making utility of a continuum of fluency-based indicators of foundational reading skills for third-grade high-stakes outcomes. *Scientific Studies of Reading, 5,* 257–288.

Huettig, F., & Altmann, G. (2005). Word meaning and the control of eye fixation: Semantic competitor effects and the visual world paradigm. *Cognition, 96,* B23–B32.

Klekotka, P. (2005, June). Beyond high school: Improving transition programs for postsecondary education. *NCREL Policy Issues, 18.* Retrieved December 28, 2010, from http://www.ncrel.org/policy/pubs/pdfs/pivol18.pdf

McClelland, J., & Elman, J. (1986). The TRACE model of speech perception. *Cognitive Psychology, 18,* 1–86.

Mirković, J., MacDonald, M., & Seidenberg, M. (2004). Where does gender come from? Evidence from a complex inflectional system. *Language and Cognitive Processes, 20,* 139–168.

Perfetti, C., & Hart, L. (2002). The lexical quality hypothesis. In L. Verhoeven, C. Elbro, & P. Reitsma (Eds.), *Precursors of functional literacy* (pp. 189–213). Amsterdam/Philadelphia: John Benjamins.

Pugh, K., & McCardle, P. (2009). Conclusion: Integration of methodologies in cognitive neuroscience—research, planning, and policy. In K. Pugh & P. McCardle (Eds.), *How children learn to read: Current issues and new directions in the integration of cognition, neurobiology, and genetics of reading and dyslexia research and practice* (pp. 301–312). New York: Psychology Press, Taylor and Francis Group.

Ramus, F., & Szenkovits, G. (2008). What phonological deficit? *Quarterly Journal of Experimental Psychology, 61,* 129–141.

Schatschneider, C.L., Wagner, R.K., & Crawford, E. (2008). The importance of measuring growth in response to intervention models: Testing a core assumption. *Learning and Individual Differences, 18,* 308–315.

Speece, D.L., & Case, L.P. (2001). Classification in context: An alternative approach to identifying early reading disability. *Journal of Educational Psychology, 93,* 735–749.

Strauss, T., Harris, H., & Magnuson, J. (2007). jTRACE: A reimplementation and extension of the TRACE model of speech perception and spoken word recognition. *Behavior Research Methods, 39,* 19–30.

Tanenhaus, M.K., Spivey-Knowlton, M., Eberhard, K., & Sedivy, J.C. (1995). Integration of visual and linguistic information in spoken-language comprehension. *Science, 268,* 1632–1634.

Torgesen, J.K., Alexander, A.W., Wagner, R.K., Rashotte, C.A., Voeller, K.K.S., & Conway, T. (2001). Intensive remedial instruction for children with severe reading disabilities: Immediate and long-term outcomes from two instructional approaches. *Journal of Learning Disabilities, 34,* 33–58.

Vellutino, F.R., Scanlon, D.M., Sipay, E.R., Small, S.G., Chen, R., Pratt, A., et al. (1996). Cognitive profiles of difficult-to-remediate and readily remediated poor readers: Early intervention as a vehicle for distinguishing between cognitive and experiential deficits as basic causes of specific reading disability. *Journal of Educational Psychology, 88,* 601–638.

Waesche, J.B., Schatschneider, C., Maner, J.K., Ahmed, Y., & Wagner, R.K. (in press). Agreement and longitudinal stability among traditional and RTI-based definitions of reading disability.

Genetics and Neurobiology

遺傳與神經生物

PART IV CONTENTS

CHAPTER 13

Neurogenetic Contribution to Developmental Reading Disorders

Albert M. Galaburda, R. Holly Fitch, Joseph J. LoTurco, and Glenn D. Rosen

THE PHENOTYPE: DEVELOPMENTAL DYSLEXIA

Reading requires the mapping of language sounds (reducible to phonemes) onto visual representations of these sounds (graphemes). This mapping, at least where it concerns regular orthographies in which the sound–letter correspondence is consistent, presupposes conscious awareness of the phonological structure of the language to be read. Such awareness arises after a few years of exposure to the native language in children (usually around 5 years of age, on average), which probably reflects issues of brain maturation, because adults who are illiterate often learn to read in a much shorter time. In the most common form of the reading disorder—phonological dyslexia—children display a difficulty with this consciousness-dependent phonological awareness (Bradley & Bryant, 1981; Mody, Studdert-Kennedy, & Brady, 1997; Ramus, 2004; Shankweiler et al., 1995; Snowling, 2001), which is considered to be the deficit immediately proximal to learning to read.

The developmental origin of the deficit in phonological awareness remains unclear but continues to be an area of study (Benasich, 1998; Benasich et al., 2006) limited by the difficulties that exist in identifying children at risk for dyslexia early on when phonologies are being laid down. Phonology becomes established within the first year of life (Kuhl, 1994), but there is debate regarding the preadapted, nonlinguistic sensory and perceptual capacities that precede the acquisition of phonemes (Ramus, 2004). Clearly, congenital deafness would (and does) preclude the acquisition of spoken language during the first year of life, but we know that a nonauditory language such as American Sign Language can be acquired normally, following a time course that is equivalent to that of infants acquiring a spoken language (Petitto & Marentette, 1991), indicating that language per se is not affected, but rather a particular sensory modality for its implementation—in this case, hearing.

A more difficult question to answer is the extent to which degradation of the initial auditory experience (such as by fluid in the middle ear in infants with chronic otitis media in the first year of life [Bishop & Edmunson, 1986], for instance, or a degraded thalamocortical sound map) can interfere with the development of phonemic awareness and reading. Even the question of the nature of the preconscious phonological representations in very young children who will ultimately be diagnosed as dyslexic has not been fully answered, although there is the suggestion that these representations may be normal, because they are found to be normal in older children with dyslexia (Ramus &

Szenkovits, 2008). However, everyone would agree that this question remains open to debate, because not enough research has been carried out on the nature and degree of plasticity of these sensory/perceptual systems or phonological systems early on, which may render the picture at 12 years of age difficult to interpret. Other research in children at risk for language disorders (Benasich, 1998; Benasich et al., 2006) and in animal models (see next section) would seem to suggest that auditory processing is developmentally abnormal in infants at high risk for dyslexia but can improve to a variable extent. Following this observation, the notion that comes to mind is this: If sensory/perceptual abnormalities are present during a critical stage of development, affecting the development of linked cognitive functions, then even if there is subsequent "healing" in the prerequisite sensory–perceptual systems, the dependent cognitive function may remain abnormal.

ANIMAL MODELS OF DEVELOPMENTAL DYSLEXIA

The research effort in our laboratories was initially motivated by findings in the brains of people with dyslexia studied at autopsy. In the late 1970s and early 1980s, we had the opportunity to examine the brains of nine individuals with dyslexia who had died of various causes at various ages (Galaburda, Sherman, Rosen, Aboitiz, & Geschwind, 1985). Observations of these postmortem cases revealed focal collections of abnormally placed neurons in the cerebral cortex that were suggestive of an underlying disorder in neuronal migration. These anomalies were distributed predominantly in cortical regions known to be important for language acquisition and reading (perisylvian). The anomalies, which consisted mainly of nests of neurons and glia in the uppermost cortical layer—termed *ectopias*—were more frequently seen in the left hemisphere of each brain. Although the numbers of brains examined were small and no independent study confirmed (or disconfirmed) these original findings from our laboratory, the arrival of powerful in vivo imaging tools in the clinical and research arenas led to additional discoveries of abnormal neuronal migration in humans with dyslexia (Chang et al., 2005).

The generalizability of the association of neuronal migration disorders in the dyslexic human brains is limited by the relatively small numbers of brains examined. In a control study in presumably normal brains from the Yakovlev Collection at the Armed Forces Institute of Pathology, we did not find evidence that this pattern of multiple cortical anomalies in perisylvian cortex, left more than right, however subtle, was a typical normative finding. In fact, out of 10 brains examined in detail (every serial section, roughly 1 millimeter apart, from front to back), we found only a handful of ectopias (Kaufmann & Galaburda, 1989). Nowhere in the descriptions of the collection could we ascertain that the subjects did or did not have a reading disability. Nonetheless, even if large numbers of perisylvian ectopias were not the normal pattern, as seen in the Yakovlev brains, how specific these findings were to dyslexia could not be determined; certainly a causal relationship between their presence and the reading disorder required a different type of research, one that used an engineering approach rather than an association between anatomy and behavior alone.

Such an approach could be achieved in an animal model. However, as would be obvious to anyone, a causal relation between anatomical changes in the cortex and dyslexia could not be modeled in a nonhuman animal. Instead, animal experiments were designed to mimic the neuropathological findings in brains from humans with dyslexia to get at causal and mechanistic explanations of the behaviors in individuals with dyslexia, particularly to a hypothesized abnormal auditory behavior. We chose auditory behavior on the basis of the research of Tallal (1978, 1980) that had uncovered low level auditory abnormalities in individuals with specific language impairment (SLI) of the sort that could be modeled in a rodent.

Our animal models displayed two related types of neuronal migration disorders: focal microgyria and molecular layer ectopias. Experimental production of microgyria in male and female rats leads both to local and distant changes in corticocortical connectivity—for instance, connectivity across the corpus callosum (Rosen, 2003; Sherman, Morrison, Rosen, Behan, & Galaburda, 1990). Microgyria induction leads to changes in the thalamus of male rats that are similar to those found in dyslexic thalami; comparable thalamic changes do not occur in female rats treated identically (Peiffer, Rosen, & Fitch, 2002; Rosen, Herman, & Galaburda, 1999). These results made us aware for the first time of plasticity differences in the two sexes that may help explain the sex differences often reported in dyslexia and other developmental disorders, in which more males are affected (Rosen et al., 1999; Rutter et al., 2004). Moreover, additional experiments indicated that this sex difference was, at least in part, mediated by hormones. Thus, administering testosterone to female rats with induced microgyria led to thalamic changes like those seen in the males (Rosen et al., 1999). It has been stated that boys are more vulnerable to early brain injury, mainly because of their larger size. However, differences between the sexes in developmental disorders instead may be the result of a maladaptive plasticity response to the early injury (Rosen, Burstein, & Galaburda, 2000).

At present, we believe that changes in behavior associated with induction of cortical malformations in rats are the consequence of both the initial event and the brain's plasticity, particularly the plasticity of thalamic interactions that occur following the initial event. The actual cortical malformations are small, but the resulting plasticity makes for a distributed network effect. We have shown abnormal behaviors in rats with induced malformations and in mice with spontaneously occurring malformations (Denenberg, Sherman, Schrott, Rosen, & Galaburda, 1991). Specifically, NZB/BlNJ mice with spontaneous ectopias fail nonspatial discrimination and spatial water escape tests. Performance on behavioral tests can vary among mouse strains, with malformations reflecting in part differences in the location of the malformation from strain to strain. For example, BXSB/MpJ mice with ectopias do well on the Lashley Type III maze, whereas NZB/BlNJ mice perform poorly. BXSB/MpJ mice have ectopias in the frontal cortex, whereas NZB/BlNJ mice have them in the parietal lobe. On the other hand, BXSB/MpJ mice with ectopias performed poorly on two tests of working memory, one involving an inverted Lashley Type III maze and the other a delayed-match-to-sample task, whereas they performed superiorly in learning a reference memory spatial water maze. The deficits in working memory tapped by both tasks may reflect the known abnormalities in frontal cortical pathology. On some of these tests, deficits seemed to interact with paw preference. There is no substantial difference in the behavioral changes caused by ectopias or microgyria in mice (Rosen, Waters, Galaburda, & Denenberg, 1995). Overall, lesioned mice (irrespective of hemisphere or type of damage) perform poorly in discrimination learning tasks, in a spatial Morris maze match-to-sample task, and in a Lashley Type III maze compared with sham-operated animals. In summary, focal and relatively subtle abnormalities of cortical development that arise spontaneously or are induced in the laboratory in rodents result in a range of cognitive deficits, which probably reflect secondary changes in plasticity.

The absence of anything comparable to language, let alone written language, in nonhuman animals forces us to look for preadapted behaviors that may be present in laboratory animals. To understand this link, it helps to be aware of the fact that at least some children with dyslexia exhibit deficits in rapid auditory processing, which affects auditory pathways that are also found in rodents and can be tested in our models. In fact, the cortical malformations in rodents described in the previous paragraphs can be associated with rapid auditory processing deficits in rodent models similar to those seen in dyslexic individuals (Clark, Rosen, Tallal, & Fitch, 2000; Fitch, Tallal, Brown, Galaburda, & Rosen, 1994; Peiffer, Friedman, Rosen, & Fitch, 2004). Thus, we have found that male rats with induced focal microgyria cannot perform a two-tone discrimination task when the stimulus duration is relatively short, whereas animals with sham surgery and females with microgyria do well on these tests at all stimulus durations. There is an age and task difficulty effect, with juvenile rats performing worse than adults (Peiffer et al., 2004), and with a task of greater complexity needed to elicit deficits in mature animals compared with young animals. A similar pattern has been noted in individuals with language-based learning disorders, with young males being particularly at risk (Rutter et al., 2004).

The lesion model of developmental cortical malformations in rats and mice has thus disclosed several findings that appear to hold among experimental conditions. First, there is a sex and age effect, with males, particularly young males, being susceptible out of proportion to females. The anatomical analyses in these cases point to a sex difference in the involvement of the thalamus (likely the thalamocortical circuits), which is abnormal in behaviorally affected animals. Involvement of these circuits appears to explain the presence of temporal processing difficulties in the affected animals. However, it is reasonable to add that involvement of corticocortical circuits may be shown to correlate with some known cognitive features common in dyslexia, such as working memory and higher order linguistic functions.

Before discussing the specific contributions of the study of the genetics of developmental dyslexia, a brief overview of the field of genetics is in order.

THE FIELD OF GENETICS

Genetics, and the now obligatory co-sciences of cell and molecular biology, are an active area of research, both for the understanding of normal biology and for the prevention, diagnosis, and treatment of human disorders. Genome-wide association studies (Hardy & Singleton, 2009), although they do not discover genes, are able to be used at least to pinpoint regions of the genome that statistically associate with skills or with disorders or endophenotypes thereof, in situations where the gene frequency in the population is at least 5%. Thus, they are designed to find loci that fit the common disease–common variant hypothesis (Hardy & Singleton, 2000). Additional fine mapping and the investigation of potential molecular pathways are necessary for the identification of causal genotype–phenotype relationships. Genome-wide association studies have uncovered an inordinate number of common haplotypes containing alleles that affect gene regulation, thus implicating quantity of gene expression—either increased or decreased—as well as spatial and temporal factors associated with gene expression. When these regulatory allelic variants are not lethal, they could account for a significant proportion of individual variation and frequent causes of human disease.

Despite advances in genetic epidemiology, when a single causative allele is identified it accounts for a very small proportion of the population displaying the interesting phenotype, which has prompted some experts to suggest that most human disease is caused by rare alleles that occur in single individuals or in a limited number of families. Thus, limitations of population genetics arise when there is a great amount of genetic heterogeneity found for a given disorder; for example, rare but multiple separate alleles, alone or in combination, may cause a specific disorder. Multiple mutations may exist in the same allele, and these can number in the thousands. The same mutation may result in no detectable phenotype or in several different phenotypes, or mutations in different genes may lead to the same phenotype (McClellan & King, 2010). These challenges to medical population genetics do not exempt the study of the genetics of dyslexia (see Chapter 14, this volume).

These difficulties notwithstanding, several gene loci have already been identified in association with dyslexia, and several candidate dyslexia susceptibility genes have been proposed (which we discuss later in this chapter). Again, these discoveries cannot rule out additional genes (even a huge number of additional genes) that fit the hypothesis of common disorder–rare variant; therefore, completion of a systematic genome-wide association approach will not necessarily complete the work that needs be done in dyslexia genetic epidemiology. Indeed, additional work associated with these discoveries still needs be conducted. This research should include replication in larger groups and in separate populations learning different languages and should include the investigation of the molecular pathways, anatomical and physiological phenotypes, and changes in behavior associated with the proposed allelic variants. The work reviewed later in this chapter, arising from an NICHD-funded collaboration covering these separate but complementary areas of neuroscience, attempts to address the plausibility that the proposed candidate genes could be causally involved in the production of dyslexia in human carriers. Their characterization in the laboratory also offers windows through which we can better understand normal brain development and the relationships that may exist among the different levels of description, such as the molecular, the anatomical, and the behavioral levels.

A genetic research program on dyslexia needs to solve the following problem: It needs to establish a causal link between a candidate allelic mutation or variant and the reading disorder, both during acquisition and during adult performance. In most imaginable scenarios this would require characterizing the intermediate levels of cell and molecular biology and of brain anatomy and physiology. In addition, ideally, there would be sufficient information from this neurobiological research to provide to computational biologists for use in modeling the reading deficit (Seidenberg, 2009; also see Chapter 9, this volume). Such a multidisciplinary project could shed light on the following plausible pathway: A gene variant results in decreased expression of protein x, which causes a molecular pathway to fail. This in turn results in maldevelopment of a part of the brain and its neural circuits that are necessary for learning phonemes, which also demonstrates abnormal physiology signifying abnormal codes. This causes degraded or absent phonological representations or processes, which generate an insurmountable challenge to consciousness such that conscious knowledge of the sound structure of the language does not emerge and the child finds mapping phonemes to graphemes an impossible and even illogical task.

DYSLEXIA SUSCEPTIBILITY GENES

DYX1C1, KIAA0319, DCDC2, ROBO1, MRPLI9/C2ORF3, PCNT, DIP2A, SIOOB, and *PRMT2* have been proposed as dyslexia candidate susceptibility genes (Anthoni et al., 2007; Hannula-Jouppi et al., 2005; Meng et al., 2005; Paracchini et al., 2006; Poelmans et al., 2009; Taipale et al., 2003). These genes code for proteins that appear to participate in cellular pathways implicated in neuronal migration and axon growth. This is not surprising because both neuronal migration and axon growth depend on changes in cell cytoskeleton structure and cell adhesion. This coding is also not surprising given that neuronal migration anomalies have been pointed out to underlie dyslexia since the 1980s.

As an example of the role of these genes in migration and axon growth, the proteins in the DCX family, of which DCDC2 is a member, have well-documented involvement in neuronal migration to neocortex and may also be involved in the development of the corpus callosum. Proteins in the family to which DCDC2 belongs are characterized by the presence of single or multiple DCX domains. A mutation in the gene called *DCX*, the first to be characterized in this family, causes double cortex and lissencephaly in humans (Allen, Gleeson, Shoup, & Walsh, 1998; des Portes et al., 1998). Dclk, another DCX protein family member, interacts with Dcx to promote the formation of the corpus callosum and neuronal migration to the cerebral cortex (Deuel et al., 2006; Koizumi, Tanaka, & Gleeson, 2006). After *DCDC2* was identified as a dyslexia risk gene, Dcdc2 was tested and found to participate in neocortical neuronal migration, with abnormal migration resulting from loss of function (Meng et al., 2005).

As with *DCDC2*, *KIAA0319* is located on chromosome 6p (Cope et al., 2005; Paracchini et al., 2006) where it codes for a protein with extracellular, transmembrane, and intracellular domains and is involved in cell adhesion. The role of Kiaa0319 in cellular adhesion has not yet been directly tested; however, RNA interference after intrauterine electroporation of shRNA plasmids resulting in loss of gene function demonstrates that the protein is involved in neuronal migration, and implicates an abnormal relationship between migrating neurons and radial glia (Paracchini et al., 2006).

DYX1C1 has shown increased robustness as a dyslexia risk gene after further refinement of endophenotypes and testing in large populations. Both *ROBO1* and *DYX1C1* were initially identified from chromosomal translocations in small pedigrees or by linkage disequilibrium association studies (Hannula-Jouppi et al., 2005; Taipale et al., 2003; Wigg et al., 2004). In vivo RNAi studies from our laboratories have shown that *Dyx1c1* is involved in neuronal migration (LoTurco, Wang, & Paramasivam, 2006; Wang et al., 2006), although the cellular basis for this is not clear. On the other hand, the functions of *ROBO1* in neural development are well understood and include axon growth across the midline in the commissures in the brain and spinal cord (Erskine et al., 2000; Yuan et al., 1999). *Robo1* is also implicated in neuronal migration. For example, slit, which acts on the *Robo1* receptor, repels young migrating neurons toward the neocortex and away from the proliferative zones (Zhu, Li, Zhou, Wu, & Rao, 1999).

There is no doubt that the discovery of the involvement of dyslexia risk genes in processes of neuronal migration and axonal growth gives encouragement to additional research on the function of these genes in brain development in general and in dyslexia specifically. However, much more needs to be learned. None of the genes affect coding regions and are rather more likely to be involved in spatial and temporal aspects of expression and/or change of function in the developing brain. For instance, the *KIAA0319* dyslexia variant is associated with a 40% decrease in expression in in vitro assays (Paracchini et al., 2006), but its in vivo effects are unknown. For a translational arm to arise from this research, it will be essential to know how risk variants affect protein expression in humans at risk for dyslexia, as well as the location and timing of these changes in developing and adult brains.

DYSLEXIA SUSCEPTIBILITY GENE DISRUPTION IN ANIMAL MODELS

We have also investigated the postnatal effects of embryonic knockdown or overexpression of *Kiaa0319* (Peschansky et al., 2010). We used in utero electroporation to transfect neuronal progenitors during midgestation in rats with constructs that either knocked down (*Kiaa0319* shRNA) or overexpressed Kiaa0319. We found that knockdown, but not overexpression, of Kiaa0319 resulted in large numbers of both transfected and nontransfected neurons that remained unmigrated. These collections of neurons resembled human periventricular heterotopias, which have previously been associated with developmental dyslexia (Chang et al., 2005). This suggested that *Kiaa0319* shRNA disrupts neuronal migration by direct effects on the transfected neurons, as well as by nondirect effects on the untransfected neurons. Of the *Kiaa0319* shRNA-transfected neurons that migrated into the cortical plate, most migrated to their appropriate lamina. In contrast, neurons transfected with the overexpression construct migrated to a location slightly below their expected positions. We also were able to demonstrate that there were effects of Kiaa0319 knockdown on neuronal maturation. Thus, neurons transfected with Kiaa0319 shRNA exhibited apical, but not basal, dendrite hypertrophy. The results provided evidence linking candidate dyslexia susceptibility genes to migrational disturbances during brain development, and extended the role of Kiaa0319 to include growth and differentiation of dendrites.

Knockdown of *Dyx1c1* also disrupts neuronal migration in developing embryonic neocortex (Rosen et al., 2007). As described earlier, we transfected neuronal progenitors in the rat with shRNA constructs designed to knock down *Dyx1c1* expression. Similar to knockdown of *Kiaa0319* expression described previously, knocking down *Dyx1c1* expression resulted in periventricular heterotopia. Unlike the case of Kiaa0319, the pattern of migration of transfected neurons was bimodal, with approximately 20% of the neurons migrating a short distance from their progenitor zone and another 40% that migrated past their expected position. Interestingly (see behavioral studies discussed later in this chapter), approximately 25% of the brains had hippocampal migrational anomalies. Similar results were found in another study investigating embryonic knockdown and overexpression of the homolog of the human *DCDC2* gene. Specifically, we found that knockdown of *Dcdc2* resulted in pockets of heterotopic neurons in the periventricular region. In addition, neurons transfected with Dcdc2 shRNA migrated in a bimodal pattern, with approximately 7% of the neurons migrating a short distance from the ventricular zone, and another 30% migrating past their expected lamina. These results support the claim that knockdown of *Dcdc2* expression results in neuronal migration disorders similar to those seen in the brains of individuals with dyslexia.

Recently, we studied the effects of in utero knockdown of *Dyx1c1* on auditory processing and spatial learning in rats (Threlkeld et al., 2007). Results showed that *Dyx1c1* knockdown is associated with an overall processing deficit of complex auditory stimuli in both juvenile and adult periods. In contrast, adult data alone revealed a significant processing impairment among those rats who were transfected with constructs knocking down *Dyx1c1* compared with controls, indicating an inability for *Dyx1c1* shRNA–treated rats to improve detection of complex auditory stimuli over time. Furthermore, as described previously, a subset of these rats exhibited hippocampal as well as cortical malformations. Malformations of the hippocampus were associated with robust spatial learning impairment in this subgroup.

The focal injury model of dyslexia was very powerful in its capacity to replicate in rodents anatomical and some behavioral features of human dyslexia. However, although it is not impossible that some individuals with dyslexia have focal brain lesions acquired during early development, this in all likelihood does not apply to the majority of those with dyslexia. As the genetic theory of dyslexia gains influence through the discovery of robust (replicable) candidate risk genes, animal models need to include studies on the functions of these genes on brain development, with the expectation that results of the research can be extrapolated to the dyslexic human brain. Intrauterine electroporation of gain or loss of function plasmids derived from dyslexia risk genes provides a good start for a genetic neurobiology of dyslexia, but it is unlikely to capture some important factors about the genetics of dyslexia. This is because in shRNA research the methods are necessarily focal in their effects and gene variants in dyslexic populations are likely to be acting more broadly in the brain during development, both in space and in time. However, as with other neurodevelopmental genes, wide expression need not result in broad phenotypes, as some systems may be more vulnerable to changes in a given protein translation than others. We are currently working to develop transgenic mice that should address more closely the human dyslexia biology.

CONCLUSIONS

One of the early discoveries in the present line of genetics research on brain development in dyslexia rodent models has been that all the risk genes tested so far affect neuronal migration, albeit through effects on different pathways. This does not fail to impress, as it confirms old observations about the brain in dyslexia that implicated a neuronal migration disorder. It also supports the already commonplace observation that multiple genes can separately affect a single biological system, even if in a different manner, and lead to the same disorder. We have not learned all there is to learn about how plasticity affects relevant neural circuits as a result of disturbance of cortical development from manipulation of dyslexia risk genes. However, it is expected that similar aberrations will be shown in circuit formation involving corticothalamic pathways and corticocortical pathways that can again explain, in the genetic models, the problems with temporal processing and maze task performance that are already being demonstrated in these animals. We anticipate that a genetically guided neurobiology of dyslexia using animal models will continue to provide explanatory information for the types of deficits seen in dyslexic individuals, and may help in the design of early diagnostic and treatment approaches for infants and children at risk.

ACKNOWLEDGMENTS

This work was supported by U.S. National Institutes of Health Grant HD20806 and by The Dyslexia Foundation.

REFERENCES

Allen, K.M., Gleeson, J.G., Shoup, S.M., & Walsh, C.A. (1998). A YAC contig in Xq22.3-q23, from DXS287 to DXS8088, spanning the brain-specific genes doublecortin (DCX) and PAK3. *Genomics, 52*(2), 214–218.

Anthoni, H., Zucchelli, M., Matsson, H., Muller-Myhsok, B., Fransson, I., Schumacher, J., et al. (2007). A locus on 2p12 containing the co-regulated MRPL19 and C2ORF3 genes is associated to dyslexia. *Human Molecular Genetics, 16*(6), 667–677.

Benasich, A.A. (1998). Temporal integration as an early predictor of speech and language development. In C. von Euler, I. Lunberg, & R. Llinas (Eds.), *Brain mechanisms in cognition and language—with special reference to phonological problems in dyslexia* (Vol. 70, pp. 123–142). Oxford, England: Elsevier.

Benasich, A.A., Choudhury, N., Friedman, J.T., Realpe-Bonilla, T., Chojnowska, C., & Gou, Z. (2006). The infant as a prelinguistic model for language learning impairments: Predicting from event-related potentials to behavior. *Neuropsychologia, 44*(3), 396–411.

Bishop, D.V.M., & Edmunson, A. (1986). Is otitis media a major cause of specific developmental language disorders? *British Journal of Disorders of Communication, 21,* 321–338.

Bradley, L., & Bryant, P. (1981). Visual memory and phonological skills in reading and spelling backwardness. *Psychological Research, 43*(2), 193–199.

Chang, B.S., Ly, J., Appignani, B., Bodell, A., Apse, K.A., Ravenscroft, R.S., et al. (2005).

Reading impairment in the neuronal migration disorder of periventricular nodular heterotopia. *Neurology, 64*(5), 799–803.

Clark, M.G., Rosen, G.D., Tallal, P., & Fitch, R.H. (2000). Impaired processing of complex auditory stimuli in rats with induced cerebrocortical microgyria: An animal model of developmental language disabilities. *Journal of Cognitive Neuroscience, 12*(5), 828–839.

Cope, N., Harold, D., Hill, G., Moskvina, V., Stevenson, J., Holmans, P., et al. (2005). Strong evidence that KIAA0319 on chromosome 6p is a susceptibility gene for developmental dyslexia. *American Journal of Human Genetics, 76*(4), 581–591.

Denenberg, V.H., Sherman, G.F., Schrott, L.M., Rosen, G.D., & Galaburda, A.M. (1991). Spatial learning, discrimination learning, paw preference and neocortical ectopias in two autoimmune strains of mice. *Brain Research, 562*(1), 98–104.

des Portes, V., Francis, F., Pinard, J.M., Desguerre, I., Moutard, M.L., Snoeck, I., et al. (1998). Doublecortin is the major gene causing X-linked subcortical laminar heterotopia (SCLH). *Human Molecular Genetics, 7*(7), 1063–1070.

Deuel, T.A., Liu, J.S., Corbo, J.C., Yoo, S.Y., Rorke-Adams, L.B., & Walsh, C.A. (2006). Genetic interactions between doublecortin and doublecortin-like kinase in neuronal migration and axon outgrowth. *Neuron, 49*(1), 41–53.

Erskine, L., Williams, S.E., Brose, K., Kidd, T., Rachel, R.A., Goodman, C.S., et al. (2000). Retinal ganglion cell axon guidance in the mouse optic chiasm: Expression and function of robos and slits. *Journal of Neuroscience, 20*(13), 4975–4982.

Fitch, R.H., Tallal, P., Brown, C., Galaburda, A.M., & Rosen, G.D. (1994). Induced microgyria and auditory temporal processing in rats: A model for language impairment? *Cerebral Cortex, 4*(3), 260–270.

Galaburda, A.M., Sherman, G.F., Rosen, G.D., Aboitiz, F., & Geschwind, N. (1985). Developmental dyslexia: Four consecutive cases with cortical anomalies. *Annals of Neurology, 18,* 222–233.

Hannula-Jouppi, K., Kaminen-Ahola, N., Taipale, M., Eklund, R., Nopola-Hemmi, J., Kaariainen, H., & Kere, J. (2005). The axon guidance receptor gene ROBO1 is a candidate gene for developmental dyslexia. *PLoS Genetics, 1*(4), e50.

Hardy, J., & Singleton, A. (2000). The future of genetic analysis of neurological disorders. *Neurobiology of Disease, 7,* 65–69.

Hardy, J., & Singleton, A. (2009). Genome-wide association studies and human disease. *New England Journal of Medicine, 360,* 1759–1768.

Kaufmann, W.E., & Galaburda, A.M. (1989). Cerebrocortical microdysgenesis in neurologically normal subjects: A histopathologic study. *Neurology, 39*(2), 238–244.

Koizumi, H., Tanaka, T., & Gleeson, J.G. (2006). Doublecortin-like kinase functions with doublecortin to mediate fiber tract decussation and neuronal migration. *Neuron, 49*(1), 55–66.

Kuhl, P.K. (1994). Learning and representation in speech and language. *Current Opinion in Neurobiology, 4,* 812–822.

LoTurco, J.J., Wang, Y., & Paramasivam, M. (2006). Neuronal migration and dyslexia susceptibility. In G.D. Rosen (Ed.), *The dyslexic brain: New pathways in neuroscience discovery* (pp. 119–128). Mahwah, NJ: Lawrence Erlbaum Associates.

McClellan, J., & King, M. (2010). Genetic heterogeneity in human disease. *Cell, 141,* 210–217.

Meng, H., Smith, S.D., Hager, K., Held, M., Liu, J., Olson, R.K., et al. (2005). DCDC2 is associated with reading disability and modulates neuronal development in the brain. *Proceedings of the National Academy of Sciences, USA, 102*(47), 17053–17058.

Mody, M., Studdert-Kennedy, M., & Brady, S. (1997). Speech perception deficits in poor readers: Auditory processing or phonological coding? *Journal of Experimental Child Psychology, 64*(2), 199–231.

Paracchini, S., Thomas, A., Castro, S., Lai, C., Paramasivam, M., Wang, Y., et al. (2006). The chromosome 6p22 haplotype associated with dyslexia reduces the expression of KIAA0319, a novel gene involved in neuronal migration. *Human Molecular Genetics, 15,* 1659–1666.

Peiffer, A.M., Friedman, J.T., Rosen, G.D., & Fitch, R.H. (2004). Impaired gap detection in juvenile microgyric rats. *Developmental Brain Research, 152*(2), 93–98.

Peiffer, A.M., Rosen, G.D., & Fitch, R.H. (2002). Sex differences in rapid auditory processing deficits in ectopic

BXSB/MpJ mice. *Neuroreport, 13*(17), 2277–2280.

Peschansky, V.J., Burbridge, T.J., Volz, A.J., Fiondella, C., Wissner-Gross, Z., Galaburda, A.M., et al. (2010). The effect of variation in expression of the candidate dyslexia susceptibility gene homolog Kiaa0319 on neuronal migration and dendritic morphology in the rat. *Cerebral Cortex, 20*(4), 884–897.

Petitto, L.A., & Marentette, P.F. (1991). Babbling in the manual mode: Evidence for the ontogeny of language. *Science, 251*(5000), 1493–1496.

Poelmans, G., Engelen, J.J., Van Lent-Albrechts, J., Smeets, H.J., Schoenmakers, E., Franke, B., et al. (2009). Identification of novel dyslexia candidate genes through the analysis of a chromosomal deletion. *American Journal of Medical Genetics Part B: Neuropsychiatric Genetics, 150B*(1), 140–147.

Ramus, F. (2004). Neurobiology of dyslexia: A reinterpretation of the data. *Trends in Neurosciences, 27*(12), 720–726.

Ramus, F., & Szenkovits, G. (2008). What phonological deficit? *Quarterly Journal of Experimental Psychology, 61*(1), 129–141.

Rosen, G.D. (2003). The effects of early injury to the cortical plate on callosal connectivity: Commentary on Innocenti. In E. Zaidel & M. Iacoboni (Eds.), *The cognitive neuroscience of the corpus callosum* (pp. 27–29). Cambridge, MA: The MIT Press.

Rosen, G.D., Bai, J., Wang, Y., Fiondella, C.G., Threlkeld, S.W., LoTurco, J.J., & Galaburda, A.M. (2007). Disruption of neuronal migration by targeted RNAi knockdown of Dyx1c1 results in neocortical and hippocampal malformations. *Cerebral Cortex, 17*(11), 2562–2572.

Rosen, G.D., Burstein, D., & Galaburda, A.M. (2000). Changes in efferent and afferent connectivity in rats with cerebrocortical microgyria. *Journal of Comparative Neurology, 418*(4), 423–440.

Rosen, G.D., Herman, A.E., & Galaburda, A.M. (1999). Sex differences in the effects of early neocortical injury on neuronal size distribution of the medial geniculate nucleus in the rat are mediated by perinatal gonadal steroids. *Cerebral Cortex, 9*(1), 27–34.

Rosen, G.D., Waters, N.S., Galaburda, A.M., & Denenberg, V.H. (1995). Behavioral consequences of neonatal injury of the neocortex. *Brain Research, 681*(1-2), 177–189.

Rutter, M., Caspi, A., Fergusson, D., Horwood, L.J., Goodman, R., Maughan, B., et al. (2004). Sex differences in developmental reading disability: New findings from 4 epidemiological studies. *Journal of the American Medical Association, 291*(16), 2007–2012.

Seidenberg, M.S. (2009). Taking educational research to school. *Science, 325*(5946), 1340.

Shankweiler, D., Crain, S., Katz, L., Fowler, A.E., Liberman, A.M., Brady, S.A., et al. (1995). Cognitive profiles of reading-disabled children: Comparison of language skills in phonology, morphology, and syntax. *Psychological Science, 6*(3), 149–156.

Sherman, G.F., Morrison, L., Rosen, G.D., Behan, P.O., & Galaburda, A.M. (1990). Brain abnormalities in immune defective mice. *Brain Research, 532*, 25–33.

Snowling, M.J. (2001). From language to reading and dyslexia. *Dyslexia, 7*(1), 37–46.

Taipale, M., Kaminen, N., Nopola-Hemmi, J., Haltia, T., Myllyluoma, B., Lyytinen, H., et al. (2003). A candidate gene for developmental dyslexia encodes a nuclear tetratricopeptide repeat domain protein dynamically regulated in brain. *Proceedings of the National Academy of Sciences, USA, 100*(20), 11553–11558.

Tallal, P. (1978). An experimental investigation of the role of auditory temporal processing in normal and disordered language development. In A. Caramazza & E.B. Zurif (Eds.), *Language acquisition and language breakdown: Parallels and divergences* (pp. 25–61). Baltimore: The Johns Hopkins University Press.

Tallal, P. (1980). Auditory temporal perception, phonics and reading disabilities in children. *Brain and Language, 9*, 182–198.

Threlkeld, S.W., McClure, M.M., Bai, J., Wang, Y., LoTurco, J.J., Rosen, G.D., & Fitch, R.H. (2007). Developmental disruptions and behavioral impairments in rats following in utero RNAi of Dyx1c1. *Brain Research Bulletin, 71*(5), 508–514.

Wang, Y., Paramasivam, M., Thomas, A., Bai, J., Kaminen, N., Kere, J., et al. (2006). Dyx1c1 functions in neuronal migration in developing neocortex. *Neuroscience, 143*, 515–522.

Wigg, K.G., Couto, J.M., Feng, Y., Anderson, B., Cate-Carter, T.D., Macciardi, F., et al. (2004). Support for EKN1 as the susceptibility locus for dyslexia on 15q21. *Molecular Psychiatry, 9*(12), 1111–1121.

Yuan, W., Zhou, L., Chen, J.H., Wu, J.Y., Rao, Y., & Ornitz, D.M. (1999). The mouse SLIT family: Secreted ligands for ROBO expressed in patterns that suggest a role in morphogenesis and axon guidance. *Developmental Biology, 212*(2), 290–306.

Zhu, Y., Li, H., Zhou, L., Wu, J.Y., & Rao, Y. (1999). Cellular and molecular guidance of GABAergic neuronal migration from an extracortical origin to the neocortex. *Neuron, 23*(3), 473–485.

CHAPTER 14

Human Genetic Contributions to the Neurobiology of Dyslexia

Shelley D. Smith

BEHAVIOR GENETIC STUDIES OF PHENOTYPES AND ENDOPHENOTYPES

Variation in reading ability is influenced by both genetic and environmental effects. Although there are many ways to measure reading ability, measures may differ to the degree to which they are influenced by either genes or environment, and behavior genetic methods can be used to estimate the relative magnitude and type of genetic influence. Two methods—heritability estimates and segregation analysis—have been used to identify reading phenotypes that have a substantial genetic influence.

Heritability studies estimate the proportion of variance in a phenotype that is due to genetic effects. This can be variation in an unselected group, such as reading ability in the general population, in which case the heritability is designated as h^2, or in a selected population, such as individuals with reading disability (dyslexia), designated as h^2_g. Comparison of the two types of heritability can show whether disability is affected by genetic factors more than variation in the typical range. This might be expected if there are gene mutations that specifically interfere with ability. Twin studies are usually used to estimate heritability by comparing the differences between identical versus fraternal twins. Because identical twins share all of their genes, they should be more alike for traits that have a genetic influence when compared with fraternal twins, who share only half of their genes, on average. Twins also have the advantage of being the same age, which is particularly important for traits that may change over time. Twin studies have generally produced heritability estimates for dyslexia phenotypes (h^2_g) of 0.54 to 0.84 (Astrom, Wadsworth, & DeFries, 2007; DeFries & Alarcón, 1996; DeFries, Fulker, & LaBuda, 1987; DeFries & Gillis, 1993; Gayán & Olson, 2001; Hawke, Wadsworth, & DeFries, 2006). These studies highlighted several quantitative measures of reading with substantial heritability that would be suitable for further molecular studies: a composite discriminant score (based on a function of reading and spelling achievement that discriminated readers who were typically achieving from readers with a disability), a reading recognition score, and a reading comprehension score (DeFries et al., 1987). Heritability estimates of reading scores in unselected twins are similar; in one large study, a reading recognition test had a heritability of 0.70 at age 7, but this dropped to 0.40 at age 10 with a different reading recognition test (Kovas, Haworth, Dale & Plomin, 2007).

In addition to phenotypes that directly measure reading abilities, endophenotypes of reading have also been defined; that is, component cognitive abilities that are necessary for reading and are hypothesized to be closer to the genetic mechanism (Almasy & Blangero, 2001). Examples of these are phonological coding, orthographic coding, and phonemic awareness, which showed evidence of heritabilities from 0.46–0.72 (Gayán & Olson, 2001). The assumption is that endophenotypes should be closer to the genetic effect and should therefore be better phenotypes for genetic analysis. These phenotypes and endophenotypes were used in many genetic studies of dyslexia, with some debate as to whether they may be individually influenced by different genes (see Pennington, 1997). Because the phenotypes are often highly correlated, a multivariate analysis of the phenotypes may produce better results. The discriminant score mentioned previously is one example of a composite phenotype, and a more complex multivariate linkage analysis that simultaneously evaluated the reading phenotypes and endophenotypes has been shown to produce more focused linkage results (Marlow et al., 2003).

Segregation analysis has been used to define the most likely mode of inheritance of a phenotypic trait and can also determine its suitability for genetic analysis. Although heritability can demonstrate that a phenotype has a substantial genetic influence, segregation analysis can determine whether that influence is mediated by a single gene, a few genes, or many genes acting together. For gene identification studies, phenotypes that are influenced by few genes rather than many are more appropriate. The techniques of complex segregation analysis were used with data from several family studies of dyslexia, and the results primarily supported a major gene effect with additional polygenic background (Pennington et al., 1991). Segregation analysis of a quantitative measure of reading in an unselected population supported the finding of a major gene effect (Gilger, Borecki, DeFries, & Pennington, 1994). The Monte Carlo Markov Chain method of segregation analysis can take these studies a step further and estimate the number of genes involved in a trait; when this was done with component reading phenotypes such as phonological short-term memory and phonological decoding, the results supported the existence of two or three major genes (Chapman, Raskind, Thomson, Berninger, & Wijsman, 2003; Wijsman et al., 2000).

In summary, heritability studies show that there is substantial genetic contribution to reading phenotypes, such as single word reading and spelling, and cognitive endophenotypes, such as orthographic coding, phonologic decoding, and phoneme awareness, and the segregation analyses indicate that there are a fairly small number of genes that have major influence on the phenotypes. Together, these results support the selection of reading phenotypes for molecular genetic studies to identify the influential genes.

MOLECULAR STUDIES: LINKAGE AND ASSOCIATION ANALYSIS

With this evidence for heritable phenotypes and a small number of genes, gene localization studies have a better chance of success and may not require large samples. Initial linkage studies of families with

Table 14.1. Dyslexia regions and candidate genes

Locus	Region	Candidate gene	Key references
DYX1	15q21	*DYX1C1*	Fulker et al., 1991, Grigorenko et al., 1997, Smith et al., 1983, Taipale et al., 2003, Wang et al., 2006
DYX2	6p22.2	*DCDC2, KIAA0319*	Cardon et al., 1994, 1995, Cope et al., 2005, Deffenbacher et al., 2004, Dennis et al., 2009, Francks et al., 2004, Meng et al., 2005, Paracchini et al., 2006
DYX3	2p16-p15	*MRPL19-C2ORF3*[1]	Anthoni et al., 2007, Fagerheim et al., 1999
DYX4	6q13-q16.2		Petryshen et al., 2001
DYX5	3p12-q13	*ROBO1*	Hannula-Jouppi et al., 2005, Nopola-Hemmi et al., 2001
DYX6	18p11.2		Chapman et al., 2004, Fisher et al., 2002
DYX7	11p15.5	*DRD4*[2]	Hsiung et al., 2004
DYX8	1p36	*KIAA0319L*	Couto et al., 2008, Grigorenko et al., 2001, Rabin et al., 1993, Tzenova et al., 2004
DYX9	Xq27.3		de Kovel et al., 2004, Fisher et al., 2002
	12p13.3	*SLC2A3*	Roeske et al., 2011

[1]Genes are outside the region for DYX3 and probably represent a second locus.
[2]Linkage was found to *DRD4*, but not association.

dyslexia generally involved only about 100 families, which may have contributed to some early difficulties in replicating results, but several loci have been replicated in enough studies to be considered to be reliable. Regions of linkage have been given gene designations of DYX followed by a number indicating the order of the published reports. At this time, there are 9 DYX loci. The regions and candidate genes currently reported are shown in Table 14.1. Several regions—most notably DYX1 (chromosome 15q), DYX2 (chromosome 6p), and DYX8 (chromosome 1p)—were studied extensively with linkage and association analysis.

Candidate genes have been identified within or close to some of these regions using several different methods. Two of the genes, *DYX1C1* (DYX1 candidate 1) on chromosome 15 and *ROBO1* on chromosome 3, were initially identified through chromosomal translocations. These are chromosomal rearrangements in which chromosomes break and exchange pieces. Though it may appear under the microscope that such rearrangements are balanced, meaning that no chromosome material is lost, the breakage may disrupt a gene or its regulation so that it does not function adequately. If the translocation chromosome is inherited in a family along with dyslexia, it can be a clue that a disrupted gene is influencing reading ability (Hannula-Jouppi et al., 2005; Taipale et al., 2003). The influence of these genes on dyslexia was confirmed through association with DNA variants called *single-nucleotide polymorphisms* (SNPs) in the genes using additional families that did not have translocations. The nucleotides adenine, cytosine, guanine, and thymine (sometimes referred to as *base pairs* because they pair together in the DNA helix) carry the DNA code, and a SNP is a position in which some individuals may have a particular nucleotide and other people may have a different nucleotide at that position. A difference in a particular nucleotide may actually influence the phenotype by changing the gene's DNA code or by directly affecting the regulation of the gene. Alternatively, an SNP may be in linkage disequilibrium with a nearby causal mutation, meaning that the SNP is close enough to the mutation to be inherited with it. In either case, the finding that SNPs in or around a particular gene are inherited to a statistically significant extent with a reading phenotype can point to that gene as having an influence on the phenotype.

Similarly, linkage analysis was used to localize dyslexia phenotypes to the DYX2 region on chromosome 6p22 using microsatellite repeat markers (Cardon et al., 1994, 1995; Fisher et al., 1999; Gayán et al., 1999). There markers are another form of DNA variation in which a small set of DNA nucleotides is repeated a certain number of times, and the number of repeats is inherited in families. As with SNPs, inheritance of a microsatellite marker with reading phenotypes can serve as a guidepost to a chromosomal region that would contain a candidate gene. Subsequently, two candidate genes, *DCDC2* and *KIAA0319*, were identified through association of SNPs across the linkage region (Cope et al., 2005; Deffenbacher et al., 2004; Francks et al., 2004; Kaplan et al., 2002; Schumacher et al., 2006). Similarly, the DYX3 locus on chromosome 2p was identified by linkage analysis (Fagerheim et al., 1999), and SNP association was found in proximity to the *MRPL19* and *C2ORF3* genes in that region (Anthoni et al., 2007). In contrast to the studies in which SNP analyses were used to investigate regions identified by other means (translocation or microsatellite linkage), the *SCL2A3* gene was identified directly through a whole genome association study (GWAS; Roeske et al., 2011), in which a large number of SNPs covering all of the chromosomes was assessed for association with a reading phenotype. This work is the first published GWAS in a reading-disabled population. Generally, a GWAS tests from 500,000 to millions of SNPs and requires larger sample sizes than have been reported to date for studies of dyslexia. However, a GWAS has the potential to identify new genes that were missed with earlier studies that could not cover the chromosomes as completely. With the decreases in costs of genotyping large numbers of SNPs, more genome-wide association studies of dyslexia are forthcoming.

ANALYSIS OF GENE FUNCTION

Determination of the function of genes influencing dyslexia is particularly valuable in delineating the neurobiological mechanism behind reading problems. In many cases, however, the function of a candidate gene is initially unknown or only partially known, and further studies are needed to determine the mechanism through which the gene affects the phenotype. The function of the gene *DCDC2* (doublecortin 2) has been inferred through its sequence homology to the *DCX* (doublecortin) gene on the X chromosome. Mutation of the *DYX* gene causes lissencephaly and other disorders of cortical neuronal migration in children (des Portes et al., 1998; Sossey-Alaoui et al., 1998), leading to the hypothesis that *DCDC2* might also affect migration of neurons to the cortex. This hypothesis was studied directly in humans through imaging studies comparing individuals with or without a putative deleterious deletion within *DCDC2*. This deletion of a large segment of DNA was hypothesized to decrease the amount of the doublecortin 2 protein that would be produced by the *DCDC2* gene. The investigators found an increased volume of gray matter in several brain structures related to language in individuals with the deletion (Meda et al., 2008), including cortical as well as hippocampal and caudate regions. Reading ability was not measured in this pilot study, however. Although these studies on humans can give clues toward function of a gene, ultimately the molecular mechanism of gene influence has to be tested in living cells. Studies on human brains are obviously limited, so other methods are necessary. In vitro studies of gene function in human cell lines can help determine the level of gene expression, but they may not reflect their activity in the complex environment of the developing brain. A more comprehensive view of a gene's function may be obtained in vivo with appropriate animal models. Through manipulation of gene expression (i.e., the amount of protein that the gene produces), such studies produced exciting information on the function of candidate genes for dyslexia. The expression of the homologous rat gene *Dcdc2* (in contrast to humans, rat and mouse genes are not capitalized) was decreased in rat brains at embryonic day 14 using messenger RNA *knockdown* technology, which decreases the level of messenger RNA, thus reducing the amount of the Dcdc2 protein that is produced. When the brains were examined 4 days later, there was decreased migration of neurons to the cortex when compared with control animals (Meng et al., 2005). Similarly, knockdown of the expression of *Kiaa0319* or the *Dyx1c1* genes in similar experiments with rat brains (performed in the same collaborators' laboratory) produced virtually identical decreases in neuronal migration (Paracchini et al., 2006; Wang et al., 2006). These studies strongly suggest that all three genes are involved in early neuronal migration.

Finally, studies were done to determine the changes in the genetic code that might cause decreased expression of these genes in humans. For example, the presence of a SNP genotype associated with dyslexia was found to decrease the expression of *KIAA0319* in human lymphoblasts (Paracchini et al., 2006); however, one cannot always be certain that expression in lymphoblasts is the same as expression in brain tissue, because genes may show different patterns of expression in different tissues. Further studies in neuronal cell lines partially alleviate that concern and provide even stronger evidence for reduced expression of *KIAA0319* as an influence on dyslexia: a particular SNP in the regulatory region of *KIAA0319* that was found to be associated with dyslexia was also found to disrupt a code in the DNA that binds to a transcription factor that drives the gene (Dennis et al., 2009). This disruption caused a decrease in the amount of the protein product of *KIAA0319* in neuronal as well as nonneuronal cells, making it more likely that it also regulates the gene in the brain.

Studies of long-term effects of increased or decreased expression of Kiaa0319 in rats extended the knockdown studies, showing that, at 3 weeks postnatally, rat neurons with decreased expression of Kiaa0319 became involved in periventricular heterotopias—tangles of misplaced neurons—and that overexpression produced misguided neurons at the cortex. Dendritic growth was also affected (Burbridge et al., 2008; Peschansky et al., 2010). These findings demonstrate that regulation of the amount of Kiaa0319 is critical to proper development of the brain and that too much or too little can produce abnormal results.

Although such detailed studies of gene function have not yet been published for *DCDC2*, *DYX1C1*, or *ROBO1*, it is possible that they will show similar effects. The gene *Robo1* is known to regulate axonal migration across the midline of the central nervous system in mice and *Drosophila* (Kidd et al., 1998), so it seems likely that it has a similar function in humans. Galaburda, LoTurco, Ramus, Fitch, and Rosen (2006) demonstrated how the protein products of the genes *DCDC2*, *KIAA0319*, *DYX1C1*, and *ROBO1* may work together in the cell, regulating different aspects of neuronal migration.

This type of defect in neuronal migration fits in remarkably well with human neuroanatomic studies done by Galaburda et al. starting as early as 1978 (Galaburda, 2005; Galaburda & Eidelberg, 1982; Galaburda & Kemper, 1978; Galaburda, Sherman, Rosen, Aboitiz, & Geschwind, 1985; Humphries, Kaufman, & Galaburda, 1990). These studies of the brains of individuals with dyslexia at the cellular level found areas of abnormal cortical folding (microgyri) and misplaced neurons forming heterotopias at locations throughout the brain, but particularly in the left hemisphere— similar to the migration defects and heterotopias found in the rat models of the candidate genes. Thus, there appears to be substantial convergence that at least some genes influencing dyslexia exert this influence through effects on neuronal migration in the developing brain.

Two other candidate genes suggest an additional mechanism of effect, although their role in dyslexia is less certain. *SLC2A3* was identified as a candidate gene through a genome-wide association scan of SNPs using an electrophysiological phenotype—mismatch negativity (MMN)—in children with dyslexia (Roeske et al., 2011). MMN is a component of the evoked electrophysiological response in the brain that specifically responds to a perceptible change ("oddball") in an auditory stimulus string and can be a measure of the perception of linguistic features of sound, such as a change in a consonant. A decrease in the MMN potential implies that there is weak auditory processing. Given that MMN is an accurate predictor of reading ability, this study demonstrated the potential utility of using a neurobiological endophenotype in genetic analyses, similar to the measures of gray matter in the study by Meda et al. (2008) cited earlier. The association with *SLC2A3* was not direct, however; two SNPs on chromosome 4q32.1 were found to be associated with decreased MMN, but they did not appear to affect genes in that region. Instead, they were associated with decreased expression levels of *SLC2A3*, which is on chromosome 12p13.3. This gene is known to be a glucose transporter, and the authors speculated that decreased glucose availability could explain decreased MMN. The locations on chromosomes 4 and 12 have not been detected by other scans, which could be due to the electrophysiologic phenotype rather than the cognitive phenotypes used in the other studies of dyslexia. To verify this as a candidate gene influencing dyslexia, the regulatory function of the associated SNPs needs to be established and the association needs to be replicated by an independent study. Finally, further studies on the suitability and mechanism of the MMN as a true endophenotype for dyslexia are needed.

Another gene involved in transport has also been implicated in dyslexia. A candidate gene study found linkage, but not association, with SNPs in and around the dopamine receptor *DRD4* gene, which contributes to attention-deficit/hyperactivity disorder (ADHD; see review by Gizer, Ficks, & Waldman, 2009); however, association was excluded with a particular DNA variation that has been associated with ADHD. This variation is a repeated sequence of a group of 48 nucleotides, and the 7-repeat allele (7 repeats of 48 nucleotides) has been associated with ADHD in a number of studies. The linkage of the *DRD4* SNPs with dyslexia could be due to a different genetic variation affecting the expression of *DRD4*, or the actual genetic effect could be due to a mutation affecting a nearby gene. The finding of linkage without association could also mean that there is allelic heterogeneity; that is, there are different mutations in the region that affect reading ability (Hsiung, Kaplan, Petryshen, Lu, & Field, 2004).

If these two genes are confirmed as influencing dyslexia, they would implicate a mechanism other than neuronal migration; that is, an effect on neurotransmission at the synapse. The effects could be similar: Either the neurons do not get to the proper place to make their connections, or the synaptic connections themselves are deficient. In this way, dyslexia could be seen as a "disconnection syndrome" as originally speculated by Geschwind (1965). Drawing on the findings of lesions in acquired adult alexia, he suggested that developmental dyslexia might be due to delayed maturation of connections in the angular gyrus. This interpretation of poor connections between areas of the brain is also consistent with findings in functional imaging studies in humans. These studies are described in more detail in accompanying chapters in this volume and basically demonstrate that skilled readers show sequential activation of the left hemisphere occipitotemporal, temporoparietal, and inferior frontal gyrus. However, readers with a disability tend to activate slightly different regions, including in the right hemisphere, or show differences in degree of activation, and the activation can also be more diffuse (Pugh et al., 2000). Genetic defects influencing reading may affect the circuitry of these and other regions involved in the reading process, and candidate genes could be expected to be expressed in the development of those regions. Thus, further use of neuroanatomy, neurophysiology, and gene expression could assist in triangulating on the neurobiological causes of dyslexia.

ADDITIONAL SOURCES OF GENETIC VARIATION

Overall, the DNA variations that were described in these candidate regions and genes do not account for all of the heritable variation in reading, which suggests that there are additional genes to be discovered or that there are additional types of variation in the identified genes that were not detected by the linkage, association, and DNA sequencing methods that have been used. The methods of linkage and association analysis—particularly genome-wide analyses—are dependent on the use of DNA variations, which are fairly frequent in populations. Association analysis also requires the presence of "founders" within the population of affected individuals, such that individuals from apparently unrelated families still carry a common mutation inherited from the same founder individual. Because small blocks of DNA are inherited together, people inheriting the same mutation also inherit the same SNP alleles that are located close by (linkage disequilibrium). The common mutation, or common SNPs in linkage disequilibrium with it, can then be detected on a population level. If a founder mutation is in linkage disequilibrium with a rare SNP that is not assessed on current panels, though, it may not be detected (although the increasingly dense panels available now may make this less likely). More important, if there are many founders, such that different families have different mutations in the same gene and thus have different SNP alleles surrounding the mutations, significant linkage disequilibrium will not exist, and association analysis will not detect a population-level effect of the SNP alleles on the phenotype. In contrast to association analysis, linkage analysis studies the inheritance of DNA variations within families and is not dependent on the existence of a limited number of founders, and therefore methodology is able to detect linkage to the region of the gene despite mutation heterogeneity. The disadvantage of linkage analysis is that it requires genotyping of families, so studies tend to be small and underpowered for high-resolution mapping of quantitative traits. Linkage analysis also requires variation in the linked marker (SNP or other DNA variation) within a family so that the region containing the causal gene can be shown to segregate with the phenotype. If most family members share the same allele for the linked markers, linkage will not be detected in that family.

Once a candidate gene is identified, DNA sequencing practices also may have missed DNA variations affecting the gene. Most DNA sequencing studies of candidate genes have only examined coding regions, sometimes including contiguous regulatory regions. This approach misses variations in regulatory regions within introns of a gene, which are segments of DNA that are cut out during the process of gene translation and do not contribute to the protein. Regulatory regions that are located several thousands of nucleotides from a gene are also missed by these methods. Even if they are sequenced, regulatory regions are often poorly characterized, so that interpretation of sequence variations that are discovered in these regions can be difficult. The advent of next-generation massively parallel sequencing allows more complete sequencing of entire genes and regulatory regions at reasonable cost, and may even replace array-based genotyping because all DNA variation would be assessed through sequencing the entire genome. The Thousand Genome Project, in which the entire genomes from 1,000 people of different racial and ethnic groups will be sequenced, should begin to provide the baseline data to distinguish benign variation in DNA sequences from potentially causal mutations (http://www.1000genomes.org).

Additional classes of genetic variation are also present that have not been assessed in the current publications on dyslexia. Copy number variations (CNVs) involving deletion or duplication of sequences of DNA that can be thousands or millions of nucleotides long can have deleterious effects on genes or gene expression levels. CNVs have already been associated with neurodevelopmental disorders such as autism, schizophrenia, and ADHD (Elia et al., 2009; Kirov et al., 2008; Marshall et al., 2008; Wilson et al., 2006). CNVs are generally detected using comparative genome hybridization arrays in which the number of copies of thousands of different DNA segments can be measured, but can also be detected through specially designed and analyzed SNP arrays that have more extensive coverage of the whole genome.

Abnormal methylation of a gene can also affect the degree of expression. Methylation of a gene refers to the binding of a methyl group (CH_3) to the DNA that blocks transcription of the gene, thus turning the gene off. Methylation changes are not detected by routine DNA marker or sequencing studies and may be influenced by genetic and environmental conditions. Methylation changes were recently reported in autism (Nguyen, Rauch, Pfeifer, & Hu, 2010), and it is known that mutations in genes that regulate methylation, such as *MECP2,* can affect complex neurocognitive developmental disorders, such as Rett syndrome (Amir & Zoghbi, 2000).

Overall, today's methods of detecting genes and assessing variation may be underestimating the effects of particular genes, and newer methods may identify additional sources of genetic influence that can account for the heritability of the phenotypes. In addition, most studies looked at one gene at a time, and it is likely that interactions exist among genes and between genes and environmental factors. Evidence of gene interaction has already been reported between *KIAA0319* and *DCDC2* (Harold et al., 2006). Gene–environment interaction has also been shown for dyslexia and parental education, although molecular markers were not examined (Friend, DeFries, & Olson, 2008); however, a study of chromosome 6p markers and speech sound disorder (SSD) did show that linkage was increased in families with more favorable educational environments (McGrath et al., 2007).

It is also possible that there is a significant polygenic contribution to these phenotypes, whereby variation in many different genes contributes to the phenotypic variation. The individual genes are difficult to detect without large samples, and detection is subject to the same caveats about common variants versus rare variants, which could make detection even more difficult. Focusing on the major genes that have greater individual phenotypic effects, even if they have small effect sizes at a population level, can lead to discovery of the developmental pathways that connect these genes and incorporate other genetic influences.

ADDITIONAL PHENOTYPIC VARIABILITY

It is not surprising that genes affecting neural connections important to dyslexia would also affect similar disorders that might utilize some of the same brain regions or pathways. This relationship could account for the comorbidity that is seen with reading disability and related disorders, speech sound disorder, and language impairment (LI; Pennington & Bishop, 2009). Molecular genetic studies are consistent with this hypothesis; linkage and association analyses have localized genetic influences on SSD to dyslexia candidate regions on chromosomes 1, 3, 6, and 15 (Miscimarra et al., 2007; Smith, Pennington, Boada, & Shriberg, 2005; Stein et al., 2004, 2006). Similarly, a study of LI families has replicated linkage of reading and language phenotypes to dyslexia candidate regions on chromosomes 1, 6, and 15. This study also identified association of LI phenotypes with some of the same SNPs in *KIAA0319* that showed association in dyslexia in other studies, confirming that the same gene can be involved in both disorders (Rice, Smith & Gayán, 2009).

SUMMARY: FUTURE STUDIES

By identifying the genes conferring susceptibility to dyslexia, molecular genetic studies have the potential to reveal the neurobiological mechanisms for reading and reading disability. Contemporary studies of candidate genes and their function already suggest neuronal migration impairments as a cause of dyslexia, and it is possible that additional genetic mechanisms will be identified. It can be anticipated that additional genes will be identified through genome-wide association studies, but studies should also include other sources of genetic variation such as CNV and methylation, and should include analysis of rare variants as well as common SNPs. Gene–gene and gene–environment interactions may also reveal genes that might be missed when considered separately.

Careful selection and measurement of phenotypes has always been essential to genetic analysis. With dyslexia, it is evident that some genes may affect related communication disorders as well. The synthesis of genotypic and phenotypic analyses should lead to the recognition of endophenotypes that encompass abilities contributing to different disorders such as dyslexia, LI, and SSD, and may even lead to refined definitions of these disorders.

As candidate genes are discovered that influence dyslexia, their functions on neuronal development will be assessed through manipulation of their expression in animal models. Gene interactions can be tested by manipulating the expression of several genes at a time, leading to the construction of developmental pathways. Analysis of protein interactions can determine how the protein products of the candidate genes work together.

Even more basic endophenotypes related to reading, such as electrophysiologic measures, neuroimaging, or functional magnetic resonance imaging characteristics, will also be used in genetic analyses. Functional studies of candidate genes in animal models can help determine the parts of the brain that are most likely to be involved, and these results could guide the selection of neurophysiologic or neuroanatomic measures in humans for further analysis. The combination of genetic and neurobiological research promises to lead to the discovery of the essential developmental networks for reading and related disorders.

REFERENCES

Almasy, L., & Blangero, J. (2001). Endophenotypes as quantitative risk factors for psychiatric disease: Rationale and study design. *American Journal of Medical Genetics, 105*(1), 42–44.

Amir, R.E., & Zoghbi, H.Y. (2000). Rett syndrome: Methyl-CpG-binding protein 2 mutations and phenotype-genotype correlations. *American Journal of Medical Genetics, 97*(2), 147–152.

Anthoni, H., Zucchelli, M., Matsson, H., Muller-Myhsok, B., Fransson, I., Schumacher, J., et al. (2007). A locus on 2p12 containing the co-regulated MRPL19 and C2ORF3 genes is associated to dyslexia. *Human Molecular Genetics, 16*(6), 667–677.

Astrom, R.L., Wadsworth, S.J., & DeFries, J.C. (2007). Etiology of the stability of reading difficulties: The longitudinal twin study of reading disabilities. *Twin Research and Human Genetics, 10*(3), 434–439.

Burbridge, T.J., Wang, Y., Volz, A.J., Peschansky, V.J., Lisann, L., Galaburda, A.M., et al. (2008). Postnatal analysis of the effect of embryonic knockdown and overexpression of candidate dyslexia susceptibility gene homolog Dcdc2 in the rat. *Neuroscience, 152*(3), 723–733.

Cardon, L.R., Smith, S.D., Fulker, D.W., Kimberling, W.J., Pennington, B.F., & DeFries, J.C. (1994). Quantitative trait locus for reading disability on chromosome 6. *Science, 266*(5183), 276–279.

Cardon, L.R., Smith, S.D., Fulker, D.W., Kimberling, W.J., Pennington, B.F., & DeFries, J.C. (1995). Quantitative trait locus for reading disability: Correction. *Science, 268*(5217), 1553.

Chapman, N.H., Igo, R.P., Thomson, J.B., Matsushita, M., Brkanac, Z., Holzman, T., et al. (2004). Linkage analyses of four regions previously implicated in dyslexia: Confirmation of a locus on chromosome 15q. *American Journal of Medical Genetics B Neuropsychiatric Genetics, 131B*(1), 67–75.

Cope, N., Harold, D., Hill, G., Moskvina, V., Stevenson, J., Holmans, P., et al. (2005). Strong evidence that KIAA0319 on chromosome 6p is a susceptibility gene for developmental dyslexia. *American Journal of Human Genetics, 76*(4), 581–591.

Couto, J.M., Gomez, L., Wigg, K., Cate-Carter, T., Archibald, J., Anderson, B., et al. (2008). The KIAA0319-like (KIAA0319L) gene on chromosome 1p34 as a candidate for reading disabilities. *Journal of Neurogenetics, 22*(4), 295–313.

Deffenbacher, K.E., Kenyon, J.B., Hoover, D.M., Olson, R.K., Pennington, B.F., DeFries, J.C., et al. (2004). Refinement of the 6p21.3 quantitative trait locus influencing dyslexia: Linkage and association analyses. *Human Genetics, 115*(2), 128–138.

DeFries, J.C., & Alarcón, M. (1996). Genetics of specific reading disability. *Mental Retardation and Developmental Disabilities Research Reviews, 2*, 39–47.

DeFries, J.C., Fulker, D.W., & LaBuda, M.C. (1987). Evidence for a genetic aetiology in reading disability of twins. *Nature, 329*(6139), 537–539.

DeFries, J.C., & Gillis, J.J. (1993). Genetics of reading disability. In R. Plomin & G. McClearn (Eds.), *Nature, nurture, and psychology.* Washington, DC: APA Press.

de Kovel, C.G., Hol, F.A., Heister, J.G., Willemen, J.J., Sandkuijl, L.A., Franke, B., et al. (2004). Genomewide scan identifies susceptibility locus for dyslexia on Xq27 in an extended Dutch family. *Journal of Medical Genetics, 41*(9), 652–657.

Dennis, M.Y., Paracchini, S., Scerri, T.S., Prokunina-Olsson, L., Knight, J.C., Wade-Martins, R., et al. (2009). A common variant associated with dyslexia reduces expression of the KIAA0319 gene. *Public Library of Science Genetics, 5*(3), e1000436.

des Portes, V., Francis, F., Pinard, J.M., Desguerre, I., Moutard, M.L., Snoeck, I., et al. (1998). Doublecortin is the major gene causing X-linked subcortical laminar heterotopia (SCLH). *Human Molecular Genetics, 7*(7), 1063–1070.

Elia, J., Gai, X., Xie, H.M., Perin, J.C., Geiger, E., Glessner, J.T., et al. (2009). Rare structural variants found in attention-deficit hyperactivity disorder are preferentially associated with neurodevelopmental genes. *Molecular Psychiatry, (15)*6, 637–646.

Fagerheim, T., Raeymaekers, P., Tonnessen, F.E., Pedersen, M., Tranebjaerg, L., & Lubs, H.A. (1999). A new gene (DYX3) for dyslexia is located on chromosome 2. *Journal of Medical Genetics, 36*(9), 664–669.

Fisher, S.E., Marlow, A.J., Lamb, J., Maestrini, E., Williams, D.F., Richardson, A.J., et al. (1999). A quantitative-trait locus on chromosome 6p influences different aspects of developmental dyslexia. *American Journal of Human Genetics, 64*(1), 146–156.

Fisher, S.E., Francks, C., Marlow, A.J., MacPhie, I.L., Newbury, D.F., Cardon, L.R., et al. (2002). Independent genome-wide scans identify a chromosome 18 quantitative-trait locus influencing dyslexia. *Nature Genetics, 30*(1), 86–91.

Francks, C., Paracchini, S., Smith, S.D., Richardson, A.J., Scerri, T.S., Cardon, L.R., et al. (2004). A 77-kilobase region of chromosome 6p22.2 is associated with dyslexia in families from the United Kingdom and from the United States.

American Journal of Human Genetics, 75(6), 1046–1058.

Friend, A., DeFries, J.C., & Olson, R.K. (2008). Parental education moderates genetic influences on reading disability. Psychological Science, 19(11), 1124–1130.

Fulker, D.W., Cardon, L.R., DeFries, J.C., Kimberling, W.J., Pennington, B.F., & Smith, S.D. (1991). Multiple regression of sib-pair data on reading to detect quantitative trait loci. Reading and Writing: An Interdisciplinary Journal, 3, 299–313.

Galaburda, A.M. (2005). Dyslexia: A molecular disorder of neuronal migration. The 2004 Norman Geschwind Memorial Lecture. Annals of Dyslexia, 55(2), 151–165.

Galaburda, A.M., & Eidelberg, D. (1982). Symmetry and asymmetry in the human posterior thalamus. II. Thalamic lesions in a case of developmental dyslexia. Archives of Neurology, 39(6), 333–336.

Galaburda, A.M., & Kemper, T.L. (1978). Auditory cytoarchitectonic abnormalities in a case of familial developmental dyslexia. Transactions of the American Neurological Association, 103, 262–265.

Galaburda, A.M., LoTurco, J., Ramus, F., Fitch, R.H., & Rosen, G.D. (2006). From genes to behavior in developmental dyslexia. Nature Neuroscience, 9(10), 1213–1217.

Galaburda, A.M., Sherman, G.F., Rosen, G.D., Aboitiz, F., & Geschwind, N. (1985). Developmental dyslexia: Four consecutive patients with cortical anomalies. Annals of Neurology, 18(2), 222–233.

Gayán, J., & Olson, R.K. (2001). Genetic and environmental influences on orthographic and phonological skills in children with reading disabilities. Developmental Neuropsychology, 20(2), 483–507.

Gayán, J., Smith, S.D., Cherny, S.S., Cardon, L.R., Fulker, D.W., Brower, A.M., et al. (1999). Quantitative-trait locus for specific language and reading deficits on chromosome 6p. American Journal of Human Genetics, 64(1), 157–164.

Geschwind, N. (1965). Disconnexion syndromes in animals and man. Brain, 88, 237–294.

Gilger, J.W., Borecki, I.B., DeFries, J.C., & Pennington, B.F. (1994). Commingling and segregation analysis of reading performance in families of normal reading probands. Behavior Genetics, 24(4), 345–355.

Gizer, I.R., Ficks, C., & Waldman, I.D. (2009). Candidate gene studies of ADHD: A meta-analytic review. Human Genetics, 126(1), 51–90.

Grigorenko, E.L., Wood, F.B., Meyer, M.S., Hart, L.A., Speed, W.C., Shuster, A., et al. (1997). Susceptibility loci for distinct components of developmental dyslexia on chromosomes 6 and 15. American Journal of Human Genetics, 60(1), 27–39.

Grigorenko, E.L., Wood, F.B., Meyer, M.S., Pauls, J.E., Hart, L.A., & Pauls, D.L. (2001). Linkage studies suggest a possible locus for developmental dyslexia on chromosome 1p. American Journal of Medical Genetics, 105(1), 120–129.

Hannula-Jouppi, K., Kaminen-Ahola, N., Taipale, M., Eklund, R., Nopola-Hemmi, J., Kaariainen, H., et al. (2005). The axon guidance receptor gene ROBO1 is a candidate gene for developmental dyslexia. Public Library of Science Genetics, 1(4), e50.

Harold, D., Paracchini, S., Scerri, T., Dennis, M., Cope, N., Hill, G., et al. (2006). Further evidence that the KIAA0319 gene confers susceptibility to developmental dyslexia. Molecular Psychiatry, 11(12), 1085–1091.

Hawke, J.L., Wadsworth, S.J., & DeFries, J.C. (2006). Genetic influences on reading difficulties in boys and girls: The Colorado twin study. Dyslexia, 12(1), 21–29.

Hsiung, G.Y., Kaplan, B.J., Petryshen, T.L., Lu, S., & Field, L.L. (2004). A dyslexia susceptibility locus (DYX7) linked to dopamine D4 receptor (DRD4) region on chromosome 11p15.5. American Journal of Medical Genetics Part B: Neuropsychiatric Genetics, 125B(1), 112–119.

Humphreys, P., Kaufmann, W.E., & Galaburda, A.M. (1990). Developmental dyslexia in women: Neuropathological findings in three patients. Annals of Neurology, 28(6), 727–738.

Kaplan, D.E., Gayan, J., Ahn, J., Won, T.W., Pauls, D., Olson, R.K., et al. (2002). Evidence for linkage and association with reading disability on 6p21.3–22. American Journal of Human Genetics, 70(5), 1287–1298.

Kirov, G., Gumus, D., Chen, W., Norton, N., Georgieva, L., Sari, M., et al. (2008). Comparative genome hybridization suggests a role for NRXN1 and APBA2 in schizophrenia. *Human Molecular Genetics, 17*(3), 458–465.

Kovas, Y., Haworth, C.M., Dale, P.S., & Plomin, R. (2007). The genetic and environmental origins of learning abilities and disabilities in the early school years. *Monographs of the Society for Research in Child Development, 72*(3), 1–144.

Marlow, A.J., Fisher, S.E., Francks, C., MacPhie, I.L., Cherny, S.S., Richardson, A.J., et al. (2003). Use of multivariate linkage analysis for dissection of a complex cognitive trait. *American Journal of Human Genetics, 72*(3), 561–570.

Marshall, C.R., Noor, A., Vincent, J.B., Lionel, A.C., Feuk, L., Skaug, J., et al. (2008). Structural variation of chromosomes in autism spectrum disorder. *American Journal of Human Genetics, 82*(2), 477–488.

McGrath, L.M., Pennington, B.F., Willcutt, E.G., Boada, R., Shriberg, L.D., & Smith, S.D. (2007). Gene x environment interactions in speech sound disorder predict language and preliteracy outcomes. *Development and Psychopathology, 19*(4), 1047–1072.

Meda S.A., Gelernter, J., Gruen, J.R., Calhoun, V.D., Meng, H., Cope, N.A., et al. (2008). Polymorphism of DCDC2 reveals differences in cortical morphology of healthy individuals: A preliminary voxel based morphometry study. *Brain Imaging and Behavior, 2*(1), 21–26.

Meng, H., Smith, S.D., Hager, K., Held, M., Liu, J., Olson, R.K., et al. (2005). DCDC2 is associated with reading disability and modulates neuronal development in the brain. *Proceedings of the National Academy of Sciences, USA, 102*(47), 17053–17058.

Miscimarra, L., Stein, C., Millard, C., Kluge, A., Cartier, K., Freebairn, L., et al. (2007). Further evidence of pleiotropy influencing speech and language: Analysis of the DYX8 region. *Human Heredity, 63*(1), 47–58.

Nguyen, A., Rauch, T.A., Pfeifer, G.P., & Hu, V.W. (2010). Global methylation profiling of lymphoblastoid cell lines reveals epigenetic contributions to autism spectrum disorders and a novel autism candidate gene, RORA, whose protein product is reduced in autistic brain. *The FASEB Journal, 24*(8), 3036–3051.

Nopola-Hemmi, J., Myllyluoma, B., Haltia, T., Taipale, M., Ollikainen, V., Ahonen, T., et al. (2001). A dominant gene for developmental dyslexia on chromosome 3.

Journal of Medical Genetics, 38(10), 658–664.

Paracchini, S., Thomas, A., Castro, S., Lai, C., Paramasivam, M., Wang, Y., et al. (2006). The chromosome 6p22 haplotype associated with dyslexia reduces the expression of KIAA0319, a novel gene involved in neuronal migration. *Human Molecular Genetics, 15*(10), 1659–1666.

Pennington, B.F. (1997). Using genetics to dissect cognition. *American Journal of Human Genetics, 60*(1), 13–16.

Pennington, B.F., & Bishop, D.V. (2009). Relations among speech, language, and reading disorders. *Annual Review of Psychology, 60*, 283–306.

Pennington, B.F., Gilger, J.W., Pauls, D., Smith, S.A., Smith, S.D., & DeFries, J.C. (1991). Evidence for major gene transmission of developmental dyslexia. *Journal of the American Medical Association, 266*(11), 1527–1534.

Peschansky, V.J., Burbridge, T.J., Volz, A.J., Fiondella, C., Wissner-Gross, Z., Galaburda, A.M., et al. (2010). The effect of variation in expression of the candidate dyslexia susceptibility gene homolog Kiaa0319 on neuronal migration and dendritic morphology in the rat. *Cerebral Cortex, 20*(4), 884–897.

Petryshen, T.L., Kaplan, B.J., Fu Liu, M., de French, N.S., Tobias, R., Hughes, M.L., et al. (2001). Evidence for a susceptibility locus on chromosome 6q influencing phonological coding dyslexia. *American Journal of Medical Genetics, 105*(6), 507–517.

Pugh, K.R., Mencl, W.E., Jenner, A.R., Katz, L., Frost, S.J., Lee, J.R., et al. (2000). Functional neuroimaging studies of reading and reading disability (developmental dyslexia). *Mental Retardation and Developmental Disabilities Research Reviews, 6*(3), 207–213.

Rabin, M., Wen, X.L., Hepburn, M., Lubs, H.A., Feldman, E., & Duara, R. (1993). Suggestive linkage of developmental dyslexia to chromosome 1p34-p36. *Lancet, 342*(8864), 178.

Rice, M.L., Smith, S.D., & Gayán, J. (2009). Convergent genetic linkage and associations to language, speech, and reading measures in families of probands with specific language impairment. *Journal of Neurodevelopmental Disorders, 1*(4), 264–282.

Roeske, D., Ludwig, K.U., Neuhoff, N., Becker, J., Bartling, J., Bruder, J., et al. (2011). First genome-wide association scan on neurophysiological endophenotypes points to trans-regulation effects on SLC2A3 in dyslexic children. *Molecular Psychiatry, 16*(1), 97–107.

Schumacher, J., Anthoni, H., Dahdouh, F., Konig, I.R., Hillmer, A.M., Kluck, N., et al. (2006). Strong genetic evidence of DCDC2 as a susceptibility gene for dyslexia. *American Journal of Human Genetics, 78*(1), 52–62.

Smith, S.D., Kimberling, W.J., Pennington, B.F., & Lubs, H.A. (1983). Specific reading disability: Identification of an inherited form through linkage analysis. *Science, 219*(4590), 1345–1347.

Smith, S.D., Pennington, B.F., Boada, R., & Shriberg, L.D. (2005). Linkage of speech sound disorder to reading disability loci. *Journal of Child Psychology and Psychiatry, 46*(10), 1057–1066.

Sossey-Alaoui, K., Hartung, A.J., Guerrini, R., Manchester, D.K., Posar, A., Puche-Mira, A., et al. (1998). Human double-cortin (DCX) and the homologous gene in mouse encode a putative Ca2+-dependent signaling protein which is mutated in human X-linked neuronal migration defects. *Human Molecular Genetics, 7*(8), 1327–1332.

Stein, C.M., Millard, C., Kluge, A., Miscimarra, L.E., Cartier, K.C., Freebairn, L.A., et al. (2006). Speech sound disorder influenced by a locus in 15q14 region. *Behavior Genetics, 36*(6), 858–868.

Stein, C.M., Schick, J.H., Gerry Taylor, H., Shriberg, L.D., Millard, C., Kundtz-Kluge, A., et al. (2004). Pleiotropic effects of a chromosome 3 locus on speech-sound disorder and reading. *American Journal of Human Genetics, 74*(2), 283–297.

Taipale, M., Kaminen, N., Nopola-Hemmi, J., Haltia, T., Myllyluoma, B., Lyytinen, H., et al. (2003). A candidate gene for developmental dyslexia encodes a nuclear tetratricopeptide repeat domain protein dynamically regulated in brain. *Proceedings of the National Academy of Sciences, USA, 100*(20), 11553–11558.

Tzenova, J., Kaplan, B.J., Petryshen, T.L., & Field, L.L. (2004). Confirmation of a dyslexia susceptibility locus on chromosome 1p34-p36 in a set of 100 Canadian families. *American Journal of Medical Genetics Part B: Neuropsychiatric Genetics, 127B*(1), 117–124.

Wang, Y., Paramasivam, M., Thomas, A., Bai, J., Kaminen-Ahola, N., Kere, J., et al. (2006). DYX1C1 functions in neuronal migration in developing neocortex. *Neuroscience, 143*(2), 515–522.

Wijsman, E.M., Peterson, D., Leutenegger, A.L., Thomson, J.B., Goddard, K.A., Hsu, L., et al. (2000). Segregation analysis of phenotypic components of learning disabilities. I. Nonword memory and digit span. *American Journal of Human Genetics, 67*(3), 631–646.

Wilson, G.M., Flibotte, S., Chopra, V., Melnyk, B.L., Honer, W.G., & Holt, R.A. (2006). DNA copy-number analysis in bipolar disorder and schizophrenia reveals aberrations in genes involved in glutamate signaling. *Human Molecular Genetics, 15*(5), 743–749.

Genetics and Neurobiology

Robert Plomin and Yulia Kovas

The two chapters in this section give a sense of the breadth and depth of research on the genetics and neurobiology of reading. Chapter 13 by Galaburda, Fitch, LoTurco, and Rosen highlights the value of animal model research, focusing on brain mechanisms involved in neuronal migration and axon growth. Chapter 14 by Smith gives an overview of the explosion of molecular genetics research on reading in the human species. These two chapters come from different perspectives—from the bottom-up perspective of neurogenetics using animal models and from the top-down perspective of human population genetics, respectively—yet they converge on candidate genes for reading that involve neuronal migration early in development. This exciting advance in understanding the genetics and neurobiology of reading has already led to genetically modified rat models that under- and overexpress these gene products, which are beginning to provide a glimpse of how they affect the developing brain. Although it might seem unusual or unlikely to study rodent models of reading, this impressive body of work testifies to the importance of animal models for really understanding how genes work in the brain once genes are identified. We can expect many more examples such as this as more of the genes responsible for dyslexia are identified, such as the two candidate genes involved in neurotransmission at the synapse discussed by Smith.

However, one topic about which little is known as yet is whether the genetics of reading is similar in different cultures with different orthographies—especially the sinogram, which is vastly different from alphabetic languages, as wonderfully described in the introduction to this volume by Wang and Tsai. The most direct answers to this question will come when we have genes associated with individual differences in any aspect of reading ability or disability in any culture. Then we can test whether the same genes show similar associations in other cultures with differing orthographies. Although the chapters by Galaburda et al. and by Smith describe progress toward identifying genes associated with reading, most of this work is done in English-reading cultures. We are not aware of explicit cross-cultural comparisons, but this focus on reading in English is not surprising, given that genes identified to date have not consistently been found to replicate even within English-reading cultures. This lack of replication is not a problem specific to research on reading but is found for all common disorders and complex traits (McCarthy, Abecasis, Cardon, Goldstein, Little, Ioannidis, et al., 2008). In part, the problem occurs because the effect sizes of associations reported to date are small, typically with odds ratios of less than 1.2 for case-control studies of disorders such as dyslexia and less than 1% of the population variance for quantitative traits such as reading ability. If the largest effects are so small, it will be difficult to identify more than a small portion of the genes responsible for the heritability of reading ability and disability given current technologies. This has been called "the missing heritability" problem (Maher, 2008); many ideas have been suggested to address this problem (Manolio et al., 2009). Most hope is pinned on the possibility that current genotyping platforms which rely on common DNA variants are missing the rare and low-frequency variants that can be discovered as researchers move toward whole-genome sequencing, as indicated in the chapters by Galaburda et al. and Smith.

Most of what is known now about the genetics of reading comes from quantitative genetics (e.g., twin studies), not molecular genetics (DNA studies). Rather than reiterate the excellent points made in the chapters by Galaburda et al. and by Smith, in this brief commentary, we will highlight supplementary information from quantitative genetic research. For two reasons, the stock of quantitative genetics has increased in value as the missing heritability problem of molecular genetics becomes more apparent (Haworth & Plomin, 2010). First, quantitative genetic research can estimate the cumulative effect of genetic influence regardless of the number of genes involved or the magnitude or complexity of their effects. Second, quantitative genetic studies can be used to investigate the environment while controlling for genetics.

Following are five examples of surprising findings on the genetic and environmental etiologies of reading ability and disability from quantitative genetic research. More details and references can be found in Olson (2007) and in Haworth and Plomin (2010). These findings are largely from English-reading countries (Plomin, Haworth, & Davis, 2008), but our point is that they can serve as strong hypotheses to be tested in countries with other orthographies.

1. *The heritability of learning to read in early childhood is substantial (approximately 70%).* In early childhood, the heritability of reading is nearly twice as high as the heritability of intelligence quotient (IQ) (Kovas, Haworth, Dale, & Plomin, 2007). It is also interesting that the heritability of reading does not change from early childhood to later childhood. In contrast, the heritability of IQ increases linearly from childhood to adolescence to adulthood (Haworth et al., 2009).

2. *The same genes are responsible for the heritability of learning to read in early childhood and for reading to learn in later childhood.* The most interesting findings from quantitative genetics go beyond estimating heritability of the variance of a single trait at a single age. An important example is multivariate analyses, which analyzes the covariance between traits rather than just the variance of one trait at one age. It yields a statistic called the *genetic correlation,* which estimates the extent to which genes that affect one trait (or one age) correlate with genes that affect another trait (or another age). Longitudinal genetic analyses of reading using

these techniques have shown that genes are largely responsible for age-to-age continuity (Harlaar, Dale, & Plomin, 2007). For example, the genetic correlation from learning to read at age 7 to reading to learn at age 10 is about 0.70 in our research (Kovas et al., 2007).

3. *The genes responsible for the heritability of dyslexia are also largely responsible for normal variation in reading ability.* That is, reading disability is the quantitative extreme of the same multiple genes responsible for the normal distribution of reading ability, which necessarily follows if the heritability of reading disability and ability involves many genes of small effect (Plomin, Haworth, & Davis, 2009). This finding has profound implications for the diagnosis of dyslexia because it suggests that we should think about the etiology of common reading problems as part of the normal continuum of reading ability. Nonetheless, it is likely that there are many rare single-gene disorders whose symptoms include problems with reading even though most common reading disability is part of the normal continuum; this result has been found for hundreds of rare monogenic conditions that show lowered IQ but together account for less than 1% of the heritability of IQ (Inlow & Restifo, 2004).

4. *The genes responsible for the heritability of reading ability and disability are also largely responsible for the heritability of other learning abilities and disabilities.* Perhaps the most surprising finding from quantitative genetic research comes from multivariate genetic analyses investigating genetic links between reading and other learning abilities and disabilities, the key issue of genetic heterogeneity and comorbidity. This research consistently yields astonishingly high genetic correlations—about 0.70 on average—between reading and mathematics and between reading and language, which has been called the generalist genes hypothesis (Plomin & Kovas, 2005). The most recent study of 12-year-old twins reported a genetic correlation of 0.91 between reading and language and 0.75 between reading and mathematics (Davis, Haworth, & Plomin, 2009). This same study also found a genetic correlation of 0.88 between reading and general cognitive ability (Davis et al., 2009). In other words, most of the genetic action for reading is not specific to reading but extends to other domains of learning and cognitive abilities. Nonetheless, because genetic correlations are not 1.0, this means that there are also domain-specific genes, even though most genes are domain-general. The implications of generalist genes for cognitive and brain sciences and for education have been discussed elsewhere (Kovas & Plomin, 2006; Plomin, Kovas, & Haworth, 2007).

5. *Familial resemblance for reading ability and disability is due to shared genes rather than shared environment.* As mentioned earlier, a second advantage of quantitative genetics is that it can be used to investigate the environment while controlling for genetics. One example of the importance of this feature of quantitative genetics concerns the

interpretation of the fact that reading ability and disability run in families. It was reasonable to assume that the cause for this family resemblance is nurture rather than nature. However, despite the reasonableness of the assumption that such shared environmental factors are key for reading, quantitative genetic research indicates that shared environmental factors account for only about 10% of the variance in reading ability (Kovas et al., 2007). The environment is important, but most environmental influence is not shared (called *nonshared*) by two children growing up in the same family and attending the same schools. Just as it has been difficult to identify specific genes responsible for the heritability of reading ability and disability, it has also been difficult to identify the specific environmental factors responsible for nonshared environmental influence (Plomin, 2010). Other examples of the usefulness of quantitative genetics for understanding nurture rather than nature lie at the interface of nature and nurture—in gene–environment interaction and correlation (Plomin, DeFries, McClearn, & McGuffin, 2008).

Definitive proof of these genetic hypotheses will come when specific genes are identified that are associated with reading difficulties. The predictions are clear: There is largely one set of a presumably large number of genes that is associated with learning to read (Hypothesis 1), reading to learn (Hypothesis 2), reading ability as well as disability (Hypothesis 3), and other learning abilities and disabilities as well as reading ability and disability (Hypothesis 4). Family resemblance is due to shared genes rather than shared environment (Hypothesis 5).

However, these quantitative genetic findings are limited in an important way. Because of the need for large samples, nearly all of this research is based on psychometric tests such as tests of word fluency and comprehension that assess what the reader knows and understands *after* reading. Psychometric tests tap a broad array of skills and for this reason might yield results that implicate generalist genes. In contrast, process-based analyses of reading focus on the cognitive activities that occur *during* reading (Rapp, van den Broek, McMaster, Kendeou, & Espin, 2007). A process-based level of analysis could suggest greater domain specificity if several genetically independent component processes each contribute to performance as assessed on psychometric tests. The few quantitative genetic studies that attempt to assess reading-relevant cognitive processes such as phonological processing do not resolve this issue but hint at the possibility of greater domain specificity (Byrne et al., 2008; Gayan & Olson, 2001; Hart, Petrill, & Thompson, 2010; Tiu, Wadsworth, Olson, & DeFries, 2004). However, measures such as phonological processing are halfway between psychometric tests and process-based measures. A big part of the future of quantitative genetic analysis lies in its application to all levels of analysis, including not just the brain, but drilling all the way down to the genome through all the other -*omes* such as the proteome, the metabolome, the epigenome, and the transcriptome (Haworth & Plomin, 2010). In Chapter 14, Smith considers this topic in the discussion of endophenotypes.

As richly illustrated in the two chapters in this section, DNA will be the common denominator that brings together all of the life sciences, in which bottom-up -*omic* approaches will meet top-down behavioral approaches in the brain.

Coming back to the larger theme of this book, a major limitation of nearly all of this research is that it is limited to English. We hope that the present book motivates research that tests hypotheses about the genetic and environmental origins of dyslexia in different cultures with different orthographies.

REFERENCES

Byrne, B., Coventry, W.L., Olson, R.K., Hulslander, J., Wadsworth, S., DeFries, J.C., et al. (2008). A behaviour-genetic analysis of orthographic learning, spelling and decoding. *Journal of Research in Reading, 31*, 8–21.

Davis, O.S.P., Haworth, C.M.A., & Plomin, R. (2009). Learning abilities and disabilities: Generalist genes in early adolescence. *Cognitive Neuropsychiatry, 14*, 312–331.

Gayan, J., & Olson, R.K. (2001). Genetic and environmental influences on orthographic and phonological skills in children with reading disabilities. *Developmental Neuropsychology, 20*, 483–507.

Harlaar, N., Dale, P.S., & Plomin, R. (2007). From learning to read to reading to learn: Substantial and stable genetic influence. *Child Development, 78*, 116–131.

Hart, S.A., Petrill, S.A., & Thompson, L.A. (2010). A factorial analysis of timed and untimed measures of mathematics and reading abilities in school aged twins. *Learning and Individual Differences, 20*, 63.

Haworth, C.M.A., & Plomin, R. (2010). Quantitative genetics in the era of molecular genetics: Learning abilities and disabilities as an example. *Journal of the American Academy of Child and Adolescent Psychiatry*. Advanced online publication. doi:10.1016/j.jaac.2010.01.026

Haworth, C.M.A., Wright, M.J., Luciano, M., Martin, N.G., de Geus, E.J.C., van Beijsterveldt, C.E.M., et al. (2009). The heritability of general cognitive ability increases linearly from childhood to young adulthood. *Molecular Psychiatry*. Advanced online publication. doi:10.1038/mp.2009.55

Inlow, J.K., & Restifo, L.L. (2004). Molecular and comparative genetics of mental retardation. *Genetics, 166*, 835–881.

Kovas, Y., Haworth, C.M.A., Dale, P.S., & Plomin, R. (2007). The genetic and environmental origins of learning abilities and disabilities in the early school years. *Monographs of the Society for Research in Child Development, 72*, 1–144.

Kovas, Y., & Plomin, R. (2006). Generalist genes: Implications for cognitive sciences. *Trends in Cognitive Science, 10*, 198–203.

Maher, B. (2008). Personal genomes: The case of the missing heritability. *Nature, 456*, 18–21.

Manolio, T.A., Collins, F.S., Cox, N.J., Goldstein, D.B., Hindorff, L.A., Hunter, D.J., et al. (2009). Finding the missing heritability of complex diseases. *Nature, 461*, 747–753.

McCarthy, M.I., Abecasis, G.R., Cardon, L.R., Goldstein, D.B., Little, J., Ioannidis, J.P., et al. (2008). Genome-wide association studies for complex traits: Consensus, uncertainty and challenges. *Nature Reviews Genetics, 9*, 356–369.

Olson, R.K. (2007). Introduction to the special issue on genes, environment and reading. *Reading and Writing, 20*, 1–11.

Plomin, R. (2010). Why are children in the same family so different? Nonshared environment three decades later. *International Journal of Epidemiology, 26*, 241–243.

Plomin, R., DeFries, J.C., McClearn, G.E., & McGuffin, P. (2008). *Behavioral genetics* (5th ed.). New York: Worth Publishers.

Plomin, R., Haworth, C.M.A., & Davis, O.S.P. (2008). Genetics of learning abilities and disabilities: Recent developments from the UK and possible directions for research in China. *Acta Psychologica Sinica, 40,* 1051–1061.

Plomin, R., Haworth, C.M.A., & Davis, O.S.P. (2009). Common disorders are quantitative traits. *Nature Reviews Genetics, 10,* 872–878.

Plomin, R., & Kovas, Y. (2005). Generalist genes and learning disabilities. *Psychological Bulletin, 131,* 592–617.

Plomin, R., Kovas, Y., & Haworth, C.M.A. (2007). Generalist genes: Genetic links between brain, mind, and education. *Mind, Brain, and Education, 1,* 11–19.

Rapp, D.N., van den Broek, P., McMaster, K.L., Kendeou, P., & Espin, C.A. (2007). Higher-order comprehension processes in struggling readers: A perspective for research and intervention. *Scientific Studies of Reading, 11,* 289–312.

Tiu, R.D., Jr., Wadsworth, S.J., Olson, R.K., & DeFries, J.C. (2004). Causal models of reading disability: A twin study. *Twin Research, 7,* 275–283.

Bilingualism, Cognition, Reading, and Intervention

雙語、認知、閱讀與介入

PART V CONTENTS

CHAPTER 15

Cognitive Processes in Bilingual Reading

Debra Jared and Judith F. Kroll

L earning to read in one's native language provides a significant cognitive challenge for many children. An even greater challenge is faced by the large number of children around the world who are required to learn to read at school in a language other than the one they speak at home. Often, they face this challenge because their families are relatively recent immigrants to a new country, but for other children it is because the dialect of the language spoken at home differs from that taught at school (e.g., Arabic) or because their parents want them to learn an additional language for enrichment (e.g., French immersion programs). Many of these children will learn to read in both of their languages. Although a great deal of progress has been made in the last 30 years toward understanding how reading develops and why it sometimes fails to develop, much of this research has been conducted on individuals who speak a single language, typically English (Share, 2008). Considerably less is known about reading development and reading difficulties in young second-language learners (for a review, see August & Shanahan, 2006). A growing body of research has examined early predictors of second-language reading development (see McBride-Chang & Liu, Chapter 2, and Siegel, Chapter 17, in this volume). A goal of that work is to identify children who are likely to struggle to learn to read in a second language so that timely remedial help can be given. For example, Manis, Lindsey, and Bailey (2004) demonstrated that phonological awareness assessed in Spanish when native Spanish-speaking children were in kindergarten predicted their word reading ability in English in second grade. This finding provides evidence that phonological awareness tasks can be helpful in identifying young second-language learners who may have impairments in the basic processes needed to learn to read even before they have learned much of the language of reading instruction.

Further progress in understanding reading development in second-language learners requires a consideration of how individuals represent two languages in the mind and whether the two languages can influence one another during language tasks such as reading. Most of the research thus far on these questions has been conducted with adults who are bilingual. This chapter first reviews the literature on bilingual language processing in general and then focuses on bilingual word recognition in particular. The bilingual word recognition literature is especially relevant for children who learn to read in both of their languages. Special attention is paid to the literature on phonological processing because of the close relationship between phonological processing difficulties and dyslexia. Finally the implications of this work for learning to read in a second language are discussed.

BILINGUAL LANGUAGE REPRESENTATION AND PROCESSING

Key questions in bilingual research concern how interconnected the representations for the two languages are and to what extent representations in one language are activated when a bilingual learner performs a task in the other language. Of interest also is whether the answers to these questions depend on the linguistic characteristics of the two languages involved and the learning circumstances of the second language, such as whether it is acquired in early childhood or later on. A further question concerns whether learners who are bilingual can actively inhibit representations from one of their languages when using the other language.

Early models focused on the way in which the second language (L2) was linked to the first language (L1) and with conceptual representations to enable comprehension and production in the L2 (e.g., Potter, So, Von Eckardt, & Feldman, 1984). A key element in these models is the notion of transfer; that is, that learners come to the task of mastering the L2 by using strategies based on their knowledge in the L1. At the level of word learning, that transfer may occur via the L1 translation equivalent. At the level of the grammar, it may occur by transferring the syntactic cues that are salient in the L1 onto the L2 (e.g., MacWhinney, 2005). The Revised Hierarchical Model (see Figure 15.1) attempted to

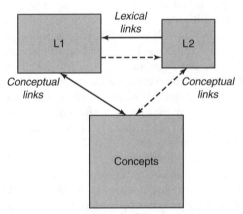

Figure 15.1. The Revised Hierarchical Model. Solid arrows represent strong connections between L1 words and concepts and between L2 words and their L1 translations. Dashed lines indicate weak connections between L2 words and concepts and between L1 words and their L2 translations. The differential strength of connections is hypothesized to create asymmetries between words and concepts for the two languages. (From Kroll, J.F., & Stewart, E. [1994]. Category interference in transition and picture naming: Evidence for asymmetric connections between bilingual memory representations. *Journal of Memory and Language, 33,* 149–174; adapted by permission.)

capture these developmental dynamics at the lexical level by assuming that early in L2 learning, adults exploit the available mappings between words and concepts in the L1 to learn the meanings of new words in the L2 (Kroll & Stewart, 1994). In this view, the L1 translation equivalent becomes a mediator for the learner to access the meaning of an L2 word. As skill in the L2 is achieved, the requirement to rely on translation mediation diminishes and there is an increase in direct conceptual processing of the L2.

A number of studies have tested the developmental predictions of the Revised Hierarchical Model (for a recent review of the controversies and evidence surrounding the model, see Brysbaert & Duyck, 2010; Kroll, van Hell, Tokowicz, & Green, 2010). For example, Sunderman and Kroll (2006) examined the performance of native English-speaking students learning Spanish in the L2. All learners performed a translation recognition task (de Groot, 1992) in which a word in Spanish was followed by an English word, and the participant had to indicate whether the English word was the correct translation of the Spanish word. In half of the trials, the English words were the correct translation of the Spanish words (e.g., *cara/face*). The critical trials in this study were those in which the English word was not the correct translation of the Spanish word but a closely related foil that was either orthographically similar to the Spanish word (e.g., *cara/card*), orthographically similar to the translation (e.g., *cara/fact*), or semantically related (e.g., *cara/head*). The time to reject the related foils as correct translations was compared with completely unrelated controls. Sunderman and Kroll found that learners at an early stage of acquiring the L2 were much more likely than more advanced learners to false-alarm for foils that were translation neighbors of the Spanish word. Curiously, both less and more proficient learners were sensitive to direct lexical neighbors and also to semantic neighbors (see Kroll et al., 2010, for additional discussion of these issues). Critically, the Sunderman and Kroll results suggest that, in keeping with the predictions of the Revised Hierarchical Model, the L1 translation equivalent may play a special role during the earliest stages of L2 learning. However, they also show that learners at all stages are sensitive to the presence of L1 lexical neighbors that are orthographically and/or phonologically similar to the L2 word. Although reliance on the L1 translation equivalent may reflect transfer during the earliest stages of learning a new language, the activation of form-related words across languages appears to be a more general feature of bilingualism that does not diminish as individuals become more skilled in the L2. That evidence is considered in the following section.

WORD READING IN ADULT BILINGUALS

Numerous studies of adult bilinguals have provided evidence that bilinguals activate lexical representations from both of their languages when reading printed words in one of their languages. For example, van Heuven, Dijkstra, and Grainger (1998) found that when Dutch–English bilinguals performed an English lexical decision task, their decision latencies to the English target words were influenced by how visually similar the words were to Dutch words. This and other findings led Dijkstra and van Heuven (1998) to propose that bilinguals have a single lexicon that is integrated across languages. In their Bilingual Interactive Activation (BIA) model, lexical nodes from both languages are activated if they share letters with the input, and activated lexical nodes compete with one another, regardless of language. The language to which a word belongs is represented by an excitatory connection to one of two language nodes. Dijkstra and van Heuven (2002) subsequently extended the model (now called the BIA+) to include sublexical and lexical phonological representations and semantic representations. A task schema was also added to account for nonlinguistic context effects (see Figure 15.2). On presentation of a word, sublexical and lexical orthographic representations become active and in turn activate associated phonological and semantic representations and the corresponding language node. As mentioned before, activation is not specific to the language of the presented word; however, Dijkstra and van Heuven assumed that because

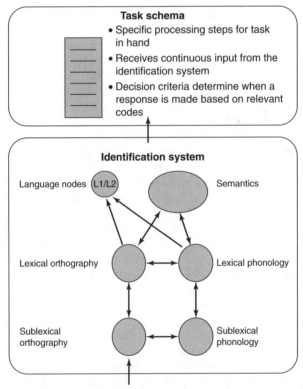

Figure 15.2. The BIA+ model. (From Dijkstra, T., & van Heuven, W.J.B. [2002]. The architecture of the bilingual word recognition system: From identification to decision. *Bilingualism: Language and Cognition, 5,* 175–197; reprinted with the permission of Cambridge University Press.)

activation levels depend in part on subjective frequency, phonological and semantic codes associated with the second language of bilinguals may be delayed in activation relative to first language codes.

Dijkstra (2005) has reviewed the evidence supporting many aspects of the BIA+. Here we focus on studies relevant to the orthographic-phonological portion of the model. Specifically, we address the question of whether bilingual readers activate phonological representations corresponding to one or both of their languages when reading in just one language. We first consider this question with respect to bilingual people whose language pairs share an alphabet, then to those whose languages use different alphabets, and finally to those who read one language that is alphabetic and another that is not.

If bilinguals read in two languages that share an alphabet, and if they activate phonological representations using knowledge of the spelling–sound correspondences from both languages, then these representations may compete with one another, which may slow processing. For example, if French spelling–sound correspondences are applied to the English word *chip*, the resulting pronunciation sounds a lot like the English word *sheep*. Of interest here is whether both phonological representations are activated when a bilingual individual reads a word in a single-language context.

It is known from the monolingual research literature on English readers that words which have letter patterns that can be pronounced more than one way—such as *glove*, which has word-body neighbors such as *stove* and *prove*—are pronounced more slowly than words with consistently pronounced word bodies (e.g., Jared, McRae, & Seidenberg, 1990). Jared and Kroll (2001) demonstrated that this spelling–sound consistency effect could also be observed across languages that share an alphabet, which in their study were English and French. Critical English words had consistent spelling–sound correspondences in English, but also had a word body that takes a different pronunciation in French (e.g., *bait*, which has the word body *-ait*, which occurs in common French words such as *fait* and *lait*). They found that French–English bilinguals made more errors on the words such as *bait* than words with bodies that do not occur in French (e.g., *bump*). This finding indicates that the French–English bilinguals activated phonological representations using knowledge of both English and French spelling–sound correspondences. No cross-language consistency effect was observed for English–French bilinguals for whom the stimuli were in their L1. However, both groups showed a large cross-language consistency effect in a second block of English trials after they had named a block of French words. These latter findings suggest that the architecture of the bilingual word recognition system allows cross-language activation of phonological representations, but that L2 phonological representations may not be sufficiently activated to influence reading L1 unless the L2 has been spoken recently.

A reason that the French neighbors of words such as English *bait* may not have had a greater impact on naming—particularly for English–French bilinguals—is that they shared only word bodies with the target English words. Jared and Szucs (2002) investigated whether a stronger influence of words in the nontarget language would be observed when these words completely overlapped in spelling with the target but had a different pronunciation in the bilingual participant's two languages, such as the case with interlingual homographs including *dent* (which means *tooth* in French). Indeed, both French–English and English–French bilinguals found interlingual homographs harder to name than matched English-only words such as *dusk*. This finding provides further evidence that bilinguals activate phonological representations from both languages when reading in one, but there are two potential sources for such an effect, according to the BIA+. Bilinguals may have activated phonological representations using knowledge of spelling–sound correspondences from each language, but they may have instead activated orthographic lexical representations in both languages, which in turn activated phonological lexical representations.

Brysbaert, van Dyck, and van de Poel (1999) devised a clever experiment to examine specifically whether bilinguals automatically activated phonological representations using knowledge of L1 spelling–sound correspondences when reading in their L2. Dutch–French bilinguals performed a perceptual identification task in which they were asked to identify briefly presented French target words that were preceded by pseudoword primes. The primes were either pseudohomophones of the target words when pronounced using Dutch spelling–sound correspondences (*soer*/SOURD) or were spelling control primes (*siard*/SOURD). Bilinguals correctly identified more of the target words that were preceded by pseudohomophone primes than control primes, leading Brysbaert et al. to conclude that participants had activated phonological representations using their knowledge of Dutch spelling–sound correspondences, even though the task was a French reading task. Rastle and Brysbaert (2006) later pointed out some limitations of the perceptual identification task, specifically that it may involve offline guessing; however, Haigh (2007) replicated Brysbaert et al.'s finding with a different task and language pair. In their experiment, French–English bilinguals had faster lexical decision latencies for English words when they were preceded by primes that were pseudohomophones of the targets when pronounced using French spelling–sound correspondences (*raille*/RYE) than when they were preceded by spelling control primes (*rauffe*/RYE). It appears, then, that bilinguals activate phonological representations using knowledge of spelling–sound relationships from their L1 when reading in their L2. It is less clear, however, whether the reverse is also true. Van Wijnendaele and Brysbaert (2002) observed that French–Dutch bilinguals were more likely to correctly identify French target words preceded by Dutch pseudohomophone primes than those preceded by graphemic control primes, but Haigh was unable to replicate this finding on L1 reading, either with a perceptual identification task or a lexical decision task. Van Wijnendaele and Brysbaert's participants were attending university in their L2, so they may have been particularly balanced bilinguals or even functionally dominant in their L2 at the time. Most bilinguals probably do not activate phonological representations using knowledge of L2 spelling–sound correspondences sufficiently to have much influence on L1 reading.

The research discussed so far has shown that when bilinguals' languages share an alphabet, phonological representations associated with the letters are activated in both languages. However, Gollan, Forster, and Frost (1997) demonstrated that languages do not need to share an alphabet in order to observe cross-language phonological priming. The participants in their study spoke English and Hebrew, which are both alphabetic languages but use different alphabets. Primes were briefly presented in one language, then masked, and targets were presented in the other language. Participants were asked to make a lexical decision to target words. Translation primes that sounded similar to the target words produced a greater priming effect than translation primes that did not share phonology with the target word. This finding was observed when participants performed the task in their L2, both for English–Hebrew and for Hebrew–English bilinguals, but not when participants performed the task in their L1. These results indicate that phonological representations were quickly activated by L1 primes, and these in turn facilitated the activation of similar-sounding target words in the participant's weaker language. Phonological representations of L2 primes were probably activated too slowly or weakly to influence reading in participants' stronger language.

Lee, Nam, and Katz (2005) further demonstrated that languages do not even need to be alphabetic languages to produce cross-language phonological priming. Participants in their study were Korean–English bilinguals. In contrast to English, Korean script represents spoken syllables. Participants were quicker to name English target words when they were preceded by a pseudoword in Korean script that sounded similar than when preceded by a Korean pseudoword that sounded different. Lee et al. further demonstrated that the same participants named Korean target words faster when preceded by English pseudohomophones than when preceded by English pseudowords. These findings provide additional evidence that phonological representations activated by the prime in one script can facilitate the activation of phonological representations in another script. However, their finding of an effect of L2 primes on first-language reading is in contrast to the results of Gollan et al. (1997). A possible reason for the discrepancy is that Lee et al.'s participants completed the L1 naming task after the L2 naming task, whereas Gollan et al. tested separate groups of bilinguals. Recent naming of L2 words may have exaggerated their influence on L1 naming responses (Jared & Kroll, 2001; Jared & Szucs, 2002).

One might argue that these cross-script phonological priming effects are found because the presence of two scripts among the experimental stimuli cues the bilingual to keep both of their languages activated while they complete the experiment. Thierry and Wu (2007) conducted a clever experiment with Chinese–English bilinguals in which words from only one language were present. Participants had to decide whether pairs of English words were semantically related (e.g., *train/ ham*). Unknown to the participants, half of the critical stimuli were pairs of words that shared a character when translated into Chinese and half did not. Both behavioral and event-related potential (ERP) data were collected. No effect of the repeated character was observed in the behavioral data, but there was a difference between the two stimulus types in the N400 responses of the ERP data. Thierry and Wu concluded that "native-language activation operates in everyday second-language use, in the absence of awareness on the part of the bilingual" (p. 12534). However, the precise locus of the repeated character effect is unclear because it could be due to either shared orthographic representations in Chinese (*train* and *ham* share the character: 火) or shared phonological representations (both share the pronunciation HUO). In a subsequent study, Wu and Thierry (2010) demonstrated that shared phonology was critical.

In summary, there is considerable evidence that adult bilinguals process words from their two languages in a single interconnected system, as proposed in the BIA+ model (Dijkstra & van Heuven, 2002). Reading in L2 is clearly influenced by the activation of L1 phonological representations, although the evidence for the reverse is inconsistent. The BIA+ was developed to explain findings from experiments in which bilinguals' two languages share an alphabet. Presumably, when a bilingual's languages have different orthographies, there are sublexical orthographic nodes for the letters or characters for each language. That is, there are more of these nodes for bilinguals whose languages have different orthographies than for those whose languages have the same orthography. Furthermore, the initial activation of lexical orthographic representations will likely differ depending on whether the languages shared orthographies. When a bilingual's two languages share an alphabet, then lexical representations from both languages are activated immediately. When languages do not share orthographic representations (e.g., Hebrew and English), then the initial activation of lexical orthographic nodes is fairly specific to the target language because it is unlikely that there would be connections between sublexical orthographic representations in the target language (e.g., Hebrew) and lexical orthographic representations in the nontarget language (e.g., English). Similarly, when languages share an alphabet, sublexical phonological representations are activated using knowledge of spelling–sound correspondences in both languages, but when the languages have different alphabets, sublexical phonological representations are activated using only knowledge of spelling–sound correspondences in the target language. The activated sublexical phonological representations in turn activate any lexical phonological representations that contain those phonemes, regardless of language. Activation of lexical phonological representations in the nontarget language is particularly strong in the case of interlingual homophones (e.g. *mow* and *mot* in English and French) or cognates with the same pronunciation in each language (as in Gollan et al.'s 1997 study). Conversely, there would be little activation of lexical phonological representations in the nontarget language if that language had few phonemes in common with the target language. Once lexical orthographic and lexical phonological nodes activate their corresponding semantic representations, these semantic representations in turn feed activation back to lexical nodes. Such feedback from semantics to orthographic lexical representations could be one source of the effect of character repetition in Thierry and Wu's (2007) study. The semantic representations of words such as *train* and *ham* could have sent feedback to Chinese orthographic nodes. A second source of the effect could have been feedback from semantics to lexical phonological nodes. If feedback from semantic nodes was the only source of activation of Chinese representations, this could account for why the effect was so subtle in Thierry and Wu's study. (It was not observed in the behavioral data, only in the ERP data.)

MODULATING CROSS-LANGUAGE INFLUENCES

A reaction to the research reviewed might reasonably be that out-of-context presentations of words in word recognition studies fail to provide the contextual cues that would otherwise normally constrain the activation of the two languages to the intended language. Although code switching between languages is a common feature of spoken language (e.g., Myers-Scotton, 2002), it is less likely that a reader will encounter a language switch as he or she is reading a sentence in text. Although understanding the way that readers handle a surprise switch of language is revealing (e.g., Moreno, Federmeier, & Kutas, 2002), the fact that most reading experience provides strong contextual cues to constrain the language in use might be taken to suggest that the system is far more selective than the word recognition studies imply.

A recent focus of research on bilingual reading has been to determine whether it is possible to reduce or eliminate the influence of the language not in use when bilinguals read in one language alone. A full review of that literature is beyond the scope of this chapter, but briefly, the results of these studies are counterintuitive. They show that when highly proficient adult bilingual readers process words in sentence context that are lexically ambiguous across languages, they appear to continue to activate both language readings even when the language cues within the sentence context are sufficient to restrict activation to one language alone (e.g., Duyck, van Assche, Drieghe, & Hartsuiker, 2007; Libben & Titone, 2009; Schwartz & Kroll, 2006; van Assche, Duyck,

Hartsuiker, & Diependaele, 2009; van Hell & de Groot, 2008). These studies demonstrate that phenomena such as facilitation in reading cognate words is still present when the words are embedded in a single-language context. Only when a sentence is highly semantically constrained can the cross-language effect be eliminated (e.g., Schwartz & Kroll, 2006; van Hell & de Groot, 2008). The persistent activation of the language not in use, even in sentence context, suggests that language nonselectivity is a central feature of reading two languages—not simply a reflection of the tasks that have been used to examine out-of-context word recognition and word decoding.

The emerging literature on sentence processing in bilingual readers also suggests that at the level of the grammar, there is permeability across the bilingual's two languages with changes that affect the bilingual's L1 as well as the L2 (e.g., Dussias, 2003). What is not known at this point is how these cross-language interactions affect the process of learning to read in two languages because most of the studies that have investigated these issues have focused on highly skilled adult bilingual readers.

LEARNING TO READ IN TWO LANGUAGES

A major limitation of the BIA+ model is that no learning mechanisms have been articulated (Jacquet & French, 2002; Thomas, 2002). Thomas and van Heuven (2005) suggested how a distributed connectionist model, such as the one first proposed by Seidenberg and McClelland (1989), might learn two languages within a single representational system. They presented the results of some preliminary simulations, but concluded that "much of the potential of distributed modeling shown in the monolingual domain remains to be exploited in the study of bilingual language processing" (p. 220). The development of formal models of bilingual reading acquisition have been hampered by the lack of research investigating whether the developing word recognition systems of beginning bilingual readers are interconnected right from the start.

Extending the study of reading development beyond children who are monolinguals learning to read in their native language is complicated by the large variety of language acquisition contexts. Most of the research literature has studied children who are learning to read in a language that is relatively new to them as a spoken language. There is much less research on reading development in children who speak two languages fluently before they begin to learn to read (for an example, see Luk & Bialystok, 2008). Some children learn to read in only one of their languages; others acquire reading skills in two languages simultaneously. Because our interest here is on how the cognitive system for reading words handles two languages, our focus is on children who are in the process of becoming biliterate. Some of these children learn to read both of their languages in bilingual school programs, whereas others learn to read one of their languages at school and the other either in an extracurricular language class, at home, or at a religious institution. Finally, the writing systems of the child's two languages can vary from being very similar (same alphabet, similar degree of orthographic transparency) to very different (one alphabetic language and one nonalphabetic language such as Chinese). All of these factors may have some influence on the nature of the child's cognitive system for reading words and the relative ease with which reading skills are acquired.

If young children who are biliterate have a single interconnected word recognition system, then one might expect correlations between word identification scores in the two languages to be fairly strong, and indeed they often are (see Table 15.1). Furthermore, one might expect that the size of the correlation would depend on the similarity of the writing systems, and an inspection of Table 15.1 suggests that this is roughly the case. However, there are several limitations of this type of evidence for making conclusions about the nature of the word recognition system of bilingual children. One limitation concerns the comparability of measures in the two languages. Geva and Siegel (2000) noted that task equivalence across languages is a perennial methodological issue in bilingual research. The study by Gottardo (2002) is an example of how correlations between word identification scores in two languages depend on the specific measures that are used. One set of measures produced a cross-language correlation of .34 for word identification scores; another set produced a correlation of .48. A second limitation is that the correlations are influenced by the similarity of the learning contexts for literacy development in each language. The correlations of English and Chinese word reading appear to be particularly affected by learning context. Children in Hong Kong are taught to read in both Chinese and English at school using the same look-and-say method. The first five studies under Chinese–English bilinguals in Table 15.1 tested such children, and the cross-language correlations in word recognition scores ranged from .32 to .63. In contrast, children in North America typically learn to read in English at school and in Chinese in a heritage language program outside regular school hours with different teachers. Cross-language correlations in word recognition scores for studies that tested these children tended to be lower, ranging from −.12 to .39 (Gottardo, Yan, Siegel, & Wade-Woolley, 2001; Luk & Bialystok, 2008; Wang, Perfetti, & Liu, 2005; Wang, Yang, & Cheng, 2009). Bialystok, McBride-Chang, and Luk (2005) directly compared the reading ability of children in the two types of settings and found a correlation of .39 between Chinese and English reading for children in Hong Kong and a correlation of .18 for children who were attending English schools in Toronto and Chinese-heritage language classes outside of regular school hours.

A third limitation of the correlational data is that cross-language correlations are likely affected by the relative amount of practice that children have in reading each language. Arab-Moghaddam and Sénéchal

Table 15.1. Cross-language correlations of word recognition scores

Language pair	Correlation	Grade	Learning context	Authors
Same alphabet				
Spanish–English	.66	1	B	Lindsey, Manis, & Bailey (2003)
	.51	1	B	Durgunoglu (1998)
	.45	1	B	Durgunoglu, Nagy, & Hancin-Bhatt (1993)
	.34, .48	1	E	Gottardo (2002)
	.41	1	E	Swanson, Sáez, Gerber, & Leafstedt (2004)
English–French	.87	1, 3, 5	B	Comeau, Cormier, Grand-maison, & Lacroix (1999)
	.85, .74, .77	1, 2, 3	B	Deacon, Wade-Woolley, & Kirby (2007)
	.65, .66, .65	1, 2, 3	B	Jared, Cormier, Levy, & Wade-Woolley (2011)
Italian–English	.56[a]	4–8	H	D'Angiulli, Siegel, & Serra (2001)
Portuguese–English	.52	4–6	H	DaFontoura & Siegel (1995)
Herero–English	.76[a]	2–5	B	Veii & Everatt (2005)
Different alphabets				
English–Hebrew	.55[a]	1–5	B	Geva & Siegel (2000)
	.60	1	B	Geva, Wade-Woolley, & Shany (1997)
Persian–English	.07[a]	2–3	H	Arab-Moghaddam & Sénéchal (2001)
	.52[a]	1–5	H	Gholamain & Geva (1999)
Arabic–English	.82	4–8	H	Abu-Rabia & Siegel (2002)
	.14[a]	3–6	B	Saiegh-Haddad & Geva (2008)
Urdu–English	.66	7–8 yrs.	HM	Mumtaz & Humphreys (2002)
Different scripts				
Korean–English	.25	3	Ex	Cho & McBride-Chang (2005)
	.36	2–4	H	Wang, Ko, & Choi (2009)
	.35	1–3	H	Wang, Park, & Lee (2006)
Chinese–English	.63	K3	B	McBride-Chang & Ho (2005)
	.52	K3	B	McBride-Chang et al. (2008)
	.58	2	B	Keung & Ho (2009)
	.41, .56	2, 5	B	Tong & McBride-Chang (2010)
	.32, .41, .45	1, 2, 3	B	Knell et al. (2007)
	.11	1	H	Wang, Yang, & Cheng (2009)
	.39	1	H	Luk & Bialystok (2008)
	.18, .39	1	H, B	Bialystok, McBride-Chang, & Luk (2005)
	−.18	2–3	H	Wang, Perfetti, & Liu (2005)
	−.04, −.12[a]	1–8	H	Gottardo, Yan, Siegel, & Wade-Woolley (2001)

Key: [a], age is partialed out; K3, third year of kindergarten (5 years old); B, bilingual schooling; E, English schooling; H, extracurricular heritage language program; HM, home and mosque; Ex, extracurricular English (L2) program.

(2001) found that parental reports of Persian–English bilingual children's exposure to print in one language were uncorrelated with word recognition ability in the other language, although within-language correlations between exposure to print and word recognition ability were significant. They concluded that language-specific print exposure is needed to develop accurate word recognition skills. Cross-language correlations in word identification scores could be high if children read equally in both languages or if the relative amount of reading in each language is similar across participants. However, cross-language correlations in the scores could be low if there is considerable variability in the relative amounts that children read in each of their languages.

If a child who is learning to read in two languages simultaneously integrates the word recognition representations for his or her two languages as proposed in the BIA+ model of bilingual word recognition, then it might be expected that the same cognitive variables would predict word reading ability in both languages, particularly if both languages were alphabetic and used the same alphabet. Many of the studies in Table 15.1 as well as other studies have investigated whether this is indeed the case, but such data are also not strong evidence concerning the nature of bilingual children's mental representations because they suffer from the same problems noted previously.

To further investigate whether young biliterate children have a single interconnected word recognition system, experiments such as those that were described earlier in the section on word recognition in adult bilinguals need to be conducted. The results of an early experimental study by Lee, Wee, Tzeng, and Hung (1992) provided evidence that biliterate children cannot selectively inhibit a nontarget language. In this study, bilingual children in Singapore performed a Stroop task in which they were asked to name the ink color of printed words in a specific language. In the critical conditions, the words were a different color word in the child's other language (e.g., the Chinese word for blue printed in red ink in the English naming task). Color naming times were slower in these incongruent conditions than in a control condition in which the stimuli were colored Xs, both when the task was performed in their native language (Chinese, Malay, or Tamil) and when it was performed in English. Furthermore, when the task was performed in English, there was no effect of the type of native language script used in the color word (Chinese logography, Tamil syllabary, or Malay alphabet). These findings suggest that the printed word automatically activated its phonological representation, which then interfered with the phonological representation that participants generated in the other language as they attempted to name the ink color.

In a more recent experiment, Jared, Cormier, Levy, and Wade-Woolly (in press) asked third-grade students who were learning to read in English and French simultaneously to name cognates, interlingual homographs, and interlingual homophones and matched control words.

Half of the children performed the task in their L1 and half performed the task in their L2. When children were reading in French—their L2—there were differences between all three word types and matched control words. In contrast, when reading in English, differences were observed only between interlingual homographs and controls. These findings indicate that young readers who are in the process of becoming biliterate have a single interconnected word recognition system—at least when their two languages share an alphabet. Stronger connections between phonological and semantic representations in their L1 than in their relatively new L2 were likely responsible for the weaker effects when reading in their L1. Further studies of this type extending the work from adult bilinguals to children is needed in order to inform a theory of bilingual reading development.

Based on the discussion in the final paragraph of the section "Word Reading in Adult Bilinguals," one could speculate about the relative difficulty that children who are becoming biliterate might have in reading as a function of the similarity of the orthographies of their two languages. If the child's two languages share an alphabet, then the correspondences between letters and sounds usually become more complex. For example, there are several pronunciations for the letter *i* in English, but if one learns French, there are additional pronunciations, such as a long *e* sound, that are also associated with this letter. Furthermore, there will be greater competition in the orthographic lexical system when the child's two languages share the same alphabet than when the languages have different orthographies. One could speculate, then, that naming times will be slower in English for children when they read another language with the same alphabet than when their other language has a different alphabet, and naming speeds might be fastest if the writing system in the other language is not an alphabet at all (see Table 17.1 in Siegel, Chapter 17, in this volume for a preliminary test of this hypothesis). A difficulty with testing this hypothesis is ensuring that children with different first-language backgrounds are matched on other relevant variables.

Although our focus has been on the nature of bilingual children's word recognition system, we close with a brief discussion of how bilingual children, or those who are beginning the process of becoming bilingual, may differ from monolingual children with respect to skills related to learning to read. In some ways, children who are learning to read in an L2 may be more prepared cognitively than monolingual children learning to read in their native language, yet they may be less prepared in other ways. On one hand, children who have been exposed to a second language may have greater metalinguistic awareness than their monolingual peers (e.g., Bruck & Genesee, 1995; Campbell & Sais, 1995; for reviews, see Bialystok, 2001, 2002). On the other hand, children learning to read in a language that is relatively new to them may be less able to distinguish sounds in the language than native speakers, which may hamper the acquisition of spelling–sound correspondences. Because of a limited spoken vocabulary, they may be less able to recognize a word when sounding it out produces only an approximation of its phonological representation, which in turn may make it harder to fine-tune their knowledge of spelling–sound correspondences. Furthermore, their limited vocabulary may make it more difficult to use context to interpret ambiguities and figure out the meanings of new words; they may be less able to parse sentences into their constituents and determine underlying propositions, which may limit their ability to hold strings of words in working memory, and they may experience interference from their native language's phonological, orthographic, morphological, syntactic, or discourse structures (Verhoeven, 2000). There may also be considerable differences between L2 learners and native speakers in exposure to print in the language of instruction. Children learning to read in an L2 may have minimal exposure to print in that language before reading instruction begins, and if they subsequently read in both of their languages, they might read less in each language than a child who is monolingual in either language. Reduced exposure to print in a language could have consequences for the development of reading fluency because reading practice is important in determining fluency (Levy, 2001; Torgesen, Rashotte, & Alexander, 2001). Indeed, Fraser (2004) has noted that developing fluent reading skills is a persistent challenge for second-language readers.

SUMMARY

The literature that has been reviewed provides strong evidence that bilinguals do not have separate language and word recognition systems for each of their languages. Instead, representations for their two languages are interconnected, and both are activated in an apparently monolingual language situation. In reading, phonological representations from both languages are activated when reading in just one language, although reading in the weaker language is affected more by activation from the bilingual's stronger language than the reverse. It appears that representations are interconnected from the start of biliterate reading acquisition, although the evidence on this point is limited thus far. There are considerable challenges in learning to read in two languages, but the benefits of being able to communicate with people in another language and having access to the written heritage of two languages is likely to be worth the effort in the long run for most children. However, children who have an impairment in basic reading processes face a much greater challenge. Whether the struggle is worth it ultimately depends on the value to the individual of being able to read in each language.

ACKNOWLEDGMENT

The writing of this article was supported by Natural Sciences and Engineering Research Council of Canada Grant RGPIN 153380-2007 to Debra Jared and National Institutes of Health Grant R01-HD053146 to Judith F. Kroll.

REFERENCES

Abu-Rabia, S., & Siegel, L.S. (2002). Reading, syntactic, orthographic, and working-memory skills of bilingual Arabic-English speaking Canadian children. *Journal of Psycholinguistic Research, 31,* 661–678.

Arab-Moghaddam, N., & Sénéchal, M. (2001). Orthographic and phonological processing skills in reading and spelling in Persian/English bilinguals. *International Journal of Behavioral Development, 25,* 140–147.

August, D., & Shanahan, T. (Eds.). (2006). *Developing literacy in second-language learners: Report of the national literacy panel on language-minority children and youth.* Mahwah, NJ: Lawrence Erlbaum Associates.

Bialystok, E. (2001). *Bilingualism in development: Language, literacy, & cognition.* Cambridge, England: Cambridge University Press.

Bialystok, E. (2002). Acquisition of literacy in bilingual children: A framework for research. *Language Learning, 52,* 159–199.

Bialystok, E., McBride-Chang, C., & Luk, G. (2005). Bilingualism, language proficiency, and learning to read in two writing systems. *Journal of Educational Psychology, 97,* 580–590.

Bruck, M., & Genesee, F. (1995). Phonological awareness in young second language learners. *Journal of Child Language, 22,* 307–324.

Brysbaert, M., & Duyck, W. (2010). Is it time to leave behind the Revised Hierarchical Model of bilingual language processing after fifteen years of service? *Bilingualism: Language and Cognition, 13,* 359–371.

Brysbaert, M., van Dyck, G., & van de Poel, M. (1999). Visual word recognition in bilinguals: Evidence from masked phonological priming. *Journal of Experimental Psychology: Human Perception and Performance, 25,* 137–148.

Campbell, R., & Sais, E. (1995). Accelerated metalinguistic (phonological) awareness in bilingual children. *British Journal of Developmental Psychology, 13,* 61–68.

Cho, J.Y., & McBride-Chang, C. (2005). Levels of phonological awareness in Korean and English: A one-year longitudinal study. *Journal of Educational Psychology, 97,* 564–571.

Comeau, L., Cormier, P., Grandmaison, É., & Lacroix, D. (1999). A longitudinal study of phonological processing skills in children learning to read in a second language. *Journal of Educational Psychology, 91,* 29–43.

DaFontoura, H.A., & Siegel, L.S. (1995). Reading, syntactic, and working memory skills of bilingual Portuguese-English Canadian children. *Reading and Writing: An Interdisciplinary Journal, 7,* 139–153.

D'Angiulli, A., Siegel, L.S., & Serra, E. (2001). The development of reading in English and Italian in bilingual children. *Applied Psycholinguistics, 22,* 479–507.

Deacon, S.H., Wade-Woolley, L., & Kirby, J. (2007). Crossover: The role of morphological awareness in French immersion children's reading. *Developmental Psychology, 43,* 732–746.

de Groot, A.M.B. (1992). Determinants of word translation. *Journal of Experimental Psychology: Learning, Memory, and Cognition, 18,* 1001–1018.

Dijkstra, T. (2005). Bilingual visual word recognition and lexical access. In J.F. Kroll & A.M.B. de Groot (Eds.), *Handbook of bilingualism: Psycholinguistic approaches* (pp. 179–201). New York: Oxford University Press.

Dijkstra, T., & van Heuven, W.J.B. (1998). The BIA-model and bilingual word recognition. In J. Grainger and A. Jacobs (Eds.), *Localist connectionist approaches to human cognition* (pp. 189–225). Mahwah, NJ: Lawrence Erlbaum Associates.

Dijkstra, T., & van Heuven, W.J.B. (2002). The architecture of the bilingual word recognition system: From identification to decision. *Bilingualism: Language and Cognition, 5,* 175–197.

Durgunoglu, A.Y. (1998). Acquiring literacy in English and Spanish in the United States. In A.Y. Durgunoglu & L. Verhoeven (Eds.), *Literacy development in a multilingual context: Cross-cultural perspectives* (pp. 135–145). Mahwah, NJ: Lawrence Erlbaum Associates.

Durgunoglu, A.Y., Nagy, W.E., & Hancin-Bhatt, B.J. (1993). Cross-language transfer of phonological awareness. *Journal of Educational Psychology, 85,* 453–465.

Dussias, P.E. (2003). Syntactic ambiguity resolution in L2 learners: Some effects of bilinguality on LI and L2 processing strategies. *Studies in Second Language Acquisition, 25,* 529–557.

Duyck, W., van Assche, E., Drieghe, D., & Hartsuiker, R.J. (2007). Recognition by bilinguals in a sentence context: Evidence for nonselective lexical access. *Journal of Experimental Psychology: Learning, Memory, and Cognition, 33,* 663–679.

Fraser, C.A. (2004). Lire avec facilité en langue seconde [Fluent reading in a second language]. *The Canadian Modern Language Review, 61,* 135–160.

Geva, E., & Siegel, L.S. (2000). Orthographic and cognitive factors in the concurrent development of basic reading skills in two languages. *Reading and Writing: An Interdisciplinary Journal, 12,* 1–30.

Geva, E., Wade-Woolley, L., & Shany, M. (1997). Development of reading efficiency in first and second language. *Scientific Studies of Reading, 1,* 119–144.

Gholamain, M., & Geva, E. (1999). Orthographic and cognitive factors in the concurrent development of basic reading skills in English and Persian. *Language Learning, 49,* 183–217.

Gollan, T.H., Forster, K.I., & Frost, R. (1997). Translation priming with different scripts: Masked priming with cognates and noncognates in Hebrew-English bilinguals. *Journal of Experimental Psychology: Learning, Memory, and Cognition, 23,* 1122–1139.

Gottardo, A. (2002). The relationship between language and reading skills in bilingual Spanish-English speakers. *Topics in Language Disorders, 22,* 46–70.

Gottardo, A., Yan, B., Siegel, L.S., & Wade-Woolley, L. (2001). Factors related to English reading performance in children with Chinese as a first language: More evidence of cross-language transfer of phonological processing. *Journal of Educational Psychology, 93,* 530–542.

Haigh, C.A. (2007). *Bilinguals' activation of phonological representations from printed words.* Unpublished doctoral dissertation, University of Western Ontario, London, ON, Canada.

Jacquet, M., & French, R.M. (2002). The BIA++: Extending the BIA+ to a dynamical distributed connectionist framework. *Bilingualism: Language and Cognition, 5,* 202–205.

Jared, D., Cormier, P., Levy, B.A., & Wade-Woolley, L. (2011). Early predictors of biliteracy development in children in French immersion: A four-year longitudinal study. *Journal of Educational Psychology, 103*(1), 119–139.

Jared, D., Cormier, P., Levy, B.A., & Wade-Woolley, L. (in press). Cross-language activation of phonology in young bilingual readers.

Jared, D., & Kroll. J. (2001). Do bilinguals activate phonological representations in one or both of their languages when naming words? *Journal of Memory and Language, 44,* 2–31.

Jared, D., McRae, K. & Seidenberg, M.S. (1990). The basis of consistency effects in word naming. *Journal of Memory and Language, 29,* 687–715.

Jared, D., & Szucs, C. (2002). Phonological activation in bilinguals: Evidence from interlingual homograph naming. *Bilingualism: Language and Cognition, 5,* 225–239.

Keung, Y.-C., & Ho, C.S.-H. (2009). Transfer of reading-related cognitive skills in learning to read Chinese (L1) and English (L2) among Chinese elementary school children. *Contemporary Educational Psychology, 34,* 103–112.

Knell, E., Siegel, L., Haiyan, Q., Lin, Z., Miao, P., Wei, Z., et al. (2007). Early English immersion and literacy in Xi'an China. *The Modern Language Journal, 91,* 395–417.

Kroll, J.F., & Stewart, E. (1994). Category interference in translation and picture naming: Evidence for asymmetric connections between bilingual memory representations. *Journal of Memory and Language, 33,* 149–174.

Kroll, J.F., van Hell, J.G., Tokowicz, N., & Green, D.W. (2010). The Revised Hierarchical Model: A critical review and assessment. *Bilingualism: Language and Cognition, 13,* 373–381.

Lee, C.H., Nam, K., & Katz, L. (2005). Nonselective access of spelling-sound knowledge for Korean-English bilinguals. *International Journal of Psychology, 40,* 407–415.

Lee, W.L., Wee, G.C., Tzeng, O.J.L., & Hung, D. (1992). A study of the interlingual and intralingual Stroop effect in three different scripts: Logograph, syllabary, and alphabet. In R.J. Harris (Ed.), *Cognitive processing in bilinguals* (pp. 427–442). Amsterdam: North Holland.

Levy, B.A. (2001). Moving the bottom. In M. Wolf (Ed.), *Dyslexia, fluency, and the brain* (pp. 357–379). Timonium, MD: York Press.

Libben, M.R., & Titone, D.A. (2009). Bilingual lexical access in context: Evidence from eye movements during reading. *Journal of Experimental Psychology. Learning, Memory, and Cognition, 35,* 381–390.

Lindsey, K.A., Manis, F.R., & Bailey, C.E. (2003). Prediction of first-grade reading in Spanish-speaking English-language learners, *Journal of Educational Psychology, 95,* 482–494.

Luk, G., & Bialystok, E. (2008). Common and distinct cognitive bases for reading in English-Cantonese bilinguals. *Applied Psycholinguistics, 29,* 269–289.

MacWhinney, B. (2005). A unified model of language acquisition. In J.F. Kroll & A.M.B. de Groot (Eds.). *Handbook of bilingualism: Psycholinguistic approaches* (pp. 49–67). New York: Oxford University Press.

Manis, F.R., Lindsey, K.A., & Bailey, C.E. (2004). Development of reading in Grades K–2 in Spanish-speaking English-language learners. *Learning Disabilities Research & Practice, 19,* 214–224.

McBride-Chang, C., & Ho, C.S.-H. (2005). Predictors of beginning reading in Chinese and English: A 2-year longitudinal study of Chinese kindergartners. *Scientific Studies of Reading, 9,* 117–144.

McBride-Chang, C., Tong, X., Shu, H., Wong, A.M.Y., Leung, K., & Tardif, T. (2008). Syllable, phoneme, and tone: Psycholinguistic units in early Chinese and English word recognition. *Scientific Studies of Reading, 12,* 171–194.

Moreno, E.M., Federmeier, K.D., & Kutas, M. (2002). Switching languages, switching palabras: An electrophysiological study of code switching. *Brain and Language, 80,* 188–207.

Mumtaz, S., & Humphreys, G.W. (2002). The effect of Urdu vocabulary size on the acquisition of single word reading in English. *Educational Psychology, 22,* 165–190.

Myers-Scotton, C. (2002). *Contact linguistics: Bilingual encounters and grammatical outcomes.* Oxford, England: Oxford University Press.

Potter, M.C., So, K.-F., Von Eckardt, B., & Feldman, L.B. (1984). Lexical and conceptual representation in beginning and more proficient bilinguals. *Journal of Verbal Learning and Verbal Behavior, 23,* 23–38.

Rastle, K., & Brysbaert, M. (2006). Masked phonological priming effects in English: Are they real? Do they matter? *Cognitive Psychology, 53,* 97–145.

Saiegh-Haddad, E., & Geva, E. (2008). Morphological awareness, phonological awareness, and reading in English-Arabic bilingual children. *Reading and Writing, 21,* 481–504.

Schwartz, A.I., & Kroll, J.F. (2006). Bilingual lexical activation in sentence context. *Journal of Memory and Language, 55,* 197–212.

Seidenberg, M.S., & McClelland, J.L. (1989). A distributed developmental model of word recognition and naming. *Psychological Review, 96,* 523–568.

Share, D.L. (2008). On the Anglocentricities of current reading research and practice: The perils of overreliance on an "outlier" orthography. *Psychological Bulletin, 134,* 584–615.

Sunderman, G., & Kroll, J.F. (2006). First language activation during second language lexical processing: An investigation of lexical form meaning and grammatical class. *Studies in Second Language Acquisition, 28,* 387–422.

Swanson, H.L., Sáez, L., Gerber, M., & Leafstedt, J. (2004). Literacy and cognitive functioning in bilingual and nonbilingual children at or not at risk for reading disabilities. *Journal of Educational Psychology, 91,* 3–18.

Thierry, G., & Wu, Y.J. (2007). Brain potentials reveal unconscious translation during foreign-language comprehension. *Proceedings of the National Academy of Sciences, USA, 104*(30), 12530–12535.

Thomas, M.S.C. (2002). Theories that develop. *Bilingualism: Language and Cognition, 5,* 216–217.

Thomas, M.S.C., & van Heuven, W.J.B. (2005). Computational models of bilingual comprehension. In J.F. Kroll & A.M.B. de Groot (Eds.), *Handbook of bilingualism: Psycholinguistic approaches.* (pp. 202–225). New York: Oxford University Press.

Tong, X., & McBride-Chang, C. (2010). Chinese-English biscriptal reading: Cognitive component skills across orthographies. *Reading & Writing, 23,* 293–310.

Torgesen, J.K., Rashotte, C.A., & Alexander, A. (2001). Principles of fluency instruction in reading: Relationships with established empirical outcomes. In M. Wolf (Ed.), *Dyslexia, fluency, and the brain* (pp. 333–355). Timonium, MD: York Press.

van Assche, E., Duyck, W., Hartsuiker, R.J., & Diependaele, K. (2009). Does bilingualism change native-language reading? Cognate effects in a sentence context. *Psychological Science, 20,* 923–927.

van Hell, J.G., & de Groot, A.M.B. (2008). Sentence context modulates visual word recognition and translation in bilinguals. *Acta Psychologica, 128*, 431–451.

van Heuven, W.J.B., Dijkstra, T., & Grainger, J. (1998). Orthographic neighborhood effects in bilingual word recognition. *Journal of Memory and Language, 39*, 458–483.

van Wijnendaele, I., & Brysbaert, M. (2002). Visual word recognition in bilinguals: Phonological priming from the second to the first language. *Journal of Experimental Psychology: Human Perception and Performance, 28*, 616–627.

Veii, K., & Everatt, J. (2005). Predictors of reading among Herero-English bilingual Namibian school children. *Bilingualism: Language and Cognition, 8*, 239–254.

Verhoeven, L. (2000). Components in early second language reading and spelling. *Scientific Studies of Reading, 4*, 313–330.

Wang, M., Ko, I.Y., & Choi, J. (2009). The importance of morphological awareness in Korean-English biliteracy acquisition. *Contemporary Educational Psychology, 34*, 132–142.

Wang, M., Park, Y., & Lee, K.R. (2006). Korean-English biliteracy acquisition: Cross-language phonological and orthographic transfer. *Journal of Educational Psychology, 98*, 148–158.

Wang, M., Perfetti, C., & Liu, Y. (2005). Chinese-English biliteracy acquisition: Cross-language and writing system transfer. *Cognition, 97*, 67–88.

Wang, M., Yang, C., & Cheng, C. (2009). The contributions of phonology, orthography, and morphology in Chinese-English biliteracy acquisition. *Applied Psycholinguistics, 30*, 291–314.

Wu, Y.J., & Thierry, G. (2010). Chinese-English bilinguals reading English hear Chinese. *The Journal of Neuroscience, 30*(22), 7646–7651.

CHAPTER 16

Language Representation and Cognitive Control in Bilinguals

Implications for Dyslexia

Gigi Luk and Ellen Bialystok

L iving in a bilingual environment has implications for the individual beyond being able to converse in more than one language. The experience of handling two languages is associated with enhanced cognitive processes that are evident in a variety of domains in addition to language. This observation comes from studies using nonverbal executive functioning tasks that require the resolution of conflict from a competing alternative. Previous research has shown that bilingual individuals perform significantly better than their monolingual peers on these nonverbal executive functioning tasks across the lifespan (see reviews in Bialystok, 2001, 2007). The interpretation of this bilingual advantage is that the experience of regularly using two language systems and the need to manage attention to those two languages enhances the general cognitive control mechanism.

The implications for language-specific processes that vary according to the unique relationship between sound and symbols in each language are more mixed. Unlike the clear cognitive advantage observed in executive functioning, the influence of bilingualism on the development of language and early literacy in children varies with different word-level processes. For phonological awareness and nonword decoding, the effect of bilingualism appears to be influenced by the relation between the orthographies used to represent the pairs of spoken languages acquired by bilingual children. In terms of receptive vocabulary, bilingual children (Oller, Pearson, & Cobo-Lewis, 2007) and young adults (Portocarrero, Burright, & Donovick, 2007) generally have weaker receptive vocabulary knowledge in each language than do their monolingual peers, irrespective of the pairs of languages. Bilingualism is also associated with weaker performance in tasks that require rapid word retrieval, such as picture naming (Gollan, Montoya, Fennema-Notestine, & Morris, 2005) and verbal fluency (Gollan, Montoya, & Werner, 2002), although some studies have reported no difference between monolinguals and bilinguals in verbal fluency (Portocarrero et al., 2007; Rosselli et al., 2002). However, with a smaller vocabulary size, it is not surprising that bilinguals perform more poorly on lexical retrieval tasks. Taken together, these factors suggest that bilingualism has opposite effects on cognitive and linguistic domains: It has a positive impact on cognitive performance but a more limiting influence on linguistic outcomes.

EARLY LITERACY AND VOCABULARY ACQUISITION

Literacy research with bilingual children typically examines whether there is a difference between monolinguals and bilinguals in the rate or timing of literacy acquisition or whether there is cross-language transfer for bilingual children. It is well documented that vocabulary size is important in literacy acquisition, yet as noted, bilinguals generally have smaller receptive vocabularies than their monolingual peers. Because bilinguals need to divide their time and exposure between two languages, such a finding is not surprising. Vocabulary is typically measured by administering standardized tests, such as the Peabody Picture Vocabulary Test (PPVT; Dunn & Dunn, 1997), which requires examinees to match one of four line drawings to a word spoken by the examiner. This test has a reported mean of 100 and a standard deviation of 15 as standardized in a North American population. In an aggregated analysis involving 1,738 children between 3 and 10 years of age (772 English monolinguals and 966 bilinguals), the central tendency measures of the performance distribution of the bilingual children were consistently 9 points lower than those measures for the monolingual children (Bialystok, Luk, Peets, & Yang, 2010). It should be noted that this finding does not indicate that bilinguals had poorer vocabulary acquisition skills; it indicates only that bilinguals showed weaker vocabulary in one of their two languages, perhaps reflecting the less intensive exposure to some of the items in the PPVT. An item analysis using a subset of the data that included only 6-year-olds categorized a portion of the items that are typically within the performance range of this age group into school-based items (e.g., astronaut, rectangle) and home-based items (e.g., squash, pitcher). In this comparison, bilinguals performed poorer on home-based items but similarly to monolinguals in school-based items, suggesting that there are culture-specific items in the PPVT that may be one of the sources of the weaker performance of bilinguals. The children typically did not speak English at home, and the PPVT was administered only in English, making such items less common in their experience. In other words, bilinguals may possess weaker language representation in one language, but this weakness in one of the two languages spoken by the bilingual children is a consequence of the nature of linguistic exposure in a diverse linguistic context rather than a limitation in learning potential. Typically, bilingual children have at least one label in each language representing the objects they encounter in everyday life. The equivalent performance in school-based items indicates that bilingual and monolingual children received similar exposure to formal classroom vocabulary in English, which was also their dominant language, but the two groups of children differed in vocabulary items related to home objects, reflecting bilingual children's diverse home linguistic environment.

In addition to vocabulary development, early literacy also requires phonological awareness and decoding skills. In this case, the effect of bilingualism changes according to the similarity between the languages spoken by the bilingual children. For phonological awareness, very young bilingual children were shown to have more advanced ability than their monolingual peers (Bruck & Genesee, 1995; Campbell & Sais, 1995; Lesaux & Siegel, 2003; Yelland, Pollard, & Mercuri, 1993), but this advantage typically disappears when children enter elementary school and begin formal reading instruction (Chiappe & Siegel, 2006; Jean & Geva, 2009). However, these studies have generally included a hetero-geneous group of bilinguals from various linguistic backgrounds or one homogeneous group of bilinguals speaking the same non-English lan-guage, making it difficult to examine the interaction between cross-linguistic literacy acquisition and bilingualism.

In order to investigate the role of bilingualism in cross-language literacy acquisition, Bialystok, Luk, and Kwan (2005) gave a series of phonological awareness and nonword decoding tasks in both English and the non-English language to Spanish–English, Hebrew–English, and Cantonese–English bilingual and English monolingual children in first grade. All the bilingual children were recruited from weekly heritage lan-guage classes, but received formal education in English during the week. Parents of the children reported the bilingual children using mostly the non-English languages, the family's major language of communication, at home. These bilingual children were chosen because the language pairs represent a systematic trend for increasingly divergent relationships between the two orthographies and spoken languages. The most similar language pair was Spanish and English because these two languages are both Indo-European, share the same writing system (alphabetic), and are represented by the same script (Roman). Although English has a more opaque relation between grapheme and phoneme, both English and Spanish are written alphabetically, and successful decoding skills rely on associating letters to sounds (Coulmas, 1991). The next pair on this scale is Hebrew and English because they share the same writing system (alphabetic) but are represented by different scripts (Hebrew uses a Semitic script). Finally, Chinese and English are completely different spo-ken languages and are represented by different writing systems (Chinese uses a morphological writing system) and, of course, different scripts. Unlike reading in English, successful reading in Chinese relies not only on phonological awareness and semantic processing (Siok & Fletcher, 2001; So & Siegel, 1997), but also on metalinguistic awareness of struc-tures *within a character,* as some parts of a character may provide infor-mation on pronunciation (Shu & Anderson, 1997). By including these bilingual children and a group of English monolingual children, it was possible to examine how writing systems and script differences affect literacy acquisition in a bilingual context.

Similar results were obtained for both phonological awareness and decoding tasks; specifically, the Spanish–English and Hebrew–English bilinguals outperformed the Cantonese–English bilinguals and English monolinguals. This pattern suggests that bilinguals who speak two languages that are represented by similar writing systems (irrespective of the script) benefit from this similarity and possibly transfer their understanding of how alphabetic words are composed of speech sounds represented by letters from one language to another. Surprisingly, the Cantonese–English bilingual participants did not suffer from handling two languages with different writing systems in which they had to learn two sets of rules to interpret written text. In fact, these children performed at the same level as the English monolinguals. Results from the group comparisons were consistent with previous research, suggesting a bilingual advantage in phonological awareness and nonword decoding but revealed conditions that modulated these effects. Specifically, this advantage was most apparent when the two languages spoken by the bilingual children shared similarities in both their writing systems and scripts.

To examine possible transfer between nonword decoding skills in bilinguals, correlations between English and non-English nonword decoding performance were examined for each bilingual group. Consistent with the level of similarity in writing systems and scripts between language pairs, there was a strong positive correlation in the Spanish–English bilinguals, a moderate positive correlation in the Hebrew–English bilinguals, and no correlation in the Cantonese–English bilinguals. Therefore, cross-language correlation between English and non-English nonword reading tasks showed that transfer of nonword decoding skills depends on the similarity between language structures and features of the writing system.

If bilinguals speaking two languages with different writing systems, such as Cantonese and English, show no transfer in nonword decoding skills, then there must be distinct cognitive processes involved in reading these divergent languages in addition to common processes involved in reading. Previous research has shown that there are cross-language correlations for measures of phonological awareness and word-decoding skills in bilinguals (Gomez & Reason, 2002; Gottardo, Yan, Siegel, & Wade-Woolley, 2001; Keung & Ho, 2009; Wang, Perfetti, & Liu, 2005). These correlations are typically strong and significant for phonological awareness in the two languages, but weaker and sometimes insignificant for decoding. Recently, Sparks, Patton, Ganschow, and Humbach (2008) reported that elementary school children's reading skills in their first language (L1; English in this case) significantly predicted reading performance in their second language (L2; German, French, and Spanish in this study) when these children were in high school. These results were interpreted as evidence for transfer of literacy skills between L1 and L2. However, because both languages are represented by an alphabetic orthography, it is unclear whether the transfer indicates shared cognitive resources that are commonly recruited for reading or similar strategies recruited to read L1 and L2.

To investigate this question, we gave a battery of literacy tasks in both English and Chinese to a group of Cantonese–English bilingual first-grade students (Luk & Bialystok, 2008). In addition, two general cognitive tasks measuring nonverbal analytic reasoning and verbal working memory were included. Consistent with previous research, these children showed significant cross-language correlation in phonological awareness tasks and word identification tasks. However, the cross-language correlation in word identification disappeared after controlling for general cognitive abilities (working memory and nonverbal reasoning), but the cross-language correlation in phonological awareness tasks remained significant. The nonverbal reasoning task, measured by the Raven's Coloured Progressive Matrices (Raven, 1998), correlated with phoneme onset deletion and word identification in both English and Cantonese; the verbal working memory correlated with phoneme onset deletion in both English and Cantonese, but only with English word identification and vocabulary. The shared variance in tasks measuring general cognitive abilities and word identification performance in both English and Cantonese contributed to the previously reported cross-language correlations in word identification (e.g., Gottardo et al., 2001).

From these studies, it is evident that the bilingual influence on phonological awareness and word decoding varies according to the similarity of written representations in the two spoken languages after controlling for general cognitive functions. In summary, the investigation of cross-language literacy development in bilinguals suggests that learning to read in two languages with different written representations requires the understanding of how words and sounds are encoded in different written forms, such as alphabets and characters, in addition to general cognitive skills, such as working memory and nonverbal reasoning. Although phonological awareness transfers between L1 and L2 irrespective of how the languages are written, transfer in L1 and L2 decoding depends on the similarity in orthographies.

LINGUISTIC AND COGNITIVE CONSEQUENCES OF BILINGUALISM

Research comparing bilingual and monolingual children on linguistic and cognitive tasks has shown better performance by bilingual children in solving problems relating to concepts of print (Bialystok, 1997, 1999; Bialystok, Shenfield, & Codd, 2000), appearance–reality isolation[1] (Study 2 in Bialystok & Senman, 2004; Goetz, 2003), cognitive flexibility[2] (Bialystok &

---

[1]In this task, children were asked to identify an object that appeared to be different from its identity, such as a sponge that is sprayed with gray paint to make it look like a rock.

[2]Cognitive flexibility was measured in a dimensional change card sort task. The cards had figures consisting of two dimensions (e.g., shape and color), and children were asked to sort the cards according to one dimension (e.g., shape). After a few trials, children were instructed to sort the card according to the other dimension (e.g., color). Cognitive flexibility was assessed as percentage of correct sorting after the switch.

Martin, 2004), and executive functions that involve conflict resolution in nonverbal tasks (Bialystok & Viswanathan, 2009; Carlson & Meltzoff, 2008). One common characteristic of the task conditions in which a bilingual advantage was found is the requirement to inhibit attention to distracting information that is presented as an alternative response. Yet, as reviewed in the previous section, bilingual children generally have weaker language proficiency in one of their languages as measured in standardized tasks such as the PPVT. Moreover, in adult populations, bilinguals generally perform more poorly than monolinguals in language production, picture naming efficiency, and lexical retrieval performance (Gollan et al., 2002; Ivanova & Costa, 2008; Portocarrero et al., 2007). However, the bilingual advantage in executive functions is rarely examined in the same paradigm as the bilingual disadvantage in language processing.

In this section, we describe how to study the positive and negative influences together using the verbal fluency paradigm. The verbal fluency paradigm is a standardized neuropsychological test that allows for the joint investigation of bilingualism, language proficiency, and executive control because of the different task demands in two conditions: letter and category fluency. In the letter fluency task, the instructions are to generate as many words as possible that begin with a specific letter and follow several explicit restrictions: no proper nouns, numbers, or variations on the same word. In the category fluency task, participants are told to say as many words in a given category (e.g., animal, clothing items) as possible within 1 minute. The standard interpretation of these conditions is that the letter task adds to the control system for monitoring and attending to lexical representations, and the category test assesses representational integrity of the linguistic system (Delis, Kaplan, & Kramer, 2001). The control demands in the letter task come from the additional restrictions and the nonintuitive generation of words from letter cues. The increased level of cognitive control in the letter fluency task has been supported by neuropsychological studies showing lower performance in letter fluency compared with category fluency (Rende, Ramsberger, & Miyake, 2002). Moreover, Paulesu et al. (1997) have shown that although letter and category fluency tasks activated some common neural regions consistent with verbal production, activation in the left inferior frontal regions was significantly higher in the letter task than in the category task. Activation in this brain region was typically higher in tasks with increased demand on cognitive control.

With adequate independent assessment of language proficiency in bilinguals and monolinguals, performance differences in category fluency should reflect the language proficiency of these participants. In other words, monolinguals and bilinguals with similar proficiency in the language of testing should also perform comparably on the category test. However, for these groups matched on language proficiency, the additional demands for executive control should favor the bilinguals, increasing their performance relative to the monolinguals on the letter task. Thus, assessing language proficiency in addition to using a verbal task with varying degrees of cognitive control would allow the dissociation of these two processes in bilinguals and monolinguals.

To date, there is no study specifically comparing bilingual and monolingual children's performance in verbal fluency, so research with adults is described here. Previous research using this paradigm has shown a bilingual disadvantage for category fluency but mixed results for letter fluency (Gollan et al., 2002; Rosselli et al., 2002). The bilingual disadvantage in category fluency may be a consequence of the bilinguals' lower language proficiency—specifically, lower vocabulary—whereas the mixed results in letter fluency may reflect the interaction between task demand of executive control (for which bilinguals enjoy a benefit) and language proficiency (for which bilinguals suffer a disadvantage). To understand the interplay among bilingualism, executive control, and language proficiency, these factors have to be considered in the same sample. However, participants' English proficiency levels have not usually been assessed in previous studies.

Some exceptions exist. Bialystok, Craik, and Luk (2008) separated bilingual young adults (around 20 years old) into two groups: the high-proficiency (HP) bilinguals, matched for English proficiency (as measured by the PPVT) to their monolingual peers, and the low-proficiency (LP) bilinguals, who attained a significantly lower PPVT score than the other two groups. Results in category fluency replicated the comparison in PPVT in which the LP bilinguals showed significantly lower performance than the HP bilinguals and monolinguals, who were not different from each other. For letter fluency, the HP bilinguals outperformed the LP bilinguals and monolinguals, with no difference between the latter two groups. In short, the bilingual advantage is apparent, even in a language production task in which bilinguals and monolinguals have comparable language proficiency. The equivalence in language proficiency becomes a stepping stone for bilinguals to exhibit a cognitive advantage in response to increased task demands of executive control.

To further examine the dissociable influences of bilingualism on executive control and linguistic processing in a verbal task, Luo, Luk, and Bialystok (2010) used a logarithmic function to model verbal responses from category and letter fluency during a 1-minute period. The initiating point of the function signifies the linguistic resources available to the individual—a measure that can be interpreted as language proficiency. The declining slope of the function indicates productivity as a function of time. This function was constructed by recording the number of correct responses—at 5-second intervals, hence generating 12 time bins for each participant in each group across the 1-minute period, for letter and category tasks separately. The group function was derived by extracting the mean performance of each task across the 20 participants in each group. In these fluency tasks, as time passes during the 1-minute period, the executive demand increases because of the diminishing available resources (participants need to filter out words that have already been said). Therefore, a steeper declining slope indicates faster depletion of performance and weaker executive control. As in the study by Bialystok et al. (2008), HP bilinguals, LP bilinguals, and monolinguals were included in the analysis and given the category and letter fluency tasks. There were no group differences in initiating point or slope for category fluency, possibly because the LP bilinguals had English proficiency (measured by PPVT) within the typical range. Consistent with the results reported in Bialystok et al. (2008) for letter fluency, the initiating point of the function reflected the high proficiency level of the HP bilinguals and monolinguals, which was higher than that of the LP bilinguals. In terms of slope, the monolinguals showed a steeper declining slope than the two bilingual groups. The interpretation is that the resources (initiating point) reflect representation and the slope represents control. Thus, these results from the verbal fluency task demonstrate the dissociability of the bilingual influence on language representation and cognitive control. Moreover, these studies also confirm the importance of assessing language proficiency in bilinguals to isolate the cognitive advantage and linguistic disadvantage in a verbal production task.

Another implication of the verbal fluency results is that a simple language production task not only involves linguistic processing, but also recruits executive functions. As with verbal production, reading ability also rests on a wide range of language and cognitive processes, including working memory (Arnell, Joanisse, Klein, Busseri, & Tannock, 2009), visual attention (Rayner, 2009), and paired associate learning of visual and verbal material (Li, Shu, McBride-Chang, Liu, & Xue, 2009). Research with bilinguals demonstrates that language experience affects cognitive processing that is not specific to the linguistic domain. Such findings point to the importance of considering these linguistic and cognitive processes when examining how reading develops in children. In the case of bilingualism, reading stands at the intersection of these linguistic and cognitive processes. Although the experience of handling two languages enhances cognitive processes, the diverse linguistic exposure simultaneously leads to weaker language proficiency in each language spoken by bilinguals. Moreover, performance reflecting these consequences of bilingualism is mediated by the task demands, as addressed in the verbal fluency paradigm. Therefore, an understanding of both the linguistic and cognitive consequences of bilingualism is essential to examining reading development in a bilingual context.

IMPLICATIONS FOR DYSLEXIA

Dyslexia, a developmental disorder that specifically affects reading ability, has been associated with poorer executive functioning (Brosnan et al., 2002; Helland & Asbjørnsen, 2000; Reiter, Tucha, & Lange, 2004). Because this is the set of processes for which bilingual advantages were reported, it is possible that dyslexia in bilingual children may entail a different profile, different severity, or require different diagnostic procedures than it does for monolingual children. In the following section, research showing the bilingual influence on cognition is reviewed, and implications of these findings are considered for research involving dyslexia in different languages and bilingual dyslexia.

Despite the increasing bilingual population, there is little research that examines whether bilingual children diagnosed with dyslexia exhibit similar or distinct behavioral profiles for the two languages and how these children differ from their monolingual peers. In the limited research to date, the profiles of bilingual children with dyslexia seem to be different for each language—a pattern that has been observed in bilingual children who speak Hindi and English (Gupta & Jamal, 2007) and Cantonese and English (Chung & Ho, 2010). Klein and Doctor (2003) reported that three English–Afrikaans bilingual adolescents with dyslexia showed similar word recognition strategies in both English and Afrikaans to the strategies proposed in a monolingual reading model. There were some differences in the strategies adopted to decode each language (lexical, whole-word approach for English and phonological sounding-out approach for Afrikaans), reflecting the different levels of transparency between script and sound, with Afrikaans having a more transparent system of phoneme–grapheme mappings. The interpretation was that bilinguals and monolinguals showed both common and distinct strategies to adapt to the orthographic and phonological features of each language in order to achieve reading accuracy.

Another possible explanation for the diverse strategies observed in these bilingual adolescents was the differences in instruction for each language. Effective instructions leading to successful literacy may involve divergent adaptation schemas to highlight the orthographic differences in these languages. Everatt, Smythe, Ocampo, and Gyarmathy (2004) pointed out the difficulty in using a general assessment for diagnosis in children speaking different languages and in bilingual children. The cross-language research in bilinguals suggests that diagnostic procedures with bilingual children should include evaluation of both of their languages to obtain the complete profile reflecting their overall reading skills.

Pursuing the importance of executive functions in successful reading, Altemeier, Abbott, and Berninger (2007) reported a longitudinal study showing the contribution of these processes to reading and writing in typical and dyslexic samples using hierarchical linear growth-curve modeling. The results showed that dyslexic children relied less on the executive function system in developing reading and writing skills than did typically developing children. Dyslexic children's weaker reliance on executive functions in reading could point to either underdeveloped executive functions or failure to recruit those cognitive resources to aid reading. Despite the importance of executive functioning for reading development, this cognitive system has rarely been included in the diagnostic assessment of dyslexia, although this may be changing. As reported earlier, bilingual children were shown to excel in cognitive tasks that require them to resolve conflict, such as ignoring distracting features in a stimulus that lead to incorrect responses (see review in Bialystok, 2007) or carrying out more efficient verbal memory retrieval that requires control of attention (Luo et al., 2010). Therefore, these cognitive advantages of bilingualism may compensate for the cognitive impairments in dyslexia. With a more complete assessment of language background (such as bilingualism), executive functioning, and reading performance, specific treatment programs may need to be developed to accommodate children with dyslexia who also have a divergent linguistic background and associated cognitive profile.

CONCLUSION

Research in bilingualism has shown that extensive experience in handling two languages leads to cognitive consequences for both verbal and nonverbal processing. Learning to read in different orthographies recruits additional or different cognitive skills (see Perfetti [Chapter 1], McBride-Chang & Liu [Chapter 2], Richardson, Aro, & Lyytinen [Chapter 4], and Padakannaya & Ramachandra [Chapter 5] in this volume; also Chung, Ho, Chan, Tsang, & Lee, 2010; Ho, Chan, Lee, Tsang, & Luan, 2004). Chung and Ho (2010) recently reported that Chinese–English bilingual children show distinct dyslexic profiles in each of their two languages, consistent with the sound–symbol relations in each language. Compared with age-matched controls, the children with dyslexia had lower reading and phonological awareness performance in both languages, but the disadvantage was more apparent in English reading (L2 for these children). Furthermore, there was a cross-linguistic contribution of L1 (Chinese) to L2 (English) word reading. These results suggest that though dyslexia affects language processing generally, different behavioral profiles are anticipated in bilingual children with dyslexia, especially when the two languages do not share the same writing system. Therefore, assessment of dyslexia in bilingual children needs to cover both languages and include measures of executive control in order to demonstrate cognitive impairments that are general across languages and specific processing difficulties for each language. If bilingualism has a positive influence on executive control, the same outcome should also apply to bilingual children with dyslexia. If that proves to be the case, then it is possible that these bilingual children perform better than their monolingual dyslexic peers on screening measures, to the extent that the disorder could go undetected. Research in bilingualism has demonstrated that the bilingual consequences are positive in the general cognitive domain but negative in the linguistic perspective. Extending these research findings to dyslexic populations suggests a need for more complete assessment in both languages as well as nonverbal assessment in executive functions.

Unlike dyslexia, which has a genetic etiology, bilingualism is experiential. With recent advances in technology, dyslexia and bilingualism can be examined using functional neuroimaging techniques, which allow researchers to isolate the contribution of the brain regions recruited for reading and to investigate how the structures and functions of these brain regions are modified with experience. Future research on bilingual children with dyslexia could provide a broader scope of research opportunity in understanding how literacy skills interact with genetics and linguistic experience. Bilingual research has opened a window for researchers to examine the interaction between language experience and cognition. Despite the recognition of dyslexia as a learning disability with a genetic etiological component, results from bilingual research should be considered to facilitate more effective assessment and provide enriched experiential treatment in both language and executive functions to help children with dyslexia achieve literacy.

ACKNOWLEDGMENTS

Preparation of this manuscript was partially supported by the National Institutes of Health Grant R01HD052523 and by the Natural Sciences and Engineering Research Council of Canada Grant A2559 to Ellen Bialystok.

REFERENCES

Altemeier, L.E., Abbott, R.D., & Berninger, V.W. (2007). Executive functions for reading and writing in typical literacy development and dyslexia. *Journal of Clinical and Experimental Neuropsychology, 30,* 588–606.

Arnell, K.M., Joanisse, M.F., Klein, R.M., Busseri, M.A., & Tannock, R. (2009). Decomposing the relation between rapid automatized naming (RAN) and reading ability. *Canadian Journal of Experimental Psychology, 63,* 173–184.

Bialystok, E. (1997). Effects of bilingualism and biliteracy on children's emerging concepts of print. *Developmental Psychology, 33,* 429–440.

Bialystok, E. (1999). Cognitive complexity and attentional control in the bilingual mind. *Child Development, 70,* 636–644.

Bialystok, E. (2001). *Bilingualism in development: Language, literacy, & cognition.* New York: Cambridge University Press.

Bialystok, E. (2007). Cognitive effects of bilingualism: How linguistic experi-

ence leads to cognitive change. *International Journal of Bilingual Education and Bilingualism, 10,* 210–223.

Bialystok, E., Craik, F.I.M., & Luk, G. (2008). Lexical access in bilinguals: Effects of vocabulary size and executive control. *Journal of Neurolinguistics, 21,* 522–538.

Bialystok, E., Luk, G., & Kwan, E. (2005). Bilingualism, biliteracy, and learning to read: Interactions among languages and writing systems. *Scientific Studies of Reading, 9,* 43–61.

Bialystok, E., Luk, G., Peets, K., & Yang, S. (2010). Receptive vocabulary differences in monolingual and bilingual children. *Bilingualism: Language and Cognition 13,* 525–531.

Bialystok, E., & Martin, M.M. (2004). Attention and inhibition in bilingual children: Evidence from the dimensional change card sort task. *Developmental Science, 7,* 325–339.

Bialystok, E., & Senman, L. (2004). Executive processes in appearance-reality tasks: The role of inhibition of attention and symbolic representation. *Child Development, 75,* 562–579.

Bialystok, E., Shenfield, T., & Codd, J. (2000). Languages, scripts, and the environment: Factors in developing concepts of print. *Developmental Psychology, 36,* 66–76.

Bialystok, E., & Viswanathan, M. (2009). Components of executive control with advantages for bilingual children in two cultures. *Cognition, 112,* 494–500.

Brosnan, M., Demetre, J., Hamill, S., Robson, K., Brockway, H., & Cody, G. (2002). Executive functioning in adults and children with dyslexia. *Neuropsychologia, 40,* 2144–2155.

Bruck, M., & Genesee, F. (1995). Phonological awareness in young second language learners. *Journal of Child Language, 22,* 307–324.

Campbell, R., & Sais, E. (1995). Accelerated metalinguistic (phonological) awareness in bilingual children. *British Journal of Developmental Psychology, 13,* 61–68.

Carlson, S.M., & Meltzoff, A.N. (2008). Bilingual experience and executive functioning in young children. *Developmental Science, 11,* 282–298.

Chiappe, P., & Siegel, L.S. (2006). A longitudinal study of reading development of Canadian children from diverse linguistic backgrounds. *The Elementary School Journal, 107*(2), 135–152.

Chung, K.K.H., & Ho, C.S.-H. (2010). Second language learning difficulties in Chinese children with dyslexia: What are the reading-related cognitive skills that contribute to English and Chinese word reading? *Journal of Learning Disabilities, 43,* 195–211.

Chung, K.K.H., Ho, C.S.-H., Chan, D.W., Tsang, S.M., & Lee, S.H. (2010). Cognitive profiles of Chinese adolescents with dyslexia. *Dyslexia, 16,* 2–23.

Coulmas, F. (1991). *The writing systems of the world.* Cambridge, MA: Blackwell.

Delis, D.C., Kaplan, E., & Kramer, J.H. (2001). *Verbal fluency subtests of the Delis-Kaplan Executive Function System.* San Antonio, TX: The Psychological Corporation.

Dunn, L.M., & Dunn, L.M. (1997). *Peabody Picture Vocabulary Test–Third Edition (PPVT-III).* Circle Pines, MN: American Guidance Service.

Everatt, J., Smythe, I., Ocampo, J., & Gyarmathy, E. (2004). Issues in the assessment of literacy-related difficulties across language backgrounds: A cross-linguistic comparison. *Journal of Research in Reading: Advances and Challenges in Assessment of Literacy, 27,* 141–151.

Goetz, P.J. (2003). The effects of bilingualism on theory of mind development. *Bilingualism: Language and Cognition, 6,* 1–15.

Gollan, T.H., Montoya, R.I., Fennema-Notestine, C., & Morris, S.K. (2005). Bilingualism affects picture naming but not picture classification. *Memory & Cognition, 33,* 1220–1234.

Gollan, T.H., Montoya, R.I., & Werner, G.A. (2002). Semantic and letter fluency in Spanish-English bilinguals. *Neuropsychology, 16,* 562–576.

Gomez, C., & Reason, R. (2002). Cross-linguistic transfer of phonological skills: A Malaysian perspective. *Dyslexia, 8,* 22–33.

Gottardo, A., Yan, B., Siegel, L.S., & Wade-Woolley, L. (2001). Factors related to English reading performance in children with Chinese as a first language: More evidence of cross-language transfer of phonological processing. *Journal of Educational Psychology, 93,* 530–542.

Gupta, A., & Jamal, G. (2007). Reading strategies of bilingual normally progressing and dyslexic readers in Hindi and English. *Applied Psycholinguistics, 28,* 47–68.

Helland, T., & Asbjørnsen, A. (2000). Executive functions in dyslexia. *Child Neuropsychology, 6,* 37–48.

Ho, C.S., Chan, D.W., Lee, S.H., Tsang, S.M., & Luan, V.H. (2004). Cognitive profiling and preliminary subtyping in Chinese developmental dyslexia. *Cognition, 91,* 43–75.

Ivanova, I., & Costa, A. (2008). Does bilingualism hamper lexical access in speech production? *Acta Psychologica, 127,* 277–288.

Jean, M., & Geva, E. (2009). The development of vocabulary in English as a second language children and its role in predicting word recognition ability. *Applied Psycholinguistics, 30,* 153–185.

Keung, Y.-C., & Ho, C.S.-H. (2009). Transfer of reading-related cognitive skills in learning to read Chinese (L1) and English (L2) among Chinese elementary school children. *Contemporary Educational Psychology, 34,* 103–112.

Klein, D., & Doctor, E.A.L. (2003). Patterns of developmental dyslexia in bilinguals. In N. Goulandris (Ed.), *Dyslexia* in different languages: Cross-linguistic comparisons (pp. 112–136). London: Whurr.

Lesaux, N.K., & Siegel, L.S. (2003). The development of reading in children who speak English as a second language. *Developmental Psychology, 39*, 1005–1019.

Li, H., Shu, H., McBride-Chang, C., Liu, H.-Y., & Xue, J. (2009). Paired associate learning in Chinese children with dyslexia. *Journal of Experimental Child Psychology, 103*, 135–151.

Luk, G., & Bialystok, E. (2008). Common and distinct cognitive bases for reading in English-Cantonese bilinguals. *Applied Psycholinguistics, 29*, 269–289.

Luo, L., Luk, G., & Bialystok, E. (2010). Effect of language proficiency and executive control on verbal fluency performance in bilinguals. *Cognition, 114*, 29–41.

Oller, D.K., Pearson, B.Z., & Cobo-Lewis, A.B. (2007). Profile effects in early bilingual language and literacy acquisition. *Applied Psycholinguistics, 28*, 191–230.

Paulesu, E., Goldacre, B., Scifo, P., Cappa, S.F., Gilardi, M.C., Castiglioni, I., et al. (1997). Functional heterogeneity of left inferior frontal cortex as revealed by fMRI. *NeuroReport, 8*, 2011–2016.

Portocarrero, J.S., Burright, R.G., & Donovick, P.J. (2007). Vocabulary and verbal fluency of bilingual and monolingual college students. *Archives of Clinical Neuropsychology, 22*, 415–422.

Raven, J.C. (1998). *Raven's Coloured Progressive Matrices*. San Antonio, TX: The Psychological Corporation.

Rayner, K. (2009). The 35th Sir Frederick Bartlett lecture: Eye movements and attention during reading, scene perception, and visual search. *Quarterly Journal of Experimental Psychology, 62*, 1457–1506.

Reiter, A., Tucha, O., & Lange, K.W. (2004). Executive functions in children with dyslexia. *Dyslexia, 10*, 364–384.

Rende, B., Ramsberger, G., & Miyake, A. (2002). Commonalities and differences in the working memory components underlying letter and category fluency tasks: A dual-task paradigm. *Neuropsychology, 16*, 309–321.

Rosselli, M., Ardila, A., Salvatierra, J., Marquez, M., Matos, L., & Weekes, V.A. (2002). A cross-linguistic comparison of verbal fluency tests. *International Journal of Neuroscience, 112*, 759–776.

Shu, H., & Anderson, R.C. (1997). Role of radical awareness in the character and word acquisition of Chinese children. *Reading Research Quarterly, 32*, 78–89.

Siok, W.T., & Fletcher, P. (2001). The role of phonological awareness and visual-orthographic skills in Chinese reading acquisition. *Developmental Psychology, 37*, 886–899.

So, D., & Siegel, L.S. (1997). Learning to read Chinese: Semantic, syntactic, phonological and working memory skills in normally achieving and poor Chinese readers. *Reading and Writing: An Interdisciplinary Journal, 9*, 1–21.

Sparks, R., Patton, J., Ganschow, L., & Humbach, N. (2008). Long-term cross-linguistic transfer of skills from L1 to L2. *Language Learning, 59*, 203–243.

Wang, M., Perfetti, C.A., & Liu, Y. (2005). Chinese-English biliteracy acquisition: Cross-language and writing system transfer. *Cognition, 97*, 67–88.

Yelland, G.W., Pollard, J., & Mercuri, A. (1993). The metalinguistic benefits of limited contact with a second language. *Applied Psycholinguistics, 14*, 423–444.

CHAPTER 17

Reducing Reading Difficulties in English L1 and L2: Early Identification and Intervention

Linda S. Siegel

T he purpose of this chapter is to consider several critical issues regarding dyslexia. One of these problems concerns the early detection of dyslexia or, more properly, children at risk for dyslexia. It is of critical importance to find reading problems early, before negative social and emotional consequences occur. Another issue concerns what constitutes effective early intervention to prevent at least some cases of dyslexia. Although there is recognition that early intervention is important, there are relatively few examples of successful intervention at the beginning stages of education. A third issue concerns language minority children; that is, children being educated in a language that is not their home language. In the study described later in this chapter, children who are being educated in English but who speak another language at home are monitored to ascertain whether any reading-related difficulties that they have are related to dyslexia or to relative lack of experience with English. These three issues are addressed with data from a longitudinal study that included both children whose first language is English and children learning English as a second language.

EARLY IDENTIFICATION OF CHILDREN AT RISK FOR DYSLEXIA

Identifying children at risk for reading difficulties and providing timely intervention is of critical importance for our society. There are many reasons why this is the case. Undetected and unremediated learning disabilities are a serious problem for our society. The social and psychological consequences of not providing effective remediation of learning disabilities, including dyslexia, are severe. For example, a high prevalence of reading disabilities has been identified among adolescent homeless youth and adolescents who have committed suicide (Barwick & Siegel, 1996; McBride & Siegel, 1997). In addition to academic problems such as grade retention (see, e.g., McLeskey & Grizzle, 1992) and school dropout (see, e.g., Lichtenstein & Zantol-Wiener, 1988; National Center for Education Statistics, 1999), students with learning disabilities are at increased risk of developing social problems (see, e.g., Sabornie, 1994; Wiener & Schneider, 2002) and emotional difficulties such as depression (see, e.g., Gregg, Hoy, King, Moreland, & Jagota, 1992). In addition, this is a population at risk for problems with self-concept (see, e.g., Boetsch, Green, & Pennington, 1996; Chapman, 1988), juvenile delinquency, and substance use and abuse (Beitchman, Wilson, Douglas, Young, & Adlaf, 2001). Obviously, early detection of children at risk for dyslexia and intervention for these children may reduce the incidence of subsequent cognitive, emotional, and social difficulties.

LONGITUDINAL STUDY

One purpose of this chapter is to summarize certain aspects of a longitudinal investigation designed to identify children at risk for dyslexia and to provide an early intervention to reduce the incidence of reading difficulties. The children in this longitudinal study were followed from kindergarten to Grade 7 (see Chiappe, Siegel, & Wade-Woolley, 2002; Lesaux, Lipka, & Siegel, 2006; Lesaux, Rupp, & Siegel, 2007; Lesaux & Siegel, 2003; Lipka & Siegel, 2007; Lipka, Siegel, and Vukovic, 2005; Siegel, 2008, 2009) and were administered tests of reading, spelling, and mathematics each year. This study was conducted in the context of a response to intervention (RTI) framework. The RTI process begins with all children receiving excellent initial classroom education, and the children who are experiencing difficulty receive help as soon as possible, often within the classroom but outside of the full classroom context if necessary. Close monitoring of basic skills is critical. Extensive testing, labeling, and identification do not occur until all other paths and resources have been exhausted.

Sample

All of the children (973 in total) who entered the North Vancouver School District in that year were included in the 1997 study. The school district is in the greater Vancouver metropolitan area and encompasses a variety of socioeconomic levels. Approximately 80% of the children came from homes in which English was spoken (L1). Approximately 20% of the children were learning English as a second language (English language learners, or ELLs). Although there were 32 languages spoken by the children in this sample, the predominant languages of the children were Cantonese, Persian (Farsi), Mandarin Chinese, and Korean. The ELL group came from homes in which a language other than English was spoken, and the children entered school with limited or no proficiency in English. The children who entered kindergarten with little or no experience with English were immersed in mainstream English classrooms with no instruction in their L1 and received no special English as a second language support.

It is important to note that the province in which this study took place, British Columbia, has a policy of universal inclusion, meaning that any student—regardless of his or her disabilities—is educated in a regular mainstream classroom. Therefore, only children with known disabilities—such as visual or hearing impairments, Down syndrome, or autism—were excluded from the study (although they were in the classroom). In addition, at the inception of this study, all ELL children entered regular classrooms; there were no segregated programs for ELLs. In Canada, children start formal schooling in kindergarten when they are 5 years old. In the province of British Columbia and other Canadian provinces, most of the children (95%–99%) attend publicly supported government schools.

Early Identification

For a screening tool to be useful, it must be brief and easy to administer. It should be completed by teachers or other school personnel and must be designed to provide useful information. In November and December of their kindergarten year, the children in this study were administered a battery of tests. In this study, students in kindergarten were identified as being at risk based on a battery of tests that included letter-naming tasks, phonological-awareness tasks, syntactic-awareness tasks, a picture-naming speed task, and a sentence-repetition task. This battery is described in detail in Lesaux and Siegel (2003). We have developed a shorter and more appropriate battery of tests that has been adapted to other languages, including Spanish and Portuguese (Reading Readiness Screening Battery, Learning Disabilities Association of Alberta, 2009).

Results

When we administered the screening battery to the children in kindergarten, we found that approximately 25% of the children who had English as a first language (L1) were at risk and that approximately 50% of the ELL students were at risk. The ascertainment of risk was based on scores 1 standard deviation (SD) or more below the mean on two or more of the screening tasks. At the end of Grade 7, we found that 1.7% of the English L1 group was dyslexic and 2.1% of the ELL was dyslexic. Dyslexia was defined as having a score at least 1 SD below the mean on the reading subtest of the Wide Range Achievement Test (WRAT) or the Woodcock-Johnson Word Identification or the Woodcock-Johnson Word Attack subtests. This definition was based on the scores in Grade 7. For reasons described in Siegel (1989, 1992), we did not use an IQ achievement discrepancy formula.

We then compared the English L1 and the ELL normally achieving readers on a variety of reading and spelling tasks. These two groups did not differ on the following tasks: WRAT reading subtest, the Woodcock-Johnson Word Identification subtests, the word and nonword reading fluency tests of the Test of Word Reading Efficiency, the Stanford Reading Comprehension Test, and the Rosner phoneme and syllable deletion test. However, the ELL group did have significantly *higher* scores than the English L1 group on the WRAT spelling subtest and the Woodcock-Johnson Word Attack subtest. In other words, within the typically achieving reader group, there were few significant differences between the ELL and English L1 groups, and the differences that we did find were in favor of the ELL group. In other studies, we have found that ELL children had higher scores than English L1 on spelling, pseudo-word reading, and word recognition tasks (Abu Rabia & Siegel, 2002; Da Fontoura & Siegel, 1995; D'Angiulli, Siegel, & Serra, 2002).

The higher performance of the ELL students on the pseudoword reading test and the spelling test might at first seem paradoxical. However, English spelling requires good phonological skills to facilitate the sounding out of words as well as good visual memory skills to remember the spelling of the many irregular words in the language. Some of the children (specifically, those whose first language was a Slavic language and who were learning Cyrillic script, or whose first language was Chinese and who were learning to read Chinese, or whose first language was Farsi and who were learning to read it in Arabic script) were exposed to an alphabetic system that is different from English. This exposure may have improved their visual memory skills and made it easier to deal with the irregularities of English spelling. All of the ELL children were exposed to two different sound systems (English and their first language), and this bilingual experience may have improved their ability to discriminate sounds.

Luk and Bialystok (Chapter 16, this volume) found some similar results. In addition to advanced concepts of print, they found that English–Spanish and English–Hebrew bilinguals had higher scores on phoneme-counting and pseudoword-reading tasks than monolinguals.

In contrast to the results of many previous studies, the ELL group was performing at age- and grade-appropriate levels, even on a reading comprehension test. We attribute these results to the extensive reading and language program used by the North Vancouver School District, which is described in detail later in this chapter.

BILINGUAL DYSLEXICS

The children with dyslexia in both the ELL and English L1 groups had significantly lower scores on all the reading, spelling, phonological, morphological, and syntactic-awareness tasks than the normally achieving readers. This pattern of results is as expected. However, a different pattern emerged in the comparison of the bilingual and monolingual children with dyslexia. The ELL students with dyslexia had significantly *higher* scores than the monolinguals with dyslexia on the following tests: Woodcock-Johnson Word Identification and Word Attack, word and pseudoword spelling, nonword-reading fluency, and phoneme deletion. This pattern of results suggests that there are significant advantages for bilingualism in students with dyslexia.

The pattern of bilingual advantage for children with dyslexia in word recognition, spelling, and pseudoword reading was also found in a number of previous studies (Abu Rabia & Siegel, 2002; Da Fontoura & Siegel, 1995; D'Angiulli et al., 2002).

SCHOOL DISTRICT READING PROGRAM

The school district to which the children belonged is one that has made a commitment to a balanced reading acquisition program that includes phonological awareness instruction. The district uses a program called Firm Foundations, which is designed to improve phonological-awareness, vocabulary, and sound-discrimination skills. The program consists of games and activities designed to improve such skills as rhyming, initial sound discrimination, syllable and phoneme segmentation, syllable and phoneme blending, and sound discrimination. There are three types of activities described in this program: Circle Time, Centre Time, and Assessment activities. Circle Time activities are designed for the entire class and generally take place in a circle, enabling the teacher to view all the children and to be aware of which students are participating and which students are engaging in problem behaviors. In Centre Time, the children work in small groups on activities designed to develop their reading and language skills. In the Assessment activities, the teacher works individually with each child.

The phonological awareness training took the form of classroom-based small-group activities for all children in kindergarten. The small groups consisted of both ELL and English L1 speakers matched on phonological awareness ability. The classroom teachers and the school resource teachers provided the intervention 3 or 4 times a week for 20 minutes. The kindergarten phonological-awareness training for all children was presented in the context of a variety of literacy activities, which included a combination of activities with an explicit emphasis on the sound–symbol relationship as well as independent activities such as cooperative story writing and journal writing using invented spelling. Given the commitment of the district to early identification and intervention for children at risk for reading failure, the phonological-awareness intervention continued into first grade for some children in the study and took the form of small-group and individually targeted interventions.

Starting in second grade (and sometimes in first grade), a program called Reading 44 was used. This program was designed to develop reading comprehension strategies and vocabulary. Information and demonstrations of these programs are available at http://www.nvsd44.bc.ca.

Following the kindergarten assessment, each teacher received feedback on the performance of the children who participated in the study. Specifically, children who were classified as at risk for reading failure were identified, and the teachers were informed about the performance (average, above average, or below average) of the student in each area.

READING COMPREHENSION

Given these linguistic and reading comprehension interventions, the ELL children in seventh grade did not perform differently on reading comprehension tests from the English L1 speakers. Although we found that it took several years for the ELL children to catch up to the English L1 speakers, they did eventually reach the same levels of reading comprehension.

Research in other contexts in which language status and low socioeconomic status (SES) may be confounded has found that language minority children are delayed in reading comprehension (Droop & Verhoeven, 2003). However, this sample of ELL children came from varied SES backgrounds, not just the lower SES backgrounds typically associated with immigrants in many countries.

This SES indicator was based on average income and other income-related measures (e.g. real estate values) for all people in each of the catchment areas (Statistics Canada, 1996). We examined the relationship between SES and ELL for each of the 30 schools. The correlation between ELL and the SES indicators was not significant at r (30) = .03. This lack of significant correlation reduced the possibility that the performance of the ELL children was confounded as a group by SES (D'Angiulli, Siegel, & Maggi, 2004).

HIGHER LANGUAGE FUNCTIONS

Although the ELL group did not differ from the English L1 speakers on most of the reading, language, and cognitive measures by seventh grade, as noted earlier, it took them several years to reach this comparable level in higher language functions. The ELL students performed more poorly than the English L1 speakers on measures of syntactic awareness and verbal working memory in fourth grade. Five years of English immersion was not sufficient to develop the ELL speakers' syntactic skills to the same degree as their English L1 peers. However, after this point, there were no significant differences between the ELL and English L1 groups.

Morphological awareness is another higher language process. Languages have different types of morphology. In English, one important aspect of morphology is derivational morphology, in which endings of words indicate their grammatical function. For example, -*ness* indicates a noun, -*ize* signifies a verb, and -*ful* signifies an adjective. When the children in this sample were in the sixth grade, we examined their morphological awareness skills. We examined these morphological skills in dyslexic and typical readers and in English L1 and ELL children. Individuals with dyslexia had lower scores on tasks measuring morphological awareness than did normally achieving readers. This relative lack of morphological awareness in the children with dyslexia may interfere with the speed and accuracy of their reading skills. Children for whom English was a second language did not have lower morphological skills than the English L1 group.

Morphological skills were significant contributors to reading and spelling skills over and above the contribution of phonological awareness and syntactic awareness skills. Therefore, understanding the morphological structure of English is related to more accurate reading and spelling skills.

The results from the present study suggest that limited early exposure to English and lack of proficiency in English on entering school do not necessarily mean that ELL children are handicapped in the acquisition of language and literacy skills in English.

INFLUENCE OF FIRST LANGUAGE

The ELL children in this study came from a variety of language backgrounds. We selected the most common language groups and compared the children's performance in third grade as a function of their language group. The children spoke a variety of first languages, and they were grouped into language families as follows: a Chinese group (Mandarin, Cantonese); Farsi; a Slavic group (Russian, Bulgarian, Serbian, Polish, Croatian); and a Romance group (French, Italian, Spanish). Each group was compared with the native English speakers.

These languages vary in the regularity of the correspondence between letters and sounds, with the exception of Chinese, which is not an alphabetic language. For example, all of the alphabetic languages of the children in this study are more predictable than English in the correspondence between letters and sounds. Experience with these languages may make it easier for children to learn the unpredictable letter–sound correspondences of English. The Chinese languages do have some indication of pronunciation (the phonetic radical) in some words, but the language is not alphabetic and words cannot be decoded in the same way that they can in an alphabetic language. Therefore, one might expect that children whose first language is Chinese would have difficulty with tasks that require decoding.

Table 17.1 shows the scores of these five groups on the reading tasks. The Slavic and Romance groups had the highest word-reading scores (higher than the native speakers), possibly because the regularity of their

Table 17.1. Comparison of the different language groups on reading, spelling, and phonological tasks

	English	Slavic	Farsi	Chinese	Romance
Reading words (percentiles)	75.0	84.0	77.0	78.0	84.0
Word reading fluency (WPM)	18.8	21.2	19.3	20.2	18.8
Pseudoword reading fluency	28.1	30.9	30.4	28.1	30.5
Pseudoword reading (percentile)	77.2	79.2	81.7	79.3	85.1
Spelling (percentile)	63.1	72.3	68.0	76.4	63.2
Phoneme deletion	4.0	5.3	4.1	3.0	5.4
Pseudoword spelling	9.2	10.4	9.3	8.1	9.2

Key: WPM, words per minute.

Table 17.2. Comparison of the language groups on syntactic and verbal memory tasks

	English	Slavic	Farsi	Chinese	Romance
Kindergarten oral cloze (number correct)	2.4	1.7	1.5	0.9	1.9
Grade 3 oral cloze (number correct)	8.0	8.6	7.6	6.5	8.0
Working memory (words)	3.6	4.2	2.7	3.4	4.0

orthography gave them greater experience with letter–sound correspondences. The Chinese and Farsi speakers had the lowest fluency of reading words, possibly because of lack of vocabulary experience. The spelling scores of the Chinese speakers were the highest and those of the native English speakers the lowest. The visual memory requirements of learning to read and write Chinese may be one explanation for these findings. As can be seen in Table 17.1, the children with a Slavic language as a first language had high scores on the phoneme-deletion and pseudoword-spelling tasks and the Chinese-speaking children had the lowest scores. This pattern would be predicted from the role of phonological processing (or relative lack of it) in the Chinese language.

Table 17.2 shows the performance on the oral cloze (a measure of syntactic awareness) and working memory tasks. In kindergarten, unsurprisingly, the native speakers had higher scores on the oral cloze task. However, in third grade, the children who spoke a Slavic or Romance language had *higher* scores on the syntactic awareness test than the native English speakers. This apparent paradox may be the result of the more heavily inflected and complex grammar systems of these languages when compared with English. The working memory task has two requirements: a language-processing requirement and a memory requirement for the language; the higher scores of the children who speak Slavic and Romance languages may also reflect their experience with complex grammatical structures. It is important to note that the Chinese speakers had the lowest scores; the Chinese languages have no verb or adjective inflections, no articles, no plurals, and no prepositions, so the structure of English presents a challenge to them. It should be noted that the working-memory task that we used was a verbal one, and the findings for spelling were based on a hypothesized superiority of visual memory.

The Role of Socioeconomic Factors in the Development of Reading Skills and Reading Difficulties

We conducted studies of the relationship between socioeconomic level and reading and spelling skills. We were able to quantify the SES of the catchment area of each school in the district. Within each school, the socioeconomic levels were relatively homogeneous, but the differences between different catchment areas were significant. As noted earlier, in many countries, studying minority language learners is complicated by the high correlation between minority language status and SES. This correlation is not true in this sample in Canada. We found that when the children entered school, there was a strong correlation between SES and basic literacy skills. The correlation was approximately .60, which is typical of that found in most studies of the relation between socioeconomic level and academic skills. After the children remained in school for a year and a half, that relationship decreased significantly, indicating powerful effects of schooling, and the correlation was nonsignificant by third grade (D'Angiulli, Siegel, & Hertzman, 2004). D'Angiulli, Siegel, and Maggi (2004) found that the lowest SES subgroups in both the ELL and the English L1 groups improved the most as a function of schooling. The prevalence of dyslexia decreased significantly with more schooling; that is, the longer the children were exposed to the districtwide reading programs. The improvement was greater for children at the lower socioeconomic levels. Systematic instruction in literacy skills was responsible in part for the decrease in influence of SES. Typically, the relationship between SES and literacy skills increases as children remain in school. However, the teaching in this district was at least partially responsible for the powerful effects.

CONCLUSION

It is possible to identify children at risk for reading disabilities in kindergarten. It may be that some of the children identified were not truly at risk. It is impossible to know, but the consequence of the identification is that the teacher paid special attention to these children and worked to help them.

It is possible to provide a classroom-based intervention to bring most of these children to at least average levels of reading. Children learning English as a second language can eventually perform at the same levels as English L1 children, and bilingualism may be an advantage.

These findings can be understood in an RTI model. In this model, children are given good classroom instruction, and—when necessary— individual or small groups of children receive more intensive intervention. This intervention starts early but does not necessarily involve withdrawal from the classroom. It also involves frequent monitoring of skills. Extensive testing and labeling did not occur.

Some caveats are necessary. The development of language and literacy skills in ELL students requires good teaching of the type used in this district. Basic-level reading skills were stressed, but higher level language and reading comprehension strategies were both used. The Canadian government encourages the maintenance of heritage languages through support for language instruction in the child's first language in after-school or weekend classes. First-language maintenance is important whenever possible to facilitate transfer from the first language to the language in which literacy skills are being learned. The literacy instruction in this district was exemplary.

The development of learning literacy skills in the first language seems to promote positive transfer to the second or additional language. Further, bilingualism facilitates a child's literacy development and is not an impediment to the development of second-language skills. Reading is built on the solid foundation of language skills; therefore, we must do what we can to ensure well-developed language skills in all children. As noted earlier, bilingualism seems to offer some added benefits in terms of language abilities. Bilingualism facilitates literacy development in dyslexics, if the instruction in the second language is carefully and comprehensively provided. Obviously, we can generalize only to the first languages of the children in this study. It is possible that it would not be true of other languages.

Finally, systematic instruction in the early years can significantly reduce but cannot completely eliminate the incidence of dyslexia and reading problems.

REFERENCES

Abu Rabia, S., & Siegel, L.S. (2002). Reading, syntactic, orthographic and working memory skills of bilingual Arabic-English speaking children. *Journal of Psycholinguistic Research, 31,* 661–678.

Barwick, M.A., & Siegel, L.S. (1996). Learning difficulties in adolescent clients of a shelter for runaway and homeless street youths. *Journal of Research on Adolescence, 6,* 649–670.

Beitchman, J.H., Wilson, B., Douglas, L., Young, A., & Adlaf, E. (2001). Substance use disorders in young adults with and without LD: Predictive and concurrent relationships. *Journal of Learning Disabilities, 34,* 317–332.

Boetsch, E.A., Green, P.A., & Pennington, B.F. (1996). Psychosocial correlates of dyslexia across the life span. *Development and Psychopathology, 8,* 536–539.

Chapman, J.W. (1988). Cognitive motivational characteristics and academic achievement of learning disabled children: A longitudinal study. *Journal of Educational Psychology, 80,* 357–365.

Chiappe, P., Siegel, L.S., & Wade-Woolley, L. (2002). Linguistic diversity and the development of reading skills: A longitudinal study. *Scientific Study of Reading, 6,* 369–400.

Da Fontoura, H.A., & Siegel, L.S. (1995). Reading, syntactic, and working memory skills of bilingual Portuguese-English Canadian children. *Reading and Writing: An Interdisciplinary Journal, 7,* 139–153.

D'Angiulli, A., Siegel, L.S., & Hertzman, C. (2004). Schooling, socioeconomic context, and literacy development. *Educational Psychology, 24*(6), 867–883.

D'Angiulli, A., Siegel, L.S., & Maggi, S. (2004). Literacy instruction, SES, and word-reading achievement in English-language learners and children with English as a first language: A longitudinal study. *Learning Disabilities Research & Practice, 19,* 202–213.

D'Angiulli, A., Siegel, L.S., & Serra, E. (2002). The development of reading in English and Italian in bilingual children. *Applied Psycholinguistics, 22,* 479–507.

Droop, M., & Verhoeven, L. (2003). Language proficiency and reading ability in first- and second-language learners. *Reading Research Quarterly, 38*(1), 78–103.

Gregg, N., Hoy, C., King, M., Moreland, C., & Jagota, M. (1992). The MMPI-2 profiles of adults with learning disabilities in university and rehabilitation settings. *Journal of Learning Disabilities, 25,* 386–395.

Lesaux, N.K., Lipka, O., & Siegel, L.S. (2006). Investigating cognitive and linguistic abilities that influence the reading comprehension skills of children from diverse linguistic backgrounds. *Reading & Writing: An Interdisciplinary Journal, 19,* 99–131.

Lesaux, N.K., Rupp, A.A., & Siegel, L.S. (2007). Growth in reading skills of children from diverse linguistic backgrounds: Findings from a 5-year longitudinal study. *Journal of Educational Psychology, 99*(4), 821–834.

Lesaux, N.K., & Siegel, L.S. (2003). The development of reading in children who speak English as a second language. *Developmental Psychology, 25*, 1005–1019.

Lichtenstein, S., & Zantol-Wiener, K. (1988). *Special education dropouts (ERIC Digest #451).* ERIC Documentation Service No. ED 295 395. Reston, VA: ERIC Clearinghouse on Handicapped and Gifted Children.

Lipka, O., & Siegel, L.S. (2007). The development of reading skills in children with English as a second language. *Scientific Studies of Reading, 11*, 105–131.

Lipka, O., Siegel, L.S., & Vukovic, R.K. (2005). The literacy skills of English language learners in lessons from research. *Learning Disabilities, 20*, 39–49. doi: 10.1111/j.1540-5826.2005.00119.x

McBride, H., & Siegel, L.S. (1997). Learning disabilities and adolescent suicide. *Journal of Learning Disabilities, 30*, 652–659.

McLeskey, J., & Grizzle, K.L. (1992). Grade retention rates among students with learning disabilities. *Exceptional Children, 58*, 548–554.

National Center for Education Statistics. (1999). *Adult literacy in America.* Washington, DC: Office of Educational Research and Improvement, U.S. Department of Education.

Sabornie, E.J. (1994). Social-affective characteristics in early adolescents identified as learning disabled and nondisabled. *Learning Disabilities Quarterly, 17*, 268–279.

Siegel, L.S. (1989). IQ is irrelevant to the definition of learning disabilities. *Journal of Learning Disabilities, 22*, 469–486.

Siegel, L.S. (1992). An evaluation of the discrepancy definition of dyslexia. *Journal of Learning Disabilities, 25*, 618–629.

Siegel, L.S. (2008). Morphological awareness skills of English language learners and children with dyslexia. *Topics in Language Disorders, 28*(1), 15–27.

Siegel, L.S. (2009). Down the garden path and into the poison ivy: IQ & LD. *New Times for DLD, 7*(3), 1–6.

Statistics Canada. (1996). National population health survey. Retrieved January 15, 2011, from http://www.statcan.gc.ca/dli-ild/data-donnees/ftp/nphs-ensp-eng.htm

Wiener, J., & Schneider, B.H. (2002). A multisource exploration of the friendship patterns of children with and without learning disabilities. *Journal of Abnormal Child Psychology, 30*, 127–141.

CHAPTER 18

Developing Oral Proficiency in Second-Language Learners in the Context of Literacy Instruction

Diane August

T his chapter first reviews the research on the role of oral language proficiency in literacy development and then describes ways in which English language learners' (ELLs) oral language proficiency has been developed in the context of developing early literacy skills. There are many advantages to developing students' oral language proficiency in the context of literacy instruction. First and foremost is that literacy instruction provides a context in which students primarily focus on meaning, which is one of the basic principles of effective pedagogy for the acquisition of a second language in classroom contexts (referred to in the literature as instructed second-language acquisition). Although a focus on meaning can be conceptualized as explicit attention to the meanings of particular words and phrases, it can also be conceptualized as immersion in activities that have a "pragmatic purpose," and reading certainly qualifies as such an activity.

Linguists generally believe that a focus on pragmatic meaning is important not only for activating the linguistic resources that have been developed through other means but also because it is the principal means by which the linguistic resources are themselves created (Ellis, 2005). In addition, for ELLs, literacy outcomes may be enhanced by focusing on oral language development. In a thorough review of literacy instruction for ELLs, August and Shanahan (2006) found that reading interventions had a lesser impact on the reading skills of ELLs than on those of students with English as their first language. This finding suggests that providing high-quality instruction in reading skills alone was insufficient to support equal academic success for ELLs in reading and that sound reading instruction should be combined with efforts to increase both the size and the sophistication of these students' oral language proficiency.

Because ELLs with dyslexia have to develop oral proficiency in a second language as well as master literacy skills that will be challenging for them, an approach that develops both oral language proficiency and literacy skills concurrently might be advantageous. Such an approach condenses oral language and literacy development in a joint target for instruction, providing more overall time for each area. Stronger oral language skills might help compensate for and support phonological processing skills, a key weakness for children with dyslexia (Lundberg, 2002; Sparks & Ganschow, 1991). In addition, recent research indicates

that oral language proficiency is an important predictor of word identification and word attack skills, also areas of weakness for these children
(Swanson, Rosston, Gerber, & Solari, 2008).

In the following section, we describe research related to the relationship between oral language proficiency and word-level and text-
level literacy skills. In the subsequent section, we describe how effective
literacy interventions have incorporated principled methods to build
students' oral language proficiency. The chapter closes with a discussion
of implications for practice, policy, and research.

THE ROLE OF ORAL LANGUAGE PROFICIENCY IN READING DEVELOPMENT

Word-Level Reading Skills

Although phonological processing skills are critical to early reading
development in both first- and second-language learners (SLLs; Gottardo,
Collins, Baciu, & Gebotys, 2008; Share & Stanovich, 1995), research also
indicates that second-language oral proficiency plays an important role,
most certainly because second-language knowledge supports SLLs'
attempts at word reading (Share & Stanovich, 1995). More specifically,
studies that have examined the relationship between English oral proficiency and English word-reading skills in elementary-age children
learning English as a second or foreign language find small but positive
relationships between these variables (Arab-Moghaddam & Sénéchal,
2001; Gottardo, 2002; Quiroga, Lemos-Britten, Mostafapour, Abbott, &
Berninger, 2002). Even when phonological processing skills are added
to the regression analyses, oral language skills are still predictive of early
reading for SLLs who have some proficiency in English (Arab-Moghaddam
& Sénéchal, 2001; Gottardo, 2002; Muter & Diethelm, 2001). In recent work
with third-grade bilingual children, Swanson et al. (2008) found that oral
language, syntax, and vocabulary played major roles in predicting word
identification and word attack. Hierarchical regression modeling indicated that oral language accounted for 21% of the unique variance in
English word identification and 31% of the unique variance in English
word attack. In contrast, phonological awareness contributed less than
10% of the unique variance across the literacy measures.

Text-Level Reading Skills

Models of reading comprehension emphasize the important role that
oral language proficiency plays in the later elementary grades for monolingual English speakers (Hoover & Gough, 1990; Perfetti, 1985). Second-
language research also indicates that second-language oral language
skills—such as oral vocabulary knowledge, listening comprehension,
oral storytelling skills, syntactic skills, and the ability to handle decon-
textualized aspects of language (such as word definitions)—are all

positively related to second-language reading comprehension (Beech & Keys, 1997; Carlisle, Beeman, Davis, & Spharim, 1999; Carlisle, Beeman, & Shah, 1996; Droop & Verhoeven, 2003; Dufva & Voeten, 1999; Goldstein, Harris, & Klein, 1993; Jiménez, García, & Pearson, 1996; Lee & Schallert, 1997; Peregoy, 1989; Peregoy & Boyle, 1991; Royer & Carlo, 1991; van Gelderen et al., 2004). Three recent studies highlight the fact that second-language reading comprehension is compromised when second-language oral skills are insufficient to support second-language text comprehension. Proctor, Carlo, August, and Snow (2005) found that both second-language decoding and oral language proficiency of fourth-grade ELLs predicted their English reading comprehension, with English vocabulary and listening comprehension playing a more prominent role than decoding. Nakamoto, Lindsey, and Manis (2008) found that third-grade English and Spanish decoding and oral language factors were both significant predictors of English reading comprehension in sixth grade in a sample of Spanish-speaking ELLs. Kieffer (2008) found that students from Spanish-speaking homes who enter kindergarten with limited English oral proficiency have different trajectories than either monolingual English speakers or language minority students who are proficient in oral English; in fifth grade, this group of students' reading achievement was significantly worse than students in the other two groups. However, it is important to keep in mind that the relationship between English oral proficiency and English reading comprehension is also mediated by contextual factors such as home language use and socioeconomic status, as well as by differences in instructional experiences (Lesaux & Geva, 2006).

Although correlational research helps us understand relationships among variables, experimental research is essential if we are to evaluate the relative effectiveness of instructional methods designed to develop literacy skills in SLLs and, in this context, also develop their oral language proficiency. In the following section, we review the experimental and quasi-experimental research in this area.

DEVELOPING ORAL LANGUAGE PROFICIENCY IN THE CONTEXT OF LITERACY INSTRUCTION

We begin this section with a brief review of findings related to effective literacy instruction for ELLs and then turn to methods used to develop students' oral language proficiency[1] in the context of this literacy instruction.[2] The review related to effective literacy instruction draws on the work of the National Literacy Panel on Language Minority Children and

---

[1]In this chapter, *oral language proficiency* is defined as phonology, vocabulary, morphology, grammar, and discourse domains; it encompasses skills in both comprehension and expression.
[2]*Literacy skills* are defined as consisting of prereading skills (e.g., concepts of print and alphabetic knowledge); word-level skills (decoding, word reading, pseudoword reading, and spelling); and text-level skills (fluency and reading comprehension).

Youth (August & Shanahan, 2006),[3] but has been updated to reflect research conducted between 2003 and 2009. Students in the studies cited were ELLs, ages 3–18 years, who were learning to read in English in English-speaking contexts. The studies included in the review used experimental designs published in peer-reviewed journals or journals that used an editorial board for review. Book chapters, literature reviews, and summary documents were used to provide context for the findings presented.

To locate relevant studies, we began with the searchable database of the National Literacy Panel (August & Shanahan, 2006), adding searches (2003–2009) using Scirus (http://www.scirus.com), Ovid, and Web of Science with restrictions on years, peer review status, and the use of specific search terms as applicable. Other references were located by subsequent searches of each table of contents available for 14 journals from 2003 to 2009 that have been frequently cited by past research focusing on the present topic. All abstracts were reviewed to determine whether they met the inclusion criteria cited earlier. Using the most inclusive criteria, abstracts for 124 studies conducted between 2003 and 2009 were reviewed. For the purposes of this chapter, studies that are included focused on developing phonological awareness, phonics, fluency, and vocabulary.

Findings from Second-Language Literacy Research

Research that is focused on developing literacy in ELLs builds on first-language reading research—most notably, *The National Reading Panel Report* (National Institute of Child Health and Human Development [NICHD], 2000)—that provided an analysis of research on the teaching of reading to native speakers of English. The report indicates that it is helpful to explicitly teach young children to hear the individual English sounds or phonemes within words (phonemic awareness); to use the letters and spelling patterns within words to decode the word's pronunciations (phonics); to read text aloud with appropriate speed, accuracy, and expression (oral reading fluency); to know the meanings of words and affixes (vocabulary); to think in particular ways during reading (reading comprehension); and to produce writing in which the organization, development, substance, and style are appropriate to the task, purpose, and audience.

The review of effective reading instruction for ELLs (August & Shanahan, 2006) indicates that the general pattern found with English-proficient students seems to hold for ELLs: explicit instruction focused on developing key aspects of literacy—phonemic awareness, phonics,

---

[3]The work is adapted from August, D., & Shanahan, T. (Eds.). (2006). Educating language minority students: Instructional approaches and professional development. Part IV of the report *Developing literacy in second language learners* (© 2006). It appears by permission of Taylor and Francis Group, LLC, a division of Informa plc.

oral reading fluency, and vocabulary—provides clear learning benefits for ELLs (August & Shanahan, 2008). Although this does not necessarily mean that English learners benefit from the same types of instructional routines and programs that are effective with native speakers of English, the analysis of research suggests that many of the instructional approaches that have been successful with native speakers of English are indeed effective with English learners, too. Although there are important similarities between the kinds of instruction that best support first- and second-language learners in their literacy development, there are also important differences.

One difference is the importance of supporting ELLs' second-language oral development in the context of second-language literacy instruction. Instructional interventions have generally had a greater impact on the decoding and spelling skills of English learners than on their reading comprehension. English learners often acquire basic skills as well as do native speakers of English (e.g., phonemic awareness, decoding, spelling), but they rarely match English-proficient students in reading comprehension. Although instruction in various basic skills provides a clear benefit to English learners (as it does with native speakers of English), the effect associated with such efforts is clearly less than occurs when English-proficient students are the target population (Shanahan & Beck, 2006). This pattern seems logical: Teaching decoding, for instance, helps by allowing the reader to produce an appropriate oral language representation of written language. But this decoding ability leads to better comprehension only if the reader can understand the oral language. Thus, phonics would help readers of English up to the level of their oral proficiency; when text difficulty exceeds the students' oral proficiency, the beneficial effects of phonics would diminish. The same pattern is evident with older native speakers; that is, phonics instruction yields less payoff for comprehension as students proceed through school because the texts they confront are more likely to present language and concepts that they cannot understand and use orally. Clearly, in order to provide maximum benefit to SLLs, instruction must do more than develop a complex array of basic literacy skills; it must also develop oral language proficiency in the second language.

Findings from Research on
Instructed Second-Language Acquisition

Several principles helpful for designing interventions that develop students' oral language proficiency emerge from the research literature on effective instructed second-language acquisition (August, Goldenberg, Saunders, & Dressler, 2010; Ellis, 2005). The first principle is that learners will learn language best if they focus predominately on meaning. According to Ellis 2005, it is important to focus on the two senses of meaning: semantic meaning (i.e., the meanings of lexical items or of specific grammatical structures) and pragmatic meaning (i.e., the highly contextualized meanings that arise in acts of communication). To the extent that students are engaged in learning to read, they are engaged in meaningful activity that makes reading a promising venue for developing second-language proficiency.

A second principle is that explicit instructional attention to grammatical features (*forms,* in the second-language literature) is likely to facilitate second-language learning in ways that solely relying on meaning- and communication-oriented instruction will not. Instruction can focus on forms in a number of ways, "through grammar lessons designed to teach specific grammatical features, through focused tasks that require learners to comprehend and process specific grammatical structures, and by such methods as time for strategic and on-line planning or corrective feedback" (Ellis, 2005, p. 35). Many of the studies that focus on form are narrow in scope (e.g., teaching a specific feature of language such as verb tense, adverb placement, or relative pronouns) and were conducted with students in the upper grades. Therefore, there is still a lot to learn about the interplay between meaning making and conscious attention to form, such as how they vary for different aspects of language, levels of second-language proficiency, the age of the learner, and the learner's first language (Spada & Lightbown, 2008). Currently, we have little empirical evidence addressing this dynamic interplay.

A third principle is that students need opportunities to interact (via speaking, listening, reading, and writing) in the second language. Speaking is important to generate feedback, force syntactic processing, and challenge students to engage at higher proficiency levels (Johnson & Swain, 1998). Extensive opportunities for listening and reading are also crucial: Substantial differences in the rate of second-language acquisition are related to the amount and quality of the input that students receive (Ellis & Wells, 1980). Some researchers recommend making this input comprehensible either through modification or the use of contextual props (Echevarria, Vogt, & Short, 2008; Krashen, 1994).

A fourth principle is that instruction needs to take into account individual differences in aptitude for language learning and motivation. To deal with individual differences in aptitude, teachers can explicitly teach students a variety of learning strategies, although it is unclear to what extent these increasingly sophisticated strategies can actually be taught—as opposed to the strategies being a by-product of increased language competence. Some studies do suggest the benefit of explicit instruction for ELLs on how to use communication strategies effectively. For example, O'Malley, Chamot, Stewner-Manzanares, Russo, and Kupper (1985) tested the effects of an 8-day (50 minutes per day) intervention designed to train high school ELLs to use metacognitive and cognitive strategies in the context of integrative tasks: listening to lectures and making oral presentations. The training produced significant effects for speaking but not for listening. With regard to motivation, Ellis (2005) makes the important point that one obvious way to increase motivation is to improve the quality of classroom teaching.

One final point is important. There has been much emphasis on the importance of building academic language, defined as the language of education (Halliday, 1994) in contrast to social language. However, we are in accord with Bailey (2007), who stressed the importance of guarding against believing that there is something inherent in social language that makes it less sophisticated or less cognitively demanding than language used in an academic context. There are times when academic discourse does not demand complex linguistic responses, and there are times when social uses of language are complex and complicated. Thus, it is most accurate to characterize the difference between academic language and social language as differences in the *relative frequency* of complex grammatical structures, specialized vocabulary, and uncommon language functions.

Developing Second-Language Oral Proficiency During Phonological Awareness, Phonics, Word Reading, and Fluency Instruction

In our review, 16 studies included a focus on phonological awareness and phonics, 5 of which also focused on developing fluency in SLLs. Two additional studies focused solely on fluency development (Koskinen et al., 2000; VanWagenen, Williams, & McLaughlin, 1994; see Appendix A of this chapter for a list of these studies). Findings across the studies indicate that explicit instruction in phonological awareness, phonics, word reading, and fluency benefits ELLs across varying samples. Many studies involved students who were struggling readers, and as such, the findings generalize to this group of students rather than the wider population. Three of the studies with younger learners (Calhoon, Al Otaiba, Cihak, King, & Avalos, 2007; Ehri, Dreyer, Flugman, & Gross, 2007; Kamps et al., 2007) focused on students who had been designated or identified as having reading difficulties; this was also the case for each of the studies that dealt with older learners (Denton, Wexler, Vaughn, & Bryan, 2008; Lovett et al., 2008; Swanson, Hodson, & Schommer-Aikins, 2005; VanWagenen, Williams, & McLaughlin, 1994). In the study by Gunn, Smolkowski, Biglan, Black, and Blair (2005), students in the study samples were high in aggressive behavior or had reading difficulties.

Many of these studies used published instructional programs (e.g., Reading Mastery, Read Naturally, Corrective Reading, Jolly Phonics, Orton-Gillingham) or methods that had been found to be effective in previous research with monolingual English speakers (e.g., use of a scope and sequence for phonics instruction that was developed by Torgesen & Bryant [1994]; the Auditory Depth and Discrimination Program, developed by Lindamood & Lindamood [1975]; the Peer-Assisted Learning Strategies [PALS], developed and adapted by Fuchs, Fuchs,

Mathes, & Simmons [1997]; and the Reading Rescue tutoring intervention, created by Ehri et al. [2007]).

In this group of studies that focused on developing phonological awareness, phonics, word reading, and fluency, two of the studies explicitly focused on oral language forms and specifically on sounds that may be challenging for SLLs because they appear in the second language but not in the first. The first study (Kramer, Schell, & Rubison, 1983) is a 4-week auditory discrimination program in which students are taught four contrasting pairs of sounds that are difficult for Spanish speakers to ensure adequate sound differentiation for letter sounds. Students involved in the auditory discrimination training performed significantly better than a control group on a 60-item researcher-developed measure. Giambo and McKinney (2004) compared phono-logical awareness instruction—which incorporated 9 of 18 English sounds, 14 of the 18 English contrast pairs, and an additional 10 pairs of English sounds that do not appear in the students' first language—with a treated control group receiving story-reading activities. Students in the phonological awareness training showed significantly greater gains in phonological awareness but not in receptive vocabulary.

Three studies used methods structured to encourage students to interact (via speaking, listening, reading, and writing) in the second language (Calhoon et al., 2007; McMaster, Kung, Han, & Cao, 2008; Saenz, Fuchs, & Fuchs, 2005). All three studies used PALS, a supplemental peer tutoring program in which teachers pair higher performing readers with lower performing readers in coach–reader roles, which are later reversed. During peer tutoring, teachers circulate among students, monitor students' feedback, and provide corrective practice. Other features of PALS consistent with effective instructed second-language acquisition include interactive teaching and frequent opportunities for accurate response (McMaster et al., 2008). It is worth noting, however, that students who were already familiar with English and started the study with established or emerging English skills were likely to benefit more than students who were less proficient (Calhoon et al., 2007); although PALS ELLs outperformed controls in phonemic awareness and letter–sound recognition, they did not outperform them in word identification, word attack, or spelling—the ultimate goals of the inter-vention (McMaster et al., 2008).

In three of the studies, explicit attention was given to ensure that students understood the meaning of what they were reading (Ehri et al., 2007; Slavin & Madden, 2000; VanWagenen, Williams, & McLaughlin, 1994). In all three studies, treatment students outperformed students in control groups on measures of early reading ability. VanWagenen et al. focused on developing fluency in SLLs by having them read a passage silently while listening to the teacher's recording, read the same passage aloud, read the passage silently three times without the tape recording, and read the passage orally a second time. Prior to fluency practice, teachers introduced and discussed new vocabulary, and each student completed written work related to the story. Written activities focused on helping students understand the meaning of words within sentences and having them answer questions that required recall, inferencing, and sequencing. Students showed improvement in reading rate, accuracy, and comprehension. In the series of studies reported by Slavin and Madden (2000), students who were ELLs participated in the same balanced literacy program as monolingual students—Success for All—but received support for English as a second language aligned with the program to ensure that they understood the meaning of the reading materials used to build phonological awareness and phonics skills. Ehri et al. (2007) used the Reading Rescue tutoring intervention model to try to improve phonological awareness, phonics, and fluency; in addition to the usual Reading Rescue tutoring, tutors introduced each book prior to reading it by talking through it with students page by page and encouraging students to talk about each page; explaining unknown vocabulary and having students record unknown words and their meanings; and asking literal, inferential, and evaluative questions after each book was read. In this study, treatment students outperformed students in the control group in a similar comprehensive early reading program in both word-level and text-level skills (reading comprehension). The tutoring program raised the majority of students' reading from below average to average. Ehri et al. attribute strong results in part to students reading text at a high level of accuracy and to one-on-one tutoring rather than small-group tutoring.

Although students in almost all of these studies were provided with instruction in one-on-one formats or in small groups (exceptions included Slavin & Madden, 2000; Stuart, 1999; Tharp, 1982), individual differences were defined by reading ability rather than ability to acquire a second language. This might be the proper approach with regard to reading outcomes, but additional support in second-language development might be provided for students who have less aptitude for learning a second language.

Developing Second-Language Oral Proficiency During Vocabulary Instruction

One method for developing reading comprehension in students is development of their vocabulary. Considerable previous research (August & Shanahan, 2006) suggests that one major determinant of poor reading comprehension for children with limited English proficiency is low vocabulary. Lack of knowledge of the academic words encountered in middle and secondary school texts impedes comprehension of those texts, which in turn impedes the natural process of learning new word meanings from exposure during reading. It is widely known that vocabulary relates to reading comprehension scores, and the presumption is that the effect is reciprocal: Greater vocabulary makes comprehension easier, and wider reading generates larger vocabularies.

Our review located 12 studies that used experimental designs and focused primarily on the vocabulary development of ELLs (see Appendix A for a list of these studies). Findings across the studies generally indicate that instruction focused on developing students' vocabulary improves their vocabulary and, in cases in which comprehension is measured, improves their comprehension. In this group of studies, students in the sample were predominately from a Spanish-speaking background and, unlike the studies reported in the section previously, generally did not have learning difficulties.[4] All studies followed principles of effective vocabulary instruction as well as effective instructed second-language acquisition, including teaching individual words, teaching word learning strategies, fostering word consciousness, and providing rich and varied language experiences that provide opportunities for meaningful interactions in the second language (Graves, 2006).

Three studies confirmed that vocabulary learning for ELLs can occur through indirect exposure during television viewing (Neuman & Koskinen, 1992; Uchikoshi, 2005) or reading (Tudor & Hafiz, 1989). Neuman and Koskinen (1992) found that ELLs who watched captioned episodes of *3-2-1 Contact* outperformed their classmates who simply read from their science textbooks on measures of word recognition, sentence anomaly, and word meaning; these students also performed better than their classmates who watched the television program without captions for some units (Neuman & Koskinen, 1992). Similarly, Uchikoshi (2005) found that watching *Arthur,* a television program that emphasizes narrative storytelling, improved ELLs' oral language development more than watching *Between the Lions,* a television program emphasizing phonics. In Tudor and Hafiz (1989), during a 12-week after-school program, students choose books, read for an hour a day, and gave a weekly oral report. Results indicated that students who participated in sustained silent reading made gains on a number of reading and writing achievement tests over the course of the intervention; the results were largely static for the control group, who received no supplementary instruction. Taken together, these studies indicate that language minority students may benefit from increased exposure to rich language experiences using multiple media. However, Uchikoshi (2005) found that higher levels of vocabulary growth were associated with higher levels of initial oral English

---

[4]The exceptions are students in studies by Bos, Allen, and Scanlon (1989) and Neuman and Koskinen (1992).

proficiency, and noted that the more linguistic competence the students had, the more they acquired. This finding supports the need for substantial direct-teacher intervention in building oral English proficiency for students who are below a threshold of linguistic competence in their new language.

In seven studies, meaning was directly taught and reinforced in the context of read-alouds, an area previously shown to lead to vocabulary acquisition in native English-speaking students (Biemiller & Boote, 2006; Carlo et al., 2004; Roberts, 2008; Roberts & Neal, 2004; Silverman, 2007; Tharp, 1982; Ulanoff & Pucci, 1999). The studies indicate that such approaches are also effective with ELLs. Roberts (2008) found that home reading in students' first language was more effective than home reading in English when both were followed by classroom storybook reading in English. Ulanoff and Pucci (1999) found that previewing and reviewing reading material in student's home language first was more effective than strategies of no prior explanation of the story or a concurrent translation; Biemiller and Boote (2006) found that more exposures to a word benefited kindergartners but not students in second grade. These results reinforce the need for careful consideration of a number of factors, including use of students' home languages to help foster second-language vocabulary and taking into account grade level in the design of vocabulary instruction.

IMPLICATIONS FOR PRACTICE, POLICY, AND RESEARCH

This chapter briefly summarized the research on effective literacy instruction for ELLs, finding that the general pattern found with students proficient in English seems to hold for ELLs: explicit instruction focused on developing key aspects of literacy—phonemic awareness, phonics, oral reading fluency, and vocabulary—provides clear learning benefits for ELLs (August & Shanahan, 2008). However, the interventions have generally had a greater impact on word-level skills than text-level skills, and August and Shanahan argue that the cause is limited English proficiency of ELLs, which needs to be addressed in the context of literacy instruction.

Although the research that formed the basis for this chapter focused on literacy instruction, the real leverage may be in the continual, systematic, everyday ways in which we engage children in learning new knowledge and information across all the content areas— not solely language arts—starting in the early years (Glaser, 1984; Neuman, 2001). Many of the techniques described in this chapter to develop oral language proficiency in language arts can also be applied to instruction in other content areas. The dual purpose of these techniques is to teach knowledge and skills in the content areas, as well as to support ongoing acquisition and learning of English as it relates to these content areas.

The likelihood of incorporating oral language development into literacy instruction as well as instruction in other content areas increases when schools and districts make it a priority. A sizable literature suggests that a sustained and coherent focus on academic goals in schools and districts is associated with higher levels of student achievement. Due to the dearth of experimental research and detailed case studies in this area, it is very difficult to draw firm conclusions about cause and effect. However, numerous dimensions of school and district functioning—leadership, common goals and curricula, professional development, ongoing support and supervision, collaboration among teachers, and regular assessments that inform instruction—are levers that school and district administrators can use to help shape the academic experiences of students (e.g., Fullan, 2007; Goldenberg, 2004; McDougall, Saunders, & Goldenberg, 2007).

Finally, as is abundantly clear from the reviews, there is a need for more intervention research focused on developing literacy in ELLs. In the components covered by this review—phonological awareness, phonics, fluency, and vocabulary—the National Reading Panel found approximately 154 studies in 2000. Our review of studies published between 1980 and 2000 located approximately 30 unique studies. There is even less research that addresses the needs of dyslexic SLLs. Though many of the phonological awareness, phonics, and fluency studies and one vocabulary study focused on students with reading difficulties, no samples were explicitly identified as dyslexic.[5] Not only is research needed to confirm the general findings accrued from a small body of research, but there is also a need to examine the effects of interventions over time, the effects for students with different levels of first- and second-language proficiency, and the effects for students with different types of learning difficulties and different first-language backgrounds. Research also should focus more explicitly on the development of oral language proficiency in the context of content-area instruction using designs that enable us to compare content-area interventions with and without oral language development. Finally, most research has targeted one or two components of literacy; interventions that are more comprehensive are needed, as are studies of how to accommodate the language learning and literacy needs of students with diverse skills and capacities within the same classroom.

---

[5]However, some students in the samples of the phonological awareness, phonics, and fluency studies may have been dyslexic because the samples of these studies included many students with reading difficulties. The same is true for one vocabulary study, as discussed previously.

REFERENCES

Arab-Moghaddam, N., & Sénéchal, M. (2001). Orthographic and phonological processing skills in reading and spelling in Persian/English bilinguals. *International Journal of Behavioral Development, 25*(2), 140–147.

August, D., Goldenberg, C., Saunders, W., & Dressler, C. (2010). Recent research on English language and literacy instruction: What we have learned to guide practice for English language learners in the 21st century. In M. Shatz and L.C. Wilkinson (Eds.), *The education of English language learners* (pp. 272–297). New York: Guilford.

August, D., & Shanahan, T. (2006). *Developing literacy in second language learners: Report of the National Literacy Panel on language minority children and youth.* Mahwah, NJ: Lawrence Erlbaum Associates.

August, D., & Shanahan, T. (2008). *Developing reading and writing in second language learners.* New York: Routledge.

Bailey, A.L. (Ed.). (2007). *Language demands of school: Putting academic English to the test.* New Haven, CT: Yale University Press.

Beech, J.R., & Keys, A. (1997). Reading, vocabulary, and language preference in 7- to 8-year-old bilingual Asian children. *British Journal of Educational Psychology, 67*(4), 405–414.

Biemiller, A., & Boote, A. (2006). An effective method for building meaning vocabulary in primary grades. *Journal of Educational Psychology, 98*(1), 44–62.

Bos, C.S., Allen, A.A., & Scanlon, D.J. (1989). Vocabulary instruction and reading comprehension with bilingual learning disabled students. *Yearbook of the National Reading Conference, 38,* 173–179.

Calhoon, M.B., Al Otaiba, S., Cihak, D., King, A., & Avalos, A. (2007). Effects of peer-mediated program on reading skill acquisition for two-way bilingual first-grade classrooms. *Learning Disability Quarterly, 30,* 169–184.

Carlisle, J.F., Beeman, M.M., Davis, L.H., & Spharim, G. (1999). Relationship of metalinguistic capabilities and reading achievement for children who are becoming bilingual. *Applied Psycholinguistics, 20*(4), 459–478.

Carlisle, J.F., Beeman, M.B., & Shah, P.P. (1996). The metalinguistic capabilities and English literacy of Hispanic high school students: An exploratory study.

Yearbook of the National Reading Conference, 45, 306–316.

Carlo, M.S., August, D., McLaughlin, B., Snow, C.E., Dressler, C., Lippman, D., et al. (2004). Closing the gap: Addressing the vocabulary needs of English language learners in bilingual and mainstream classrooms. *Reading Research Quarterly, 39*(2), 188–215.

Denton, C.A., Wexler, J., Vaughn, S., & Bryan, D. (2008). Intervention provided to linguistically diverse middle school students with severe reading difficulties. *Learning Disabilities Research & Practice, 23*(2), 79–89.

Droop, M., & Verhoeven, L.T. (2003). Language proficiency and reading ability in first and second language learners. *Reading Research Quarterly, 38*(1), 78–103.

Dufva, M., & Voeten, M.J.M. (1999). Native language literacy and phonological memory as prerequisites for learning English as a foreign language. *Applied Psycholinguistics, 20*(3), 329–348.

Echevarria, J., Vogt, M., & Short, D. (2008). *Making content comprehensible for English learners.* Boston: Pearson Education, Inc.

Ehri, L.C., Dreyer, L.G., Flugman, B., & Gross, A. (2007). Reading rescue: An effective tutoring intervention model for language-minority students who are struggling readers in first grade. *American Educational Research Journal, 44*(2), 414–448.

Ellis, R. (2005). *Instructed second language acquisition: A literature review.* Wellington, New Zealand: New Zealand Ministry of Education.

Ellis, R., & Wells, G. (1980). Enabling factors in adult-child discourse. *First Language, 1,* 46–82.

Fuchs, D., Fuchs, L.S., Mathes, P.G., & Simmons, D.C. (1997). Peer-assisted learning strategies: Making classrooms more responsive to academic diversity. *American Educational Research Journal, 34,* 174–206.

Fullan, M. (2007). Change the terms for teacher learning. *JSD: Journal of the National Staff Development Council, 28*(3), 35–36.

Giambo, D.A., & McKinney, J.D. (2004). The effects of a phonological awareness intervention on the oral English proficiency of Spanish-speaking kindergarten children. *TESOL Quarterly, 38*(1), 95–117.

Glaser, R. (1984). Education and thinking: The role of knowledge. *American Psychologist, 39,* 93–104.

Goldenberg, C. (2004). *Successful school change: Creating settings to improve teaching and learning.* New York: Teachers College Press.

Goldstein, B.C., Harris, K.C., & Klein, M.D. (1993). Assessment of oral storytelling abilities of Latino junior high school students with learning handicaps. *Journal of Learning Disabilities, 26*(2), 138–132.

Gottardo, A. (2002). The relationship between language and reading skills in bilingual Spanish-English speakers. *Topics in Language Disorders, 22*(5), 46–70.

Gottardo, A., Collins, P., Baciu, I., & Gebotys, R. (2008). Predictors of grade 2 word reading and vocabulary learning from grade 1 variables in Spanish-speaking children: Similarities and differences. *Learning Disabilities Research and Practice, 23*(1), 11–23.

Graves, M.F. (2006). *The vocabulary book.* New York: Teachers College Press.

Gunn, B., Smolkowski, K., Biglan, A., Black, C., & Blair, J. (2005). Fostering the development of reading skill through supplemental instruction: Results for Hispanic and non-Hispanic students. *Journal of Special Education, 39*(2), 66–85.

Halliday, M.A.K. (1994). *An introduction to functional grammar* (2nd ed.). London: Edward Arnold.

Hoover, W., & Gough, P.B. (1990). The simple view of reading. *Reading and Writing, 2,* 127–160.

Jiménez, R.T., García, G.E., & Pearson, D.P. (1996). The reading strategies of bilingual Latina/o students who are successful English readers: Opportunities and obstacles. *Reading Research Quarterly, 31*(1), 90–112.

Johnson, K., & Swain, M. (1998). *Immersion education: International perspectives.* Cambridge, UK: Cambridge University Press.

Kamps, D., Abbott, M., Greenwood, C., Arreaga-Mayer, C., Wills, H., Lonstaff, J., et al. (2007). Use of evidence-based, small-group reading instruction for English language learners in elementary grades: Secondary-tier intervention. *Learning Disability Quarterly, 30,* 153–168.

Kieffer, M. (2008). Catching up or falling behind? Initial English proficiency, concentrated poverty, and the reading growth of language minority learners in the United States. *Child Development, 100,* 851–868.

Koskinen, P.S., Blum, I.H., Bisson, S.A., Phillips, S.M., Creamer, T.S., & Baker, T.K. (2000). Book access, shared reading, and the audio models: The effects of supporting the literacy learning of linguistically diverse students in school and at home. *Journal of Educational Psychology, 92*(1), 23–36.

Kramer, V.R., Schell, L.M., & Rubison, R.M. (1983). Auditory discrimination training in English of Spanish-speaking children. *Reading Improvement, 20*(3), 162–168.

Krashen, S. (1994). The input hypothesis and its rivals. In N. Ellis (Ed.), *Implicit and explicit learning of languages* (pp. 45–77). London: Academic Press.

Lee, J.W., & Schallert, D.L. (1997). The relative contribution of L2 language proficiency and L1 reading ability to L2 reading performance: A test of the threshold hypothesis in an EFL context. *TESOL Quarterly, 31*(4), 713–739.

Lesaux, N., & Geva, E. (2006). Development of literacy in language minority students. In D. August & T. Shanahan (Eds.), *Developing literacy in second language learners: Report of the National Literacy Panel on language minority children and youth* (pp. 27–61). Mahwah, NJ: Lawrence Erlbaum Associates.

Lindamood, C., & Lindamood, P. (1975). *Auditory discrimination in depth.* Columbus, OH: Macmillan/McGraw-Hill.

Lovett, M.W., De Palma, M., Frijters, J., Steinbach, K., Temple, M., Benson, N., et al. (2008). Interventions for reading difficulties: A comparison of response to intervention by ELL and EFL struggling readers. *Journal of Learning Disabilities, 41*(4), 333–352.

Lundberg, I. (2002). Second language learning and reading with the additional load of dyslexia. *Annals of Dyslexia, 52,* 165–187.

McDougall, D., Saunders, W., & Goldenberg, C. (2007). Inside the black box of school reform: Explaining the how and why of change at Getting Results schools. *International Journal of Disability, Development and Education, 54,* 51–89.

McMaster, K.L., Kung, S., Han, I., & Cao, M. (2008). Peer-assisted learning strategies: A "Tier 1" approach to promoting English learners' response to intervention. *Exceptional Children, 74*(2), 194–214.

Muter, V., & Diethelm, K. (2001). The contribution of phonological skills and letter knowledge to early reading development in a multilingual population. *Language Learning, 51*(2), 187–219.

Nakamoto, J., Lindsey, K.A., & Manis, F.R. (2008). A cross-linguistic investigation of English language learners' reading comprehension in English and Spanish. *Scientific Studies of Reading, 12*(4), 351–371.

National Institute of Child Health and Human Development. (2000). Report of the National Reading Panel. *Teaching children to read: An evidence-based assessment of the scientific research literature on reading and its implications for reading instruction* (NIH Publication No. 00–4754). Washington, DC: U.S. Government Printing Office. Retrieved January 17, 2011, from http://www.nichd.nih.gov/research/supported/nrp.cfm

Neuman, S.B. (2001). Essay book review: The role of knowledge in early literacy. *Reading Research Quarterly, 36*(4), 468–475.

Neuman, S.B., & Koskinen, P. (1992). Captioned television as comprehensible input: Effects of incidental word learning from context for language minority students. *Reading Research Quarterly, 27*(1), 94–106.

O'Malley, J.M., Chamot, A.U., Stewner-Manzanares, G., Russo, R., & Kupper, L. (1985). Learning strategy applications with students of English as a second language. *TESOL Quarterly, 19*(3), 557–584.

Peregoy, S.F. (1989). Relationships between second language oral proficiency and reading comprehension of bilingual fifth grade students. *NABE: Journal of the National Association for Bilingual Education, 13*(3), 217–234.

Peregoy, S.F., & Boyle, O.F. (1991). Second language oral proficiency characteristics of low, intermediate, and high second language readers. *Hispanic Journal of Behavioral Sciences, 13*(1), 35–47.

Perfetti, C.A. (1985). *Reading ability.* New York: Oxford University Press.

Proctor, C.P., Carlo, M., August, D., & Snow, C. (2005). Native Spanish-speaking children reading in English: Toward a model of comprehension. *Journal of Educational Psychology, 97*(2), 246–256.

Quiroga, T., Lemos-Britten, Z., Mostafapour, E., Abbott, R.D., & Berninger, V.W. (2002). Phonological awareness and beginning reading in Spanish-speaking

ESL first graders: Research into practice. *Journal of School Psychology, 40*(1), 85–111.

Roberts, T. (2008). Home storybook reading in primary or second language with preschool children: Evidence of equal effectiveness for second language vocabulary acquisition. *Reading Research Quarterly, 43*(2), 103–130.

Roberts, T., & Neal, H. (2004). Relationships among preschool English language learner's oral proficiency in English, instructional experience and literacy development. *Contemporary Educational Psychology, 29,* 283–311.

Royer, J.M., & Carlo, M.S. (1991). Transfer of comprehension skills from native to second language. *Journal of Reading, 34,* 450–455.

Saenz, L., Fuchs, L.S., & Fuchs, D. (2005). Effects of peer-assisted learning strategies on English language learners: A randomized controlled study. *Exceptional Children, 71,* 231–247.

Shanahan, T., & Beck, I. (2006). Effective literacy teaching for English-language learning. In D. August & T. Shanahan (Eds.), *Developing literacy in second language learners: Report of the National Literacy Panel on language minority children and youth* (pp. 415–488). Mahwah, NJ: Lawrence Erlbaum Associates.

Share, D.L., & Stanovich, K.E. (1995). Cognitive processes in early reading development: Accommodating individual differences into a model of acquisition. *Issues in Education, 1,* 105–121.

Silverman, R.D. (2007). Vocabulary development of English language and English-only learners in kindergarten. *The Elementary School Journal, 107*(4), 365–383.

Slavin, R.E., & Madden, N. (2000). Effects of bilingual and English as a second language adaptations to Success for All on the reading achievement of students acquiring English. *Journal of the Education for Students Placed at Risk, 4*(4), 393–416.

Spada, N., & Lightbown, P.M. (2008). Form-focused instruction: Isolated or integrated? *TESOL Quarterly, 42*(2), 181–207.

Sparks, R.L., & Ganschow, L. (1991). Foreign language learning differences: Affective or native language aptitude differences? *Modern Language Journal, 75,* 3–16.

Stuart, M. (1999). Getting ready for reading: Early phoneme awareness and phonics teaching improves reading and spelling in inner-city second language learners. *British Journal of Educational Psychology, 69*(4), 587–605.

Swanson, H.L., Rosston, K., Gerber, M., & Solari, E. (2008). Influence of oral language and phonological processing on children's bilingual reading. *Journal of School Psychology, 46,* 413–429. doi:10.1016/j.jsp.2007.07.002

Swanson, T.J., Hodson, B.W., & Schommer-Aikins, M. (2005). An examination of phonological awareness treatment outcomes for seventh-grade poor readers from a bilingual community. *Language, Speech, and Hearing Services in Schools, 36,* 336–345.

Tharp, R.G. (1982). The effective instruction of comprehension: Results and descriptions of the Kamehameha Early Education Program. *Reading Research Quarterly, 17*(4), 503–527.

Torgesen, J.K., & Bryant, B.R. (1994). *Test of Phonological Awareness.* Austin, TX: PRO-ED.

Tudor, I., & Hafiz, F. (1989). Extensive reading as a means of input to L2 learning. *Journal of Research in Reading, 12*(2), 164–178.

Uchikoshi, Y. (2005). Narrative development in bilingual kindergarteners: Can *Arthur* help? *Developmental Psychology, 41*(3), 464–478.

Ulanoff, S.H., & Pucci, S.L. (1999). Learning words from books: The effects of read-aloud on second language vocabulary acquisition. *Bilingual Research Journal, 23*(4), 409–422.

van Gelderen, A., Schoonen, R., De Glopper, K., Hulstijn, J., Simis, A., Snellings, P., et al. (2004). Linguistic knowledge, processing, speed and metacognitive knowledge in first- and second-language reading comprehension: A componential analysis. *Journal of Educational Psychology, 96,* 19–30.

VanWagenen, M.A., Williams, R.L., & McLaughlin, T.F. (1994). Use of assisted reading to improve reading rate, word accuracy, and comprehension with ESL Spanish-speaking students. *Perceptual and Motor Skills, 79,* 227–230.

Data by Domain

PHONOLOGY AND PHONICS

Calhoon, M.B., Al Otaiba, S., Cihak, D., King, A., & Avalos, A. (2007). Effects of peer-mediated program on reading skill acquisition for two-way bilingual first-grade classrooms. *Learning Disability Quarterly, 30*, 169–184.

Denton, C.A., Wexler, J., Vaughn, S., & Bryan, D. (2008). Intervention provided to linguistically diverse middle school students with severe reading difficulties. *Learning Disabilities Research & Practice, 23*(2), 79–89.

Ehri, L.C., Dreyer, L.G., Flugman, B., & Gross, A. (2007). Reading rescue: An effective tutoring intervention model for language-minority students who are struggling readers in first grade. *American Educational Research Journal, 44*(2), 414–448.

Giambo, D.A., & McKinney, J.D. (2004). The effects of a phonological awareness intervention on the oral English proficiency of Spanish-speaking kindergarten children. *TESOL Quarterly, 38*(1), 95–117.

Goldenberg, C., Reese, L., & Gallimore, R. (1992). Effects of literacy materials from school on Latino children's home experiences and early reading achievement. *American Journal of Education, 100*(4), 497–536.

Gunn, B., Smolkowski, K., Biglan, A., Black, C., & Blair, J. (2005). Fostering the development of reading skill through supplemental instruction: Results for Hispanic and non-Hispanic students. *Journal of Special Education, 39*(2), 66–85.

Kamps, D., Abbott, M., Greenwood, C., Arreaga-Mayer, C., Wills, H., Lonstaff, J., et al. (2007). Use of evidence-based, small-group reading instruction for English language learners in elementary grades: Secondary-tier intervention. *Learning Disability Quarterly, 30*, 153–168.

Kramer, V.R., Schell, L.M., & Rubison, R.M. (1983). Auditory discrimination training in English of Spanish-speaking children. *Reading Improvement, 20*(3), 162–168.

Lovett, M.W., De Palma, M., Frijters, J., Steinbach, K., Temple, M., Benson, N., et al. (2008). Interventions for reading difficulties: A comparison of response to intervention by ELL and EFL struggling readers. *Journal of Learning Disabilities, 41*(4), 333–352.

McMaster, K.L., Kung, S., Han, I., & Cao, M. (2008). Peer-assisted learning strategies: A "Tier 1" approach to promoting English learners' response to intervention. *Exceptional Children, 74*(2), 194–214.

Roberts, T., & Neal, H. (2004). Relationships among preschool English language learner's oral proficiency in English, instructional experience and literacy development. *Contemporary Educational Psychology, 29*, 283–311.

Slavin, R.E., & Madden, N. (2000). Effects of bilingual and English as a second language adaptations to Success for All on the reading achievement of students acquiring English. *Journal of the Education for Students Placed at Risk, 4*(4), 393–416.

Solari, E.J., & Gerber, M.M. (2008). Early comprehension instruction for Spanish-speaking English language learners: Teaching text-level reading skills while maintaining effects on world-level skills. *Learning Disabilities Research and Practice, 23*(4), 155–168.

Stuart, M. (1999). Getting ready for reading: Early phoneme awareness and phonics teaching improves reading and spelling in inner-city second language learners. *British Journal of Educational Psychology, 69*(4), 587–605.

Swanson, T.J., Hodson, B.W., & Schommer-Aikins, M. (2005). An examination of phonological awareness treatment outcomes for seventh-grade poor readers from a bilingual community. *Language, Speech, and Hearing Services in Schools, 36*, 336–345.

Troia, G.A. (2004). Migrant students with limited English proficiency: Can Fast ForWord Language™ make a difference in their language skills and academic achievement? *Remedial and Special Education, 25*(6), 353–366.

FLUENCY

Calhoon, M.B., Al Otaiba, S., Cihak, D., King, A., & Avalos, A. (2007). Effects of peer-mediated program on reading skill acquisition for two-way bilingual first-grade classrooms. *Learning Disability Quarterly, 30,* 169–184.

Denton, C.A., Wexler, J., Vaughn, S., & Bryan, D. (2008). Intervention provided to linguistically diverse middle school students with severe reading difficulties. *Learning Disabilities Research & Practice, 23*(2), 79–89.

Gunn, B., Smolkowski, K., Biglan, A., Black, C., & Blair, J. (2005). Fostering the development of reading skill through supplemental instruction: Results for Hispanic and non-Hispanic students. *Journal of Special Education, 39*(2), 66–85.

Kamps, D., Abbott, M., Greenwood, C., Arreaga-Mayer, C., Wills, H., Lonstaff, J., et al. (2007). Use of evidence-based, small-group reading instruction for English language learners in elementary grades: Secondary-tier intervention. *Learning Disability Quarterly, 30,* 153–168.

Koskinen, P.S., Blum, I.H., Bisson, S.A., Phillips, S.M., Creamer, T.S., & Baker, T.K. (2000). Book access, shared reading, and the audio models: The effects of supporting the literacy learning of linguistically diverse students in school and at home. *Journal of Educational Psychology, 92*(1), 23–36.

McMaster, K.L., Kung, S., Han, I., & Cao, M. (2008). Peer-assisted learning strategies: A "Tier 1" approach to promoting English learners' response to intervention. *Exceptional Children, 74*(2), 194–214.

VanWagenen, M.A., Williams, R.L., & McLaughlin, T.F. (1994). Use of assisted reading to improve reading rate, word accuracy, and comprehension with ESL Spanish-speaking students. *Perceptual and Motor Skills, 79,* 227–230.

VOCABULARY

Biemiller, A., & Boote, A. (2006). An effective method for building meaning vocabulary in primary grades. *Journal of Educational Psychology, 98*(1), 44–62.

Bos, C.S., Allen, A.A., & Scanlon, D.J. (1989). Vocabulary instruction and reading comprehension with bilingual learning disabled students. *Yearbook of the National Reading Conference, 38,* 173–179.

Carlo, M.S., August, D., McLaughlin, B., Snow, C.E., Dressler, C., Lippman, D., et al. (2004). Closing the gap: Addressing the vocabulary needs of English language learners in bilingual and mainstream classrooms. *Reading Research Quarterly, 39*(2), 188–215.

Giambo, D.A., & McKinney, J.D. (2004). The effects of a phonological awareness intervention on the oral English proficiency of Spanish-speaking kindergarten children. *TESOL Quarterly, 38*(1), 95–117.

Neuman, S.B., & Koskinen, P. (1992). Captioned television as comprehensible input: Effects of incidental word learning from context for language minority students. *Reading Research Quarterly, 27*(1), 94–106.

Roberts, T. (2008). Home storybook reading in primary or second language with preschool children: Evidence of equal effectiveness for second language vocabulary acquisition. *Reading Research Quarterly, 43*(2), 103–130.

Roberts, T., & Neal, H. (2004). Relationships among preschool English language learner's oral proficiency in English, instructional experience and literacy development. *Contemporary Educational Psychology, 29,* 283–311.

Silverman, R.D. (2007). Vocabulary development of English language and English-only learners in kindergarten. *The Elementary School Journal, 107*(4), 365–383.

Tharp, R.G. (1982). The effective instruction of comprehension: Results and descriptions of the Kamehameha Early Education Program. *Reading Research Quarterly, 17*(4), 503–527.

Tudor, I., & Hafiz, F. (1989). Extensive reading as a means of input to L2 learning. *Journal of Research in Reading, 12*(2), 164–178.

Uchikoshi, Y. (2005). Narrative development in bilingual kindergarteners: Can *Arthur* help? *Developmental Psychology, 41*(3), 464–478.

Ulanoff, S.H., & Pucci, S.L. (1999). Learning words from books: The effects of read-aloud on second language vocabulary acquisition. *Bilingual Research Journal, 23*(4), 409–422.

Bilingualism, Cognition, Reading, and Intervention

Peggy McCardle and Brett Miller

Bilingual people have been noted to have both advantages (cognitive) and disadvantages (linguistic) associated with their bilingualism (or, in the case of speakers of more than two languages, their multilingualism). Children who are bilingual or are becoming bilingual may differ from their monolingual peers in ways that can affect literacy development: they may have greater metalinguistic awareness due to their exposure to more than one language system; they may be less able to distinguish sounds in the second language and therefore have difficulty learning the second language's sound–symbol correspondences; their limited vocabulary in the second language may hinder both word recognition and the ability to use context to interpret ambiguities; and their limited familiarity with syntactic differences may slow their ability to learn concepts, thus slowing their growth in both oral and reading comprehension. How much of this is due to the brain's efforts to manage two languages, and how much is due to the circumstances of the linguistic, social, and educational environment is important for reading development and for the identification, prevention, and intervention of reading disabilities.

If people who are bilingual activate lexical representations from both languages when they read printed words in one language, their language processing may be slower than would be seen in a monolingual person. In fact, some differences in aspects of language processing related to reading have been observed. In Chapter 15, Jared and Kroll discuss two models of bilingualism that might account for this difference. One model posits that adults use their first language to mediate the learning of the second language early in the process of learning a second language (Revised Hierarchical Model); the other model holds that rather than using a *translation function* to learn languages, speakers have a single lexicon that is integrated across languages (Bilingual Interactive Activation [BIA] model). Jared and Kroll examine this theoretical debate in the adult bilingualism literature as well as in their own work with both adults and children, and they consider the implications for children developing literacy in two languages.

Jared and Kroll cite research indicating that in bilinguals who speak two languages that share an alphabet, phonological representations of the words being read are activated in both languages. However, studies of Hebrew–English and Korean–English bilinguals have demonstrated that this effect can be observed even in languages that do not share an alphabet. Further, the activation of both languages has been shown in psycholinguistic experiments to not be restricted to the level of reading single words; even when reading words in sentence contexts, bilingual adult readers take longer to process word ambiguity. This finding suggests a single, interconnected system such as that posited in the BIA model.

Given this evidence in adults, the question becomes whether bilingual children have a single word recognition system from the onset of reading; Jared and Kroll assert that they do, at least when the two languages share an alphabet. However, they note that, much of the data being brought to bear on this subject is hindered by three issues: the comparability of language measures in the two languages, the sensitivity of correlations to the learning contexts (instructional settings and approaches), and the influence of the relative amount of experience they have had in reading each language (which can contribute to vocabulary, syntax, and language proficiency). Therefore, the authors call for additional research that takes into account these factors in developing bilingual readers.

Jared and Kroll raise interesting theoretical issues about bilingual reading based on the adult psycholinguistic research and speculate about implications for children. In Chapter 16, Luk and Bialystok examine recent and current research on child bilingualism and reading, including their own work, and discuss the implications of the cognitive advantages and disadvantages that have been demonstrated in bilinguals for the identification and remediation of dyslexia in different languages. Bilinguals (both children and adults) have been shown to have weaker receptive vocabularies than their monolingual peers, as demonstrated on tasks such as picture naming and verbal fluency; they also have been found to have an advantage when compared with monolinguals in cognitive flexibility (Bialystok & Martin, 2004),[1] as measured in a sorting task in which children are asked to sort the same items according to different dimensions and in executive functions (Bialystok & Viswanathan, 2009; Carlson & Meltzoff, 2008). Luk and Bialystok point out that these and other tasks that have shown such cognitive flexibility have in common a requirement to inhibit attention to distracting information presented as an alternative response.

Luk and Bialystok make the important point that although bilinguals may have relatively weaker language abilities in one of their two languages, this finding is directly related in most cases to linguistic exposure, not a limitation in learning potential. Thus language experience—an

---

[1]Spiro and Jehng (1990) defined cognitive flexibility as adaptively reassembling elements of knowledge to fit the requirements of a particular problem-solving task. Deák defined it as "the dynamic reconstruction of representations and responses based on information (i.e., similarities, cues, relations) selected from the linguistic and nonlinguistic environment" (2005, p. 5). Deák went on to explain that flexible thinkers are able to examine and then delimit the various ways to grasp and respond to a problem, shifting their cognitive focus as the task demands change.

important factor also noted by Jared and Kroll that should be but is not always taken into account in bilingualism research—must be considered in assessing bilingual individuals for possible language or reading problems. When individuals are learning to read in two alphabetic languages, one can logically expect that they may be able to recruit common strategies for reading both languages; in fact, the Revised Hierarchical Model discussed by Jared and Kroll assumes a translation function in sequential language learning in adults. Luk and Bialystok point out that positive correlations have been found for nonword decoding in languages with similar language structures and writing systems (strong for English and Spanish, moderate for English and Hebrew). They further sought to determine whether readers are transferring strategies from one language to another across similar languages or whether they might be tapping a more general cognitive resource. Based on data from English–Cantonese bilingual children, Luk and Bialystok observe that correlations for decoding (a reading skill) depend heavily on the structural and orthographic similarities across languages and writing systems, and that phonological awareness (a language skill that is foundational but not specific to reading) appears to call on a more general shared cognitive resource and is not dependent on the specific characteristics of a given language. Thus the Bilingual Interactive Activation model seems most promising.

Additional data on how bilingualism might affect reading and reading disability is presented by Siegel in Chapter 17. When following children from kindergarten to seventh grade in the North Vancouver School District, she uncovered some interesting differences in native English-speaking and English language–learning students. Although there were a few significant differences between the native English speakers and those learning English as a second language who were typical readers, the differences that did emerge (English spelling, pseudoword reading, and word recognition) favored the English learners. Because the predominant first languages among these students were Cantonese, Farsi, Mandarin, and Korean (with some Slavic language speakers), Siegel reasons that exposure to two scripts (e.g., Chinese, Arabic, Cyrillic) may have improved the children's visual memory skills and that the exposure to two different sounds systems may have done the same for their sound discrimination abilities. Siegel also noted that those English learning students with reading problems in seventh grade fared better on word attack, nonword fluency, word and pseudoword spelling, and phoneme deletion than did native English speakers with reading impairments. Though there are other problems that English learners may experience in reading, these particular skills are the ones most often targeted early in reading intervention. Siegel speculates that bilingualism may therefore provide advantages to students with dyslexia.

In Chapter 18, August presents information on the role of language proficiency in the literacy development of English learners. Based on earlier work by August and Shanahan on the National Literacy Panel on Language Minority Children and Youth (August & Shanahan, 2006) and more recent literature, they synthesize studies in two areas: the role of oral proficiency in the reading development of English learners and the development of oral proficiency itself in the context of literacy instruction for English learners. Oral language skills have been shown in several studies to be predictive of early reading for second-language learners, although—as August points out—confirmation of these correlational findings is needed through experimental studies.

Early reading depends on and benefits from the acquisition of phonological skills in reading (e.g., phoneme awareness, decoding) and spelling. However, as students progress, these effects diminish, and vocabulary, the ability to comprehend more complex concepts, and the syntax associated with the expression of more complex ideas become increasingly important. August argues, citing research literature on instructed second-language acquisition, that the path to higher level reading skills must include targeted efforts at developing oral second-language proficiency. She draws from that literature five principles to keep in mind when designing oral language interventions for second-language learners: focus predominantly on meaning (both via semantics and syntax, and within the context of communication activities; that is, pragmatically); explicitly address grammatical features of the language; provide opportunities to interact in the language (both orally and via reading and writing); take into account individual differences in student aptitude and motivation; and attend to both academic and social discourse because both involve levels of complexity that can challenge and build language abilities. In reviewing the studies that examine attempts to build oral second-language proficiency, August concludes that interventions that have been shown to be successful with native English speakers have also been valuable with English learners, but adds that those focused on phonemic awareness, phonics, oral reading fluency, and vocabulary have had a greater impact on word-level abilities than on text-level abilities for English learners. She attributes this limited effect to limited English proficiency and advocates for future research to confirm correlational findings; this confirmatory research must take into account levels of oral language proficiency. The lack of consistent text-level benefits may not be surprising, given that these successful interventions have focused much more heavily on word-level processing and fluency and included a lesser focus on reading comprehension. An integrative focus on reading comprehension may help us achieve increased text-level skills for English learners.

The cognitive flexibility noted to occur in bilingual individuals may be masked by the frequent failure to control for the language proficiency and language experience of research participants in each of their languages in studies comparing bilinguals with monolinguals. Furthermore, characteristics of bilingual participants' cognitive flexibility lie in what are referred to as *executive functions*, yet executive functions are generally not examined in the same studies, samples, or individuals being studied to examine the bilingual language-processing disadvantage. Luk and Bialystok have been able to demonstrate, at least in a preliminary way, that the bilingual advantage seen in nonverbal tasks can be seen also in language tasks if language proficiency levels are accounted for. Siegel has seen preliminary evidence of bilingual advantage in children coping with reading disabilities. Given that a reading ability depends on both language and cognitive processes, measuring both aspects together in individuals is crucial in identifying and remediating children with reading disabilities. Luk and Bialystok point out that this need is especially crucial in assessing bilingual children for reading problems. Siegel's findings also indicate that taking a close look at specific reading tasks and linking these abilities to visual memory and language abilities should provide us with possible insights. Exploring psycholinguistic theories such as those discussed by Jared and Kroll, with developmental data collected longitudinally not only on reading but also on language and executive functions, appears to hold great promise.

A premise of this volume is that we can learn much about the nature and manifestations of dyslexia by studying reading and reading difficulties across languages, especially across languages with differing orthographies. The profiles of dyslexics may also differ within a single language if we are comparing monolingual individuals with bilingual individuals. To truly understand the impact of bilingualism (and of second-language development that is coincident with literacy instruction) on children's literacy development, we must more fully understand bilingualism. This understanding is essential if we are to avoid both false positive and false negative diagnoses of dyslexia. To accomplish these several goals, we must find ways to compare studies of children and youths at various ages and educational levels and at various stages of bilingual or second-language development. Studies need to take into account language proficiency, which means agreeing on what is meant by the term and finding valid and reliable ways to assess both oral and reading proficiency. Identifying or developing comparable measures in various languages will be challenging, and determining what results mean across languages, within groups and within individuals, and across studies will be difficult. Many factors could influence outcomes, such as language exposure and opportunities for interaction in each of a bilingual person's languages, the age at which exposure to the second or additional language began, and so forth. Therefore, because it is clear that both language proficiency and more general cognitive abilities—specifically, executive functions—are important to reading and are key factors in bilingual reading and reading disabilities, measuring these factors in the same individuals and studies is crucial.

What we will ultimately learn through better designed and better controlled research will inform the development of interventions that can then be studied and can feed back to inform theory. Theory and practice should mutually inform one another. To more fully understand the processes involved when bilingual children are becoming biliterate, we also should heed Jared and Kroll's recommendation that we begin to use data on children to explore and modify current models of bilingualism.

REFERENCES

August, D., & Shanahan, T. (Eds.). (2006). *Developing literacy in second language learners: Report of the National Literacy Panel on language minority children and youth*. Mahwah, NJ: Lawrence Erlbaum Associates.

Bialystok, E., & Martin, M.M. (2004). Attention and inhibition in bilingual children: Evidence from the dimensional change card sort task. *Developmental Science, 7*, 325–339.

Bialystok, E., & Viswanathan, M. (2009). Components of executive control with advantages for bilingual children in two cultures. *Cognition, 112*, 494–500.

Carlson, S.M., & Meltzoff, A.N. (2008). Bilingual experience and executive functioning in young children. *Developmental Science, 11*, 282–298.

Deák, G.O. (2005). *The development of cognitive flexibility and language abilities*. Amsterdam: Elsevier.

Spiro, R., & Jehng, J. (1990). Cognitive flexibility and hypertext: Theory and technology for the nonlinear and multidimensional traversal of complex subject matter. In D. Nix and R. Spiro (Eds.), *Cognition, education, and multimedia: Exploring ideas in high technology* (pp. 163–205). Hillsdale, NJ: Lawrence Erlbaum Associates.

CONCLUSION

Future Directions in Research on Dyslexia Across Languages and Orthographies

Peggy McCardle, Jun Ren Lee, Brett Miller, and Ovid Tzeng

T his book presents a cross-section of the current research on reading, writing, and reading disabilities (dyslexia), including behavioral studies of typical development, intervention, brain imaging, and genetics. In the introduction, Wang and Tsai present some history of the development of written language, both in English and Chinese, with reference to other languages as well, and some basics about the structure of these languages. They point out broadly the need for future research to enable us to better understand the many factors— orthographic and linguistic, socioeconomic and educational, cultural, genetic and neurobiological—that can deepen our understanding of reading and writing. Such understanding should lead to improvements in reading and writing education for both typically developing and dyslexic readers, as well as add to our basic understanding of how the brain functions during these essential activities.

Frost, in a summary of Part I, points out the theoretical importance of the question of how the linguistic environment influences reading and writing. Cross-linguistic research has expanded recently, especially in the area of reading research; comparing reading behaviors across languages requires taking into consideration the characteristics of the languages involved and how they affect both typical and impaired reading processes. One major factor in comparing how children develop reading abilities across alphabetic languages is transparency, or orthographic depth; in transparent or orthographically shallow languages, a grapheme maps directly to a particular phoneme. Many nonalphabetic languages such as Chinese, however, lack a systematic correspondence between the written symbol and its pronunciation. Thus we need to look at other bases for cross-language comparison. In emphasizing the importance of the link between the characteristics of the language itself and reading theory, Frost notes that statistical regularities rely on morphological data because it is morphology that modulates the correlation between form and meaning. Ultimately, concludes Frost, to model reading processes and problems, we must consider the totality of the linguistic environment, not simply the sound–symbol relationship.

How the brain functions as individuals read or struggle to read has been an area of focused attention for more than two decades. It continues to intrigue and challenge researchers. Examining brain function in readers of alphabetic and nonalphabetic languages holds promise for deepening our understanding of the brain's activity during reading. Pugh's summary of and commentary on the chapters in Part II highlight the value of cognitive neuroscience and its potential to support plausible theory development, heighten sensitivity to individual differences that may be present, and help us better target both early identification and the remediation of reading and learning problems. Together, the author of this summary and those of the corresponding chapters addressing brain studies highlight and emphasize the value of using neuroimaging approaches in concert with behavioral data to examine research questions focused on cross-linguistic comparisons, bilingualism and dyslexia, and orthographic differences. To date, the research field has not paid sufficient attention to how reading in different writing systems might affect which neural regions are involved in reading and their functional organization, as well as how writing systems might affect more general aspects of reading development and the manifestation of dyslexia. As we look across writing systems, Pugh cautions that the common or overlapping neural substrates for reading and writing that are being found do not necessarily imply commonalities in successful instruction or remediation approaches. We must examine such possibilities, and Pugh calls for a new generation of longitudinal studies that employ comparable tasks and measures and well-matched samples.

In the summary and discussion of Part III, which discusses modeling of language and reading processes, Miller, McCardle, and Lee highlight the value of computational and statistical modeling. Modeling can be used to further elucidate the nature of the underlying cognitive structure or architecture involved in reading and to more generally inform theory and practice in reading and reading disability. Part of the value of model development and testing lies in the requirement of significantly greater specificity than previous theoretical accounts would necessitate, as highlighted in the modeling chapters. In addition, researchers are taking advantage of the modeling architecture to help differentiate between possible accounts or explanations of empirical data obtained, whether their own or others', and to help identify possible cognitive organizational levels that might be involved in reading or language processing in light of their findings. This section and its summary highlight the need for additional research to construct developmental accounts of learning to read across the lifespan. Although the chapters demonstrate the potential of applying adult models to developmental data, we need accounts that are sensitive to children's emerging skills and the developmental learning trajectory through adulthood that are also sensitive to individual differences. Clearly, additional research is needed to inform work on these models; in particular, research on the development of reading comprehension skills and research that more generally addresses reading and writing in typical, struggling, and disabled individuals from preadolescence into adulthood.

Finally, Miller et al. highlight work reported in Chapter 12 by Wagner, Waesche, Schatschneider, Maner, and Ahmed that emphasizes the need for an additional focus on how we think about the identification of reading disability and the delivery of reading instruction in a response to intervention (RTI) context. With the widespread introduction of RTI in kindergarten through 12th grade, research is needed to examine whether students respond well to instruction in order to make meaningful decisions about when to increase the intensity and/or performance monitoring and when to refer students for formal learning disabilities evaluations. Miller et al. also highlight the need for further research on classification and identification of reading disabilities given the lack of convergence on which individuals are identified as having a disability and the instability of these decisions over time. Additional emphasis on computational and statistical modeling that integrates with empirical research can help bring us a richer understanding of reading development and the unfolding of reading disability. As we move toward a greater data-based understanding of how individuals acquire reading skills and when and how students struggle to do so, we must also examine what factors put some children at risk for reading difficulties. These factors include genetics and neurobiology.

As Plomin and Kovas point out in their summary and commentary on Chapter 13 by Galaburda, Fitch, LoTurco, and Rosen, and Chapter 14 by Smith in Part IV, the convergence between findings from animal models and findings from population genetics is striking. They highlight the value of an animal model for reading disability, especially in light of the genes shown to relate to synaptic neurotransmission cited in Smith's chapter. As Plomin and Kovas note, most of the population genetics work has been done in English-speaking groups. This lack of explicit cross-cultural comparisons could prove limiting when and if we find consistently replicable genes associated with English reading. Plomin and Kovas also provide information about quantitative genetics, which can be used to estimate the cumulative effect from genes and to investigate environmental effects. They point out that the future of quantitative genetic analysis will likely be multilevel and will link top-down behavioral research approaches to bottom-up "-omic" approaches. Clearly, further work is needed on the genetics of reading and reading disability with the use of animal models and human populations, implementation of molecular and quantitative behavioral genetics, and the linking of genetics and neurobiology, as has already begun. Bringing together disciplines that study reading and reading disability and having them communicate, collaborate, and engage in interdisciplinary studies that can make these links is crucial to the future understanding of the genetics underlying these skills and disabilities.

Any discussion of reading and writing research across languages must consider the data on bilingualism and cognition. A premise of this book is that dyslexia may manifest differently when filtered through different languages, and recognizing dyslexia in developing children may be even more challenging when looking not only across different languages but also across different orthographies. In Part V, four chapters by leaders in bilingualism research, along with a summary by McCardle and Miller, lay out some of what is known about the advantages and limitations of bilingualism, both for language processing more generally and for reading, as well as the implications of these factors for identifying and remediating reading disabilities in bilingual and second-language learners. These chapters address current theoretical debates as well as data on what cognitive differences exist in bilinguals and how these differences may affect a child's ability to respond to intervention. Although it appears that bilingualism may confer advantages specific to dyslexics, it is clear that proficiency in speaking each of the bilingual individual's languages must be considered in any assessment or intervention and in work that seeks to confirm or disconfirm theories. In fact, failure to take language proficiency into account may mask aspects of performance and thus alter research findings. Another key area that must be integrated into research on bilingualism and reading is that of executive functions. How and what to assess to account for executive functions is under general debate; calls for a core set of common measures across studies to allow for comparability of data is not unique to executive functions' role in reading or in bilingualism, but such a core set is crucial to consider. As McCardle and Miller point out in their summary, what is learned about bilingualism and reading through well-designed and tightly controlled studies can inform both theory and the development of interventions. Research on the effectiveness of those interventions and how and why they work will provide feedback to inform stronger theories. The mutual benefit of research on theory and practice is clear.

Overall, all chapters in this book grew out of the preparations that researchers made to engage in debate of key questions that were posed to participants of the 11th symposium of The Dyslexia Foundation on which this book is based. These questions, which were discussed in some depth at that meeting, remain important questions for the field. They were embraced, dissected, augmented, and reformulated to be part of a research agenda to share broadly:

- Does the manifestation of reading difficulties differ in languages with nonalphabetic and alphabetic languages and across varying orthographic depths, and if so, how? What are the roles of phonology and language impairments in reading problems across orthographies; do nonalphabetic languages tap different phonological or morphological abilities than do alphabetic languages? Is it possible that dyslexia could arise from different etiologies, and if so, how would these differential etiologies relate to differing languages and cultures, the presence or absence of comorbid conditions, and the design and effectiveness of intervention approaches?

- If genes associated with dyslexia put children at risk for reading difficulties, how does the genetic profile interact with environment (early language input, language development, instructional input, socioeconomic status, native language and cultural influences, and so forth) to influence the manifestation of reading ability or difficulty? Can that same genetic makeup also predict other aspects of cognitive development, such as differential areas of superiority or problems, including visual-spatial ability, cognitive organizational ability, mathematics, and working memory? How do crucial language and cultural differences between alphabetic and nonalphabetic languages manifest in this regard?

- Are there unique neurobiological and/or behavioral characteristics that are thought to be universal to dyslexia? If so, how might these best be confirmed across languages? Are there language-invariant characteristics of dyslexic or poor readers?

- Are there certain abilities related to learning to read nonalphabetic orthographies that might have increased association with the etiology or manifestations of dyslexia in those languages, such as visual-spatial analysis or morphological abilities? What are the theoretical and practical implications of such hypotheses? What data exist that might be brought to bear on such questions? How could such hypotheses be studied empirically and systematically across languages and within bilinguals proficient in both alphabetic and nonalphabetic languages, and among those proficient in a nonalphabetic (or alphabetic) language but in the process of learning a second language with a different type of orthography?

- Prevalence rates of dyslexia appear to differ in languages with nonalphabetic orthographies and those with alphabetic orthographies. Are these differences robust, or do they reflect difficulties of matching on assessment and diagnostic methodologies? If these differences are robust, what might account for the contrasts? To what extent can orthographic or other linguistic differences account for these differences, and what role do factors such as cultural, environmental (socioeconomic status, educational exposure), or genetic or neurobiological differences play? Do these factors, individually or in combination, amplify or reduce the impact of dyslexia? Are there groups that are economically disadvantaged or that have pronounced cultural differences (e.g., aboriginal groups) that might increase risk of an individual's identification as someone who requires reading intervention?

- The nature of poor reading in languages with differing orthographies (alphabetic versus nonalphabetic and with varying orthographic depths) should be examined with respect to differences in accuracy and speed at the word and character level (fluency versus phonologically mediated problems) and differences in comprehension at the sentence level (including the relation of listening comprehension to reading comprehension). A broad range of reading components must be examined in this cross-language research.

- A neglected area across all languages is the role of writing in reading intervention. Looking at how writing is learned and taught across alphabetic and nonalphabetic languages in both proficient and struggling readers could offer significant insights into both writing itself and its contribution to reading ability.

- What factors might explain response to instruction or intervention? How are nonresponders characterized in order to set decision rules for changes in intervention, and how might these be different or similar for different languages, for example, those with alphabetic and nonalphabetic orthographies and with different orthographic depths? The role of assessment in identifying students, monitoring their progress, and tailoring instruction to individual student needs must be carefully documented if we are to accurately gauge response to instruction or intervention. We cannot determine at which point remediation can most effectively be delivered and at what costs without careful measurement and documentation.

- How can technology enhance remediation and learning? How can we use technology to simultaneously deliver an intervention, collect data on individual student performance, and facilitate analysis of these data to determine the effectiveness of the intervention? How can we use technology to refine and enhance interventions and tailor interventions to student profiles to better meet student needs?

In closing, we offer the following next steps for research on reading, writing, and dyslexia across the world's languages and orthographies. Although it is clear that the phonology of languages remains highly important to research on the precursors of reading and, in both alphabetic and nonalphabetic languages, to identifying and remediating dyslexia, there are other bases for cross-language comparisons that are proving fruitful in some languages, such as morphology in Hebrew. In examining the statistical regularities of language and in modeling reading, we must consider the entire linguistic environment, not just the sound system. Cross-linguistic and bilingual neuroimaging studies are needed to determine what links exist between common neural substrates for reading and writing across languages and orthographies, and the identification and remediation of reading and writing difficulties. Modeling work should be integrated with neurobiological and genetic research. Animal models have already been used to explore the genetics and neurobiology of typical and impaired learning; more such work is needed. Linking studies through core sets of common measures to allow for cross-study comparisons, sharing new analytic approaches and research methods as they are developed, and building collaborations across disciplines appear to be key to progressing in the field's quest to better understand the basic cognition, genetics, and neurobiology of reading, writing, and dyslexia as well as the earlier and more accurate identification and remediation of dyslexia for all children and youth. We need to recognize how children learn to read and how best to ensure their access to academic learning, regardless of language and across orthographies!

Index

Tables and figures are indicated by *t* and *f* respectively.